# CONSCIENCE, CONSENSUS, AND THE DEVELOPMENT OF DOCTRINE

# CONSCIENCE, CONSENSUS, AND THE DEVELOPMENT OF DOCTRINE

REVOLUTIONARY TEXTS BY

## JOHN HENRY CARDINAL NEWMAN

THE THEORY OF DEVELOPMENTS IN RELIGIOUS DOCTRINE

AN ESSAY ON THE DEVELOPMENT OF CHRISTIAN DOCTRINE

ON CONSULTING THE FAITHFUL IN MATTERS OF DOCTRINE

A LETTER ADDRESSED TO HIS GRACE THE DUKE OF NORFOLK

WITH COMMENTARY AND NOTES BY JAMES GAFFNEY

IMAGE BOOKS
DOUBLEDAY
NEW YORK  LONDON  TORONTO  SYDNEY  AUCKLAND

An Image Book
PUBLISHED BY DOUBLEDAY
a division of Bantam Doubleday Dell Publishing Group, Inc.
666 Fifth Avenue, New York, New York 10103

Image and Doubleday are trademarks of Doubleday,
a division of Bantam Doubleday Dell Publishing Group, Inc.

This Image Original edition published May 1992.

Library of Congress Cataloging-in-Publication Data
Newman, John Henry, 1801–1890.
    Conscience, consensus, and the development of
    doctrine / by John Henry Newman; with commentary
    and notes by James Gaffney.
        p.  cm.
    Includes bibliographical references and index.
    1. Dogma, Development of.  2. Conscience—Religious
aspects—Catholic Church.  3. Catholic Church—
Infallibility.  4. Popes—Infallibility.  5. Laity—Catholic Church.
6. Catholic Church—Doctrines.  I. Gaffney, James.
II. Title.
BT21.N49   1992        91-38844
262.9—dc20              CIP
ISBN 0-385-42280-6

# CONTENTS

# FOREWORD

John Henry Newman's life nearly spanned the nineteenth century (1801–1890), and his celebrated transition from the Church of England to the Church of Rome occurred at its very midpoint (1845).

The literary monument of that transition, and fullest record of the argument of which it was for Newman the compelling practical conclusion, was *An Essay on the Development of Christian Doctrine*, a book-length treatise published in 1845. The *Essay* was revised slightly for a second edition in the following year, and much more extensively for a third one in 1878. It is this third edition which is reproduced in the present volume, as being not only Newman's final statement on the subject, but also the text of that work that has most influenced students and critics of his thought.

Two years before writing the *Essay*, Newman had treated the same subject much more briefly and in much more general terms in the last of *Fifteen Sermons Preached Before the University of Oxford*, entitled "The Theory of Developments in Religious Doctrine." That sermon (really a lecture) is here included not only as an eloquent prelude to the work more than ten times its length, but as incorporating a significantly different approach to the subject.

The two other works here presented come from the Roman Catholic half of Newman's life. They deal respectively with how doctrinal development is, or should be, influenced at the upper and lower extremities of Roman Catholicism's hierarchical society. The first, or "lowermost" of these is the laity. Newman contended (and was severely censured for contending) in an 1859 article, "On Consulting the Faithful in Matters of Doctrine," that the contribution of laypersons to the shaping of church doctrine is neither abnormal nor insignificant. The second, "uppermost" ecclesiastical stratum is that of the papacy. In 1875 Newman argued in what is actually a short book, formulated for political reasons as a "Letter Addressed to His Grace the Duke of Norfolk," that the scope of papal authority in determining the belief of Catholics is not indefinite or unlimited, and is predicated on the inviolable moral sovereignty of conscience.

The thematic thread that links all four of these works—and many other expressions of Newman's thought through much of his life—is that of how God's revelation is apprehended and elaborated, validly and faithfully, in the social and historical context of the Christian Church. That supernatural divine revelation is a reality, and that Christ founded a Church to receive, preserve, and transmit it, is not here in question—although Newman discussed those presuppositions critically in some of his other writings. Here he is arguing as a Christian with Christians, presuming divinely inspired Scriptures and an apostolically instituted Church, authorized by Christ to teach, rule, and sanctify, in his name. What is mainly at issue in all four of these works is the reliability of the Church's teaching function, and how the fidelity of that function is discerned and preserved.

Evidently, Church teachings had never been restricted to simple reiterations or even modest paraphrases of what the New Testament records as teachings of Christ or his apostles. Indeed, the very authority attributed to the New Testament is itself a Church teaching undiscoverable in the New Testament's pages. And, over the course of nearly two millennia, statements of Church doctrine have continued to accumulate, claiming normative status for believing Christians as expressing divinely revealed truth. In every age, some Christians challenged and repudiated certain of these Church doctrines as mere human inventions usurping the prerogatives of divine revelations. Likewise in every age, certain Christians or groups of Christians put forward statements of belief that they regarded as components or implications of Christian faith, only to have those cherished beliefs stigmatized as heretical by Church authorities. Thus the elaboration of orthodoxy has been frequently punctuated by the emergence of heterodoxy, generating conflicts that often resulted in ecclesiastical fragmentation.

The most momentously divisive of such episodes was, of course, the Protestant Reformation of the sixteenth century, after which nearly all of Western Christianity has been popularly regarded as divided between Protestants and Catholics. The most notable exception to that broad division has been the Church of England, which originated in a dispute that was primarily political and only incidentally doctrinal. As a result Anglicanism, detached from papal jurisdiction, has shown, from age to age and from faction to faction, alternate learnings towards Protestant (Calvinist and Lutheran) or Roman Catholic conceptions of Christian orthodoxy.

Newman's decisive conversion from scepticism to Christianity took place when he was only fifteen years old. He was never, as an adult Christian, tempted by Continental Protestantism, which he regarded as departing radically from "the Church of the Fathers." The latter phrase he applied to that period of early Christianity, mainly in the fourth and fifth centuries, when the main lines of Christian belief and worship were definitively laid down. In the course of his career as an Anglican, Newman at first assumed, hoped, and argued, but later doubted and at last denied, that the Church of England in his own day was the legitimate heir of the Church of the Fathers. *Simultaneously*, he found himself compelled to reexamine, revise, and ultimately repudiate his own arguments denying that that legacy belonged instead to the Church of Rome. Newman's *Essay on the Development of Christian Doctrine* is his fullest account of this revisionary reading and practical reinterpretation of the historical evidence. The book ends, accordingly, in a way most uncharacteristic of historical treatises, with an impassioned exhortation to readers not to ignore the argument or doubt its motives, and to recognize that what is at issue reaches not only time but eternity. How deeply the work's outcome eased its author's own spirit finds expression in its concluding sentence, cited in Latin from the Gospel hymn, *Nunc dimittis*: "Lord, now lettest thou thy servant depart in peace, according to thy word; for mine eyes have seen thy salvation . . ." It is very characteristic of Newman, for whom theological inquiry was never a dispassionate academic exercise, but always a deeply personal religious undertaking.

Newman's most homely way of explaining what he attempted to do in the *Essay* on development was to say that he was trying to decide where, among the multidenominational churches of Victorian England, a reincarnated St. Athanasius or St. Ambrose might find himself religiously at home. No doubt, time-travellers from the Church of the Fathers would encounter puzzling novelties at whatever parish they chose to visit. But, given the gospel's assurance that Christ's Church would endure until the end of history, Newman was confident that in some contemporary churches they would not fail to recognize the worship and teaching they knew as Christian, and would even perceive that less familiar features were natural outgrowths of authentically Christian roots. In other churches they would be disquieted by the omission of essential things and the inclusion of incongruous ones.

Throughout his Anglican career, Newman remained persuaded that a visitor from the Church of the Fathers would find that essential omissions disqualified Protestantism, while incongruous additions discredited Roman Catholicism. Between those two extremes of doctrinal barrenness and overgrowth there lay, he hoped, a middle ground, what he called a *via media*, within the Church of England. Newman's dedication to the Oxford Movement was in great part an effort to preserve and share that hope, resisting those forces of Protestant and Liberal (or rationalistic) thought that threatened to carry Anglicanism far to the left of its middle ground, while attempting to assemble traditional elements of Anglican doctrine and worship into a plausible facsimile of the Church of the Fathers. The resulting synthesis, Newman was compelled to acknowledge, was a purely theoretical construction, an ideal Church of England that had never been realized and that had poor prospects of being realized by forces prevailing in that Church in the nineteenth century. At the same time, his critics within the Church of England became apprehensive that Newman's reinterpretation and reconstruction of the Church of England, whether or not it bore any significant likeness to the Church of the Fathers, resembled increasingly the Church of Rome. To most Anglicans of the Victorian age, what the Church of Rome chiefly connoted were superstition, authoritarianism, and foreignness. To the average Englishman, religious deserts of Protestantism seemed easier to traverse than jungles of Roman Catholicism, and the secularizing drift of rationalism appeared less threatening than mindless subservience to an Italian theocrat. If Newman felt otherwise, let him go quietly and alone from the lovely decent Englishness of Oxford into ecclesiastical haunts of eccentric pre-Elizabethan diehards, vulgar Irish immigrants, jail-like nunneries, and exotic clergymen whose very accents marked them as agents of a foreign power. To Newman, an utterly domesticated Oxonian and Victorian, it could come as no surprise that in the view of colleagues and compatriots the path to Rome led to a kind of ecclesiastical slumming. Nevertheless, elegance of churchly lifestyle was beside the point. The point was to identify in mid-nineteenth century the church that had arisen in response to Christ's message preached by Christ's apostles. That Christ had founded such a church Newman did not question. That the church he founded had afterwards ceased to exist, and been succeeded only by false pretenders, he admitted to be abstractly possible, but dismissed as an "unnatural" assumption. The "natural" assumption was that a religion professed uninterruptedly for eighteen centuries had existed throughout that time. But since those who currently professed it disallowed one another's claims to legitimacy, how was one to identify the real thing? One proposal for doing so was to identify the doctrines of the primitive church, regarding anything added to them as corruptions and, setting the corruptions aside, to recover what, according to the formula of authenticity given by Vincent of Lerins, "had been believed always, everywhere, and by all."

Without disputing the truth of this "Vincentian Canon," Newman doubted its concrete applicability. Applied strictly, it would exclude even articles of the Creeds professed by all Christians, for they were not explicitly formulated for centuries after Christ. If applied expansively, it could not effectively discriminate between disputed doctrines of Anglicans and Roman Catholics. A usable criterion must be one that acknowledged doctrinal changes evidenced by history, while at the same time distinguishing continuity from discontinuity underlying the changes. The notion of essential continuity underlying a succession of changes was, after all, a perfectly familiar idea. It was the idea of growth, evolution, development—the very opposite of corruption, indicative not of disintegration but of life.

This is, of course, a metaphorical way of thinking and arguing, and the metaphor is, basically, a biological one. It has often been remarked that Newman, like so many other nineteenth-century thinkers, exhibits a certain temperamental affinity to their famous contemporary Darwin by his readiness to regard the objects of his study as emerging and evolving, rather than as fixed and finished realities. Nevertheless, although "to live is to change" is one of Newman's most quoted phrases, the analogue most present to his thought is not biological but psychological; what he has chiefly in mind are not organisms but ideas. Indeed, although evolutionary thought was definitely in the air since the previous century, the *Essay on Development* appeared more than a decade before the *Origin of Species*. Newman had little interest in biological evolutionary theory, which, moreover, he did not think conflicted in any way with belief in divine creation.

Newman did not think his understanding of development was original or unique. He even suggested that it had "at all times, perhaps, been implicitly adopted by theologians" and mentioned its use by Maistre and Möhler among his contemporaries. Newman's own use of it reflects the influence on him, which he acknowledged to be very great, of the eighteenth-century Anglican philosopher of religion, Bishop Joseph Butler, who argued in his book, *The Analogy of Religion*, that many objections to religious doctrines lose much of their force when we observe how closely those doctrines parallel ordinary natural phenomena that we readily take for granted. In the same vein, Newman argues that the sort of development he believes to have taken place in Christian doctrine is simply the counterpart, in the history of revealed religion, of what normally occurs in the history of "any philosophy or polity which takes possession of the intellect and heart, and has had any wide or extended dominion." The reason why it occurs is because "from the nature of the human mind, time is necessary for the full comprehension and perfection of great ideas." Applying these observations to Christian doctrinal tradition, one should not be surprised that "the highest and most wonderful truths, though communicated to the world once for all by inspired teachers, could not be comprehended all at once by the recipients, but, as being received and transmitted by minds not inspired and through media which were human, have required only the longer time and deeper thought for their full elucidation." "This," says Newman, "may be called the *Theory of Development of Doctrine*."

Evidently, the most such a theory could account for is the fact that Christian doctrine does seem to expand over the course of time. By the same token, the only objection it could meet is that later Christians seem to insist upon a number of beliefs that earlier Christians, though closer in time to the source of their revelation, seem to have ignored. The theory as stated here does not offer any help towards deciding *which* of these beliefs insisted upon by later Christians really are elucidations of those truths "communicated to the world once for all by inspired teachers." To do that, the theory would have to be elaborated, and much of that elaboration is undertaken in Newman's *Essay on Development*. The simpler form of the theory, as stated above, is expounded eloquently in Newman's fifteenth *University Sermon*, which accordingly provides an excellent introduction to the larger work, but is by no means a synopsis of it.

# I

## THE THEORY OF DEVELOPMENTS
## IN RELIGIOUS DOCTRINE

*(February 2, 1843)*

# LIFE AND GROWTH IN RELIGIOUS DOCTRINE

The development of doctrine seems to have become a major theoretical preoccupation of Newman's in 1842, and his first major statement on that subject was the last of his *Fifteen Sermons Preached Before the University of Oxford*, delivered at St. Mary's Church in February of the following year. University sermons were not liturgical homilies but religious lectures. This last one of Newman's was his longest, having occupied a full hour and a half.

Newman's first appointment to preach a university sermon was in 1826, but despite their having spanned seventeen years he found sufficient connectedness among them to publish them all in a single volume which he thought would be his "best book" to date. Some have thought it even excelled much more famous later works. It contains significant anticipations of all of them, but most conspicuously of the *Essay in Aid of a Grammar of Assent* and the *Essay on the Development of Christian Doctrine*. Newman considered "faith and reason" to be the general subject matter common to all the sermons. He later remarked that the most representative of them incorporated "the two principles which are so prominent in the *Essay* (on Development), that no idea can be comprehended in all its bearings at once" and that "the main instrument of proof in matters of life is antecedent probability." It is especially the first of those principles that underlies the argument of the university sermon on "The Theory of Developments in Religious Doctrine," which is reproduced in the following pages.

As a sermon, the discourse is introduced with a biblical text. Newman chose, as appropriate to both the day, the Feast of the Purification, and his theme, doctrinal development, the Lucan passage, "Mary kept all these things, pondering them in her heart." Essentially, what the sermon is about is what happens, normally and naturally, when a profound idea, and in particular a revealed religious truth, is pondered in the hearts of devout believers. Newman was always impressed by the way that great ideas comprise innumerable aspects and entail innumerable implications. His very concept of an educated person was that of one who could progressively consider those aspects and draw out those implications. Great ideas, therefore, once taken into the mind, appeared to come alive, to expand, extend, and differentiate themselves in ways analogous to organic growth.

This general view of how great truths progressively unfold within receptive minds was Newman's basic answer to the question of how Christian belief proceeded from embracing the simple words of the Gospel to generate an unending proliferation of credal formulae, dogmatic pronouncements, and theological speculations. That, in his view, was simply the counterpart in a tradition of religious believers, of what always happened when great, living ideas were meditated long and seriously. Ideas that exhibited no such fertility when planted in the mind were dead ideas. Accordingly, for Newman, the growth and differentiation of doctrinal expression over the course of history was not a betrayal of the original idea, but a sign that the Word of God was indeed a living word that communicated an idea which, being alive, grew, unforeseeably and yet coherently.

Within Christian tradition, orthodoxy represented the fullness of life in the Christian idea, and therefore its richest growth. Heresies were mutilations of the idea, which either by killing it precluded development or allowed only partial and lopsided growth. Protestantism seemed to Newman always discredited by signs of arrested or distorted development.

Newman's sermon concentrates on his conviction that living ideas develop in a receptive mind, and his inference that if Christian faith embraces a living idea, development is only to be expected. Persuasive as his psychological analogies are, however, at least two questions are likely to remain in readers' minds. First, can the unfolding of an idea in an individual mind really be likened, in a more than superficial way, to the proliferation of doctrinal statements in a church comprising great numbers of individuals in many successive generations? That is, how meaningfully can one argue, on premises drawn from individual psychology, about processes in the "mind" of a church? And second, even granting the naturalness of development as an unfolding from within, must one not also admit the possibility of accretions from without, and of processes of change that are better likened to corruption than to maturation? Is there not a problem of overdevelopment, or hypertrophy, as well as one of atrophy, or underdevelopment?

Clearly, Newman's case for the propriety of doctrinal development needed to be supplemented with criteria for distinguishing healthy developments from unwholesome ones, and the criteria needed to be applied to the data of history. To these tasks he would address himself a few years later in his major work on this subject, the centerpiece of the present collection.

# The Theory of Developments
# in Religious Doctrine

(Preached on the Purification, 1843.)

LUKE ii. 19.
*"But Mary kept all these things,*
*and pondered them in her heart."*

Little is told us in Scripture concerning the Blessed Virgin, but there is one grace of which the Evangelists make her the pattern, in a few simple sentences—of Faith. Zacharias questioned the Angel's message, but "Mary said, Behold the handmaid of the Lord; be it unto me according to thy word." Accordingly Elisabeth, speaking with an apparent allusion to the contrast thus exhibited between her own highly-favoured husband, righteous Zacharias, and the still more highly-favoured Mary, said, on receiving her salutation, "Blessed art thou among women, and blessed is the fruit of thy womb; Blessed is she that believed for there shall be a performance of those things which were told her from the Lord."

2. But Mary's faith did not end in a mere acquiescence in Divine providences and revelations: as the text informs us, she "pondered" them. When the shepherds came, and told of the vision of Angels which they had seen at the time of the Nativity, and how one of them announced that the Infant in her arms was "the Saviour, which is Christ the Lord," while others did but wonder, "Mary kept all these things, and pondered them in her heart." Again, when her Son and Saviour had come to the age of twelve years, and had left her for awhile for His Father's service, and had been found, to her surprise, in the Temple, amid the doctors, both hearing them and asking them questions, and had, on her addressing Him, vouchsafed to justify His conduct, we are told, "His mother kept all these sayings in her heart." And accordingly, at the marriage-feast in Cana, her faith anticipated His first miracle, and she said to the servants, "Whatsoever He saith unto you, do it."

3. Thus St. Mary is our pattern of Faith, both in the reception and

in the study of Divine Truth. She does not think it enough to accept, she dwells upon it; not enough to possess, she uses it; not enough to assent, she developes it; not enough to submit the Reason, she reasons upon it; not indeed reasoning first, and believing afterwards, with Zacharias, yet first believing without reasoning, next from love and reverence, reasoning after believing. And thus she symbolizes to us, not only the faith of the unlearned, but of the doctors of the Church also, who have to investigate, and weigh, and define, as well as to profess the Gospel; to draw the line between truth and heresy; to anticipate or remedy the various aberrations of wrong reason; to combat pride and recklessness with their own arms; and thus to triumph over the sophist and the innovator.

4. If, then, on a Day dedicated to such high contemplations as the Feast which we are now celebrating, it is allowable to occupy the thoughts with a subject not of a devotional or practical nature, it will be some relief of the omission to select one in which St. Mary at least will be our example,—the use of Reason in investigating the doctrines of Faith; a subject, indeed, far fitter for a volume than for the most extended notice which can here be given to it; but one which cannot be passed over altogether in silence, in any attempt at determining the relation of Faith to Reason.

5. The overthrow of the wisdom of the world was one of the earliest, as well as the noblest of the triumphs of the Church; after the pattern of her Divine Master, who took His place among the doctors before He preached His new Kingdom, or opposed Himself to the world's power. St. Paul, the learned Pharisee, was the first fruits of that gifted company, in whom the pride of science is seen prostrated before the foolishness of preaching. From his day to this the Cross has enlisted under its banner all those great endowments of mind, which in former times had been expended on vanities, or dissipated in doubt and speculation. Nor was it long before the schools of heathenism took the alarm, and manifested an unavailing jealousy of the new doctrine, which was robbing them of their most hopeful disciples. They had hitherto taken for granted that the natural home of the Intellect was the Garden or the Porch; and it reversed their very first principles to be called on to confess, what yet they could not deny, that a Superstition, as they considered it, was attracting to itself all the energy, the keenness, the originality, and the eloquence of the age. But these aggressions upon heathenism were only the beginning of the Church's conquests; in the course of time the whole mind of the world, as I may say, was absorbed into the philosophy of the Cross, as the element in

which it lived, and the form upon which it was moulded. And how many centuries did this endure, and what vast ruins still remain of its dominion! In the capitals of Christendom the high cathedral and the perpetual choir still witness to the victory of Faith over the world's power. To see its triumph over the world's wisdom, we must enter those solemn cemeteries in which are stored the relics and the monuments of ancient Faith—our libraries. Look along their shelves, and every name you read there is, in one sense or other, a trophy set up in record of the victories of Faith. How many long lives, what high aims, what single-minded devotion, what intense contemplation, what fervent prayer, what deep erudition, what untiring diligence, what toilsome conflicts has it taken to establish its supremacy! This has been the object which has given meaning to the life of Saints, and which is the subject-matter of their history. For this they have given up the comforts of earth and the charities of home, and surrendered themselves to an austere rule, nay, even to confessorship and persecution, if so be they could make some small offering, or do some casual service, or provide some additional safeguard towards the great work which was in progress. This has been the origin of controversies, long and various, yes, and the occasion of much infirmity, the test of much hidden perverseness, and the subject of much bitterness and tumult. The world has been moved in consequence of it, populations excited, leagues and alliances formed, kingdoms lost and won: and even zeal, when excessive, evinced a sense of its preciousness; nay, even rebellions in some sort did homage to it, as insurgents imply the actual sovereignty of the power which they are assailing. Meanwhile the work went on, and at length a large fabric of divinity was reared, irregular in its structure, and diverse in its style, as beseemed the slow growth of centuries; nay, anomalous in its details, from the peculiarities of individuals, or the interference of strangers, but still, on the whole, the development of an idea, and like itself, and unlike anything else, its most widely-separated parts having relations with each other, and betokening a common origin.

6. Let us quit this survey of the general system, and descend to the history of the formation of any Catholic dogma. What a remarkable sight it is, as almost all unprejudiced persons will admit, to trace the course of the controversy, from its first disorders to its exact and determinate issue. Full of deep interest, to see how the great idea takes hold of a thousand minds by its living force, and will not be ruled or stinted, but is "like a burning fire," as the Prophet speaks, "shut up" within them, till they are "weary of forbearing, and cannot stay," and

grows in them, and at length is born through them, perhaps in a long course of years, and even successive generations; so that the doctrine may rather be said to use the minds of Christians, than to be used by them. Wonderful it is to see with what effort, hesitation, suspense, interruption,—with how many swayings to the right and to the left—with how many reverses, yet with what certainty of advance, with what precision in its march, and with what ultimate completeness, it has been evolved; till the whole truth "self-balanced on its centre hung," part answering to part, one, absolute, integral, indissoluable, while the world lasts! Wonderful, to see how heresy has but thrown that idea into fresh forms, and drawn out from if farther developments, with an exuberance which exceeded all questioning, and a harmony which baffled all criticism, like Him, its Divine Author, who, when put on trial by the Evil One, was but fortified by the assault, and is ever justified in His sayings, and overcomes when He is judged.

7. And this world of thought is the expansion of a few words, uttered, as if casually, by the fishermen of Galilee. Here is another topic which belongs more especially to that part of the subject to which I propose to confine myself. Reason has not only submitted, it has ministered to Faith; it has illustrated its documents; it has raised illiterate peasants into philosophers and divines; it has elicited a meaning from their words which their immediate hearers little suspected. Stranger surely is it that St. John should be a theologian, than that St. Peter should be a prince. This is a phenomenon proper to the Gospel, and a note of divinity. Its half sentences, its overflowings of language, admit of development[1]; they have a life in them which shows itself in progress; a truth, which has the token of consistency; a reality, which is fruitful in resources; a depth, which extends into mystery: for they are representations of what is actual, and has a definite location and necessary bearings and a meaning in the great system of things, and a harmony in what it is, and a compatibility in what it involves. What form of Paganism can furnish a parallel? What philosopher has left his words to posterity as a talent which could be put to usury, as a mine which could be wrought? Here, too, is the badge of heresy; its dogmas are unfruitful; it has no theology; so far forth as it is heresy, it has none. Deduct its remnant of Catholic theology, and what remains? Polemics, explanations, protests. It turns to Biblical Criticism, or to the Evidences of Religion, for want of a province. Its *formulæ* end in themselves, without development, because they are words; they are

[1] Vide Butler's Analogy, part ii. ch. iii.

barren, because they are dead. If they had life, they would increase and multiply; or, if they do live and bear fruit, it is but as "sin, when it is finished, bringeth forth death." It developes into dissolution; but it creates nothing, it tends to no system, its resultant dogma is but the denial of all dogmas, any theology, under the Gospel. No wonder it denies what it cannot attain.

8. Heresy denies to the Church what is wanting in itself. Here, then, we are brought to the subject to which I wish to give attention. It need not surely formally be proved that this disparagement of doctrinal statements, and in particular of those relating to the Holy Trinity and Incarnation, is especially prevalent in our times. There is a suspicion widely abroad,—felt, too, perhaps, by many who are unwilling to confess it,—that the development of ideas and formation of dogmas is a mere abuse of Reason, which, when it attempted such sacred subjects, went beyond its powers, and could do nothing more than multiply words without meaning, and deductions which come to nothing. The conclusion follows, that such an attempt does but lead to mischievous controversy, from that discordance of doctrinal opinions, which is its immediate consequence; that there is, in truth, no necessary or proper connexion between inward religious belief and scientific expositions; and that charity, as well as good sense, is best consulted by reducing creeds to the number of private opinions, which, if individuals will hold for themselves, at least they have no right to impose upon others.

9. It is my purpose, then, in what follows, to investigate the connexion between Faith and Dogmatic Confession, as far as relates to the sacred doctrines which were just now mentioned, and to show the office of the Reason in reference to it; and, in doing so, I shall make as little allusion as may be to erroneous views on the subject, which have been mentioned only for the sake of perspicuity; following rather the course which the discussion may take, and pursuing those issues on which it naturally opens. Nor am I here in any way concerned with the question, who is the legitimate framer and judge of these dogmatic inferences under the Gospel, or if there be any. Whether the Church is infallible, or the individual, or the first ages, or none of these, is not the point here, but the theory of developments itself.

10. Theological dogmas are propositions expressive of the judgments which the mind forms, or the impressions which it receives, of Revealed Truth. Revelation sets before it certain supernatural facts and actions, beings and principles; these make a certain impression or image upon it; and this impression spontaneously, or even necessarily,

becomes the subject of reflection on the part of the mind itself, which proceeds to investigate it, and to draw it forth in successive and distinct sentences. Thus the Catholic doctrine of Original Sin, or of Sin after Baptism, or of the Eucharist, or of Justification, is but the expression of the inward belief of Catholics on these several points, formed upon an analysis of that belief[2]. Such, too, are the high doctrines with which I am especially concerned.

11. Now, here I observe, first of all, that, naturally as the inward idea of divine truth, such as has been described, passes into explicit form by the activity of our reflective powers, still such an actual delineation is not essential to its genuineness and perfection. A peasant may have such a true impression, yet be unable to give any intelligible account of it, as will easily be understood. But what is remarkable at first sight is this, that there is good reason for saying that the impression made upon the mind need not even be recognized by the parties possessing it. It is no proof that persons are not possessed, because they are not conscious, of an idea. Nothing is of more frequent occurrence, whether in things sensible or intellectual, than the existence of such unperceived impressions. What do we mean when we say, that certain persons do not know themselves, but that they are ruled by views, feelings, prejudices, objects which they do not recognize? How common is it to be exhilarated or depressed, we do not recollect why, though we are aware that something has been told us, or has happened, good or bad, which accounts for our feeling, could we recall it! What is memory itself, but a vast magazine of such dormant, but present and excitable ideas? Or consider, when persons would trace the history of their own opinions in past years, how baffled they are in the attempt to fix the date of this or that conviction, their system of thought having been all the while in continual, gradual, tranquil expansion; so that it were as easy to follow the growth of the fruit of the earth, "first the blade, then the ear, after that the full corn in the ear," as to chronicle changes, which involved no abrupt revolution, or reaction, or fickleness of mind, but have been the birth of an idea, the development, in explicit form, of what was already latent within it. Or, again, critical disquisitions are often written about the idea which this or that poet might have in his mind in certain of his compositions and characters; and we call such analysis the philosophy of poetry, not implying

---

[2] The controversy between the English Church and the Church of Rome lies, it is presumed, *in the matter of fact*, whether such and such developments are true, (e.g. Purgatory a true development of the doctrine of sin after baptism,) not in the *principle* of development itself.

thereby of necessity that the author wrote upon a theory in his actual delineation, or knew what he was doing; but that, in matter of fact, he was possessed, ruled, guided by an unconscious idea. Moreover, it is a question whether that strange and painful feeling of unreality, which religious men experience from time to time, when nothing seems true, or good, or right, or profitable, when Faith seems a name, and duty a mockery, and all endeavours to do right, absurd and hopeless, and all things forlorn and dreary, as if religion were wiped out from the world, may not be the direct effect of the temporary obscuration of some master vision, which unconsciously supplies the mind with spiritual life and peace.

12. Or, to take another class of instances which are to the point so far as this, that at least they are real impressions, even though they be not influential. How common is what is called vacant vision, when objects meet the eye, without any effort of the judgment to measure or locate them; and that absence of mind, which recollects minutes afterwards the occurrence of some sound, the striking of the hour, or the question of a companion, which passed unheeded at the time it took place! How, again, happens it in dreams, that we suddenly pass from one state of feeling, or one assemblage of circumstances to another, without any surprise at the incongruity, except that, while we are impressed first in this way, then in that, we take no active cognizance of the impression? And this, perhaps, is the life of inferior animals, a sort of continuous dream, impressions without reflections; such, too, seems to be the first life of infants; nay, in heaven itself, such may be the high existence of some exalted orders of blessed spirits, as the Seraphim, who are said to be, not Knowledge, but all Love.

13. Now, it is important to insist on this circumstance, because it suggests the reality and permanence of inward knowledge, as distinct from explicit confession. The absence, or partial absence, or incompleteness of dogmatic statements is no proof of the absence of impressions or implicit judgments, in the mind of the Church. Even centuries might pass without the formal expression of a truth, which had been all along the secret life of millions of faithful souls. Thus, not till the thirteenth century was there any direct and distinct avowal, on the part of the Church, of the numerical Unity of the Divine Nature, which the language of some of the principal Greek fathers, *primâ facie*, though not really, denies. Again, the doctrine of the Double Procession was no Catholic dogma in the first ages, though it was more or less clearly stated by individual Fathers; yet, if it is now to be received, as

surely it must be, as part of the Creed, it was really held every where from the beginning, and therefore, in a measure, held as a mere religious impression, and perhaps an unconscious one.

14. But, further, if the ideas may be latent in the Christian mind, by which it is animated and formed, it is less wonderful that they should be difficult to elicit and define; and of this difficulty we have abundant proof in the history whether of the Church, or of individuals. Surely it is not at all wonderful, that, when individuals attempt to analyze their own belief, they should find the task arduous in the extreme, if not altogether beyond them; or, again, a work of many years; or, again, that they should shrink from the true developments, if offered to them, as foreign to their thoughts. This may be illustrated in a variety of ways.

15. It will often happen, perhaps from the nature of things, that it is impossible to master and express an idea in a short space of time. As to individuals, sometimes they find they cannot do so at all; at length, perhaps, they recognize, in some writer they meet, with the very account of their own thoughts, which they desiderate; and then they say, that "here is what they have felt all along, and wanted to say, but could not," or "what they have ever maintained, only better expressed." Again, how many men are burdened with an idea, which haunts them through a great part of their lives, and of which only at length, with much trouble, do they dispossess themselves? I suppose most of us have felt at times the irritation, and that for a long period, of thoughts and views which we felt, and felt to be true, only dimly showing themselves, or flitting before us; which at length we understood must not be forced, but must have their way, and would, if it were so ordered, come to light in their own time. The life of some men, and those not the least eminent among divines and philosophers, has centred in the development of one idea; nay, perhaps has been too short for the process. Again, how frequently it happens, that, on first hearing a doctrine propounded, a man hesitates, first acknowledges, then disowns it; then says that he has always held it, but finds fault with the mode in which it is presented to him, accusing it of paradox or over-refinement; that is, he cannot at the moment analyze his own opinions, and does not know whether he holds the doctrine or not, from the difficulty of mastering his thoughts.

16. Another characteristic, as I have said, of dogmatic statements, is the difficulty of recognizing them, even when attained, as the true representation of our meaning. This happens for many reasons; sometimes, from the faint hold we have of the impression itself, whether its

nature be good or bad, so that we shrink from principles in substance, which we acknowledge in influence. Many a man, for instance, is acting on utilitarian principles, who is shocked at them in set treatises, and disowns them. Again, in sacred subjects, the very circumstance that a dogma professes to be a direct contemplation, and, if so be, a definition of what is infinite and eternal, is painful to serious minds. Moreover, from the hypothesis, it is the representation of an idea in a medium not native to it, not as originally conceived, but, as it were, in projection; no wonder, then, that, though there be an intimate correspondence, part by part, between the impression and the dogma, yet there should be an harshness in the outline of the latter; as, for instance, a want of harmonious proportion; and yet this is unavoidable, from the infirmities of our intellectual powers.

17. Again, another similar peculiarity in developments in general, is the great remoteness of the separate results of a common idea, or rather at first sight the absence of any connexion. Thus it often happens that party spirit is imputed to persons, merely because they agree with one another in certain points of opinion and conduct, which are thought too minute, distant, and various, in the large field of religious doctrine and discipline, to proceed from any but an external influence and a positive rule; whereas an insight into the wonderfully expansive power and penetrating virtue of theological or philosophical ideas would have shown, that what is apparently arbitrary in rival or kindred schools of thought, is after all rigidly determined by the original hypothesis. The remark has been made, for instance, that rarely have persons maintained the sleep of the soul before the Resurrection, without falling into more grievous errors; again, those who deny the Lutheran doctrine of Justification, commonly have tendencies towards a ceremonial religion; again, it is a serious fact that Protestantism has at various times unexpectedly developed into an allowance or vindication of polygamy; and heretics in general, however opposed in tenets, are found to have an inexplicable sympathy for each other, and never wake up from their ordinary torpor, but to exchange courtesies and meditate coalitions. One other remark is in point here, and relates to the length to which statements run, though, before we attempted them, we fancied our idea could be expressed in one or two sentences. Explanations grow under our hands, in spite of our effort at compression. Such, too, is the contrast between conversation and epistolary correspondence. We speak our meaning with little trouble; our voice, manner, and half words completing it for us; but in writing, when details must be drawn out, and misapprehensions anticipated, we seem never

to be rid of the responsibility of our task. This being the case, it is surprising that the Creeds are so short, nor surprising that they need a comment.

18. The difficulty, then, and hazard of developing doctrines implicitly received, must be fully allowed; and this is often made a ground for inferring that they have no proper developments at all; that there is no natural connexion between certain dogmas and certain impressions; and that theological science is a matter of time, and place, and accident, though inward belief is ever and every where one and the same. But surely the instinct of every Christian revolts from such a position; for the very first impulse of his faith is to try to express itself about the "great sight" which is vouchsafed to it; and this seems to argue that a science there is, whether the mind is equal to its discovery or no. And, indeed, what science is open to every chance inquirer? which is not recondite in its principles? which requires not special gifts of mind for its just formation? All subject-matters admit of true theories and false, and the false are no prejudice to the true. Why should this class of ideas be different from all other? Principles of philosophy, physics, ethics, politics, taste, admit both of implicit reception and explicit statement; why should not the ideas, which are the secret life of the Christian, be recognized also as fixed and definite in themselves, and as capable of scientific analysis? Why should not there be that real connexion between science and its subject-matter in religion, which exists in other departments of thought? No one would deny that the philosophy of Zeno or Pythagoras was the exponent of a certain mode of viewing things; or would affirm that Platonist and Epicurean acted on one and the same idea of nature, life, and duty, and meant the same thing, though they verbally differed, merely because a Plato or an Epicurus was needed to detect the abstruse elements of thought, out of which each philosophy was eventually constructed. A man surely may be a Peripatetic or an Academic in his feelings, views, aims, and acts, who never heard the names. Granting, then, extreme cases, when individuals who would analyze their views of religion are thrown entirely upon their own reason, and find that reason unequal to the task, this will be no argument against a general, natural, and ordinary correspondence between the dogma and the inward idea. Surely, if Almighty God is ever one and the same, and is revealed to us as one and the same, the true inward impression of Him, made on the recipient of the revelation, must be one and the same; and, since human nature proceeds upon fixed laws, the statement of that impression must be one and the same, so that we may as well say that there are two Gods

as two Creeds. And considering the strong feelings and energetic acts and severe sufferings which age after age have been involved in the maintenance of the Catholic dogmas, it is surely a very shallow philosophy to account such maintenance a mere contest about words, and a very abject philosophy to attribute it to mere party spirit, or to personal rivalry, or to ambition, or to covetousness.

19. Reasonable, however, as is this view of doctrinal developments in general, it cannot be denied that those which relate to the Objects of Faith, of which I am particularly speaking, have a character of their own, and must be considered separately. Let us, then, consider how the case stands, as regards the sacred doctrines of the Trinity and the Incarnation.

20. The Apostle said to the Athenians, "Whom ye ignorantly worship, Him declare I unto you;" and the mind which is habituated to the thought of God, of Christ, of the Holy Spirit, naturally turns, as I have said, with a devout curiosity to the contemplation of the Object of its adoration, and begins to form statements concerning Him before it knows whither, or how far, it will be carried. One proposition necessarily leads to another, and a second to a third; then some limitation is required; and the combination of these opposites occasions some fresh evolutions from the original idea, which indeed can never be said to be entirely exhausted. This process is its development, and results in a series, or rather body of dogmatic statements, till what was at first an impression on the Imagination has become a system or creed in the Reason.

21. Now such impressions are obviously individual and complete above other theological ideas, *because* they are the impressions of Objects. Ideas and their developments are commonly not identical, the development being but the carrying out of the idea into its consequences. Thus the doctrine of Penance may be called a development of the doctrine of Baptism, yet still is a distinct doctrine; whereas the developments in the doctrines of the Holy Trinity and the Incarnation are mere portions of the original impression, and modes of representing it. As God is one, so the impression which He gives us of Himself is one; it is not a thing of parts; it is not a system; nor is it any thing imperfect, and needing a counterpart. It is the vision of an object. When we pray, we pray, not to an assemblage of notions, or to a creed, but to One Individual Being; and when we speak of Him we speak of a Person, not of a Law or a Manifestation. This being the case, all our attempts to delineate our impression of Him go to bring out one idea,

not two or three or four; not a philosophy, but an individual idea in its separate aspects.

22. This may be fitly compared to the impressions made on us through the senses. Material objects are whole, and individual; and the impressions which they make on the mind, by means of the senses, are of a corresponding nature, complex and manifold in their relations and bearings, but considered in themselves integral and one. And in like manner the ideas which we are granted of Divine Objects under the Gospel, from the nature of the case and because they are ideas, answer to the Originals so far as this, that they are whole, indivisible, substantial, and may be called real, as being images of what is real. Objects which are conveyed to us through the senses, stand out in our minds, as I may say, with dimensions and aspects and influences various, and all of these consistent with one another, and many of them beyond our memory or even knowledge, while we contemplate the objects themselves; thus forcing on us a persuasion of their reality from the spontaneous congruity and coincidence of these accompaniments, as if they could not be creations of our minds, but were the images of external and independent beings. This of course will take place in the case of the sacred ideas which are the objects of our faith. Religious men, according to their measure, have an idea or vision of the Blessed Trinity in Unity, of the Son Incarnate and of His Presence, not as a number of qualities, attributes, and actions, not as the subject of a number of propositions, but as one, and individual, and independent of words, as an impression conveyed through the senses.

23. Particular propositions, then, which are used to express portions of the great idea vouchsafed to us, can never really be confused with the idea itself, which all such propositions taken together can but reach, and cannot exceed. As definitions are not intended to go beyond their subject, but to be adequate to it, so the dogmatic statements of the Divine Nature used in our confessions, however multiplied, cannot say more than is implied in the original idea, considered in its completeness, without the risk of heresy. Creeds and dogmas live in the one idea which they are designed to express, and which alone is substantive; and are necessary only because the human mind cannot reflect upon that idea, except piecemeal, cannot use it in its oneness and entireness, nor without resolving it into a series of aspects and relations. And in matter of fact these expressions are never equivalent to it; we are able, indeed, to define the creations of our own minds, for they are what we make them and nothing else; but it were as easy to create what is real as to

define it; and thus the Catholic dogmas are, after all, but symbols of a Divine fact, which, far from being compassed by those very propositions, would not be exhausted, nor fathomed, by a thousand.

24. Now of such sacred ideas and their attendant expressions, I observe:—

(1.) First, that an impression of this intimate kind seems to be what Scripture means by "knowledge." "This is life eternal," says our Saviour, "that they might know Thee the only True God, and Jesus Christ whom Thou hast sent." In like manner St. Paul speaks of willingly losing all things, "for the excellency of the knowledge of Christ Jesus;" and St. Peter of "the knowledge of Him who hath called us to glory and virtue[3]." Knowledge is the possession of those living ideas of sacred things, from which alone change of heart or conduct can proceed. This awful vision is what Scripture seems to designate by the phrases "Christ in us," "Christ dwelling in us by faith," "Christ formed in us," and "Christ manifesting Himself unto us." And though it is faint and doubtful in some minds, and distinct in others, as some remote object in the twilight or in the day, this arises from the circumstances of the particular mind, and does not interfere with the perfection of the gift itself.

25. (2.) This leads me next, however, to observe, that these religious impressions differ from those of material objects, in the mode in which they are made. The senses are direct, immediate, and ordinary informants, and act spontaneously without any will or effort on our part; but no such faculties have been given us, as far as we know, for realizing the Objects of Faith. It is true that inspiration may be a gift of this kind to those who have been favoured with it; nor would it be safe to deny to the illuminating grace of Baptism a power, at least of putting the mind into a capacity for receiving impressions; but the former of these is not ordinary, and both are supernatural. The secondary and intelligible means by which we receive the impression of Divine Verities, are, for instance, the habitual and devout perusal of Scripture, which gradually acts upon the mind; again, the gradual influence of intercourse with those who are in themselves in possession of the sacred ideas; again, the study of Dogmatic Theology, which is our present subject; again, a continual round of devotion; or again, sometimes, in minds both fitly disposed and apprehensive, the almost instantaneous operation of a keen faith. This obvious distinction follows between sensible and religious ideas, that we put the latter into lan-

[3] John xvii. 3. Phil. iii. 8. 2 Pet. i. 3.

guage in order to fix, teach, and transmit them, but not the former. No one defines a material object by way of conveying to us what we know so much better by the senses, but we form creeds as a chief mode of perpetuating the impression.

26. (3.) Further, I observe, that though the Christian mind reasons out a series of dogmatic statements, one from another, this it has ever done, and always must do, not from those statements taken in themselves, as logical propositions, but as being itself enlightened and (as if) inhabited by that sacred impression which is prior to them, which acts as a regulating principle, ever present, upon the reasoning, and without which no one has any warrant to reason at all. Such sentences as "the Word was God," or "the Only-begotten Son who is in the bosom of the Father," or "the Word was made flesh," or "the Holy Ghost which proceedeth from the Father," are not a mere letter which we may handle by the rules of art at our own will, but august tokens of most simple, ineffable, adorable facts, embraced, enshrined according to its measure in the believing mind. For though the development of an idea is a deduction of proposition from proposition, these propositions are ever formed in and round the idea itself (so to speak), and are in fact one and all only aspects of it. Moreover, this will account both for the mode of arguing from particular texts or single words of Scripture, practised by the early Fathers, and for their fearless decision in practising it; for the great Object of Faith on which they lived both enabled them to appropriate to itself particular passages of Scripture, and became to them a safeguard against heretical deductions from them. Also, it will account for the charge of weak reasoning, commonly brought against those Fathers; for never do we seem so illogical to others as when we are arguing under the continual influence of impressions to which they are insensible.

27. (4.) Again, it must of course be remembered, as I have just implied, (though as being an historical matter it hardly concerns us here), that Revelation itself has provided in Scripture the main outlines and also large details of the dogmatic system. Inspiration has superseded the exercise of human Reason in great measure, and left it but the comparatively easy task of finishing the sacred work. The question, indeed, at first sight occurs, why such inspired statements are not enough without further developments; but in truth, when Reason has once been put on the investigation, it cannot stop till it has finished it; one dogma creates another, by the same right by which it was itself created; the Scripture statements are sanctions as well as informants in the inquiry; they begin and they do not exhaust.

28. (5.) Scripture, I say, begins a series of developments which it does not finish; that is to say, in other words, it is a mistake to look for every separate proposition of the Catholic doctrine in Scripture. This is plain from what has gone before. For instance, the Athanasian Creed professes to lay down the right faith, which we must hold on its most sacred subjects, in order to be saved. This must mean that there is one view concerning the Holy Trinity, or concerning the Incarnation, which is true, and distinct from all others; one definite, consistent, entire view, which cannot be mistaken, not contained in any certain number of propositions, but held as a view by the believing mind, and not held, but denied by Arians, Sabellians, Tritheists, Nestorians, Monophysites, Socinians, and other heretics. That idea is not enlarged, if propositions are added, nor impaired if they are withdrawn: if they are added, this is with a view of conveying that one integral view, not of amplifying it. That view does not depend on such propositions: it does not consist in them; they are but specimens and indications of it. And they may be multiplied without limit. They are necessary, but not needful to it, being but portions or aspects of that previous impression which has at length come under the cognizance of Reason and the terminology of science. The question, then, is not whether this or that proposition of the Catholic doctrine is *in terminis* in Scripture, unless we would be slaves to the letter, but whether that one view of the Mystery, of which all such are the exponents, be not there; a view which would be some other view, and not itself, if any one of such propositions, if any one of a number of similar propositions, were not true. Those propositions imply each other, as being parts of one whole; so that to deny one is to deny all, and to invalidate one is to deface and destroy the view itself. One thing alone has to be impressed on us by Scripture, the Catholic idea, and in it they all are included. To object, then, to the number of propositions, upon which an anathema is placed, is altogether to mistake their use; for their multiplication is not intended to enforce many things, but to express one,—to form within us that one impression concerning Almighty God, as the ruling principle of our minds, and that, whether we can fully recognize our own possession of it or no. And surely it is no paradox to say that such ruling ideas may exert a most powerful influence, at least in their various aspects, on our moral character, and on the whole man: as no one would deny in the case of belief or disbelief of a Supreme Being.

29. (6.) And here we see the ordinary mistake of doctrinal innovators, viz. to go away with this or that proposition of the Creed, instead of embracing that one idea which all of them together are meant to

convey; it being almost a definition of heresy, that it fastens on some one statement as if the whole truth, to the denial of all others, and as the basis of a new faith; erring rather in what it rejects, than in what it maintains: though, in truth, if the mind deliberately rejects any portion of the doctrine, this is a proof that it does not really hold even that very statement for the sake of which it rejects the others. Realizing is the very life of true developments; it is peculiar to the Church, and the justification of her definitions.

30. Enough has now been said on the distinction, yet connexion, between the implicit knowledge and the explicit confession of the Divine Objects of Faith, as they are revealed to us under the Gospel. An objection, however, remains, which cannot be satisfactorily treated in a few words. And what is worse than prolixity, the discussion may bear with it some appearance of unnecessary or even wanton refinement; unless, indeed, it is thrown into the form of controversy, a worse evil. Let it suffice to say, that my wish is, not to discover difficulties in any subject, but to solve them.

31. It may be asked, then, whether the mistake of words and names for things is not incurred by orthodox as well as heretics, in dogmatizing at all about the "secret things which belong unto the Lord our God," inasmuch as the idea of a supernatural object must itself be supernatural, and since no such ideas are claimed by ordinary Christians, no knowledge of Divine Verities is possible to them. How should any thing of this world convey ideas which are beyond and above this world? How can teaching and intercourse, how can human words, how can earthly images, convey to the mind an idea of the Invisible? They cannot rise above themselves. They can suggest no idea but what is resolvable into ideas natural and earthly. The words "Person," "Substance," "Consubstantial," "Generation," "Procession," "Incarnation," "Taking of the manhood into God," and the like, have either a very abject and human meaning, or none at all. In other words, there is no such inward view of these doctrines, distinct from the dogmatic language used to express them, as was just now supposed. The metaphors by which they are signified are not mere symbols of ideas which exist independently of them, but their meaning is coincident and identical with the ideas. When, indeed, we have knowledge of a thing from other sources, then the metaphors we may apply to it are but accidental appendages to that knowledge; whereas our ideas of Divine things are just coextensive with the figures by which we express them, neither more nor less, and without them are not; and when we draw inferences from those figures, we are not illustrating one existing idea, but draw-

ing mere logical inferences. We speak, indeed, of material objects freely, because our senses reveal them to us apart from our words; but as to these ideas about heavenly things, we learn them from words, yet (it seems) we are to say what we, without words, conceive of them, as if words could convey what they do not contain. It follows that our anathemas, our controversies, our struggles, our sufferings, are merely about the poor ideas conveyed to us in certain figures of speech.

32. Some obvious remarks suggest themselves in answer to this representation. First, it is difficult to determine what divine grace may not do for us, if not in immediately implanting new ideas, yet in refining and elevating those which we gain through natural informants. If, as we all acknowledge, grace renews our moral feelings, yet through outward means, if it opens upon us new ideas about virtue and goodness and heroism and heavenly peace, it does not appear why, in a certain sense, it may not impart ideas concerning the nature of God. Again, the various terms and figures which are used in the doctrine of the Holy Trinity or of the Incarnation, surely may by their combination create ideas which will be altogether new, though they are still of an earthly character. And further, when it is said that such figures convey no knowledge of the Divine Nature itself, beyond those figures, whatever they are, it should be considered whether our senses can be proved to suggest any real idea of matter. All that we know, strictly speaking, is the existence of the impressions our senses make on us; and yet we scruple not to speak as if they conveyed to us the knowledge of material substances. Let, then, the Catholic dogmas, as such, be freely admitted to convey no true idea of Almighty God, but only an earthly one, gained from earthly figures, provided it be allowed, on the other hand, that the senses do not convey to us any true idea of matter, but only an idea commensurate with sensible impressions.

33. Nor is there any reason why this should not be fully granted. Still there may be a certain correspondence between the idea, though earthly, and its heavenly archetype, such, that that idea belongs to the archetype, in a sense in which no other earthly idea belongs to it, as being the nearest approach to it which our present state allows. Indeed Scripture itself intimates the earthly nature of our present ideas of Sacred Objects, when it speaks of our now "seeing in a glass *darkly*, ἐν αἰνίγματι, but then face to face" and it has ever been the doctrine of divines that the Beatific Vision, or true sight of Almighty God, is reserved for the world to come. Meanwhile we are allowed such an approximation to the truth as earthly images and figures may supply to us.

34. It must not be supposed that this is the only case in which we are obliged to receive information needful to us, through the medium of our existing ideas, and consequently with but a vague apprehension of its subject-matter. Children, who are made our pattern in Scripture, are taught, by an accommodation, on the part of their teachers, to their immature faculties and their scanty vocabulary. To answer their questions in the language which we should use towards grown men, would be simply to mislead them, if they could construe it at all. We must dispense and "divide" the word of truth, if we would not have it changed, as far as they are concerned, into a word of falsehood; for what is short of truth in the letter may be to them the most perfect truth, that is, the nearest approach to truth, compatible with their condition[4]. The case is the same as regards those who have any natural defect or deprivation which cuts them off from the circle of ideas common to mankind in general. To speak to a blind man of light and colours, in terms proper to those phenomena, would be to mock him; we must use other media of information accommodated to his circumstances, according to the well-known instance in which his own account of scarlet was to liken it to the sound of a trumpet. And so again, as regards savages, or the ignorant, or weak, or narrow-minded, our representations and arguments must take a certain form, if they are to gain admission into their minds at all, and to reach them. Again, what impediments do the diversities of language place in the way of communicating ideas! Language is a sort of analysis of thought; and, since ideas are infinite, and infinitely combined, and infinitely modified, whereas language is a method definite and limited, and confined to an arbitrary selection of a certain number of these innumerable materials, it were idle to expect that the courses of thought marked out in one language should, except in their great outlines and main centres, correspond to those of another. Multitudes of ideas expressed in the one do not even enter into the other, and can only be conveyed by some economy or accommodation, by circumlocutions, phrases, limiting words, figures, or some bold and happy expedient. And sometimes, from the continual demand, foreign words become naturalized. Again, the difficulty is extreme, as all persons know, of leading certain individuals (to use a familiar phrase) to understand one another; their habits of thought turning apparently on points of mutual repulsion. Now this

---

[4]Hence it is not more than an hyperbole to say that, in certain cases, a lie is the nearest approach to the truth. [Vide Hist. of Arians, p. 67, &c. Edit. 3.] We are told that "God is not the son of man, that He should repent;" yet "it repented the Lord that He had made man."

is always in a measure traceable to moral diversities between the
parties; still, in many cases, it arises mainly from difference in the
principle on which they have divided and subdivided that world of
ideas, which comes before them both. They seem ever to be dodging
each other, and need a common measure or economy to mediate
between them.

35. Fables, again, are economies or accommodations, being truths
and principles cast into that form in which they will be most vividly
recognized; as in the well-known instance attributed to Menenius
Agrippa. Again, mythical representations, at least in their better form,
may be considered facts or narratives, untrue, but like the truth, intended to bring out the action of some principle, point of character,
and the like. For instance, the tradition that St. Ignatius was the child
whom our Lord took in His arms, may be unfounded; but it realizes
to us his special relation to Christ and His Apostles, with a keenness
peculiar to itself. The same remark may be made upon certain narratives of martyrdoms, or of the details of such narratives, or of certain
alleged miracles, or heroic acts, or speeches, all which are the spontaneous produce of religious feeling under imperfect knowledge. If the
alleged facts did not occur, they ought to have occurred (if I may so
speak); they are such as might have occurred, and would have occurred, under circumstances; and they belong to the parties to whom
they are attributed, potentially, if not actually; or the like of them did
occur; or occurred to others similarly circumstanced, though not to
those very persons. Many a theory or view of things, on which an
institution is founded, or a party held together, is of the same kind.
Many an argument, used by zealous and earnest men, has this economical character, being not the very ground on which they act, (for they
continue in the same course, though it be refuted,) yet, in a certain
sense, a representation of it, a proximate description of their feelings
in the shape of argument, on which they can rest, to which they can
recur when perplexed, and appeal when questioned. Now, in this
reference to accommodation or economy in human affairs, I do not
meddle with the question of casuistry, viz. which of such artifices, as
they may be called, are innocent, or where the line is to be drawn.
That some are immoral, common sense tells us; but it is enough for
my purpose, if some are necessary, as the same common sense will
allow; and then the very necessity of the use will account for the abuse
and perversion.

36. Even between man and man, then, constituted, as men are, alike,
various distinct instruments, keys, or *calculi* of thought obtain, on

which their ideas and arguments shape themselves respectively, and which we must use, if we would reach them. The cogitative method, as it may be called, of one man is notoriously very different from that of another; of the lawyer from that of the soldier, of the rich from that of the poor. The territory of thought is portioned out in a hundred different ways. Abstractions, generalizations, definitions, propositions, all are framed on distinct standards; and if this is found in matters of this world between man and man, surely much more must it exist between the ideas of men, and the thoughts, ways, and works of God.

37. One of the obvious instances of this contrariety is seen in the classifications we make of the subjects of the animal or vegetable kingdoms. Here a very intelligible order has been observed by the Creator Himself; still one of which we have not, after all, the key. We are obliged to frame one of our own; and when we apply it, we find that it will not exactly answer the Divine idea of arrangement, as it discovers itself to us; there being phenomena which we cannot locate, or which, upon our system of division, are anomalies in the general harmony of the Creation.

38. Mathematical science will afford us a more extended illustration of this distinction between supernatural and eternal laws, and our attempts to represent them, that is, our economies. Various methods or *calculi* have been adopted to embody those immutable principles and dispositions of which the science treats, which are really independent of any, yet cannot be contemplated or pursued without one or other of them. The first of these instruments of investigation employs the medium of extension; the second, that of number; the third, that of motion; the fourth proceeds on a more subtle hypothesis, that of increase. These methods are very distinct from each other, at least the geometrical and the differential; yet they are, one and all, analyses, more or less perfect, of those same necessary truths, for which we have not a name, of which we have no idea, except in the terms of such economical representations. They are all developments of one and the same range of ideas; they are all instruments of discovery as to those ideas. They stand for real things, and we can reason with them, though they be but symbols, as if they were the things themselves, for which they stand. Yet none of them carries out the lines of truth to their limits; first, one stops in the analysis, then another; like some calculating tables which answer for a thousand times, and miss in the thousand and first. While they answer, we can use them just as if they were the realities which they represent, and without thinking of those realities; but at length our instrument of discovery issues in some great impossi-

bility or contradiction, or what we call in religion, a mystery. It has run its length; and by its failure shows that all along it has been but an expedient for practical purposes, not a true analysis or adequate image of those recondite laws which are investigated by means of it. It has never fathomed their depth, because it now fails to measure their course. At the same time, no one, because it cannot do every thing, would refuse to use it within the range in which it will act; no one would say that it was a system of empty symbols, though it be but a shadow of the unseen. Though we use it with caution, still we use it, as being the nearest approximation to the truth which our condition admits.

39. Let us take another instance, of an outward and earthly form, or economy, under which great wonders unknown seem to be typified; I mean musical sounds, as they are exhibited most perfectly in instrumental harmony. There are seven notes in the scale; make them fourteen; yet what a slender outfit for so vast an enterprise! What science brings so much out of so little? Out of what poor elements does some great master in it create his new world! Shall we say that all this exuberant inventiveness is a mere ingenuity or trick of art, like some game or fashion of the day, without reality, without meaning? We may do so; and then, perhaps, we shall also account the science of theology to be a matter of words; yet, as there is a divinity in the theology of the Church, which those who feel cannot communicate, so is there also in the wonderful creation of sublimity and beauty of which I am speaking. To many men the very names which the science employs are utterly incomprehensible. To speak of an idea or a subject seems to be fanciful or trifling, to speak of the views which it opens upon us to be childish extravagance; yet is it possible that that inexhaustible evolution and disposition of notes, so rich yet so simple, so intricate yet so regulated, so various yet so majestic, should be a mere sound, which is gone and perishes? Can it be that those mysterious stirrings of heart, and keen emotions, and strange yearnings after we know not what, and awful impressions from we know not whence, should be wrought in us by what is unsubstantial, and comes and goes, and begins and ends in itself? It is not so; it cannot be. No; they have escaped from some higher sphere; they are the outpourings of eternal harmony in the medium of created sound; they are echoes from our Home; they are the voice of Angels, or the Magnificat of Saints, or the living laws of Divine Governance, or the Divine Attributes; something are they besides themselves, which we cannot compass, which we

cannot utter,—though mortal man, and he perhaps not otherwise distinguished above his fellows, has the gift of eliciting them.

40. So much on the subject of musical sound; but what if the whole series of impressions, made on us through the senses, be, as I have already hinted, but a Divine economy suited to our need, and the token of realities distinct from themselves, and such as might be revealed to us, nay, more perfectly, by other senses, different from our existing ones as they from each other? What if the properties of matter, as we conceive of them, are merely relative to us, so that facts and events, which seem impossible when predicated concerning it in terms of those impressions, are impossible only in those terms, not in themselves,— impossible only because of the imperfection of the idea, which, in consequence of those impressions, we have conceived of material substances? If so, it would follow that the laws of physics, as we consider them, are themselves but generalizations of economical exhibitions, inferences from figure and shadow, and not more real than the phenomena from which they are drawn. Scripture, for instance, says that the sun moves and the earth is stationary; and science, that the earth moves, and the sun is comparatively at rest. How can we determine which of these opposite statements is the very truth, till we know what motion is? If our idea of motion be but an accidental result of our present senses, neither proposition is true, and both are true; neither true philosophically, both true for certain practical purposes in the system in which they are respectively found; and physical science will have no better meaning when it says that the earth moves, than plane astronomy when it says that the earth is still.

41. And should any one fear lest thoughts such as these should tend to a dreary and hopeless scepticism, let him take into account the Being and Providence of God, the Merciful and True; and he will at once be relieved of his anxiety. All is dreary till we believe, what our hearts tell us, that we are subjects of His Governance; nothing is dreary, all inspires hope and trust, directly we understand that we are under His hand, and that whatever comes to us is from Him, as a method of discipline and guidance. What is it to us whether the knowledge He gives us be greater or less, if it be He who gives it? What is it to us whether it be exact or vague, if He bids us trust it? What have we to care whether we are or are not given to divide substance from shadow, if He is training us heavenwards by means of either? Why should we vex ourselves to find whether our deductions are philosophical or no, provided they are religious? If our senses supply the media by which

we are put on trial, by which we are all brought together, and hold intercourse with each other, and are disciplined and are taught, and enabled to benefit others, it is enough. We have an instinct within us, impelling us, we have external necessity forcing us, to trust our senses, and we may leave the question of their substantial truth for another world, "till the day break, and the shadows flee away[5]." And what is true of reliance on our senses, is true of all the information which it has pleased God to vouchsafe to us, whether in nature or in grace.

42. Instances, then, such as these, will be found both to sober and to encourage us in our theological studies,—to impress us with a profound sense of our ignorance of Divine Verities, when we know most; yet to hinder us from relinquishing their contemplation, though we know so little. On the one hand, it would appear that even the most subtle questions of the schools may have a real meaning, as the most intricate *formulæ* in analytics; and, since we cannot tell how far our instrument of thought reaches in the process of investigation, and at what point it fails us, no questions may safely be despised. "Whether God was any where before creation?" "whether He knows all creatures in Himself?" "whether the blessed see all things possible and future in Him?" "whether relation is the form of the Divine Persons?" "in what sense the Holy Spirit is Divine Love?" these, and a multitude of others, far more minute and remote, are all sacred from their subject.

43. On the other hand, it must be recollected that not even the Catholic reasonings and conclusions, as contained in Confessions, and most thoroughly received by us, are worthy of the Divine Verities which they represent, but are the truth only in as full a measure as our minds can admit it; the truth as far as they go, and under the conditions of thought which human feebleness imposes. It is true that God is without beginning, if eternity may worthily be considered to imply succession; in every place, if He who is a Spirit can have relations with space. It is right to speak of His Being and Attributes, if He be not rather super-essential; it is true to say that He is wise or powerful, if we may consider Him as other than the most simple Unity. He is truly

[5 The senses convey to the mind "substantial truth," in so far as they bring home to us that certain things are, and *in confuso* what they are. But has a man born blind, by means of hearing, smelling, taste, and touch, such an idea of physical nature, as may be called *substantially* true, or, on the contrary, an idea which at best is but the *shadow* of the truth? for, in whichever respect, whether as in substance or by a shadow, the blind man knows the objects of sight, in the same are those things, in "which eye has not seen, nor ear heard," apprehended by us now, "in a glass darkly," *per speculum, in ænigmate.*]

Three, if He is truly One; He is truly One, if the idea of Him falls under earthly number. He has a triple Personality, in the sense in which the Infinite can be understood to have Personality at all. If we know anything of Him,—if we may speak of Him in any way,—if we may emerge from Atheism or Pantheism into religious faith,—if we would have any saving hope, any life of truth and holiness within us,—this only do we know, with this only confession, we must begin and end our worship—that the Father is the One God, the Son the One God, and the Holy Ghost the One God; and that the Father is not the Son, the Son not the Holy Ghost, and the Holy Ghost not the Father.

44. The fault, then, which we must guard against in receiving such Divine intimations, is the ambition of being wiser than what is written; of employing the Reason, not in carrying out what is told us, but in impugning it; not in support, but in prejudice of Faith. Brilliant as are such exhibitions of its powers, they bear no fruit. Reason can but ascertain the profound difficulties of our condition, it cannot remove them; it has no work, it makes no beginning, it does but continually fall back, till it is content to be a little child, and to follow where Faith guides it.

45. What remains, then, but to make our prayer to the Gracious and Merciful God, the Father of Lights, that in all our exercises of Reason, His gift, we may thus use it,—as He would have us, in the obedience of Faith, with a view to His glory, with an aim at His Truth, in dutiful submission to His will, for the comfort of His elect, for the edification of Holy Jerusalem, His Church, and in recollection of His own solemn warning, "Every idle word that men shall speak, they shall give account thereof in the day of judgment; for by the words thou shalt be justified, and by thy words thou shalt be condemned."

# II

# AN ESSAY ON THE DEVELOPMENT OF CHRISTIAN DOCTRINE

*(3rd edition, February 2, 1878)*
*(First published October 6, 1845)*

# A THEORY WITH A METHOD

What Newman called the Theory of Development was introduced in his University Sermon by the psychological analogy of how a great truth, once apprehended by an individual human mind, is afterwards increasingly comprehended. As a result, later enunciations of that truth will be notably more elaborate than earlier ones. Meanings will be increasingly clarified, implications will be successively drawn out, and connections will be progressively discovered. In other words, the original idea will develop, in the sense that its full amplitude and relevance will be increasingly appreciated.

This sermon of Newman's is a masterpiece of intellectual introspection and psychological description. That ideas do indeed develop in the way that it describes would be difficult to deny. And yet, as an analogy, it is hardly sufficient to account for the authentic development of Christian doctrine. After all, even individual minds doing their best may progressively *mis*understand a profound idea, resulting in the elaboration not of truth but of error; indeed that is presumably what Newman must suppose to have happened in the elaboration of Protestant belief. More important still, Christianity does not simply unfold within some individual mind, but occupies multitudes of enormously various minds, in numerous, prolonged succession. One may indeed speak of the "mind" of the Church, but in a literal sense there is no such thing, and the metaphorical sense will scarcely support rigorous argumentation. Many of us have participated in a popular classroom psychology experiment, in which some relatively simple report is whispered to a student, who is instructed to whisper it in turn to another, and so on until the last recipient reports to the whole group what is almost invariably a garbled rather than an elucidated version of the original message. Every teacher of ordinary students has, all too often, the dismal experience of reading or hearing conscientious accounts of a carefully imparted lesson that seem almost perverse by the extent of their misunderstanding. Newman needed a theory that would persuade Christians that Christ's lessons had a happier fate than those of lesser teachers, and that would enable them to discern where, among contemporary claimants to Christian tradition, that happier fate was realized. Accordingly, in the *Essay*, although his argument is still essentially analogical, the analogy has become much more complex, envisaging a variety of social processes of development, not simply a typically individual psychology. And along with this expansion of the analogy, there is now built into the argument a set of criteria for distinguishing true developments that elucidate an original idea, from corruptions that distort it.

The very notion of an "original idea" of Christianity, which "develops" over the course of time into ever more elaborate formulations of doctrine, may be perplexing. What idea? Is there some marvellously concise primordial notion, recoverable through a study of history, to which all subsequent authentic dogmas are, at least in principle, reducible? Newman points to nothing of the sort. And indeed, when Newman refers to the "idea" of Christianity, he most typically understands "idea" not as a gist, or pith, from which developments emanate, but as the exhaustive representation towards which they tend. "The idea which represents an object or supposed object is commensurate with the sum total of its possible aspects, however they may vary in the separate consciousness of individuals; and in proportion to the variety of aspects under which it presents itself to various minds is its force and depth, and the argument for its reality." This rather Platonic usage of Newman's invalidates one objection frequently raised, that he never tells us what the "idea" of Christianity is that he regards as developing. For Newman, on the contrary, it is precisely the development that progressively discloses the idea.

One may still ask if Newman thought the "whole" idea of Christianity had ever been contained in any individual human mind. His most forthright answer to that question was given only many years later, in an 1868 paper on papal infallibility. There he tells us that the Apostles "had the fullness of revealed knowledge," but possessed it in a way that was "latent or implicit." Thus, if it were possible to submit later doctrinal disputes to the Apostles in terms they could understand, they would recognize as correct the dogmatic definitions that settled them. This same capacity, which the Apostles enjoyed habitually, Newman supposes to be possessed by a pope, teaching ex cathedra, or by an ecumenical council at the point of dogmatic definition. This ability to give the right answer, in the light of revelation, does not imply, for Apostles, councils, or popes, any comparable ability to support the answer with the best reasons. Infallible teachings may, therefore, be accompanied by entirely fallible, indeed faulty theology.

Newman does not, of course, attempt to prove that the Apostles' minds contained, however implicitly, the whole revelation. He is arguing on Christian premises, and considers it common Christian belief that revelation was complete—in some sense—with the Apostles. What he first attempts to show, in general but with specific illustrations, is that development, understood as gradual, consistent, progressive elucidation, is only to be expected. He then attempts to show further that a definite pattern of such development is discernible in history, and distinguishable by definite criteria from mere doctrinal innovations and retrenchments. Thus we find in the first part of the *Essay* something like a philosophy of the history of ideas, and in the second part a selective review of data from the history of Christian doctrine in the perspective furnished by that philosophy.

It has surprised some readers that in Newman's general account of developments he early argues that an infallible authority for authenticating true developments is one of the things only to be expected. Thus the doctrine of infallibility is itself a development, but once it is accepted all other criteria might seem superfluous. In fact Newman believed that for the generality of Christians Church authority, immune from error, would be the only practical guide to right belief.

In the same connection it has been objected that since Newman only shows, at best, that an infallible authority is probable, reliance upon such an authority cannot be altogether freed from doubt. To regard an authority as probably infallible would seem to support only the conclusion that teachings of that authority are probably true—hence, possibly false. Newman's answer to such objections, as given in the *Essay*, is to the effect that probabilities, received in faith, can generate certainty, an anticipation of some of his later writings on religious certitude, especially in his *Grammar of Assent*. Newman did not believe that certainties of religious life, any more than what we regard as certainties in everyday secular life, made doubt absolutely impossible, but only that doubting them was unnatural, unhelpful, fanatical. It was in that sense that he shared the view he cited from Bishop Butler, that "probability is the guide of life."

The historical portion of the *Essay*, comprising about two-thirds of it, is organized around a set of seven "notes" that serve as criteria for distinguishing developments from corruptions. Each note is described in a general way, usually with secular illustrations as well as religious ones, and then each of them in turn is applied to historical instances of what appear to be doctrinal changes. How far the *Essay* is from being a finished comprehensive treatise can be surmised from the fact that Newman devotes progressively fewer pages to his treatment of each successive note, to the extent that fifteen times as much space is given to the first of them as to the last. The book is indeed what it is called, an essay. It is pointing directions of argument and anticipating their outcome, rather than carrying them out to comprehensive conclusions. Moreover, Newman is hastening to a practical conclusion which for him has very personal urgency. Certainly he did not intend by applying his notes to demonstrate incontrovertibly the authenticity of every disputed Catholic dogma.

Whether Newman's readers consider the *Essay* a success or a failure depends in part on what question they want him to answer. If the main question is whether or not any *new* doctrines have become established at various times in the history of the Catholic (or any other) Church, Newman's negative answer (in the case of Catholicism) may be more perplexing than convincing. Implicit in his thought seems to be a distinction between new doctrines and developments of old ones that seemed much sharper to him than it may to some of us. For most of us, the same thing may be accurately described as both a novelty and a development. "Something new has developed" does not seem to us a paradoxical phrase. Indeed we expect novelties to be developments at least in the sense that they are effects of antecedent causes. At the same time, for most of us the distinction between healthy developments and unhealthy ones is perfectly meaningful, inasmuch as some changes enhance the systems out of which they arise, whereas others are detrimental to them. Newman's contrast between developments and corruptions—the one he chiefly emphasizes and systematically pursues—appears to be a much clearer and more usable one than the less explicit contrast between developments and novelties. Newman leaves his readers little room for believing that Christian doctrine has been, or even could have been, finally fixed and static over the course of its long history. And he leaves them good grounds for believing that later orthodoxy, at least in many respects, exhibits a vital congruity and kinship with early teachings. And yet, for new ideas to be congruously and constructively related to older ones in the same tradition does not keep them from being truly new. Apart from his unargued and seemingly indemonstrable belief that all doctrine was, somehow, in the Apostles' minds, Newman's case for development does not add up to a case against novelty.

A question that should also be raised about the upshot of Newman's argument is whether he does not somewhat rashly assume that the developments and corruptions of Christian doctrine must all fall respectively on one side and the other of existing ecclesiastical boundaries. Is it, on his premises, simply inconceivable that Catholics should have accumulated some of both—and that the same could be said, in varying measures, of various Christian denominations? Newman himself once noted with wry regret that although Wesleyan Methodism had indubitably gone astray from true apostolicity, it did seem somehow to cultivate true Christian holiness to a degree unmatched in Newman's own communion. Probably, in doctrinal matters, Newman's confident belief in an infallible teaching authority forbade him to suppose that any true developments could be excluded from the church possessing that authority, or any corruptions included within it. And yet Newman himself thought the actual exercise of infallibility occurred only infrequently and in quite special circumstances.

One surprising thing about the reception given to Newman's *Essay on Development* is that, praised as it usually is among Catholics, it is so little imitated or extended by them. It is, after all, essentially the demonstration of a method. But even of those who regard it as an ingenious and effective method, few make any use of it beyond that which Newman himself made. Yet if Newman's "notes of genuine developments" possess any validity for criticizing apparent doctrinal changes in the past, they should have similar validity in evaluating prospective doctrinal changes. How, for example, might those notes be applied to a hypothetical future teaching that women are ordainable to the priesthood? Or that regional episcopal conferences exercise apostolic teaching authority? Or that papal government admits the form of a constitutional monarchy? Or any of numerous other controversial proposals for the development of Catholic doctrine? It is hard to see why, if Newman's criteria help us trace the course of authentic Christian beliefs through the past, they should not be helpful in charting their course into the proximate future.

# An Essay on the Development of Christian Doctrine

TO THE
REV. SAMUEL WILLIAM WAYTE, B.D.
PRESIDENT OF TRINITY COLLEGE, OXFORD.

My dear President,

Not from any special interest which I anticipate you will take in this volume, or any sympathy you will feel in its argument, or intrinsic fitness of any kind in my associating you and your fellows with it,—

But, because I have nothing besides it to offer you, in token of my sense of the gracious compliment which you and they have paid me in making me once more a member of a college dear to me from undergraduate memories;—

Also, because of the happy coincidence, that whereas its first publication was contemporaneous with my leaving Oxford, its second becomes, by virtue of your act, contemporaneous with a recovery of my position there:—

Therefore it is that, without your leave or your responsibility, I take the bold step of placing your name in the first pages of what, at my age, I must consider the last print or reprint on which I shall ever be engaged.

I am, my dear President,
Most sincerely yours,
JOHN H. NEWMAN.

February 23, 1878.

# CONTENTS

# PREFACE TO THE EDITION OF 1878

The following pages were not in the first instance written to prove the divinity of the Catholic religion, though ultimately they furnish a positive argument in its behalf, but to explain certain difficulties in its history, felt before now by the author himself, and commonly insisted on by Protestants in controversy, as serving to blunt the force of its prima facie and general claims on our recognition.

However beautiful and promising that religion is in theory, its history, we are told, is its best refutation; the inconsistencies, found age after age in its teaching, being as patent as the simultaneous contrarieties of religious opinion manifest in the High, Low, and Broad branches of the Church of England.

In reply to this specious objection, it is maintained in this essay that, granting that some large variations of teaching in its long course of eighteen hundred years exist, nevertheless, these, on examination, will be found to arise from the nature of the case, and to proceed on a law, and with a harmony and a definite drift, and with an analogy to Scripture revelations, which, instead of telling to their disadvantage, actually constitute an argument in their favour, as witnessing to a super-intending Providence and a great Design in the mode and in the circumstances of their occurrence.

Perhaps his confidence in the truth and availableness of this view has sometimes led the author to be careless and over-liberal in his concessions to Protestants of historical fact.

If this be so anywhere, he begs the reader in such cases to understand him as speaking hypothetically, and in the sense of an *argumentum ad hominem* and a fortiori. Nor is such hypothetical reasoning out of place in a publication which is addressed, not to theologians, but to those who as yet are not even Catholics, and who, as they read history, would scoff at any defence of Catholic doctrine which did not go the length of covering admissions in matters of fact as broad as those which are here ventured on.

In this new edition of the essay various important alterations have been made in the arrangement of its separate parts, and some, not indeed in its matter, but in its text.

February 2, 1878.

# ADVERTISEMENT TO THE FIRST EDITION

OCULI MEI DEFECERUNT IN SALUTARE TUUM.*

It is now above eleven years since the writer of the following pages, in one of the early numbers of the *Tracts for the Times*, expressed himself thus:—

"Considering the high gifts, and the strong claims of the Church of Rome and her dependencies on our admiration, reverence, love, and gratitude, how could we withstand her, as we do; how could we refrain from being melted into tenderness, and rushing into communion with her, but for the words of Truth, which bid us prefer Itself to the whole world? 'He that loveth father or mother more than Me, is not worthy of Me.' How could we learn to be severe, and execute judgment, but for the warning of Moses against even a divinely-gifted teacher who should preach new gods, and the anathema of St. Paul even against Angels and Apostles who should bring in a new doctrine?"[1]

He little thought, when he so wrote, that the time would ever come when he should feel the obstacle, which he spoke of as lying in the way of communion with the Church of Rome, to be destitute of solid foundation.

The following work is directed towards its removal.

Having, in former publications, called attention to the supposed difficulty, he considers himself bound to avow his present belief that it is imaginary.

He has neither the ability to put out of hand a finished composition nor the wish to make a powerful and moving representation on the great subject of which he treats. His aim will be answered if he succeeds in suggesting thoughts which in God's good time may quietly bear fruit in the minds of those to whom that subject is new; and which may carry forward inquirers who have already put themselves on the course.

If at times his tone appears positive or peremptory, he hopes this will be imputed to the scientific character of the work, which requires

---

* Psalm 119:123: "My eyes fail with watching for thy salvation." Compare this opening biblical citation with the closing one, on the book's final page (458).

[1] Records of the Church, xxiv. p. 7.

a distinct statement of principles and of the arguments which recommend them.

He hopes too he shall be excused for his frequent quotations from himself; which are necessary in order to show how he stands at present in relation to various of his former publications.

Littlemore,
October 6, 1845.

## Postscript.

Since the above was written, the author has joined the Catholic Church. It was his intention and wish to have carried his volume through the press before deciding finally on this step. But when he had got some way in the printing, he recognized in himself a conviction of the truth of the conclusion to which the discussion leads so clear as to supersede further deliberation. Shortly afterwards circumstances gave him the opportunity of acting upon it, and he felt that he had no warrant for refusing to do so.

His first act on his conversion was to offer his work for revision to the proper authorities; but the offer was declined on the ground that it was written and partly printed before he was a Catholic, and that it would come before the reader in a more persuasive form, if he read it as the author wrote it.

It is scarcely necessary to add that he now submits every part of the book to the judgment of the Church, with whose doctrine, on the subjects of which he treats, he wishes all his thoughts to be coincident.

# PART I

*Doctrinal Developments Viewed in Themselves*

# INTRODUCTION

Christianity has been long enough in the world to justify us in dealing with it as a fact in the world's history. Its genius and character, its doctrines, precepts, and objects cannot be treated as matters of private opinion or deduction unless we may reasonably so regard the Spartan institutions or the religion of Mahomet. It may indeed legitimately be made the subject matter of theories; what is its moral and political excellence, what its due location in the range of ideas or of facts which we possess, whether it be divine or human, whether original or eclectic, or both at once, how far favourable to civilization or to literature, whether a religion for all ages or for a particular state of society, these are questions upon the fact, or professed solutions of the fact, and belong to the province of opinion; but to a fact do they relate, on an admitted fact do they turn, which must be ascertained as other facts and surely has on the whole been so ascertained unless the testimony of so many centuries is to go for nothing. Christianity is no theory of the study or the cloister. It has long since passed beyond the letter of documents and the reasonings of individual minds and has become public property. Its "sound has gone out into all lands," and its "words unto the ends of the world." It has from the first had an objective existence, and has thrown itself upon the great concourse of men. Its home is in the world; and to know what it is we must seek it in the world and hear the world's witness of it.

## 2.

The hypothesis, indeed, has met with wide reception in these latter times, that Christianity does not fall within the province of history— that it is to each man what each man thinks it to be, and nothing else; and thus in fact is a mere name for a cluster or family of rival religions all together, religions at variance one with another, and claiming the same appellation, not because there can be assigned any one and the same doctrine as the common foundation of all, but because certain points of agreement may be found here and there of some sort or other by which each in its turn is connected with one or other of the rest.

Or again, it has been maintained, or implied, that all existing denominations of Christianity are wrong, none representing it as taught by Christ and His Apostles; that the original religion has gradually decayed or become hopelessly corrupt; nay, that it died out of the world at its birth, and was forthwith succeeded by a counterfeit or counterfeits which assumed its name, though they inherited at best but some fragments of its teaching; or rather that it cannot even be said either to have decayed or to have died, because historically it has no substance of its own, but from the first and onwards it has, on the stage of the world, been nothing more than a mere assemblage of doctrines and practices derived from without, from oriental, Platonic, polytheistic sources, from Buddhism, Essenism, Manicheeism; or that, allowing true Christianity still to exist, it has but a hidden and isolated life, in the hearts of the elect, or again as a literature or philosophy, not certified in any way, much less guaranteed, to come from above, but one out of the various separate informations about the Supreme Being and human duty, with which an unknown Providence has furnished us, whether in nature or in the world.

### 3.

All such views of Christianity imply that there is no sufficient body of historical proof to interfere with, or at least to prevail against, any number whatever of free and independent hypotheses concerning it. But this surely is not self-evident, and has itself to be proved. Till positive reasons grounded on facts are adduced to the contrary, the most natural hypothesis, the most agreeable to our mode of proceeding in parallel cases, and that which takes precedence of all others, is to consider that the society of Christians which the Apostles left on earth were of that religion to which the Apostles had converted them; that the external continuity of name, profession, and communion, argues a real continuity of doctrine; that, as Christianity began by manifesting itself as of a certain shape and bearing to all mankind, therefore it went on so to manifest itself; and that the more, considering that prophecy had already determined that it was to be a power visible in the world and sovereign over it, characters which are accurately fulfilled in that historical Christianity to which we commonly give the name. It is not a violent assumption, then, but rather mere abstinence from the wanton admission of a principle which would necessarily lead to the most vexatious and preposterous scepticism, to take it for granted, before proof to the contrary, that the Christianity of the second, fourth, seventh, twelfth, sixteenth, and intermediate centuries is in its substance the very religion which Christ and His Apostles taught in the first, whatever may be the modifications for good or for evil which lapse of years, or the vicissitudes of human affairs, have impressed upon it.

Of course I do not deny the abstract possibility of extreme changes. The substitution is certainly, in idea, supposable of a counterfeit Christianity—superseding the original, by means of the adroit innovations of seasons, places, and persons, till, according to the familiar illustration, the "blade" and the "handle" are alternately renewed, and identity is lost without the loss of continuity. It is possible; but it must not be assumed. The *onus probandi* is with those who assert what it is unnatural to expect; to be just able to doubt is no warrant for disbelieving.

## 4.

Accordingly, some writers have gone on to give reasons from history for their refusing to appeal to history. They aver that, when they come to look into the documents and literature of Christianity in times past, they find its doctrines so variously represented, and so inconsistently maintained by its professors, that, however natural it be a priori, it is useless, in fact, to seek in history the matter of that Revelation which has been vouchsafed to mankind; that they cannot be historical Christians if they would. They say, in the words of Chillingworth, "There are popes against popes, councils against councils, some fathers against others, the same fathers against themselves, a consent of fathers of one age against a consent of fathers of another age, the Church of one age against the Church of another age"—hence they are forced, whether they will or not, to fall back upon the Bible as the sole source of Revelation, and upon their own personal private judgment as the sole expounder of its doctrine. This is a fair argument if it can be maintained, and it brings me at once to the subject of this essay. Not that it enters into my purpose to convict of misstatement, as might be done, each separate clause of this sweeping accusation of a smart but superficial writer; but neither on the other hand do I mean to deny everything that he says to the disadvantage of historical Christianity. On the contrary, I shall admit that there are in fact certain apparent variations in its teaching, which have to be explained; thus I shall begin, but then I shall attempt to explain them to the exculpation of that teaching in point of unity, directness, and consistency.

## 5.

Meanwhile, before setting about this work, I will address one remark to Chillingworth and his friends: Let them consider that if they can criticize history, the facts of history certainly can retort upon them. It might, I grant, be clearer on this great subject than it is. This is no great concession. History is not a creed or a catechism, it gives lessons rather than rules; still no one can mistake its general teaching in this matter, whether he accept it or stumble at it. Bold outlines and broad masses of colour rise out of the records of the past. They may be dim, they may be incomplete; but they are definite. And this one thing at least is certain; whatever history teaches, whatever it omits, whatever it exaggerates or extenuates, whatever it says and unsays, at least the Christianity of history is not Protestantism. If ever there were a safe truth, it is this.

And Protestantism has ever felt it so. I do not mean that every writer on the Protestant side has felt it; for it was the fashion at first, at least as a rhetorical argument against Rome, to appeal to past ages, or to some of them; but Protestantism as a whole feels it, and has felt it. This is shown in the determination already referred to of dispensing with historical Christianity altogether and of forming a Christianity from the Bible alone: men never would have put it aside, unless they had despaired of it. It is shown by the long neglect of ecclesiastical history in England, which prevails even in the English Church. Our popular religion scarcely recognizes the fact of the twelve long ages which lie between the Councils of Nicæa and Trent, except as affording one or two passages to illustrate its wild interpretations of certain prophecies of St. Paul and St. John. It is melancholy to say it, but the chief, perhaps the only English writer who has any claim to be considered an ecclesiastical historian is the unbeliever Gibbon. To be deep in history is to cease to be a Protestant.

## 6.

And this utter incongruity between Protestantism and historical Christianity is a plain fact, whether the latter be regarded in its earlier or in its later centuries. Protestants can as little bear its Antenicene as its Posttridentine period. I have elsewhere observed on this circumstance: "So much must the Protestant grant, that if such a system of doctrine as he would now introduce ever existed in early times, it has been clean swept away as if by a deluge, suddenly, silently, and without memorial; by a deluge coming in a night, and utterly soaking, rotting, heaving up, and hurrying off every vestige of what it found in the Church, before cock-crowing: so that 'when they rose in the morning' her true seed 'were all dead corpses'—Nay dead and buried—and without gravestone. 'The waters went over them; there was not one of them left; they sunk like lead in the mighty waters.' Strange antitype, indeed, to the early fortunes of Israel!—then the enemy was drowned, and 'Israel saw them dead upon the sea shore.' But now, it would seem, water proceeded as a flood 'out of the serpent's mouth,' and covered all the witnesses, so that not even their dead bodies lay in the streets of the great city.' Let him take which of his doctrines he will, his peculiar view of self-righteousness, of formality, of superstition; his notion of faith, or of spirituality in religious worship; his denial of the virtue of the sacraments, or of the ministerial commission, or of the visible Church; or his doctrine of the divine efficacy of the Scriptures as the one appointed instrument of religious teaching; and let him consider how far antiquity, as it has come down to us, will countenance him in it. No; he must allow that the alleged deluge has done its work; yes, and has in turn disappeared itself; it has been swallowed up by the earth, mercilessly as itself was merciless."[1]

That Protestantism, then, is not the Christianity of history, it is easy to determine, but to retort is a poor reply in controversy to a question of fact, and whatever be the violence or the exaggeration of writers like Chillingworth, if they have raised a real difficulty, it may claim a real answer, and we must determine whether on the one hand Christianity is still to represent to us a definite teaching from above, or whether on the other its utterances have been from time to time so strangely at variance that we are necessarily thrown back on our own judgment individually to determine what the revelation of God is, or rather if in fact there is, or has been, any revelation at all.

### 7.

Here then I concede to the opponents of historical Christianity that there are to be found, during the eighteen hundred years through which it has lasted, certain apparent inconsistencies and alterations in its doctrine and its worship such as irresistibly attract the attention of all who inquire into it. They are not sufficient to interfere with the general character and course of the religion, but they raise the question how

[1] Church of the Fathers [Hist. Sketches, vol. 1. p. 418].

they came about, and what they mean, and have in consequence supplied matter for several hypotheses.

Of these one is to the effect that Christianity has even changed from the first and ever accommodates itself to the circumstances of times and seasons; but it is difficult to understand how such a view is compatible with the special idea of revealed truth, and in fact its advocates more or less abandon, or tend to abandon the supernatural claims of Christianity; so it need not detain us here.

A second and more plausible hypothesis is that of the Anglican divines, who reconcile and bring into shape the exuberant phenomena under consideration by cutting off and casting away as corruptions all usages, ways, opinions, and tenets, which have not the sanction of primitive times. They maintain that history first presents to us a pure Christianity in East and West, and then a corrupt; and then of course their duty is to draw the line between what is corrupt and what is pure, and to determine the dates at which the various changes from good to bad were introduced. Such a principle of demarcation, available for the purpose, they consider they have found in the dictum of Vincent of Lerins that revealed and Apostolic doctrine is *quod semper, quod ubique, quod ab omnibus*,* a principle infallibly separating, on the whole field of history, authoritative doctrine from opinion, rejecting what is faulty, and combining and forming a theology. That "Christianity is what has been held always, everywhere, and by all" certainly promises a solution of the perplexities, an interpretation of the meaning, of history. What can be more natural than that divines and bodies of men should speak sometimes from themselves, sometimes from tradition; what more natural than that individually they should say many things on impulse, or under excitement, or as conjectures, or in ignorance; what more certain than that they must all have been instructed and catechized in the Creed of the Apostles; what more evident than that what was their own would in its degree be peculiar and differ from what was similarly private and personal in their brethren; what more conclusive than that the doctrine that was common to all at once was not really their own but public property in which they had a joint interest, and was proved by the concurrence of so many witnesses to have come from an Apostolical source? Here, then, we have a short and easy method for bringing the various informations of ecclesiastical history under that antecedent

---

* A fifth-century monk, Vincent of Lerins, in a work entitled *Commonitorium*, proposed what has come to be called the Vincentian Canon, a threefold criterion of authenticty in Catholic traditions, namely, "what has been believed everywhere, always, and by all."

probability in its favour, which nothing but its actual variations would lead us to neglect. Here we have a precise and satisfactory reason why we should make much of the earlier centuries, yet pay no regard to the later, why we should admit some doctrines and not others, why we refuse the Creed of Pius IV and accept the Thirty-nine Articles.

8.

Such is the rule of historical interpretation which has been professed in the English school of divines; and it contains a majestic truth, and offers an intelligible principle, and wears a reasonable air. It is congenial or, as it may be said, native to the Anglican mind, which takes up a middle position, neither discarding the Fathers nor acknowledging the Pope. It lays down a simple rule by which to measure the value of every historical fact, as it comes, and thereby it provides a bulwark against Rome, while it opens an assault upon Protestantism. Such is its promise; but its difficulty lies in applying it in particular cases. The rule is more serviceable in determining what is not than what is Christianity; it is irresistible against Protestantism, and in one sense indeed it is irresistible against Rome also, but in the same sense it is irresistible against England. It strikes at Rome through England. It admits of being interpreted in one of two ways: if it be narrowed for the purpose of disproving the catholicity of the Creed of Pope Pius, it becomes also an objection to the Athanasian; and if it be relaxed to admit the doctrines retained by the English Church, it no longer excludes certain doctrines of Rome which that Church denies. It cannot at once condemn St. Thomas and St. Bernard, and defend St. Athanasius and St. Gregory Nazianzen.

This general defect in its serviceableness has been heretofore felt by those who appealed to it. It was said by one writer; "The Rule of Vincent is not of a mathematical or demonstrative character, but moral, and requires practical judgment and good sense to apply it. For instance, what is meant by being 'taught *always*'? does it mean in every century, or every year, or every month? Does '*everywhere*' mean in every country, or in every diocese? and does 'the *Consent of Fathers*' require us to produce the direct testimony of every one of them? How many Fathers, how many places, how many instances, constitute a fulfilment of the test proposed? It is, then, from the nature of the case, a condition which never can be satisfied as fully as it might have been. It admits of various and unequal application in various instances; and what degree of application is enough, must be decided by the same principles which guide us in the conduct of life, which determine us in politics, or trade, or war, which lead us to accept Revelation at all, (for which we have but probability to show at most,) nay, to believe in the existence of an intelligent Creator."[2]

### 9.

So much was allowed by this writer; but then he added:

"This character, indeed, of Vincent's Canon, will but recommend it to the disciples of the school of Butler, from its agreement with the analogy of nature; but it affords a ready loophole for such as do not wish to be persuaded, of which both Protestants and Romanists are not slow to avail themselves."

This surely is the language of disputants who are more intent on assailing others than on defending themselves; as if similar loopholes were not necessary for Anglican theology.

He elsewhere says: "What there is not the shadow of a reason for saying that the Fathers held, what has not the faintest pretensions of being a Catholic truth, is this, that St. Peter or his successors were and are universal Bishops, that they have the whole of Christendom for their one diocese in a way in which other Apostles and Bishops had and have not."[3] Most true, if, in order that a doctrine be considered Catholic, it must be formally stated by the Fathers generally from the very first; but on the same understanding the doctrine also of the apostolical succession in the episcopal order "has not the faintest pretensions of being a Catholic truth."

Nor was this writer without a feeling of the special difficulty of his school; and he attempted to meet it by denying it. He wished to maintain that the sacred doctrines admitted by the Church of England into her Articles were taught in primitive times with a distinctness which no one could fancy to attach to the characteristic tenets of Rome.

"We confidently affirm," he said in another publication, "that there is not an article in the Athanasian Creed concerning the Incarnation which is not anticipated in the controversy with the Gnostics. There is no question which the Apollinarian or the Nestorian heresy raised, which may not be decided in the words of Ignatius, Irenæus and Tertullian."[4]

---

[2] Proph. Office [Via Med. vol. i. pp. 55, 56].
[3] Ibid. p. 181.
[4] British Critic, July, 1836, p. 193. Vid. supr. vol. i. p. 130.

## 10.

This may be considered as true. It may be true also, or at least shall here be granted as true, that there is also a consensus in the Antenicene Church for the doctrines of our Lord's Consubstantiality and Coeternity with the Almighty Father. Let us allow that the whole circle of doctrines, of which our Lord is the subject, was consistently and uniformly confessed by the Primitive Church, though not ratified formally in Council. But it surely is otherwise with the Catholic doctrine of the Trinity. I do not see in what sense it can be said that there is a consensus of primitive divines in its favour, which will not avail also for certain doctrines of the Roman Church which will presently come into mention. And this is a point which the writer of the above passages ought to have more distinctly brought before his mind and more carefully weighed; but he seems to have fancied that Bishop Bull proved the primitiveness of the Catholic doctrine concerning the Holy Trinity as well as that concerning our Lord.

Now it should be clearly understood what it is which must be shown by those who would prove it. Of course the doctrine of our Lord's divinity itself partly implies and partly recommends the doctrine of the Trinity; but implication and suggestion belong to another class of arguments which has not yet come into consideration. Moreover the statements of a particular father or doctor may certainly be of a most important character; but one divine is not equal to a *catena*. We must have a whole doctrine stated by a whole Church. The Catholic Truth in question is made up of a number of separate propositions, each of which, if maintained to the exclusion of the rest, is a heresy. In order then to prove that all the Antenicene writers taught the dogma of the Holy Trinity, it is not enough to prove that each still has gone far enough to be only a heretic—not enough to prove that one has held that the Son is God (for so did the Sabellian, so did the Macedonian) and another that the Father is not the Son (for so did the Arian) and another that the Son is equal to the Father (for so did the Tritheist) and another that there is but One God (for so did the Unitarian)—not enough that many attached in some sense a Threefold Power to the idea of the Almighty (for so did almost all the heresies that ever existed, and could not but do so, if they accepted the New Testament at all); but we must show that all these statements at once, and others too, are laid down by as many separate testimonies as may fairly be taken to constitute a "consensus of doctors." It is true indeed that the subsequent profession of the doctrine in the Universal Church creates a presumption that it was held even before it was professed; and it is fair to interpret the early Fathers by the later. This is true, and admits of application to certain other doctrines besides that of the Blessed Trinity in Unity; but there is as little room for such antecedent probabilities as for the argument from suggestions and intimations in the precise and imperative *quod semper, quod ubique, quod ab omnibus*, as it is commonly understood by English divines, and is by them used against the later Church and the See of Rome. What we have a right to ask, if we are bound to act upon Vincent's rule in regard to the Trinitarian dogma, is a sufficient number of Antenicene statements, each distinctly anticipating the Athanasian Creed.

## 11.

Now let us look at the leading facts of the case, in appealing to which I must not be supposed to be ascribing any heresy to the holy men whose words have not always been sufficiently full or exact to preclude the imputation. First, the Creeds of that early day make no mention in their letter of the Catholic doctrine at all. They make mention indeed of a Three; but that there is any mystery in the doctrine, that the Three are One, that They are coequal, coeternal, all increate, all omnipotent, all incomprehensible, is not stated and never could be gathered from them. Of course we believe that they imply it, or rather intend it. God forbid we should do otherwise! But nothing in the mere letter of those documents leads to that belief. To give a deeper meaning to their letter, we must interpret them by the times which came after.

Again, there is one and one only great doctrinal council in Antenicene times. It was held at Antioch in the middle of the third century on occasion of the incipient innovations of the Syrian heretical school. Now the Fathers there assembled, for whatever reason, condemned, or at least withdrew, when it came into the dispute, the word "Homoüsion," which was afterwards received at Nicæa as the special symbol of Catholicism against Arius.[5]

Again, the six great bishops and Saints of the Antenicene Church were St. Irenæus, St. Hippolytus, St. Cyprian, St. Gregory Thaumatur-

---

[5] This of course has been disputed, as is the case with almost all facts which bear upon the decision of controversies. I shall not think it necessary to notice the possibility or the fact of objections on questions upon which the world may now be said to be agreed; *e.g.* the arianizing tone of Eusebius.

gus, St. Dionysius of Alexandria, and St. Methodius. Of these, St. Dionysius is accused by St. Basil of having sown the first seeds of Arianism;[6] and St. Gregory is allowed by the same learned Father to have used language concerning our Lord which he only defends on the plea of an economical object in the writer.[7] St. Hippolytus speaks as if he were ignorant of our Lord's Eternal Sonship;[8] St. Methodius speaks incorrectly at least upon the Incarnation;[9] and St. Cyprian does not treat of theology at all. Such is the incompleteness of the extant teaching of these true saints and, in their day, faithful witnesses of the Eternal Son.

Again, Athenagoras, St. Clement, Tertullian, and the two SS. Dionysii would appear to be the only writers whose language is at any time exact and systematic enough to remind us of the Athanasian Creed. If we limit our view of the teaching of the Fathers by what they expressly state, St. Ignatius may be considered as a Patripassian, St. Justin arianizes, and St. Hippolytus is a Photinian.

Again, there are three great theological authors of the Antenicene centuries, Tertullian, Origen, and, we may add, Eusebius, though he lived some way into the fourth. Tertullian is heterodox on the doctrine of our Lord's divinity,[10] and, indeed, ultimately fell altogether into heresy or schism; Origen is, at the very least, suspected, and must be

[6] σχεδὸν ταυτησὶ τῆς νῦν περιθυλλουμένης ἀσεβείας, τῆς κατὰ τὸ Ἀνόμοιον λέγω, οὗτος ἐστὶν, ὅσα γε ἡμεῖς ἴδυεν, ὁ πρῶτος ἀνθρώποις τὰ σπέρματα παρασχών. ["He was, as far as we know, the first to furnish men with seeds of that impious doctrine—I mean the Unlikeness [of Father and Son]—with which our ears are now assailed."] Ep. ix. 2.

[7] Bull, Defens. F.N.

[8] "The authors who make the generation temporary, and speak not expressly of any other, are these following: Justin, Athenagoras, Theophilus, Tatian, Tertullian, and Hippolytus."—*Waterland*, vol. i. part 2, p. 104.

[9] "Levia sunt," says Maran in his defence, "quae in Sanctissimam Trinitatem hic liber peccare dicitur, paulo graviora quae in mysterium Incarnationis." ["This book's offenses agaisnt the Trinity are trivial, but somewhat more serious are those against the mystery of the Incarnation."]—*Div. Jes. Christ* p. 527. Shortly after, p. 530, "In tertiâ oratione nonnulla legimus Incarnationem Domini spectantia, quae subabsurdè dicta fateor, nego impie cogitata." ["In his third discourse we do read some things about the Incarnation which I confess to be worse than absurd, but I deny that they are products of any irreverence of thought."]

[10] Bishop Bull, who is tender towards him, allows, "Ut quod res est dicam, cum Valentinianis hic et reliquo gnosticorum grege aliquatenus locutus est Tertullianus; in re ipsâ tamen cum Catholicis omninò sensit." ["He did express himself somewhat in the manner of the Valentinians and other Gnostics, but his sentiments were really always with the Catholics."] Defens. F. N. iii. 10, § 15.

defended and explained rather than cited as a witness of orthodoxy; and Eusebius was a Semi-Arian.

## 12.

Moreover, it may be questioned whether any Antenicene father distinctly affirms either the numerical Unity or the Co-equality of the Three Persons; except perhaps the heterodox Tertullian, and that chiefly in a work written after he had become a Montanist:[11] yet to satisfy the Anti-roman use of *quod semper*, etc., surely we ought not to be left for these great articles of doctrine to the testimony of a later age.

Further, Bishop Bull allows that "nearly all the ancient Catholics who preceded Arius have the appearance of being ignorant of the invisible and incomprehensible (*immensam*) nature of the Son of God";[12] an article expressly taught in the Athanasian Creed under the sanction of its anathema.

It must be asked, moreover, how much direct and literal testimony the Antenicene Fathers give, one by one, to the divinity of the Holy Spirit? This alone shall be observed, that St. Basil, in the fourth century, finding that, if he distinctly called the Third Person in the Blessed Trinity by the Name of God, he should be put out of the Church by the Arians, pointedly refrained from doing so on an occasion on which his enemies were on the watch; and that, when some Catholics found fault with him, St. Athanasius took his part.[13] Could this possibly have been the conduct of any true Christian, not to say Saint, of a later age; that is, whatever be the true account of it, does it not suggest to us that the testimony of those early times lies very unfavourably for the application of the rule of Vincentius?

## 13.

Let it not be for a moment supposed that I impugn the orthodoxy of the early divines or the cogency of their testimony among *fair* inquirers; but I am trying them by that *unfair* interpretation of Vincentius, which is necessary in order to make him available against

[11] Adv. Praxeam.
[12] Defens. F. N. iv. 3, § 1.
[13] Basil, ed. Ben. vol. 3, p. xcvi.

the Church of Rome. And now, as to the positive evidence which those Fathers offer in behalf of the Catholic doctrine of the Trinity, it has been drawn out by Dr. Burton and seems to fall under two heads. One is the general *ascription of glory* to the Three Persons together, both by fathers and churches, and that on continuous tradition and from the earliest times. Under the second fall certain *distinct statements* of *particular* fathers; thus we find the word "Trinity" used by St. Theophilus, St. Clement, St. Hippolytus, Tertullian, St. Cyprian, Origen, St. Methodius; and the Divine *Circumincessio*, the most distinctive portion of the Catholic doctrine, and the unity of power, or again, of substance, are declared with more or less distinctness by Athenagoras, St. Irenæus, St. Clement, Tertullian, St. Hippolytus, Origen, and the two SS. Dionysii. This is pretty much the whole of the evidence.

## 14.

Perhaps it will be said we ought to take the Antenicene Fathers as a whole, and interpret one of them by another. This is to assume that they are all of one school, which of course they are, but which in controversy is a point to be proved; but it is even doubtful whether, on the whole, such a procedure would strengthen the argument. For instance, as to the second head of the positive evidence noted by Dr. Burton, Tertullian is the most formal and elaborate of these Fathers in his statements of the Catholic doctrine. "It would hardly be possible," says Dr. Burton, after quoting a passage, "for Athanasius himself, or the compiler of the Athanasian Creed, to have delivered the doctrine of the Trinity in stronger terms than these."[14] Yet Tertullian must be considered heterodox on the doctrine of our Lord's eternal generation.[15] If then we are to argue from his instance to that of the other

---

[14] Antenicene Test. to the Trinity, p. 69.

[15] "Quia et Pater Deus est, et judex Deus est, non tamen ideo Pater et judex semper, quia Deus semper. Nam nec Pater potuit esse ante Filium, nec judex ante delictum. Fuit autem tempus, cum et delictum et Filius non fuit, quod judicem, et qui Patrem Dominum faceret." ["Although God is father and judge, it does not follow that because he was always God he was always father and always judge. For he could not be father before there was any son, nor could he be judge before there was any offense. And there was a time when there was neither offense nor son to make the Lord both judge and father."] *Contr. Herm.* 3.

Fathers, we shall be driven to the conclusion that even the most exact statements are worth nothing more than their letter, are a warrant for nothing beyond themselves, and are consistent with heterodoxy where they do not expressly protest against it.

And again, as to the argument derivable from the Doxologies, it must not be forgotten that one of the passages in St. Justin Martyr includes the worship of the Angels. "We worship and adore," he says, "Him, and the Son who came from Him and taught us these things, and the host of those other good Angels, who follow and are like Him, and the Prophetic Spirit."[16] A Unitarian might argue from this passage that the glory and worship which the early Church ascribed to our Lord was not more definite than that which St. Justin was ready to concede to creatures.

## 15.

Thus much on the doctrine of the Holy Trinity. Let us proceed to another example. There are two doctrines which are generally associated with the name of a Father of the fourth and fifth centuries, and which can show little definite, or at least but partial, testimony in their behalf before his time—Purgatory and Original Sin. The dictum of Vincent admits both or excludes both, according as it is or is not rigidly taken; but, if used by Aristotle's "Lesbian Rule," then, as Anglicans would wish, it can be made to admit Original Sin and exclude Purgatory.

On the one hand, some notion of suffering, or disadvantage, or punishment after this life, in the case of the faithful departed, or other vague forms of the doctrine of Purgatory, has in its favour almost a consensus of the four first ages of the Church, though some Fathers state it with far greater openness and decision than others. It is, as far as words go, the confession of St. Clement of Alexandria, Tertullian, St. Perpetua, St. Cyprian, Origen, Lactantius, St. Hilary, St. Cyril of Jerusalem, St. Ambrose, St. Basil, St. Gregory of Nazianzus, and of Nyssa, St. Chrysostom, St. Jerome, St. Paulinus, and St. Augustine. And so, on the other hand, there is a certain agreement of Fathers from the first that mankind has derived some disadvantage from the sin of Adam.

---

[16] Vid. infra, towards the end of the Essay, ch. x., where more will be said on the passage.

## 16.

Next, when we consider the two doctrines more distinctly—the doctrine that between death and judgment there is a time or state of punishment; and the doctrine that all men, naturally propagated from fallen Adam, are in consequence born destitute of original righteousness—we find, on the one hand, several, such as Tertullian, St. Perpetua, St. Cyril, St. Hilary, St. Jerome, St. Gregory Nyssen, as far as their words go, definitely declaring a doctrine of Purgatory: whereas no one will say that there is a testimony of the Fathers, equally strong, for the doctrine of Original Sin, though it is difficult here to make any definite statement about their teaching without going into a discussion of the subject.

On the subject of Purgatory there were, to speak generally, two schools of opinion: the Greek, which contemplated a trial of fire at the last day through which all were to pass; and the African, resembling more nearly the present doctrine of the Roman Church. And so there were two principal views of Original Sin, the Greek and the African or Latin. Of the Greek, the judgment of Hooker is well known, though it must not be taken in the letter: "The heresy of freewill was a millstone about those Pelagians' neck; shall we therefore give sentence of death inevitable against all those Fathers in the Greek Church which, being mispersuaded, died in the error of freewill?"[17] Bishop Taylor, arguing for an opposite doctrine, bears a like testimony: "Original Sin," he says, "as it is at this day commonly explicated, was not the doctrine of the primitive Church; but when Pelagius had puddled the stream, St. Austin was so angry that he stamped and disturbed it more. And truly . . . I do not think that the gentlemen that urged against me St. Austin's opinion do well consider that I profess myself to follow those Fathers who were before him; and whom St. Austin did forsake, as I do him, in the question."[18] The same is asserted or allowed by Jansenius, Petavius, and Walch,[19]

[17] Of Justification, 26.
[18] Works, vol. ix. p. 396.
[19] "Quamvis igitur quam maximè fallantur Pelagiani, quum asserant, peccatum originale ex Augustini profluxisse ingenio, antiquam vero ecclesiam illud plane nescivisse; diffiteri tamen nemo potest, apud Græcos patres imprimis inveniri loca, quæ Pelagianismo favere videntur. Hinc et C. Jansenius, 'Græci,' inquit, 'nisi caute legantur et intelligantur, præbere possunt occasionem errori Pelagiano'; et D. Petavius dicit, 'Græci originalis fere criminis raram, nec

men of such different schools that we may surely take their agreement
as a proof of the fact. A late writer, after going through the testimonies of the Fathers one by one, comes to the conclusion, first, that
"the Greek Church in no point favoured Augustine, except in teaching that from Adam's sin came death, and (after the time of Methodius) an extraordinary and unnatural sensuality also"; next, that
"the Latin Church affirmed, in addition, that a corrupt and contaminated soul, and that, by generation, was carried on to his posterity";[20] and, lastly, that neither Greeks nor Latins held the doctrine
of imputation. It may be observed, in addition, that, in spite of the
forcible teaching of St. Paul on the subject, the doctrine of Original
Sin appears neither in the Apostles' nor the Nicene Creed.

## 17.

One additional specimen shall be given as a sample of many others:
I betake myself to one of our altars to receive the Blessed Eucharist; I
have no doubt whatever on my mind about the Gift which that Sacrament contains; I confess to myself my belief, and I go through the steps
on which it is assured to me. "The Presence of Christ is here, for It
follows upon Consecration; and Consecration is the prerogative of
Priests; and Priests are made by Ordination; and Ordination comes in
direct line from the Apostles. Whatever be our other misfortunes, every
link in our chain is safe; we have the Apostolic Succession, we have a
right form of consecration: therefore we are blessed with the great
Gift." Here the question rises in me, "Who told you about that Gift?"
I answer, "I have learned it from the Fathers: I believed the Real
Presence because they bear witness to it. St. Ignatius calls it 'the medicine of immortality': St. Irenæus says that 'our flesh becomes incorrupt,
and partakes of life, and has the hope of the resurrection,' as 'being
nourished from the Lord's Body and Blood'; that the Eucharist 'is
made up of two things, an earthly and an heavenly':[21] perhaps Origen,

disertam, mentionem scriptis suis attigerunt.' " ["Although the Pelagians were
seriously mistaken in saying original sin issued from the mind of Augustine,
and was something of which the ancient Church had no awareness, it remains
undeniable that there are passages in the Greek fathers that seem very congenial to Pelagianism. Jansenius accordingly observed that 'unless the Greeks
are read and interpreted cautiously, they can give occasion for the Pelagian
error,' and Petavius declared that 'writings of the Greeks touched only rarely
and unclearly on original sin.' "]—*Walch, Miscell. Sacr.* p. 607.

[20]Horn, Comment. de Pecc. Orig. 1801; p. 98.
[21]Hær. iv. 18, § 5.

and perhaps Magnes, after him, say that It is not a type of our Lord's Body, but His Body: and St. Cyprian uses language as fearful as can be spoken, of those who profane it. I cast my lot with them, I believe as they." Thus I reply, and then the thought comes upon me a second time, "And do not the same ancient Fathers bear witness to another doctrine, which you disown? Are you not as a hypocrite, listening to them when you will, and deaf when you will not? How are you casting your lot with the Saints, when you go but halfway with them? For of whether of the two do they speak the more frequently, of the Real Presence in the Eucharist, or of the Pope's supremacy? You accept the lesser evidence, you reject the greater."

### 18.

In truth, scanty as the Antenicene notices may be of the Papal supremacy, they are both more numerous and more definite than the adducible testimonies in favour of the Real Presence. The testimonies to the latter are confined to a few passages such as those just quoted. On the other hand, of a passage in St. Justin, Bishop Kaye remarks, "Le Nourry infers that Justin maintained the doctrine of Transubstantiation; it might in my opinion be more plausibly urged in favour of Consubstantiation, since Justin calls the consecrated elements Bread and Wine, though not common bread and wine.[22] . . . We may therefore conclude that, when he calls them the Body and Blood of Christ, he speaks figuratively." "Clement," observes the same author, "says that the Scripture calls wine a mystic *symbol* of the holy blood. . . . Clement gives various interpretations of Christ's expressions in John vi. respecting His flesh and blood; but in no instance does he interpret them literally. . . . His notion seems to have been that, by partaking of the bread and wine in the Eucharist, the soul of the believer is united to the Spirit, and that by this union the principle of immortality is imparted to the flesh."[23] "It has been suggested by some," says Waterland, "that Tertullian understood John vi merely of faith, or doctrine, or spiritual actions; and it is strenuously denied by others." After quoting the passage, he adds, "All that one can justly gather from this confused passage is that Tertullian interpreted the bread of life in John vi of the word, which he sometimes makes to be vocal, and sometimes substantial, blending the ideas in a very perplexed manner; so that he

[22] Justin Martyr, ch. 4.
[23] Clem. Alex. ch. 11.

is no clear authority for construing John vi of doctrines, &c. All that is certain is that he supposes the Word made flesh, the Word incarnate to be the heavenly bread spoken of in that chapter."[24] "Origen's general observation relating to that chapter is, that it must not be literally, but figuratively understood."[25] Again, "It is plain enough that Eusebius followed Origen in this matter, and that both of them favoured the same mystical or allegorical construction; whether constantly and uniformly I need not say."[26] I will but add the incidental testimony afforded on a late occasion: how far the Anglican doctrine of the Eucharist depends on the times before the Nicene Council, how far on the times after it, may be gathered from the circumstance that, when a memorable sermon[27] was published on the subject, out of about one hundred and forty passages from the Fathers appended in the notes, not in formal proof, but in general illustration, only fifteen were taken from Antenicene writers.

With such evidence, the Antenicene testimonies which may be cited in behalf of the authority of the Holy See need not fear a comparison. Faint they may be one by one, but at least we may count seventeen of them, and they are various, and are drawn from many times and countries, and thereby serve to illustrate each other, and form a body of proof. Whatever objections may be made to this or that particular fact, and I do not think any valid ones can be raised, still, on the whole, I consider that a cumulative argument rises from them in favour of the ecumenical and the doctrinal authority of Rome stronger than any argument which can be drawn from the same period for the doctrine of the Real Presence. I shall have occasion to enumerate them in the fourth chapter of this essay.

## 19.

If it be said that the Real Presence appears, by the liturgies of the fourth or fifth century, to have been the doctrine of the earlier, since those very forms probably existed from the first in Divine worship, this is doubtless an important truth; but then it is true also that the writers of the fourth and fifth centuries fearlessly assert or frankly allow that the prerogatives of Rome were derived from apostolic times, and that because it was the See of St. Peter.

[24] Works, vol. vii. pp. 118–20.
[25] Ibid. p. 121.
[26] Ibid. p. 127.
[27] Dr. Pusey's University Sermon of 1843.

Moreover, if the resistance of St. Cyprian and Firmilian to the Church of Rome, in the question of baptism by heretics, be urged as an argument against her primitive authority, or the earlier resistance of Polycrates of Ephesus, let it be considered, first, whether all authority does not necessarily lead to resistance; next, whether St. Cyprian's own doctrine, which is in favour of Rome, is not more weighty than his act, which is against her; thirdly, whether he was not already in error in the main question under discussion, and Firmilian also; and lastly, which is the chief point here, whether, in like manner, we may not object on the other hand against the Real Presence the words of Tertullian, who explains, "This is my Body," by "a figure of my Body," and of Origen, who speaks of "our drinking Christ's Blood not only in the rite of the Sacraments, but also when we receive His discourses,"[28] and says that "that Bread which God the Word acknowledges as His Body is the Word which nourishes souls"[29]— passages which admit of a Catholic interpretation when the Catholic doctrine is once proved, but which prima facie run counter to that doctrine.

It does not seem possible, then, to avoid the conclusion that, whatever be the proper key for harmonizing the records and documents of the early and later Church, and true as the dictum of Vincentius must be considered in the abstract, and possible as its application might be in his own age, when he might almost ask the primitive centuries for their testimony, it is hardly available now, or effective of any satisfactory result. The solution it offers is as difficult as the original problem.

### 20.

Another hypothesis for accounting for a want of accord between the early and the late aspects of Christianity is that of the *Disciplina Arcani*, put forward on the assumption that there has been no variation in the teaching of the Church from first to last. It is maintained that doctrines which are associated with the later ages of the Church were really in the Church from the first, but not publicly taught, and that for various reasons: as, for the sake of reverence, that sacred subjects might not be profaned by the heathen; and for the sake of catechumens, that they might not be oppressed or carried away by a sudden commu-

[28]Numer. Hom. xvi. 9.
[29]Interp. Com. in Matt. 85.

nication of the whole circle of revealed truth. And indeed the fact of this concealment can hardly be denied, in whatever degree it took the shape of a definite rule, which might vary with persons and places. That it existed even as a rule, as regards the Sacraments, seems to be confessed on all hands. That it existed in other respects, as a practice, is plain from the nature of the case, and from the writings of the Apologists. Minucius Felix and Arnobius, in controversy with pagans, imply a denial that then the Christians used altars; yet Tertullian speaks expressly of the *Ara Dei* in the Church. What can we say, but that the Apologists deny altars *in the sense* in which they ridicule them; or, that they deny that altars *such as* the pagan altars were tolerated by Christians? And, in like manner, Minucius allows that there were no temples among Christians; yet they are distinctly recognized in the edicts of the Diocletian era, and are known to have existed at a still earlier date. It is the tendency of every dominant system, such as the paganism of the Antenicene centuries, to force its opponents into the most hostile and jealous attitude, from the apprehension which they naturally feel, lest if they acted otherwise, in those points in which they approximate towards it, they should be misinterpreted and over-borne by its authority. The very fault now found with clergymen of the Anglican Church, who wish to conform their practices to her rubrics, and their doctrines to her divines of the seventeenth century, is, that, whether they mean it or no, whether legitimately or no, still, in matter of fact, they will be sanctioning and encouraging the religion of Rome, in which there are similar doctrines and practices, more definite and more influential; so that, at any rate, it is inexpedient at the moment to attempt what is sure to be mistaken. That is, they are required to exercise a *disciplina arcani*; and a similar reserve was inevitable on the part of the Catholic Church, at a time when priests and altars and rites all around it were devoted to malignant and incurable superstitions. It would be wrong indeed to deny, but it was a duty to withhold, the ceremonial of Christianity; and Apologists might be sometimes tempted to deny absolutely what at furthest could only be denied under conditions. An idolatrous paganism tended to repress the externals of Christianity, as, at this day, the presence of Protestantism is said to repress, though for another reason, the exhibition of the Roman Catholic religion.

On various grounds, then, it is certain that portions of the Church system were held back in primitive times, and of course this fact goes some way to account for that apparent variation and growth of doctrine, which embarrasses us when we would consult history for the true idea of Christianity; yet it is no key to the whole difficulty, as we find it, for obvious reasons: because the variations continue beyond the time when it is conceivable that the discipline was in force, and because they manifest themselves on a law, not abruptly, but by a visible growth which has persevered up to this time without any sign of its coming to an end.[30]

## 21.

The following essay is directed towards a solution of the difficulty which has been stated—the difficulty, as far as it exists, which lies in the way of our using in controversy the testimony of our most natural informant concerning the doctrine and worship of Christianity, viz., the history of eighteen hundred years. The view on which it is written has at all times, perhaps, been implicitly adopted by theologians, and, I believe, has recently been illustrated by several distinguished writers of the continent, such as De Maistre and Möhler: viz., that the increase and expansion of the Christian Creed and ritual, and the variations which have attended the process in the case of individual writers and Churches, are the necessary attendants on any philosophy or polity which takes possession of the intellect and heart, and has had any wide or extended dominion; that, from the nature of the human mind, time is necessary for the full comprehension and perfection of great ideas; and that the highest and most wonderful truths, though communicated to the world once for all by inspired teachers, could not be comprehended all at once by the recipients, but, as being received and transmitted by minds not inspired and through media which were human, have required only the longer time and deeper thought for their full elucidation. This may be called the *Theory of Development of Doctrine*; and, before proceeding to treat of it, one remark may be in place.

It is undoubtedly an hypothesis to account for a difficulty; but such too are the various explanations given by astronomers from Ptolemy to Newton of the apparent motions of the heavenly bodies, and it is as unphilosophical on that account to object to the one as to object to the other. Nor is it more reasonable to express surprise that at this time of day a theory is necessary, granting for argument's sake that the theory is novel, than to have directed a similar wonder in disparagement of the theory of gravitation, or the Plutonian theory in geology. Doubtless, the theory of the secret and the theory of doctrinal develop-

---

[30] Vid. Apolog., p. 198, and Difficulties of Angl. vol. i. xii. 7.

ments are expedients, and so is the dictum of Vincentius; so is the art of grammar or the use of the quadrant; it is an expedient to enable us to solve what has now become a necessary and an anxious problem. For three hundred years the documents and the facts of Christianity have been exposed to a jealous scrutiny; works have been judged spurious which once were received without a question; facts have been discarded or modified which were once first principles in argument; new facts and new principles have been brought to light; philosophical views and polemical discussions of various tendencies have been maintained with more or less success. Not only has the relative situation of controversies and theologies altered, but infidelity itself is in a different—I am obliged to say in a more hopeful position—as regards Christianity. The facts of revealed religion, though in their substance unaltered, present a less compact and orderly front to the attacks of its enemies now than formerly, and allow of the introduction of new inquiries and theories concerning its sources and its rise. The state of things is not as it was when an appeal lay to the supposed works of the Areopagite, or to the primitive decretals, or to St. Dionysius's answers to Paul, or to the Cœna Domini of St. Cyprian. The assailants of dogmatic truth have got the start of its adherents of whatever creed; philosophy is completing what criticism has begun; and apprehensions are not unreasonably excited lest we should have a new world to conquer before we have weapons for the warfare. Already infidelity has its views and conjectures, on which it arranges the facts of ecclesiastical history; and it is sure to consider the absence of any antagonist theory as an evidence of the reality of its own. That the hypothesis, here to be adopted, accounts not only for the Athanasian Creed, but for the Creed of Pope Pius, is no fault of those who adopt it. No one has power over the issues of his principles: we cannot manage our argument, and have as much of it as we please and no more. An argument is needed, unless Christianity is to abandon the province of argument; and those who find fault with the explanation here offered of its historical phenomena will find it their duty to provide one for themselves.

And as no special aim at Roman Catholic doctrine need be supposed to have given a direction to the inquiry, so neither can a reception of that doctrine be immediately based on its results. It would be the work of a life to apply the theory of developments so carefully to the writings of the Fathers, and to the history of controversies and councils, as thereby to vindicate the reasonableness of every decision of Rome; much less can such an undertaking be imagined by one who, in the middle of his days, is beginning life again. Thus much, however, might be gained even from an essay like the present, an explanation of so many of the reputed corruptions, doctrinal and practical, of Rome, as might serve as a fair ground for trusting her in parallel cases where the investigation had not been pursued.

# CHAPTER I

# ON THE DEVELOPMENT OF IDEAS

## SECTION I

### ON THE PROCESS OF DEVELOPMENT IN IDEAS

It is the characteristic of our minds to be ever engaged in passing judgment on the things which come before us. No sooner do we apprehend than we judge; we allow nothing to stand by itself; we compare, contrast, abstract, generalize, connect, adjust, classify; and we view all our knowledge in the associations with which these processes have invested it.

Of the judgments thus made, which become aspects in our minds of the things which meet us, some are mere opinions which come and go, or which remain with us only till an accident displaces them, whatever be the influence which they exercise meanwhile. Others are firmly fixed in our minds, with or without good reason, and have a hold upon us, whether they relate to matters of fact, or to principles of conduct, or are views of life and the world, or are prejudices, imaginations, or convictions. Many of them attach to one and the same object, which is thus variously viewed, not only by various minds, but by the same. They sometimes lie in such near relation that each implies the others; some are only not inconsistent with each other, in that they have a common origin; some, as being actually incompatible with each other, are, one or other, falsely associated in our minds with their object, and in any case they may be nothing more than ideas which we mistake for things.

Thus Judaism is an idea which once was objective, and Gnosticism is an idea which was never so. Both of them have various aspects: those of Judaism were such as monotheism, a certain ethical discipline, a ministration of divine vengeance, a preparation for Christianity; those of the Gnostic idea are such as the doctrine of two principles, that of emanation, the intrinsic malignity of matter, the inculpability of sensual indulgence, or the guilt of every pleasure of sense, of which last two one or other must be in the Gnostic a false aspect and subjective only.

## 2.

The idea which represents an object or supposed object is commensurate with the sum total of its possible aspects, however they may vary in the separate consciousness of individuals; and in proportion to the variety of aspects under which it presents itself to various minds is its force and depth, and the argument for its reality. Ordinarily an idea is not brought home to the intellect as objective except through this variety; like bodily substances, which are not apprehended except under the clothing of their properties and results, and which admit of being walked round, and surveyed on opposite sides, and in different perspectives, and in contrary lights, in evidence of their reality. And as views of a material object may be taken from points so remote or so opposed that they seem at first sight incompatible, and especially as their shadows will be disproportionate or even monstrous, and yet all these anomalies will disappear and all these contrarieties be adjusted on ascertaining the point of vision or the surface of projection in each case; so also all the aspects of an idea are capable of coalition, and of a resolution into the object to which it belongs; and the prima facie dissimilitude of its aspects becomes, when explained, an argument for its substantiveness and integrity, and their multiplicity for its originality and power.

## 3.

There is no one aspect deep enough to exhaust the contents of a real idea, no one term or proposition which will serve to define it; though of course one representation of it is more just and exact than another, and though when an idea is very complex, it is allowable, for the sake of convenience, to consider its distinct aspects as if separate ideas. Thus, with all our intimate knowledge of animal life and of the structure of particular animals, we have not arrived at a true definition of any one of them, but are forced to enumerate properties and accidents by way of description. Nor can we inclose in a formula that intellectual fact, or system of thought, which we call the Platonic philosophy, or that historical phenomenon of doctrine and conduct which we call the heresy of Montanus or of Manes. Again, if Protestantism were said to lie in its theory of private judgment, and Lutheranism in its doctrine of justification, this indeed would be an approximation to the truth; but it is plain that to argue or to act as if the one or the other aspect were a sufficient account of those forms of religion severally would be a serious mistake. Sometimes an attempt is made to determine the "leading idea," as it has been called, of Christianity, an ambitious essay as employed on a supernatural work, when, even as regards the visible creation and the inventions of man, such a task is beyond us. Thus its one idea has been said by some to be the restoration of our fallen race, by others philanthropy, by others the tidings of immortality, or the spirituality of true religious service, or the salvation of the elect, or mental liberty, or the union of the soul with God. If, indeed, it is only thereby meant to use one or other of these as a central idea for convenience, in order to group others around it, no fault can be found with such a proceeding; and in this sense I should myself call the Incarnation the central aspect of Christianity, out of which the three main aspects of its teaching take their rise, the sacramental, the hierarchical, and the ascetic. But one aspect of Revelation must not be allowed to exclude or to obscure another; and Christianity is dogmatical, devotional, practical all at once; it is esoteric and exoteric; it is indulgent and strict; it is light and dark; it is love, and it is fear.

## 4.

When an idea, whether real or not, is of a nature to arrest and possess the mind, it may be said to have life, that is, to live in the mind which is its recipient. Thus mathematical ideas, real as they are, can hardly properly be called living, at least ordinarily. But when some great enunciation, whether true or false, about human nature, or present good, or government, or duty, or religion is carried forward into the public throng of men and draws attention, then it is not merely received passively in this or that form into many minds, but it becomes an active principle within them, leading them to an ever new contemplation of itself, to an application of it in various directions, and a propagation of it on every side. Such is the doctrine of the divine right of kings, or of the rights of man, or of the anti-social bearings of a priesthood, or utilitarianism, or free trade, or the duty of benevolent enterprises, or the philosophy of Zeno or Epicurus, doctrines which are of a nature to attract and influence, and have so far a prima facie reality, that they may be looked at on many sides and strike various minds very variously. Let one such idea get possession of the popular mind, or the mind of any portion of the community, and it is not difficult to understand what will be the result. At first men will not fully realize what it is that moves them, and will express and explain themselves inadequately. There will be a general agitation of thought, and an action of mind upon mind. There will be a time of confusion, when conceptions and misconceptions are in conflict, and it is uncertain whether anything is to come of the idea at all, or which view of it is to get the start of the others. New lights will be brought to bear upon the original statements of the doctrine put forward; judgments and aspects will accumulate. After a while some definite teaching emerges; and as time proceeds, one view will be modified or expanded by another, and then combined with a third; till the idea to which these various aspects belong will be to each mind separately what at first it was only to all together. It will be surveyed too in its relation to other doctrines or facts, to other natural laws or established customs, to the varying circumstances of times and places, to other religions, polities, philosophies, as the case may be. How it stands affected towards other systems, how it affects them, how far it may be made to combine with them, how far it tolerates them, when it interferes with them, will be gradually wrought out. It will be interrogated and criticized by enemies, and defended by well-wishers. The multitude of opinions formed concerning it in these respects and many others will be collected, compared, sorted, sifted, selected, rejected, gradually attached to it, separated from it, in the minds of individuals and of the community. It will, in proportion to its native vigour and subtlety, introduce itself into the framework and details of social life, changing public opinion, and strengthening or undermining the foundations of established order. Thus in time it will have grown into an ethical code, or into a system of government, or into a theology, or into a ritual, according to its capabilities; and this body of thought, thus laboriously gained, will after all be little more than the proper representative of one idea, being in substance what that idea meant from the first, its complete image as seen in a combination of diversified aspects, with the suggestions and corrections of many minds, and the illustration of many experiences.

## 5.

This process, whether it be longer or shorter in point of time, by which the aspects of an idea are brought into consistency and form, I call its development, being the germination and maturation of some truth or apparent truth on a large mental field. On the other hand this process will not be a development, unless the assemblage of aspects which constitute its ultimate shape really belongs to the idea from which they start. A republic, for instance, is not a development from a pure monarchy, though it may follow upon it; whereas the Greek "tyrant" may be considered as included in the idea of a democracy. Moreover a development will have this characteristic, that, its action being in the busy scene of human life, it cannot progress at all without cutting across, and thereby destroying or modifying and incorporating with itself existing modes of thinking and operating. The development then of an idea is not like an investigation worked out on paper, in which each successive advance is a pure evolution from a foregoing, but it is carried on through and by means of communities of men and their leaders and guides; and it employs their minds as its instruments, and depends upon them while it uses them. And so, as regards existing opinions, principles, measures, and institutions of the community which it has invaded; it develops by establishing relations between itself and them; it employs itself, in giving them a new meaning and direction, in creating what may be called a jurisdiction over them, in throwing off whatever in them it cannot assimilate. It grows when it incorporates, and its identity is found not in isolation, but in continuity and sovereignty. This it is that imparts to the history both of states and of religions its specially turbulent and polemical character. Such is the explanation of the wranglings, whether of schools or of parliaments. It is the warfare of ideas under their various aspects striving for the mastery, each of them enterprising, engrossing, imperious, more or less incompatible with the rest, and rallying followers or rousing foes, according as it acts upon the faith, the prejudices, or the interest of parties or classes.

### 6.

Moreover, an idea not only modifies but is modified, or at least influenced, by the state of things in which it is carried out, and is dependent in various ways on the circumstances which surround it. Its development proceeds quickly or slowly, as it may be; the order of succession in its separate stages is variable; it shows differently in a small sphere of action and in an extended; it may be interrupted, retarded, mutilated, distorted, by external violence; it may be enfeebled by the effort of ridding itself of domestic foes; it may be impeded and swayed or even absorbed by counter energetic ideas; it may be coloured by the received tone of thought into which it comes, or depraved by the intrusion of foreign principles, or at length shattered by the development of some original fault within it.

## 7.

But whatever be the risk of corruption from intercourse with the world around, such a risk must be encountered if a great idea is duly to be understood, and much more if it is to be fully exhibited. It is elicited and expanded by trial, and battles into perfection and supremacy. Nor does it escape the collision of opinion even in its earlier years, nor does it remain truer to itself, and with a better claim to be considered one and the same, though externally protected from vicissitude and change. It is indeed sometimes said that the stream is clearest near the spring. Whatever use may fairly be made of this image, it does not apply to the history of a philosophy or belief, which on the contrary is more equable, and purer, and stronger when its bed has become deep, and broad, and full. It necessarily rises out of an existing state of things, and for a time savours of the soil. Its vital element needs disengaging from what is foreign and temporary, and is employed in efforts after freedom which become more vigorous and hopeful as its years increase. Its beginnings are no measure of its capabilities, nor of its scope. At first no one knows what it is, or what it is worth. It remains perhaps for a time quiescent; it tries, as it were, its limbs, and proves the ground under it, and feels its way. From time to time it makes essays which fail, and are in consequence abandoned. It seems in suspense which way to go; it wavers, and at length strikes out in one definite direction. In time it enters upon strange territory; points of controversy alter their bearing; parties rise and fall around it; dangers and hopes appear in new relations; and old principles reappear under new forms. It changes with them in order to remain the same. In a higher world it is otherwise, but here below to live is to change, and to be perfect is to have changed often.

## SECTION II

### ON THE KINDS OF DEVELOPMENT IN IDEAS

To attempt an accurate analysis or complete enumeration of the processes of thought, whether speculative or practical, which come under the notion of development, exceeds the pretensions of an essay like the present; but, without some general view of the various mental exercises which go by the name we shall have no security against confusion in our reasoning and necessary exposure to criticism.

1. First, then, it must be borne in mind that the word is commonly used, and is used here, in three senses indiscriminately, from defect of our language; on the one hand for the process of development, on the other for the result; and again either generally for a development, true or not true (that is, faithful or unfaithful to the idea from which it started) or exclusively for a development deserving the name. A false or unfaithful development is more properly to be called a corruption.

2. Next, it is plain that *mathematical* developments, that is, the system of truths drawn out from mathematical definitions or equations, do not fall under our present subject, though altogether analogous to it. There can be no corruption in such developments, because they are conducted on strict demonstration; and the conclusions in which they terminate, being necessary, cannot be declensions from the original idea.

3. Nor, of course, do *physical* developments, as the growth of animal or vegetable nature, come into consideration here; excepting that, together with mathematical, they may be taken as illustrations of the general subject to which we have to direct our attention.

4. Nor have we to consider *material* developments, which, though effected by human contrivance, are still physical; as the development, as it is called, of the national resources. We speak, for instance, of Ireland, the United States, or the valley of the Indus, as admitting of a great development; by which we mean, that those countries have fertile tracts, or abundant products, or broad and deep rivers, or central positions for commerce, or capacious and commodious harbours, the materials and instruments of wealth, and these at present turned to insufficient account. Development in this case will proceed by establishing marts, cutting canals, laying down railroads, erecting factories, forming docks, and similar works, by which the natural riches of the country may be made to yield the largest return and to exert the greatest influence. In this sense, art is the development of nature, that is, its adaptation to the purposes of utility and beauty, the human intellect being the developing power.

### 2.

5. When society and its various classes and interests are the subject matter of the ideas which are in operation, the development may be called *political*; as we see it in the growth of states or the changes of

a constitution. Barbarians descend into southern regions from cupidity, and their warrant is the sword; this is no intellectual process, nor is it the mode of development exhibited in civilized communities. Where civilization exists, reason, in some shape or other, is the incentive or the pretence of development. When an empire enlarges, it is on the call of its allies, or for the balance of power, or from the necessity of a demonstration of strength, or from a fear for its frontiers. It lies uneasily in its territory, it is ill-shaped, it has unreal boundary lines, deficient communication between its principal points, or defenceless or turbulent neighbours. Thus, of old time, Eubœa was necessary for Athens, and Cythera for Sparta; and Augustus left his advice, as a legacy, to confine the Empire between the Atlantic, the Rhine and Danube, the Euphrates, and the Arabian and African deserts. In this day, we hear of the Rhine being the natural boundary of France, and the Indus of our Eastern empire; and we predict that, in the event of a war, Prussia will change her outlines in the map of Europe. The development is material; but an idea gives unity and force to its movement.

And so to take a case of national politics, a late writer remarks of the Parliament of 1628–29, in its contest with Charles, that, so far from encroaching on the just powers of a limited monarch, it never hinted at the securities which were necessary for its measures. However, "twelve years more of repeated aggressions," he adds, "taught the Long Parliament what a few sagacious men might perhaps have already suspected; that they must recover more of their ancient constitution, from oblivion; that they must sustain its partial weakness by new securities; that, in order to render the existence of monarchy compatible with that of freedom, they must not only strip it of all it had usurped, but of something that was its own."[1] Whatever be the worth of this author's theory, his facts or representations are an illustration of a political development.

Again, at the present day, that Ireland should have a population of one creed and a Church of another is felt to be a political arrangement so unsatisfactory that all parties seem to agree that either the population will develop in power or the Establishment in influence.

Political developments, though really the growth of ideas, are often capricious and irregular from the nature of their subject matter. They are influenced by the character of sovereigns, the rise and fall of statesmen, the fate of battles, and the numberless vicissitudes of the world.

[1] Hallam's Constit. Hist. ch. vii. p. 572.

"Perhaps the Greeks would be still involved in the heresy of the Mono-physites," says Gibbon, "if the Emperor's horse had not fortunately stumbled. Theodosius expired, his orthodox sister succeeded to the throne."[2]

<h2 style="text-align:center">3.</h2>

Again, it often happens, or generally, that various distinct and in-compatible elements are found in the origin or infancy of politics, or indeed of philosophies, some of which must be ejected before any satisfactory developments, if any, can take place. And they are com-monly ejected by the gradual growth of the stronger. The reign of Charles the First, just referred to, supplies an instance in point.

Sometimes discordant ideas are for a time connected and concealed by a common profession or name. Such is the case of coalitions in politics and comprehensions in religion, of which commonly no good is to be expected. Such is an ordinary function of committees and boards, and the sole aim of conciliations and concessions, to make contraries look the same, and to secure an outward agreement where there is no other unity.

Again, developments, reactions, reforms, revolutions, and changes of various kinds are mixed together in the actual history of states, as of philosophical sects, so as to make it very difficult to exhibit them in any scientific analysis.

Often the intellectual process is detached from the practical, and posterior to it. Thus it was after Elizabeth had established the Reforma-tion that Hooker laid down his theory of Church and State as one and the same, differing only in idea; and after the Revolution and its political consequences that Warburton wrote his "Alliance." And now again a new theory is needed for the constitutional lawyer in order to reconcile the existing political state of things with the just claims of religion. And so, again, in Parliamentary conflicts, men first come to their conclusions by the external pressure of events or the force of principles, they do not know how; then they have to speak, and they look about for arguments; and a pamphlet is published on the subject in debate, or an article appears in a review, to furnish commonplaces for the many.

Other developments, though political, are strictly subjected and con-sequent to the ideas of which they are the exhibitions. Thus Locke's

[2] ch. xlvii.

philosophy was a real guide, not a mere defence of the Revolution era, operating forcibly upon Church and Government in and after his day. Such too were the theories which preceded the overthrow of the old regime in France and other countries at the end of the last century.

Again, perhaps there are polities founded on no ideas at all but on mere custom, as among the Asiatics.

### 4.

6. In other developments the intellectual character is so prominent that they may even be called *logical*, as in the Anglican doctrine of the Royal Supremacy, which has been created in the courts of law, not in the cabinet or on the field. Hence it is carried out with a consistency and minute application which the history of constitutions cannot exhibit. It does not only exist in statutes, or in articles, or in oaths, it is realized in details: as in the *congé d'élire* and letter-missive on appointment of a bishop; in the forms observed in Privy Council on the issuing of State Prayers; in certain arrangements observed in the Prayer-book, where the universal or abstract Church precedes the King but the national or really existing body follows him; in printing his name in large capitals, while the Holiest Names are in ordinary type, and in fixing his arms in churches instead of the Crucifix; moreover, perhaps, in placing "sedition, privy conspiracy and rebellion," before "false doctrine, heresy, and schism" in the Litany.

Again, when some new philosophy or its instalments are introduced into the measures of the legislature, or into the concessions made to a political party, or into commercial or agricultural policy, it is often said, "We have not seen the end of this"; "It is an earnest of future concessions"; "Our children will see." We feel that it has unknown bearings and issues.

The admission of Jews to municipal offices has lately been defended[3] on the ground that it is the introduction of no new principle, but a development of one already received; that its great premises have been decided long since; and that the present age has but to draw the conclusion; that it is not open to us to inquire what ought to be done in the abstract, since there is no ideal model for the infallible guidance of nations; that change is only a question of time, and that there is a time for all things; that the application of principles ought not to go beyond the actual case, neither preceding nor coming after an impera-

---

[3] *Times* newspaper of March, 1845.

tive demand; that in point of fact Jews have lately been chosen for offices, and that in point of principle the law cannot refuse to legitimate such elections.

### 5.

7. Another class of developments may be called *historical*; being the gradual formation of opinion concerning persons, facts, and events. Judgments which were at one time confined to a few at length spread through a community and attain general reception by the accumulation and concurrence of testimony. Thus some authoritative accounts die away; others gain a footing, and are ultimately received as truths. Courts of law, Parliamentary proceedings, newspapers, letters and other posthumous documents, the industry of historians and biographers, and the lapse of years which dissipates parties and prejudices, are in this day the instruments of such development. Accordingly the poet makes Truth the daughter of Time.[4] Thus at length approximations are made to a right appreciation of transactions and characters. History cannot be written except in an after-age. Thus by development the Canon of the New Testament has been formed. Thus public men are content to leave their reputation to posterity; great reactions take place in opinion; nay, sometimes men outlive opposition and obloquy. Thus Saints are canonized in the Church long after they have entered into their rest.

### 6.

8. *Ethical* developments are not properly matter for argument and controversy, but are natural and personal, substituting what is congruous, desirable, pious, appropriate, generous, for strictly logical inference. Bishop Butler supplies us with a remarkable instance in the beginning of the second part of his "Analogy." As principles imply applications, and general propositions include particulars, so, he tells us, do certain relations imply correlative duties, and certain objects demand certain acts and feelings. He observes that, even though we were not enjoined to pay divine honours to the Second and Third Persons of the Holy Trinity, what is predicated of Them in Scripture would be an abundant warrant, an indirect command, nay, a ground in reason for doing so. "Does not," he asks, "the duty of religious

[4] Crabbe's Tales.

regards to both these Divine Persons as immediately arise, to the view of reason, out of the very nature of these offices and relations, as the inward good-will and kind intention which we owe to our fellow creatures arises out of the common relations between us and them?" He proceeds to say that he is speaking of the inward religious regards of reverence, honour, love, trust, gratitude, fear, hope. "In what external manner this inward worship is to be expressed, is a matter of pure revealed command; . . . but the worship, the internal worship itself, to the Son and Holy Ghost, is no further matter of pure revealed command than as the relations they stand in to us are matter of pure revelation; for, the relations being known, the obligations to such internal worship are obligations of reason, arising out of those relations themselves." Here is a development of doctrine into worship of which parallel instances are obviously to be found in the Church of Rome.

## 7.

A development converse to that which Butler speaks of must next be mentioned. As certain objects excite certain emotions and sentiments, so do sentiments imply objects and duties. Thus conscience, the existence of which we cannot deny, is a proof of the doctrine of a Moral Governor, which alone gives it a meaning and a scope; that is, the doctrine of a Judge and Judgment to come is a development of the phenomenon of conscience. Again, it is plain that passions and affections are in action in our minds before the presence of their proper objects; and their activity would of course be an antecedent argument of extreme cogency in behalf of the real existence of those legitimate objects, supposing them unknown. And so again, the social principle, which is innate in us, gives a divine sanction to society and to civil government. And the usage of prayers for the dead implies certain circumstances of their state upon which such devotions bear. And rites and ceremonies are natural means through which the mind relieves itself of devotional and penitential emotions. And sometimes the cultivation of awe and love towards what is great, high, and unseen, has led a man to the abandonment of his sect for some more Catholic form of doctrine.

Aristotle furnishes us with an instance of this kind of development in his account of the happy man. After showing that his definition of happiness includes in itself the pleasurable, which is the most obvious and popular idea of happiness, he goes on to say that still external goods are necessary to it, about which, however, the definition said nothing; that is, a certain prosperity is by moral fitness, not by logical necessity, attached to the happy man. "For it is impossible," he observes, "or not easy, to practise high virtue without abundant means. Many deeds are done by the instrumentality of friends, wealth and political power; and of some things the absence is a cloud upon happiness, as of noble birth, of hopeful children, and of personal appearance: for a person utterly deformed, or low-born, or bereaved and childless, cannot quite be happy: and still less if he have very worthless children or friends, or they were good and died."[5]

## 8.

This process of development has been well delineated by a living French writer, in his lectures on European civilization, who shall be quoted at some length. "If we reduce religion," he says, "to a purely religious sentiment . . . it appears evident that it must and ought to remain a purely personal concern. But I am either strangely mistaken, or this religious sentiment is not the complete expression of the religous nature of man. Religion is, I believe, very different from this, and much more extended. There are problems in human nature, in human destinies, which cannot be solved in this life, which depend on an order of things unconnected with the visible world, but which unceasingly agitate the human mind with a desire to comprehend them. The solution of these problems is the origin of all religion; her primary object is to discover the creeds and doctrines which contain, or are supposed to contain it.

"Another cause also impels mankind to embrace religion . . . From whence do morals originate? whither do they lead? is this self-existing obligation to do good, an isolated fact, without an author, without an end? does it not conceal, or rather does it not reveal to man, an origin, a destiny, beyond this world? The science of morals, by these spontaneous and inevitable questions, conducts man to the threshold of religion, and displays to him a sphere from whence he has not derived it. Thus the certain and never-failing sources of religion are, on the one hand, the problems of our nature; on the other, the necessity of seeking for morals a sanction, an origin, and an aim. It therefore assumes many other forms beside that of a pure sentiment; it appears

[5] Eth. Nic. i. 8.

a union of doctrines, of precepts, of promises. This is what truly constitutes religion; this is its fundamental character; it is not merely a form of sensibility, an impulse of the imagination, a variety of poetry.

"When thus brought back to its true elements, to its essential nature, religion appears no longer a purely personal concern, but a powerful and fruitful principle of association. Is it considered in the light of a system of belief, a system of dogmas? Truth is not the heritage of any individual, it is absolute and universal; mankind ought to seek and profess it in common. Is it considered with reference to the precepts that are associated with its doctrines? A law which is obligatory on a single individual, is so on all; it ought to be promulgated, and it is our duty to endeavour to bring all mankind under its dominion. It is the same with respect to the promises that religion makes, in the name of its creeds and precepts; they ought to be diffused; all men should be incited to partake of their benefits. A religious society, therefore, naturally results from the essential elements of religion, and is such a necessary consequence of it that the term which expresses the most energetic social sentiment, the most intense desire to propagate ideas and extend society, is the word *proselytism*, a term which is especially applied to religious belief, and in fact consecrated to it.

"When a religious society has ever been formed, when a certain number of men are united by a common religious creed, are governed by the same religious precepts, and enjoy the same religious hopes, some form of government is necessary. No society can endure a week, nay more, no society can endure a single hour, without a government. The moment, indeed, a society is formed, by the very fact of its formation, it calls forth a government,—a government which shall proclaim the common truth which is the bond of the society, and promulgate and maintain the precepts that this truth ought to produce. The necessity of a superior power, of a form of government, is involved in the fact of the existence of a religious, as it is in that of any other society.

"And not only is a government necessary, but it naturally forms itself. . . . When events are suffered to follow their natural laws, when force does not interfere, power falls into the hands of the most able, the most worthy, those who are most capable of carrying out the principles on which the society was founded. Is a warlike expedition in agitation? The bravest take the command. Is the object of the association learned research, or a scientific undertaking? The best informed will be the leader. . . . The inequality of faculties and influence, which is the foundation of power in civil life, has the same effect in a religious society . . . Religion has no sooner arisen in the human mind than a religious society appears; and immediately a religious society is formed, it produces its government."[6]

## 9.

9. It remains to allude to what, unless the word were often so vaguely and variously used, I should be led to call *metaphysical* developments; I mean such as are a mere analysis of the idea contemplated, and terminate in its exact and complete delineation. Thus Aristotle draws the character of a magnanimous or of a munificent man; thus Shakespeare might conceive and bring out his Hamlet or Ariel; thus Walter Scott gradually enucleates his James, or Dalgetty as the action of his story proceeds; and thus, in the sacred province of theology, the mind may be employed in developing the solemn ideas, which it has hitherto held implicitly and without subjecting them to its reflecting and reasoning powers.

I have already treated of this subject at length, with a reference to the highest theological subject, in a former work, from which it will be sufficient here to quote some sentences in explanation:

"The mind which is habituated to the thought of God, of Christ, of the Holy Spirit, naturally turns with a devout curiosity to the contemplation of the object of its adoration, and begins to form statements concerning it, before it knows whither, or how far, it will be carried. One proposition necessarily leads to another, and a second to a third; then some limitation is required; and the combination of these opposites occasions some fresh evolutions from the original idea, which indeed can never be said to be entirely exhausted. This process is its development, and results in a series, or rather body, of dogmatic statements, till what was an impression on the Imagination has become a system or creed in the Reason.

"Now such impressions are obviously individual and complete above other theological ideas, because they are the impressions of Objects. Ideas and their developments are commonly not identical, the development being but the carrying out of the idea into its consequences. Thus the doctrine of Penance may be called a development of the doctrine of Baptism, yet still is a distinct doctrine; whereas the developments in the doctrines of the Holy Trinity and the Incarnation are mere portions of the original impression, and modes of representing

[6] Guizot, Europ. Civil., Lect. v., Beckwith's Translation.

it. As God is one, so the impression which He gives us of Himself is one; it is not a thing of parts; it is not a system; nor is it anything imperfect and needing a counterpart. It is the vision of an object. When we pray, we pray, not to an assemblage of notions or to a creed, but to One Individual Being; and when we speak of Him, we speak of a Person, not of a Law or Manifestation . . . Religious men, according to their measure, have an idea or vision of the Blessed Trinity in Unity, of the Son Incarnate, and of His Presence, not as a number of qualities, attributes, and actions, not as the subject of a number of propositions, but as one and individual, and independent of words, like an impression conveyed through the senses. . . . Creeds and dogmas live in the one idea which they are designed to express, and which alone is substantive; and are necessary, because the human mind cannot reflect upon that idea except piecemeal, cannot use it in its oneness and entireness, or without resolving it into a series of aspects and relations."[7]

## 10.

So much on the development of ideas in various subject matters: it may be necessary to add that, in many cases, *development* simply stands for *exhibition*, as in some of the instances adduced above. Thus both Calvinism and Unitarianism may be called developments, that is, exhibitions, of the principle of private judgment, though they have nothing in common viewed as doctrines.

As to Christianity, supposing the truths of which it consists to admit of development, that development will be one or other of the last five kinds. Taking the Incarnation as its central doctrine, the Episcopate, as taught by St. Ignatius, will be an instance of political development, the *Theotokos* of logical, the determination of the date of our Lord's birth of historical, the Holy Eucharist of moral, and the Athanasian Creed of metaphysical.

[7]Univ. Serm. xv. 20–23, pp. 329–32, ed. 3.

# CHAPTER II

# ON THE ANTECEDENT ARGUMENT IN BEHALF OF DEVELOPMENTS IN CHRISTIAN DOCTRINE

## SECTION I

### DEVELOPMENTS OF DOCTRINE TO BE EXPECTED

1. If Christianity is a fact and impresses an idea of itself on our minds and is a subject matter of exercises of the reason, that idea will in course of time expand into a multitude of ideas, and aspects of ideas, connected and harmonious with one another, and in themselves determinate and immutable, as is the objective fact itself which is thus represented. It is a characteristic of our minds that they cannot take an object in which is submitted to them simply and integrally. We conceive by means of definition or description; whole objects do not create in the intellect whole ideas, but are, to use a mathematical phrase, thrown into series, into a number of statements, strengthening, interpreting, correcting each other, and with more or less exactness approximating, as they accumulate, to a perfect image. There is no other way of learning or of teaching. We cannot teach except by aspects or views which are not identical with the thing itself which we are teaching. Two persons may each convey the same truth to a third, yet by methods and through representations altogether different. The same person will treat the same argument differently in an essay or speech, according to the accident of the day of writing, or of the audience, yet it will be substantially the same.

And the more claim an idea has to be considered living, the more various will be its aspects; and the more social and political is its nature, the more complicated and subtle will be its issues, and the longer and more eventful will be its course. And in the number of these special ideas, which from their very depth and richness cannot be fully understood at once, but are more and more clearly expressed and taught the longer they last—having aspects many and bearings many, mutually connected and growing one out of another, and all parts of a whole, with a sympathy and correspondence keeping pace with the ever changing necessities of the world, multiform, prolific, and ever resourceful—among these great doctrines surely we Christians shall not refuse a foremost place to Christianity. Such previously to the determination of the fact must be our anticipation concerning it from a contemplation of its initial achievements.

## 2.

It may be objected that its inspired documents at once determine the limits of its mission without further trouble; but ideas are in the writer and reader of the revelation, not the inspired text itself; and the question is whether those ideas which the letter conveys from writer to reader, reach the reader at once in their completeness and accuracy on his first perception of them, or whether they open out in his intellect and grow to perfection in the course of time. Nor could it surely be maintained without extravagance that the letter of the New Testament, or of any assignable number of books, comprises a delineation of all possible forms which a divine message will assume when submitted to a multitude of minds.

Nor is the case altered by supposing that inspiration provided in behalf of the first recipients of the Revelation, what the Divine Fiat effected for herbs and plants in the beginning, which were created in maturity. Still, the time at length came when its recipients ceased to be inspired; and on these recipients the revealed truths would fall, as in other cases, at first vaguely and generally, though in spirit and in truth, and would afterwards be completed by developments.

Nor can it fairly be made a difficulty that thus to treat of Christianity is to level it in some sort to sects and doctrines of the world, and to impute to it the imperfections which characterize the productions of man. Certainly it is a sort of degradation of a divine work to consider it under an earthly form; but it is no irreverence, since our Lord Himself, its Author and Guardian, bore one also. Christianity differs from other religions and philosophies, in what is superadded to earth from heaven; not in kind, but in origin; not in its nature, but in its personal characteristics; being informed and quickened by what is more than intellect, by a divine spirit. It is externally what the Apostle calls an "earthen vessel," being the religion of men. And, considered as such, it grows "in wisdom and stature"; but the powers which it wields, and the words which proceed out of its mouth attest its miraculous nativity.

Unless then some special ground of exception can be assigned, it is as evident that Christianity, as a doctrine and worship, will develop in the minds of recipients, as that it conforms in other respects, in its external propagation or its political framework, to the general methods by which the course of things is carried forward.

### 3.

2. Again, if Christianity be an universal religion, suited not simply to one locality or period but to all times and places, it cannot but vary in its relations and dealings towards the world around it, that is, it will develop. Principles require a very various application according as persons and circumstances vary, and must be thrown into new shapes according to the form of society which they are to influence. Hence all bodies of Christians, orthodox or not, develop the doctrines of Scripture. Few but will grant that Luther's view of justification had never been stated in words before his time; that his phraseology and his positions were novel, whether called for by circumstances or not. It is equally certain that the doctrine of justification defined at Trent was, in some sense, new also. The refutation and remedy of errors cannot precede their rise; and thus the fact of false developments or corruptions involves the correspondent manifestation of true ones. Moreover, all parties appeal to Scripture, that is, argue from Scripture; but argument implies deduction, that is, development. Here there is no difference between early times and late, between a Pope ex cathedra and an individual Protestant, except that their authority is not on a par. On either side the claim of authority is the same, and the process of development.

Accordingly, the common complaint of Protestants against the Church of Rome is not simply that she has added to the primitive or the Scriptural doctrine (for this they do themselves) but that she contradicts it, and moreover imposes her additions as fundamental truths under sanction of an anathema. For themselves they deduce by quite as subtle a method, and act upon doctrines as implicit and on reasons as little analyzed in time past, as Catholic schoolmen. What prominence has the Royal Supremacy in the New Testament, or the lawfulness of bearing arms, or the duty of public worship, or the substitution of the first day of the week for the seventh, or infant baptism, to say nothing of the fundamental principle that the Bible and the Bible only is the religion of Protestants? These doctrines and usages, true or not, which is not the question here, are surely not gained by the direct use and immediate application of Scripture, nor by a mere exercise of argument upon words and sentences placed before the eyes, but by the unconscious growth of ideas suggested by the letter and habitual to the mind.

### 4.

3. And, indeed, when we turn to the consideration of particular doctrines on which Scripture lays the greatest stress, we shall see that it is absolutely impossible for them to remain in the mere letter of Scripture, if they are to be more than mere words, and to convey a definite idea to the recipient. When it is declared that "the Word became flesh," three wide questions open upon us on the very announcement. What is meant by "the Word," what by "flesh," what by "became"? The answers to these involve a process of investigation, and are developments. Moreover, when they have been made, they will suggest a series of secondary questions; and thus at length a multitude of propositions is the result, which gather round the inspired sentence of which they come, giving it externally the form of a doctrine, and creating or deepening the idea of it in the mind.

It is true that so far as such statements of Scripture are mysteries, they are relatively to us but words, and cannot be developed. But as a mystery implies in part what is incomprehensible or at least unknown, so does it in part imply what is not so; it implies a partial manifestation, or a representation by economy. Because then it is in a measure understood, it can so far be developed, though each result in the process will partake of the dimness and confusion of the original impression.

### 5.

4. This moreover should be considered—that great questions exist in the subject matter of which Scripture treats which Scripture does not solve; questions too so real, so practical, that they must be answered, and, unless we suppose a new revelation, answered by means of the revelation which we have, that is, by development. Such is the question of the Canon of Scripture and its inspiration: that is, whether Christianity depends upon a written document as Judaism; if so, on what writings and how many; whether that document is self-interpreting,

or requires a comment, and whether any authoritative comment or commentator is provided; whether the revelation and the document are commensurate, or the one outruns the other; all these questions surely find no solution on the surface of Scripture, nor indeed under the surface in the case of most men, however long and diligent might be their study of it. Nor were these difficulties settled by authority, as far as we know, at the commencement of the religion; yet surely it is quite conceivable that an Apostle might have dissipated them all in a few words, had Divine Wisdom thought fit. But in matter of fact the decision has been left to time, to the slow process of thought, to the influence of mind upon mind, the issues of controversy, and the growth of opinion.

### 6.

To take another instance just now referred to: if there was a point on which a rule was desirable from the first, it was concerning the religious duties under which Christian parents lay as regards their children. It would be natural indeed in any Christian father, in the absence of a rule, to bring his children for baptism; such in this instance would be the practical development of his faith in Christ and love for his offspring; still a development it is—necessarily required, yet, as far as we know, not provided for his need by direct precept in the Revelation as originally given.

Another very large field of thought, full of practical considerations, yet, as far as our knowledge goes, but only partially occupied by any Apostolical judgment, is that which the question of the effects of baptism opens upon us. That they who came in repentance and faith to that Holy Sacrament received remission of sins is undoubtedly the doctrine of the Apostles; but is there any means of a second remission for sins committed after it? St. Paul's Epistles, where we might expect an answer to our inquiry, contain no explicit statement on the subject; what they do plainly say does not diminish the difficulty: viz., first, that baptism is intended for the pardon of sins before it, not in prospect; next, that those who have received the gift of baptism in fact live in a state of holiness, not of sin. How do statements such as these meet the actual state of the Church as we see it at this day?

Considering that it was expressly predicted that the Kingdom of Heaven, like the fisher's net, should gather of every kind, and that the tares should grow with the wheat until the harvest, a graver and more practical question cannot be imagined than that which it has pleased the Divine Author of the Revelation to leave undecided, unless indeed there be means given in that Revelation of its own growth or development. As far as the letter goes of the inspired message, every one who holds that Scripture is the rule of faith, as all Protestants do, must allow that "there is not one of us but has exceeded by transgression its revealed Ritual, and finds himself in consequence thrown upon those infinite resources of Divine Love which are stored in Christ, but have not been drawn out into form in the appointments of the Gospel."[1] Since then Scripture needs completion, the question is brought to this issue, whether defect or inchoateness in its doctrines be or be not an antecedent probability in favour of a development of them.

### 7.

There is another subject, though not so immediately practical, on which Scripture does not, strictly speaking, keep silence, but says so little as to require, and so much as to suggest, information beyond its letter—the intermediate state between death and the Resurrection. Considering the long interval which separates Christ's first and second coming, the millions of faithful souls who are waiting it out, and the intimate concern which every Christian has in the determination of its character, it might have been expected that Scripture would have spoken explicitly concerning it, whereas in fact its notices are but brief and obscure. We might indeed have argued that this silence of Scripture was intentional, with a view of discouraging speculations upon the subject, except for the circumstance that, as in the question of our post-baptismal state, its teaching seems to proceed upon an hypothesis inapplicable to the state of the Church after the time when it was delivered. As Scripture contemplates Christians not as backsliders but as saints, so does it apparently represent the Day of Judgment as immediate, and the interval of expectation as evanescent. It leaves on our minds the general impression that Christ was returning on earth at once, "the time short," worldly engagements superseded by "the present distress," persecutors urgent, Christians, as a body, sinless and expectant, without home, without plan for the future, looking up to heaven. But outward circumstances have changed, and with the change, a different application of the revealed word has of necessity been demanded, that is, a development. When the nations were converted and offences abounded, then the Church came out to view on

[1] Doctrine of Justification, Lect. xiii.

the one hand as a temporal establishment, on the other as a remedial system, and passages of Scripture aided and directed the development which before were of inferior account. Hence the doctrine of Penance as the complement of Baptism, and of Purgatory as the explanation of the intermediate state. So reasonable is this expansion of the original creed, that, when some ten years since the true doctrine of Baptism was expounded among us without any mention of Penance, our teacher was accused by many of us of Novatianism; while, on the other hand, heterodox divines have before now advocated the doctrine of the sleep of the soul because they said it was the only successful preventive of belief in Purgatory.

8.

Thus developments of Christianity are proved to have been in the contemplation of its Divine Author, by an argument parallel to that by which we infer intelligence in the system of the physical world. In whatever sense the need and its supply are a proof of design in the visible creation, in the same do the gaps, if the word may be used, which occur in the structure of the original creed of the Church, make it probable that those developments, which grow out of the truths which lie around it, were intended to fill them up.

Nor can it be fairly objected that in thus arguing we are contradicting the great philosopher, who tells us, that "upon supposition of God affording us light and instruction by revelation, additional to what He has afforded us by reason and experience, we are in no sort judges by what methods, and in what proportion, it were to be expected that this supernatural light and instruction would be afforded us,"[2] because he is speaking of our judging before a revelation is given. He observes that "we have no principles of reason upon which to judge *beforehand*, how it were to be expected Revelation should have been left, or what was most suitable to the divine plan of government," in various respects; but the case is altogether altered when a Revelation is vouchsafed, for then a new precedent, or what he calls "principle of reason," is introduced, and from what is actually put into our hands we can form a judgment whether more is to be expected. Butler, indeed, as a well-known passage of his work shows, is far from denying the principle of progressive development.

[2]Butler's Anal. ii. 3.

## 9.

5. The method of revelation observed in Scripture abundantly confirms this anticipation. For instance, prophecy, if it had so happened, need not have afforded a specimen of development; separate predictions might have been made to accumulate as time went on, prospects might have opened, definite knowledge might have been given, by communications independent of each other, as St. John's Gospel or the Epistles of St. Paul are unconnected with the first three Gospels, though the doctrine of each Apostle is a development of their matter. But the prophetic Revelation is, in matter of fact, not of this nature but a process of development; the earlier prophecies are pregnant texts out of which the succeeding announcements grow; they are types. It is not that first one truth is told, then another; but the whole truth or large portions of it are told at once, yet only in their rudiments, or in miniature, and they are expanded and finished in their parts, as the course of revelation proceeds. The Seed of the woman was to bruise the serpent's head; the sceptre was not to depart from Judah till Shiloh came, to whom was to be the gathering of the people. He was to be Wonderful, Counsellor, the Prince of Peace. The question of the Ethiopian rises in the reader's mind, "Of whom speaketh the Prophet this?" Every word requires a comment. Accordingly, it is no uncommon theory with unbelievers, that the Messianic idea, as they call it, was gradually developed in the minds of the Jews by a continuous and traditional habit of contemplating it, and grew into its full proportions by a mere human process; and so far seems certain, without trenching on the doctrine of inspiration, that the books of Wisdom and Ecclesiasticus are developments of the writings of the Prophets, expressed or elicited by means of current ideas in the Greek philosophy, and ultimately adopted and ratified by the Apostle in his Epistle to the Hebrews.

## 10.

But the whole Bible, not its prophetical portions only, is written on the principle of development. As the Revelation proceeds, it is ever new, yet ever old. St. John, who completes it, declares that he writes no "new commandment unto his brethren," but an old commandment which they "had from the beginning." And then he adds, "A new commandment I write unto you." The same test of development is suggested in our Lord's words on the Mount, as has already been noticed, "Think not that I am come to destroy the Law and the Prophets; I am not come to destroy, but to fulfil." He does not reverse but perfect what has gone before. Thus with respect to the evangelical view of the rite of sacrifice, first the rite is enjoined by Moses; next Samuel says, "to obey is better than sacrifice"; then Hosea, "I will have mercy and not sacrifice"; Isaiah, "Incense is an abomination unto me"; then Malachi, describing the times of the Gospel, speaks of the "pure offering" of wheatflour; and our Lord completes the development, when He speaks of worshipping "in spirit and in truth." If there is anything here left to explain, it will be found in the usage of the Christian Church immediately afterwards, which shows that sacrifice was not removed, but truth and spirit added.

Nay, the *effata* of our Lord and His Apostles are of a typical structure, parallel to the prophetic announcements above mentioned, and predictions as well as injunctions of doctrine. If then the prophetic sentences have had that development which has really been given them, first by succeeding revelations and then by the event, it is probably antecedently that those doctrinal, political, ritual, and ethical sentences, which have the same structure, should admit the same expansion. Such are, "This is My Body," or "Thou art Peter, and upon this Rock I will build My Church," or "The meek shall inherit the earth," or "Suffer little children to come unto Me," or "The pure in heart shall see God."

## 11.

On this character of our Lord's teaching, the following passage may suitably be quoted from a writer already used. "His recorded words and works when on earth ... come to us as the declarations of a Lawgiver. In the Old Covenant, Almighty God first of all spoke the Ten Commandments from Mount Sinai, and afterwards wrote them. So our Lord first spoke His own Gospel, both of promise and of precept, on the Mount, and His Evangelists have recorded it. Further, when He delivered it, He spoke by way of parallel to the Ten Commandments. And His style, moreover, corresponds to the authority which He assumes. It is of that solemn, measured, and severe character, which bears on the face of it tokens of its belonging to One who spake as none other man could speak. The Beatitudes, with which His Sermon opens, are an instance of this incommunicable style, which befitted, as far as human words could befit, God Incarnate.

"Nor is this style peculiar to the Sermon on the Mount. All through the Gospels it is discernible, distinct from any other part of Scripture, showing itself in solemn declarations, canons, sentences, or sayings, such as legislators propound, and scribes and lawyers comment on. Surely everything our Saviour did and said is characterized by mingled simplicity and mystery. His emblematical actions, His typical miracles, His parables, His replies, His censures, all are evidences of a legislature in germ, afterwards to be developed, a code of divine truth which was ever to be before men's eyes, to be the subject of investigation and interpretation, and the guide in controversy. 'Verily, verily, I say unto you'—'But, I say unto you'—are the tokens of a supreme Teacher and Prophet.

"And thus the Fathers speak of His teaching. 'His sayings,' observes St. Justin, 'were short and concise; for He was no rhetorician, but His word was the power of God.' And St. Basil, in like manner, 'Every deed and every word of our Saviour Jesus Christ is a canon of piety and virtue. When then thou hearest word or deed of His, do not hear it as by the way, or after a simple and carnal manner, but enter into the depth of His contemplations, become a communicant in truths mystically delivered to thee.' "[3]

## 12.

Moreover, while it is certain that developments of Revelation proceeded all through the Old Dispensation down to the very end of our Lord's ministry, on the other hand, if we turn our attention to the beginnings of Apostolical teaching after His ascension, we shall find ourselves unable to fix an historical point at which the growth of doctrine ceased, and the rule of faith was once for all settled. Not on the day of Pentecost, for St. Peter had still to learn at Joppa that he was to baptize Cornelius; not at Joppa and Cæsarea, for St. Paul had to write his Epistles; not on the death of the last Apostle, for St. Ignatius had to establish the doctrine of Episcopacy; not then, nor for centuries after, for the Canon of the New Testament was still undetermined. Not in the Creed, which is no collection of definitions, but a summary of certain *credenda*, an incomplete summary, and, like the Lord's Prayer or the Decalogue, a mere sample of divine truths, especially of the more elementary. No one doctrine can be named which starts complete at first, and gains nothing afterwards from the

[3] Proph. Office, Lect. xii. [Via Med. vol. i. pp. 292–93].

investigations of faith and the attacks of heresy. The Church went forth from the old world in haste, as the Israelites from Egypt "with their dough before it was leavened, their kneading troughs being bound up in their clothes upon their shoulders."

## 13.

Further, the political developments contained in the historical parts of Scripture are as striking as the prophetical and the doctrinal. Can any history wear a more human appearance than that of the rise and growth of the chosen people to whom I have just referred? What had been determined in the counsels of the Lord of heaven and earth from the beginning, what was immutable, what was announced to Moses in the burning bush, is afterwards represented as the growth of an idea under successive emergencies. The Divine Voice in the bush had announced the exodus of the children of Israel from Egypt and their entrance into Canaan; and added, as a token of the certainty of His purpose, "When thou hast brought forth the people out of Egypt, ye shall serve God upon this mountain." Now this sacrifice or festival, which was but incidental and secondary in the great deliverance, is for a while the ultimate scope of the demands which Moses makes upon Pharaoh. "Thou shalt come, thou and the elders of Israel unto the King of Egypt, and ye shall say unto him, The Lord God of the Hebrews hath met with us, and now let us go, we beseech thee, three days' journey into the wilderness, that we may sacrifice to the Lord our God." It had been added that Pharaoh would first refuse their request, but that after miracles he would let them go altogether, nay with "jewels of silver and gold, and raiment."

Accordingly the first request of Moses was, "Let us go, we pray thee, three days' journey into the desert, and sacrifice unto the Lord our God." Before the plague of frogs the warning is repeated, "Let My people go that they may serve Me"; and after it Pharaoh says, "I will let the people go, that they may do sacrifice unto the Lord." It occurs again before the plague of flies; and after it Pharaoh offers to let the Israelites sacrifice in Egypt, which Moses refuses on the ground that they will have to "sacrifice the abomination of the Egyptian before their eyes." "We will go three days' journey into the wilderness," he proceeds, "and sacrifice to the Lord our God"; and Pharaoh then concedes their sacrificing in the wilderness, "only," he says, "you shall not go very far away." The demand is repeated separately before the plagues of murrain, hail, and locusts, no mention being yet made of anything beyond a service or sacrifice in the wilderness. On the last of these interviews, Pharaoh asks an explanation, and Moses extends his claim: "We will go with our young and with our old, with our sons and with our daughters, with our flocks and with our herds will we go, for we must hold a feast unto the Lord." That it was an extension seems plain from Pharaoh's reply: "Go now ye that are men, and serve the Lord, for that ye did desire." Upon the plague of darkness Pharaoh concedes the extended demand, excepting the flocks and herds; but Moses reminds him that they were implied, though not expressed, in the original wording: "Thou must give us also sacrifices and burnt offerings, that we may sacrifice unto the Lord our God." Even to the last, there was no intimation of their leaving Egypt for good; the issue was left to be wrought out by the Egyptians. "All these thy servants," says Moses, "shall come down unto me, and bow down themselves unto me, saying, Get thee out and all the people that follow thee, and after that I will go out"; and, accordingly, after the judgment on the firstborn, they were thrust out at midnight, with their flocks and herds, their kneading troughs and their dough, laden, too, with the spoils of Egypt, as had been foreordained, yet apparently by a combination of circumstances, or the complication of a crisis. Yet Moses knew that their departure from Egypt was final, for he took the bones of Joseph with him; and that conviction broke on Pharaoh soon, when he and his asked themselves, "Why have we done this, that we have let Israel go from serving us?" But this progress of events, vague and uncertain as it seemed to be, notwithstanding the miracles which attended it, had been directed by Him who works out gradually what He has determined absolutely; and it ended in the parting of the Red Sea, and the destruction of Pharaoh's host, on his pursuing them.

Moreover, from what occurred forty years afterwards, when they were advancing upon the promised land, it would seem that the original grant of territory did not include the country east of Jordan, held in the event by Reuben, Gad, and half the tribe of Manasseh; at least they undertook at first to leave Sihon in undisturbed possession of his country, if he would let them pass through it, and only on his refusing his permission did they invade and appropriate it.

## 14.

6. It is in point to notice also the structure and style of Scripture, a structure so unsystematic and various and a style so figurative and indirect that no one would presume at first sight to say what is in it

and what is not. It cannot, as it were, be mapped, or its contents catalogued; but after all our diligence, to the end of our lives and to the end of the Church, it must be an unexplored and unsubdued land, with heights and valleys, forests and streams, on the right and left of our path and close about us, full of concealed wonders and choice treasures. Of no doctrine whatever, which does not actually contradict what has been delivered, can it be peremptorily asserted that it is not in Scripture; of no reader, whatever be his study of it, can it be said that he has mastered every doctrine which it contains. Butler's remarks on this subject were just now referred to. "The more distinct and particular knowledge," he says, "of those things, the study of which the Apostle calls 'going on unto perfection,'" that is, of the more recondite doctrines of the Gospel, "and of the prophetic parts of revelation, like many parts of natural and even civil knowledge, may require very exact thought and careful consideration. The hindrances too of natural and of supernatural light and knowledge have been of the same kind. And as it is owned the whole scheme of Scripture is not yet understood, so, if it ever comes to be understood, before the 'restitution of all things,' and without miraculous interpositions, it must be in the same way as natural knowledge is come at, by the continuance and progress of learning and of liberty, and by particular persons attending to, comparing, and pursuing intimations scattered up and down it, which are overlooked and disregarded by the generality of the world. For this is the way in which all improvements are made, by thoughtful men tracing on obscure hints, as it were, dropped us by nature accidentally, or which seem to come into our minds by chance. Nor is it at all incredible that a book, which has been so long in the possession of mankind, should contain many truths as yet undiscovered. For all the same phenomena, and the same faculties of investigation, from which such great discoveries in natural knowledge have been made in the present and last age, were equally in the possession of mankind several thousand years before. And possibly it might be intended that events, as they come to pass, should open and ascertain the meaning of several parts of Scripture."[4] Butler of course was not contemplating the case of new articles of faith, or developments imperative on our acceptance, but he surely bears witness to the probability of developments taking place in Christian doctrine considered in themselves, which is the point at present in question.

[4] ii. 3; vid. also ii. 4, fin.

## 15.

It may be added that, in matter of fact, all the definitions or received judgments of the early and medieval Church rest upon definite, even though sometimes obscure sentences of Scripture. Thus Purgatory may appeal to the "saving by fire," and "entering through much tribulation into the kingdom of God"; the communication of the merits of the Saints to our "receiving a prophet's reward" for "receiving a prophet in the name of a prophet," and "a righteous man's reward" for "receiving a righteous man in the name of a righteous man"; the Real Presence to "This is My Body"; Absolution to "Whosesoever sins ye remit, they are remitted"; Extreme Unction to "Anointing him with oil in the Name of the Lord"; Voluntary poverty to "Sell all that thou hast"; obedience to "He was in subjection to His parents"; the honour paid to creatures, animate or inanimate, to *Laudate Dominum in sanctis Ejus*, and *Adorate scabellum pedum Ejus*; and so of the rest.

## 16.

7. Lastly, while Scripture nowhere recognizes itself or asserts the inspiration of those passages which are most essential, it distinctly anticipates the development of Christianity, both as a polity and as a doctrine. In one of our Lord's parables "the Kingdom of Heaven" is even compared to "a grain of mustard-seed, which a man took and hid in his field; which indeed is the least of all seeds, but when it is grown it is the greatest among herbs, and becometh a tree," and, as St. Mark words it, "shooteth out great branches, so that the birds of the air come and lodge in the branches thereof." And again, in the same chapter of St. Mark, "So is the kingdom of God, as if a man should cast seed into the ground, and should sleep, and rise night and day, and the seed should spring and grow up, he knoweth not how; for the earth bringeth forth fruit of herself." Here an internal element of life, whether principle or doctrine, is spoken of rather than any mere external manifestation; and it is observable that the spontaneous, as well as the gradual, character of the growth is intimated. This description of the process corresponds to what has been above observed respecting development, viz., that it is not an effect of wishing and resolving, or of forced enthusiasm, or of any mechanism of reasoning, or of any mere subtlety of intellect; but comes of its own innate power of expansion within the mind in its season, though with the use

of reflection and argument and original thought, more or less as it may happen, with a dependence on the ethical growth of the mind itself, and with a reflex influence upon it. Again, the Parable of the Leaven describes the development of doctrine in another respect, in its active, engrossing, and interpenetrating power.

### 17.

From the necessity, then, of the case, from the history of all sects and parties in religion, and from the analogy and example of Scripture, we may fairly conclude that Christian doctrine admits of formal, legitimate, and true developments, that is, of developments contemplated by its Divine Author.

The general analogy of the world, physical and moral, confirms this conclusion, as we are reminded by the great authority who has already been quoted in the course of this section. "The whole natural world and government of it," says Butler, "is a scheme or system; not a fixed, but a progressive one; a scheme in which the operation of various means takes up a great length of time before the ends they tend to can be attained. The change of seasons, the ripening of the fruits of the earth, the very history of a flower is an instance of this; and so is human life. Thus vegetable bodies, and those of animals, though possibly formed at once, yet grow up by degrees to a mature state. And thus rational agents, who animate these latter bodies, are naturally directed to form each his own manners and character by the gradual gaining of knowledge and experience, and by a long course of action. Our existence is not only successive, as it must be of necessity, but one state of our life and being is appointed by God to be a preparation for another; and that to be the means of attaining to another succeeding one: infancy to childhood, childhood to youth, youth to mature age. Men are impatient, and for precipitating things; but the Author of Nature appears deliberate throughout His operations, accomplishing His natural ends by slow successive steps. And there is a plan of things beforehand laid out, which, from the nature of it, requires various systems of means, as well as length of time, in order to the carrying on its several parts into execution. Thus, in the daily course of natural providence, God operates in the very same manner as in the dispensation of Christianity, making one thing subservient to another; this, to somewhat farther; and so on, through a progressive series of means, which extend, both backward and forward, beyond our utmost view.

Of this manner of operation, everything we see in the course of nature is as much an instance as any part of the Christian dispensation."[5]

## SECTION II

### AN INFALLIBLE DEVELOPING AUTHORITY TO BE EXPECTED

It has now been made probable that developments of Christianity were but natural, as time went on, and were to be expected; and that these natural and true developments, as being natural and true, were of course contemplated and taken into account by its Author, who in designing the work designed its legitimate results. These, whatever they turn out to be, may be called absolutely "the developments" of Christianity. That beyond reasonable doubt there are such is surely a great step gained in the inquiry; it is a momentous fact. The next question is, *What* are they? and to a theologian, who could take a general view, and also possessed an intimate and minute knowledge, of its history, they would doubtless on the whole be easily distinguishable by their own characters, and require no foreign aid to point them out, no external authority to ratify them. But it is difficult to say who is exactly in this position. Considering that Christians, from the nature of the case, live under the bias of the doctrines, and in the very midst of the facts, and during the process of the controversies, which are to be the subject of criticism, since they are exposed to the prejudices of birth, education, place, personal attachment, engagements, and party, it can hardly be maintained that in matter of fact a true development carries with it always its own certainty even to the learned, or that history, past or present, is secure from the possibility of a variety of interpretations.

### 2.

I have already spoken on this subject, and from a very different point of view from that which I am taking at present:
"Prophets or Doctors are the interpreters of the revelation; they unfold and define its mysteries, they illuminate its documents, they

[5] *Analogy*, ii. 4, *ad fin.*

harmonize its contents, they apply its promises. Their teaching is a vast system, not to be comprised in a few sentences, not be embodied in one code of treatise, but consisting of a certain body of Truth, pervading the Church like an atmosphere, irregular in its shape from its very profusion and exuberance; at times separable only in idea from Episcopal Tradition, yet at times melting away into legend and fable; partly written, partly unwritten, partly the interpretation, partly the supplement of Scripture, partly preserved in intellectual expressions, partly latent in the spirit and temper of Christians; poured to and fro in closets and upon the housetops, in liturgies, in controversial works, in obscure fragments, in sermons, in popular prejudices, in local customs. This I call Prophetical Tradition, existing primarily in the bosom of the Church itself, and recorded in such measure as Providence has determined in the writings of eminent men. Keep that which is committed to thy charge, is St. Paul's injunction to Timothy; and for this reason, because from its vastness and indefiniteness it is especially exposed to corruption, if the Church fails in vigilance. This is that body of teaching which is offered to all Christians even at the present day, though in various forms and measures of truth, in different parts of Christendom, partly being a comment, partly an addition upon the articles of the Creed."[6]

If this be true, certainly some rule is necessary for arranging and authenticating these various expressions and results of Christian doctrine. No one will maintain that all points of belief are of equal importance. "There are what may be called minor points, which we may hold to be true without imposing them as necessary"; "there are greater truths and lesser truths, points which it is necessary, and points which it is pious to believe."[7] The simple question is, How are we to discriminate the greater from the less, the true from the false.

### 3.

This need of an authoritative sanction is increased by considering, after M. Guizot's suggestion, that Christianity, though represented in prophecy as a kingdom, came into the world as an idea rather than an institution, and has had to wrap itself in clothing and fit itself with armour of its own providing, and to form the instruments and methods of its prosperity and warfare. If the developments which have above

[6] Proph. Office, x. [Via Med. p. 250].
[7] Ibid. pp. 247, 254.

been called *moral* are to take place to any great extent, and without them it is difficult to see how Christianity can exist at all, if only its relations towards civil government have to be ascertained, or the qualifications for the profession of it have to be defined, surely an authority is necessary to impart decision to what is vague, and confidence to what is empirical, to ratify the successive steps of so elaborate a process, and to secure the validity of inferences which are to be made the premises of more remote investigations.

Tests, it is true, for ascertaining the correctness of developments in general may be drawn out, as I shall show in the sequel; but they are insufficient for the guidance of individuals in the case of so large and complicated a problem as Christianity, though they may aid our inquiries and support our conclusions in particular points. They are of a scientific and controversial, not of a practical character, and are instruments rather than warrants of right decisions. Moreover, they rather serve as answers to objections brought against the actual decisions of authority, than as proofs of the correctness of those decisions. While, then, on the one hand, it is probable that some means will be granted for ascertaining the legitimate and true developments of Revelation, it appears, on the other, that these means must of necessity be external to the developments themselves.

### 4.

Reasons shall be given in this section for concluding that, in proportion to the probability of true developments of doctrine and practice in the Divine Scheme, so is the probability also of the appointment in that scheme of an external authority to decide upon them, thereby separating them from the mass of mere human speculation, extravagance, corruption, and error, in and out of which they grow. This is the doctrine of the infallibility of the Church; for by infallibility I suppose is meant the power of deciding whether this, that, and a third, and any number of theological or ethical statements are true.

### 5.

1. Let the state of the case be carefully considered. If the Christian doctrine, as originally taught, admits of true and important developments, as was argued in the foregoing section, this is a strong antecedent argument in favour of a provision in the Dispensation for putting a seal of authority upon those developments. The probability of their

being known to be true varies with that of their truth. The two ideas indeed are quite distinct, I grant, of revealing and of guaranteeing a truth, and they are often distinct in fact. There are various revelations all over the earth which do not carry with them the evidence of their divinity. Such are the inward suggestions and secret illuminations granted to so many individuals; such are the traditionary doctrines which are found among the heathen, that "vague and unconnected family of religious truths, originally from God, but sojourning, without the sanction of miracle or a definite home, as pilgrims up and down the world, and discernible and separable from the corrupt legends with which they are mixed, by the spiritual mind alone."[8] There is nothing impossible in the notion of a revelation occurring without evidences that it is a revelation; just as human sciences are a divine gift, yet are reached by our ordinary powers and have no claim on our faith. But Christianity is not of this nature; it is a revelation which comes to us as a revelation, as a whole, objectively, and with a profession of infallibility; and the only question to be determined relates to the matter of the revelation. If then there are certain great truths, or duties, or observances, naturally and legitimately resulting from the doctrines originally professed, it is but reasonable to include these true results in the idea of the revelation itself, to consider them parts of it, and if the revelation be not only true but guaranteed as true, to anticipate that they too will come under the privilege of that guarantee. Christianity, unlike other revelations of God's will, except the Jewish, of which it is a continuation, is an objective religion, or a revelation with credentials; it is natural, I say, to view it wholly as such, and not partly *sui generis*, partly like others. Such as it begins, such let it be considered to continue; granting that certain large developments of it are true, they must surely be accredited as true.

### 6.

2. An objection, however, is often made to the doctrine of infallibility *in limine*, which is too important not to be taken into consideration. It is urged that, as all religious knowledge rests on moral evidence, not on demonstration, our belief in the Church's infallibility must be of this character; but what can be more absurd than a probable infallibility, or a certainty resting on doubt?—I believe, because I am sure; and I am

[8] Arians, ch. i. sect. 3 [p. 82, ed. 3].

sure, because I suppose. Granting then that the gift of infallibility be adapted, when believed, to unite all intellects in one common confession, the fact that it is given is as difficult of proof as the developments which it is to prove, and nugatory therefore, and in consequence improbable in a Divine Scheme. The advocates of Rome, it has been urged, "insist on the necessity of an infallible guide in religious matters, as an argument that such a guide has really been accorded. Now it is obvious to inquire how individuals are to know with certainty that Rome *is* infallible . . . how any ground can be such as to bring home to the mind infallibly that she is infallible; what conceivable proof amounts to more than a probability of the fact; and what advantage is an infallible guide, if those who are to be guided have, after all, no more than an opinion, as the Romanists call it, that she is infallible?"[9]

### 7.

This argument, however, except when used, as is intended in this passage, against such persons as would remove all imperfection in the proof of religion, is certainly a fallacious one. For since, as all allow, the Apostles were infallible, it tells against their infallibility, or the infallibility of Scripture, as truly as against the infallibility of the Church; for no one will say that the Apostles were made infallible for nothing, yet we are only morally certain that they were infallible. Further, if we have but probable grounds for the Church's infallibility, we have but the like for the impossibility of certain things, the necessity of others, the truth, the certainty of others; and therefore the words *infallibility, necessity, truth,* and *certainty* ought all of them to be banished from the language. But why is it more inconsistent to speak of an uncertain infallibility than of a doubtful truth or a contingent necessity, phrases which present ideas clear and undeniable? In sooth we are playing with words when we use arguments of this sort. When we say that a person is infallible, we mean no more than that what he says is always true, always to be believed, always to be done. The term is resolvable into these phrases as its equivalents; either then the phrases are inadmissible, or the idea of infallibility must be allowed. A probable infallibility is a probable gift of never erring; a reception of the doctrine of a probable infallibility is faith and obedience towards a person founded on the probability of his never erring in his declara-

[9]Proph. Office [Via Med. vol. i. p. 122].

tions or commands. What is inconsistent in this idea? Whatever then be the particular means of determining infallibility, the abstract objection may be put aside.[10]

### 8.

3. Again, it is sometimes argued that such a dispensation would destroy our probation, as dissipating doubt, precluding the exercise of faith, and obliging us to obey whether we wish it or no; and it is urged that a Divine Voice spoke in the first age, and difficulty and darkness rest upon all subsequent ones; as if infallibility and personal judgment were incompatible; but this is to confuse the subject. We must distinguish between a revelation and a reception of it, not between its earlier and later stages. A revelation, in itself divine, and guaranteed as such, may from first to last be received, doubted, argued against, perverted, rejected, by individuals according to the state of mind of each. Ignorance, misapprehension, unbelief, and other causes do not at once cease to operate because the revelation is in itself true and in its proofs irrefragable. We have then no warrant at all for saying that an accredited revelation will exclude the existence of doubts and difficulties on the part of those whom it addresses, or dispense with anxious diligence on their part, though it may in its own nature tend to do so. Infallibility does not interfere with moral probation; the two notions are absolutely distinct. It is no objection then to the idea of a peremptory authority, such as I am supposing, that it lessens the task of personal inquiry, unless it be an objection to the authority of Revelation altogether. A

[10] "It is very common to confuse infallibility with certitude, but the two words stand for things quite distinct from each other. I remember for certain what I did yesterday, but still my memory is not infallible. I am quite clear that two and two makes four, but I often make mistakes in long addition sums. I have no doubt whatever that John or Richard is my true friend; but I have before now trusted those who failed me, and I may do so again before I die. I am quite certain that Victoria is our sovereign, and not her father, the Duke of Kent, without any claim myself to the gift of infallibility, as I may do a virtuous action, without being impeccable. I may be certain that the Church is infallible, while I am myself a fallible mortal; otherwise I cannot be certain that the Supreme Being is infallible, unless I am infallible myself. Certitude is directed to one or other definite concrete proposition. I am certain of propositions one, two, three, four, or five, one by one, each by itself. I can be certain of one of them, without being certain of the rest: that I am certain of the first makes it neither likely nor unlikely that I am certain of the second: but, were I infallible, then I should be certain, not only of one of them, but of all."— *Essay on Assent*, ch. vii. sect. 2.

church, or a council, or a pope, or a consent of doctors, or a consent of Christendom, limits the inquiries of the individual in no other way than Scripture limits them: it does limit them; but, while it limits their range, it preserves intact their probationary character; we are tried as really, though not on so large a field. To suppose that the doctrine of a permanent authority in matters of faith interferes with our free will and responsibility is, as before, to forget that there were infallible teachers in the first age, and heretics and schismatics in the ages subsequent. There may have been at once a supreme authority from first to last, and a moral judgment from first to last. Moreover, those who maintain that Christian truth must be gained solely by personal efforts are bound to show that methods, ethical and intellectual, are granted to individuals sufficient for gaining it; else the mode of probation they advocate is less, not more, perfect than that which proceeds upon external authority. On the whole, then, no argument against continuing the principle of objectiveness into the developments of Revelation arises out of the conditions of our moral responsibility.

## 9.

4. Perhaps it will be urged that the analogy of Nature is against our anticipating the continuance of an external authority which has once been given; because in the words of the profound thinker who has already been cited, "We are wholly ignorant what degree of new knowledge it were to be expected God would give mankind by revelation, upon supposition of His affording one; or how far, and in what way, He would interpose miraculously to qualify them to whom He should originally make the revelation for communicating the knowledge given by it, and to secure their doing it to the age in which they should live, and to secure its being transmitted to posterity"; and because "we are not in any sort able to judge whether it were to be expected that the revelation should have been committed to writing, or left to be handed down, and consequently corrupted, by verbal tradition, and at length sunk under it."[11] But this reasoning does not apply here, as has already been observed; it contemplates only the abstract hypothesis of a revelation, not the fact of an existing revelation of a particular kind, which may of course in various ways modify our state of knowledge, by settling some of those very points which, before it was given, we had no means of deciding. Nor can it, as I think, be

[11] Anal. ii. 3.

fairly denied that the argument from analogy in one point of view tells against anticipating a revelation at all, for an innovation upon the physical order of the world is by the very force of the terms inconsistent with its ordinary course. We cannot then regulate our antecedent view of the character of a revelation by a test which, applied simply, overthrows the very notion of a revelation altogether. Any how, analogy is in some sort violated by the fact of a revelation, and the question before us only relates to the extent of that violation.

## 10.

I will hazard a distinction here between the facts of revelation and its principles: the argument from analogy is more concerned with its principles than with its facts. The revealed facts are special and singular, not analogous, from the nature of the case; but it is otherwise with the revealed principles; these are common to all the works of God: and if the Author of Nature be the Author of Grace, it may be expected that, while the two systems of facts are distinct and independent, the principles displayed in them will be the same, and form a connecting link between them. In this identity of principle lies the Analogy of Natural and Revealed Religion, in Butler's sense of the word. The doctrine of the Incarnation is a fact, and cannot be paralleled by anything in nature; the doctrine of mediation is a principle, and is abundantly exemplified in its provisions. Miracles are facts; inspiration is a fact; divine teaching once for all, and a continual teaching, are each a fact; probation by means of intellectual difficulties is a principle both in nature and in grace, and may be carried on in the system of grace either by a standing ordinance of teaching or by one definite act of teaching, and that with an analogy equally perfect in either case to the order of nature; nor can we succeed in arguing from the analogy of that order against a standing guardianship of revelation without arguing also against its original bestowal. Supposing the order of nature once broken by the introduction of a revelation, the continuance of that revelation is but a question of degree; and the circumstance that a work has begun makes it more probable than not that it will proceed. We have no reason to suppose that there is so great a distinction of dispensation between ourselves and the first generation of Christians, as that they had a living infallible guidance and we have not.

The case then stands thus: Revelation has introduced a new law of divine governance over and above those laws which appear in the natural course of the world; and in consequence we are able to argue for the existence of a standing authority in matters of faith on the analogy of Nature, and from the fact of Christianity. Preservation is involved in the idea of creation. As the Creator rested on the seventh day from the work which He had made, yet He "worketh hitherto"; so He gave the Creed once for all in the beginning, yet blesses its growth still, and provides for its increase. His word "shall not return unto Him void, but accomplish" His pleasure. As creation argues continual governance, so are Apostles harbingers of Popes.

### 11.

5. Moreover, it must be borne in mind that as the essence of all religion is authority and obedience, so the distinction between natural religion and revealed lies in this, that the one has a subjective authority and the other an objective. Revelation consists in the manifestation of the Invisible Divine Power, or in the substitution of the voice of a Lawgiver for the voice of conscience. The supremacy of conscience is the essence of natural religion; the supremacy of Apostle, or Pope, or Church, or bishop is the essence of revealed; and when such external authority is taken away, the mind falls back again of necessity upon that inward guide which it possessed even before Revelation was vouchsafed. Thus, what conscience is in the system of nature, such is the voice of Scripture, or of the Church, or of the Holy See, as we may determine it, in the system of Revelation. It may be objected, indeed, that conscience is not infallible; it is true, but still it is ever to be obeyed. And this is just the prerogative which controversialists assign to the See of St. Peter; it is not in all cases infallible, it may err beyond its special province, but it has in all cases a claim on our obedience. "All Catholics and heretics," says Bellarmine, "agree in two things: first, that it is possible for the Pope, even as pope, and with his own assembly of councillors, or with General Council, to err in particular controversies of fact, which chiefly depend on human information and testimony; secondly, that it is possible for him to err as a private Doctor, even in universal questions of right, whether of faith or of morals, and that from ignorance, as sometimes happens to other doctors. Next, all Catholics agree in other two points, not, however, with heretics, but solely with each other: first, that the Pope with General Council cannot err, either in framing decrees of faith or general precepts of morality; secondly, that the Pope when determining anything in a doubtful matter, whether by himself or with his own particular

Council, *whether it is possible for him to err or not, is to be obeyed
by all the faithful.*"[12] And as obedience to conscience, even supposing
conscience ill-informed, tends to the improvement of our moral nature,
and ultimately to our knowledge, so obedience to our ecclesiastical
superior may subserve our growth in illumination and sanctity, even
though he should command what is extreme or inexpedient, or teach
what is external to his legitimate province.

## 12.

6. The common sense of mankind does but support a conclusion
thus forced upon us by analogical considerations. It feels that the very
idea of revelation implies a present informant and guide, and that an
infallible one; not a mere abstract declaration of truths unknown
before to man, or a record of history, or the result of an antiquarian
research, but a message and a lesson speaking to this man and that.
This is shown by the popular notion which has prevailed among us
since the Reformation, that the Bible itself is such a guide; and which
succeeded in overthrowing the supremacy of Church and Pope, for the
very reason that it was a rival authority, not resisting merely, but
supplanting it. In proportion, then, as we find, in matter of fact, that
the inspired volume is not adapted or intended to subserve that purpose, are we forced to revert to that living and present Guide, who, at
the era of our rejection of her, had been so long recognized as the
dispenser of Scripture, according to times and circumstances, and the
arbiter of all true doctrine and holy practice to her children. We feel
a need, and she alone of all things under heaven supplies it. We are
told that God has spoken. Where? In a book? We have tried it and it
disappoints; it disappoints us, that most holy and blessed gift, not
from fault of its own, but because it is used for a purpose for which
it was not given. The Ethiopian's reply, when St. Philip asked him if
he understood what he was reading, is the voice of nature: "How can
I, unless some man shall guide me?" The Church undertakes that
office; she does what none else can do, and this is the secret of her
power. "The human mind," it has been said, "wishes to be rid of
doubt in religion; and a teacher who claims infallibility is readily
believed on his simple word. We see this constantly exemplified in

[12]De Rom. Pont. iv. 2. [Seven years ago, it is scarcely necessary to say, the
Vatican Council determined that the Pope, *ex cathedra*, has the same infallibility as the Church. This does not affect the argument in the text.]

the case of individual pretenders among ourselves. In Romanism the Church pretends to it; she rids herself of competitors by forestalling them. And probably, in the eyes of her children, this is not the least persuasive argument for her infallibility, that she alone of all Churches dares claim it, as if a secret instinct and involuntary misgivings restrained those rival communions which go so far towards affecting it."[13] These sentences, whatever be the errors of their wording, surely express a great truth. The most obvious answer, then, to the question, why we yield to the authority of the Church in the questions and developments of faith, is, that some authority there must be if there is a revelation given, and other authority there is none but she. A revelation is not given if there be no authority to decide what it is that is given. In the words of St. Peter to her Divine Master and Lord, "To whom shall we go?" Nor must it be forgotten in confirmation, that Scripture expressly calls the Church "the pillar and ground of the Truth," and promises her as by covenant that "the Spirit of the Lord that is upon her, and His words which He has put in her mouth shall not depart out of her mouth, nor out of the mouth of her seed, nor out of the mouth of her seed's seed, from henceforth and for ever."[14]

## 13.

7. And if the very claim to infallible arbitration in religious disputes is of so weighty importance and interest in all ages of the world, much more is it welcome at a time like the present, when the human intellect is so busy, and thought so fertile, and opinion so manifold. The absolute need of a spiritual supremacy is at present the strongest of arguments in favour of the fact of its supply. Surely, either an objective revelation has not been given, or it has been provided with means for impressing its objectiveness on the world. If Christianity be a social religion, as it certainly is, and if it be based on certain ideas acknowledged as divine, or a creed (which shall here be assumed) and if these ideas have various aspects, and make distinct impressions on different minds, and issue in consequence in a multiplicity of developments, true, or false, or mixed, as has been shown, what power will suffice to meet and to do justice to these conflicting conditions but a supreme authority ruling and reconciling individual judgments by a divine right and a recognized wisdom? In barbarous times the will is reached

[13] Proph. Office [Via Med. vol. i. p. 117].
[14] Tim. iii. 15; Isa. lix. 21.

through the senses; but in an age in which reason, as it is called, is the standard of truth and right, it is abundantly evident to any one who mixes ever so little with the world that, if things are left to themselves, every individual will have his own view of them, and take his own course; that two or three will agree today to part company tomorrow; that Scripture will be read in contrary ways, and history, according to the apologue, will have to different comers its silver shield and its golden; that philosophy, taste, prejudice, passion, party, caprice will find no common measure, unless there be some supreme power to control the mind and to compel agreement.

There can be no combination on the basis of truth without an organ of truth. As cultivation brings out the colours of flowers, and domestication changes the character of animals, so does education of necessity develop differences of opinion; and while it is impossible to lay down first principles in which all will unite, it is utterly unreasonable to expect that this man should yield to that, or all to one. I do not say there are no eternal truths, such as the poet proclaims,[15] which all acknowledge in private, but that there are none sufficiently commanding to be the basis of public union and action. The only general persuasive in matters of conduct is authority; that is (when truth is in question) a judgment which we feel to be superior to our own. If Christianity is both social and dogmatic, and intended for all ages, it must humanly speaking have an infallible expounder. Else you will secure unity of form at the loss of unity of doctrine, or unity of doctrine at the loss of unity of form; you will have to choose between a comprehension of opinions and a resolution into parties, between latitudinarian and sectarian error. You may be tolerant or intolerant of contrarieties of thought, but contrarieties you will have. By the Church of England a hollow uniformity is preferred to an infallible chair; and by the sects of England an interminable division. Germany and Geneva began with persecution and have ended in scepticism. The doctrine of infallibility is a less violent hypothesis than this sacrifice either of faith or of charity. It secures the object, while it gives definiteness and force to the matter, of the Revelation.

### 14.

8. I have called the doctrine of Infallibility an hypothesis: let it be so considered for the sake of argument, that is, let it be considered to

---

[15] Οὐ γάρ τι νῦν γε κἀχθές, κ.τ.λ. ["For (they are) not merely of today

be a mere position, supported by no direct evidence, but required by the facts of the case, and reconciling them with each other. That hypothesis is indeed, in matter of fact, maintained and acted on in the largest portion of Christendom, and from time immemorial; but let this coincidence be accounted for by the need. Moreover, it is not a naked or isolated fact but the animating principle of a large scheme of doctrine which the need itself could not simply create; but again, let this system be merely called its development. Yet even as an hypothesis which has been held by one out of various communions it may not be lightly put aside. Some hypothesis, this or that, all parties, all controversialists, all historians must adopt, if they would treat of Christianity at all. Gieseler's *Text Book* bears the profession of being a dry analysis of Christian history; yet on inspection it will be found to be written on a positive and definite theory, and to bend facts to meet it. An unbeliever, as Gibbon, assumes one hypothesis, and an Ultramontane, as Baronius, adopts another. The school of Hurd and Newton hold, as the only true view of history, that Christianity slept for centuries upon centuries, except among those whom historians call heretics. Others speak as if the oath of supremacy or the *congé d'élire* could be made the measure of St. Ambrose, and they fit the Thirty-nine Articles on the fervid Tertullian. The question is which of all these theories is the simplest, the most natural, the most persuasive. Certainly the notion of development under infallible authority is not a less grave, a less winning hypothesis than the chance and coincidence of events, or the oriental philosophy, or the working of Antichrist, to account for the rise of Christianity and the formation of its theology.

## SECTION III

### THE EXISTING DEVELOPMENTS OF DOCTRINE THE PROBABLE FULFILMENT OF THAT EXPECTATION

I have been arguing, in respect to the revealed doctrine, given to us from above in Christianity, first, that, in consequence of its intellectual character, and as passing through the minds of so many generations

---

or yesterday . . ." —a fragment of a passage in Sophocles' *Antigone* (456) in which the heroine affirms that the laws of the gods are eternal, and cannot be overridden by the legislation of mortals.]

of men, and as applied by them to so many purposes, and as investigated so curiously as to its capabilities, implications, and bearings, it could not but grow or develop, as time went on, into a large theological system; next, that, if development must be, then, whereas Revelation is a heavenly gift, He who gave it virtually has not given it, unless He has also secured it from perversion and corruption, in all such development as comes upon it by the necessity of its nature or, in other words, that that intellectual action through successive generations, which is the organ of development, must, so far forth as it can claim to have been put in charge of the Revelation, be in its determinations infallible.

Passing from these two points, I come next to the question whether in the history of Christianity there is any fulfilment of such anticipation as I have insisted on, whether in matter-of-fact doctrines, rites, and usages have grown up round the Apostolic Creed and have interpenetrated its Articles, claiming to be part of Christianity and looking like those additions which we are in search of. The answer is, that such additions there are, and that they are found just where they might be expected, in the authoritative seats and homes of old tradition, the Latin and Greek Churches. Let me enlarge on this point.

## 2.

I observe, then, that if the idea of Christianity, as originally given to us from heaven, cannot but contain much which will be only partially recognized by us as included in it and only held by us unconsciously; and if again, Christianity being from heaven, all that is necessarily involved in it, and is evolved from it, is from heaven, and if, on the other hand, large accretions actually do exist, professing to be its true and legitimate results, our first impression naturally is, that these must be the very developments which they profess to be. Moreover, the very scale on which they have been made, their high antiquity yet present promise, their gradual formation yet precision, their harmonious order, dispose the imagination most forcibly towards the belief that a teaching so consistent with itself, so well balanced, so young and so old, not obsolete after so many centuries, but vigorous and progressive still, is the very development contemplated in the Divine Scheme. These doctrines are members of one family, and suggestive, or correlative, or confirmatory, or illustrative of each other. One furnishes evidence to another, and all to each of them; if this is proved, that becomes probable; if this and that are both probable, but for different reasons, each adds to the other its own probability. The Incarnation is the antecedent of the doctrine of Mediation, and the archetype both of the Sacramental principle and of the merits of Saints. From the doctrine of Mediation follow the Atonement, the Mass, the merits of Martyrs and Saints, their invocation and *cultus*. From the Sacramental principle come the Sacraments properly so called; the unity of the Church and the Holy See as its type and centre; the authority of Councils; the sanctity of rites; the veneration of holy places, shrines, images, vessels, furniture, and vestments. Of the Sacraments, Baptism is developed into Confirmation on the one hand; into Penance, Purgatory, and Indulgences on the other; and the Eucharist into the Real Presence, adoration of the Host, Resurrection of the body, and the virtue of relics. Again, the doctrine of the Sacraments leads to the doctrine of Justification; Justification to that of Original Sin; Original Sin to the merit of Celibacy. Nor do these separate developments stand independent of each other, but by cross relations they are connected, and grow together while they grow from one. The Mass and Real Presence are parts of one; the veneration of Saints and their relics are parts of one; their intercessory power and the Purgatorial State, and again the Mass and that state are correlative; Celibacy is the characteristic mark of Monachism and of the Priesthood. You must accept the whole or reject the whole; attenuation does but enfeeble, and amputation mutilate. It is trifling to receive all but something which is as integral as any other portion; and, on the other hand, it is a solemn thing to accept any part, for, before you know where you are, you may be carried on by a stern logical necessity to accept the whole.

### 3.

Next, we have to consider that from first to last other developments there are none, except those which have possession of Christendom; none, that is, of prominence and permanence sufficient to deserve the name. In early times the heretical doctrines were confessedly barren and short-lived, and could not stand their ground against Catholicism. As to the medieval period I am not aware that the Greeks present more than a negative opposition to the Latins. And now in like manner the Tridentine Creed is met by no rival developments; there is no antagonist system. Criticisms, objections, protests there are in plenty, but little of positive teaching anywhere; seldom an attempt on the part of any opposing school to master its own doctrines, to investigate their sense and bearing, to determine their relation to the decrees of Trent and their distance from them. And when at any time this attempt is by chance in any measure made, then an incurable contrariety does but come to view between portions of the theology thus developed, and a war of principles; an impossibility moreover of reconciling that theology with the general drift of the formularies in which its elements occur, and a consequent appearance of unfairness and sophistry in adventurous persons who aim at forcing them into consistency;[16] and, further, a prevalent understanding of the truth of this representation, authorities keeping silence, eschewing a hopeless enterprise and discouraging it in others, and the people plainly intimating that they think both doctrine and usage, antiquity and development, of very little matter at all; and, lastly, the evident despair of even the better sort of men, who, in consequence, when they set great schemes on foot, as for the conversion of the heathen world, are afraid to agitate the question of the doctrines to which it is to be converted, lest through the opened door they should lose what they have, instead of gaining what they have not. To the weight of recommendation which this contrast throws upon the developments commonly called Catholic must be added the argument which arises from the coincidence of their consistency and permanence, with their claim of an infallible sanction—a claim, the existence of which, in some quarter or other of the Divine Dispensation, is, as we have already seen, antecedently probable. All these things being considered, I think few persons will deny the very strong presumption which exists, that, if there must be and are in fact developments in Christianity, the doctrines propounded by successive Popes and Councils, through so many ages, are they.

### 4.

A further presumption in behalf of these doctrines arises from the general opinion of the world about them. Christianity being one, all its doctrines are necessarily developments of one, and, if so, are of necessity consistent with each other, or form a whole. Now the world fully enters into this view of those well-known developments which claim the name of Catholic. It allows them that title, it considers them to belong to one family, and refers them to one theological system. It is scarcely necessary to set about proving what is urged by their opponents even more strenuously than by their champions. Their opponents avow that they protest, not against this doctrine or that, but against

[16] Vid. Via Med. vol. ii. pp. 251–341.

one and all; and they seem struck with wonder and perplexity, not to say with awe, at a consistency which they feel to be superhuman, though they would not allow it to be divine. The system is confessed on all hands to bear a character of integrity and indivisibility upon it, both at first view and on inspection. Hence such sayings as the *Tota jacet Babylon* of the distich. Luther did but a part of the work, Calvin another portion, Socinus finished it. To take up with Luther, and to reject Calvin and Socinus, would be, according to that epigram, like living in a house without a roof to it. This, I say, is no private judgment of this man or that, but the common opinion and experience of all countries. The two great divisions of religion feel it, Roman Catholic and Protestant, between whom the controversy lies; sceptics and liberals, who are spectators of the conflict, feel it; philosophers feel it. A school of divines there is, I grant, dear to memory, who have not felt it; and their exception will have its weight—till we reflect that the particular theology which they advocate has not the prescription of success, never has been realized in fact, or, if realized for a moment, had no stay; moreover that, when it has been enacted by human authority, it has scarcely travelled beyond the paper on which it was printed, or out of the legal forms in which it was embodied. But, putting the weight of these revered names at the highest, they do not constitute more than an exception to the general rule, such as is found in every subject that comes into discussion.

## 5.

And this general testimony to the oneness of Catholicism extends to its past teaching relatively to its present, as well as to the portions of its present teaching one with another. No one doubts, with such exception as has just been allowed, that the Roman Catholic communion of this day is the successor and representative of the medieval Church, or that the medieval Church is the legitimate heir of the Nicene; even allowing that it is a question whether a line cannot be drawn between the Nicene Church and the Church which preceded it. On the whole, all parties will agree that, of all existing systems, the present communion of Rome is the nearest approximation in fact to the Church of the Fathers, possible though some may think it, to be nearer still to that Church on paper. Did St. Athanasius or St. Ambrose come suddenly to life, it cannot be doubted what communion he would take to be his own. All surely will agree that these Fathers, with whatever opinions of their own, whatever protests, if we will, would find themselves more at home with such men as St. Bernard or St. Ignatius Loyola, or with the lonely priest in his lodging, or the holy sisterhood of mercy, or the unlettered crowd before the altar, than with the teachers or with the members of any other creed. And may we not add, that were those same Saints, who once sojourned, one in exile, one on embassy, at Treves, to come more northward still, and to travel until they reached another fair city, seated among groves, green meadows, and calm streams, the holy brothers would turn from many a high aisle and solemn cloister which they found there, and ask the way to some small chapel where mass was said in the populous alley or forlorn suburb? And, on the other hand, can any one who has but heard his name, and cursorily read his history, doubt for one instant how, in turn, the people of England, "we, our princes, our priests, and our prophets," Lords and Commons, Universities, Ecclesiastical Courts, marts of commerce, great towns, country parishes, would deal with Athanasius—Athanasius, who spent his long years in fighting against sovereigns for a theological term?

# CHAPTER III

# ON THE HISTORICAL ARGUMENT IN BEHALF OF THE EXISTING DEVELOPMENTS

## SECTION I

### METHOD OF PROOF

It seems, then, that we have to deal with a case something like the following: Certain doctrines come to us, professing to be Apostolic, and possessed of such high antiquity that, though we are only able to assign the date of their formal establishment to the fourth, or the fifth, or the eighth, or the thirteenth century, as it may happen, yet their substance may, for what appears, be coeval with the Apostles, and be expressed or implied in texts of Scripture. Further, these existing doctrines are universally considered, without any question, in each age to be the echo of the doctrines of the times immediately preceding them, and thus are continually thrown back to a date indefinitely early, even though their ultimate junction with the Apostolic Creed be out of sight and unascertainable. Moreover, they are confessed to form one body one with another, so that to reject one is to disparage the rest; and they include within the range of their system even those primary articles of faith, as the Incarnation, which many an impugner of the said doctrinal system, as a system, professes to accept, and which, do what he will, he cannot intelligibly separate, whether in point of evidence or of internal character, from others which he disavows. Further, these doctrines occupy the whole field of theology, and leave nothing to be supplied, except in detail, by any other system; while, in matter of fact, no rival system is forthcoming, so that we have to choose between this theology and none at all. Moreover, this theology alone makes provision for that guidance of opinion and conduct, which seems externally to be the special aim of Revelation; and fulfils the promises of Scripture, by adapting itself to the various problems of thought and practice which meet us in life. And, further, it is the nearest approach, to say the least, to the religious sentiment, and what is called *ethos*, of the early Church, nay, to that of the Apostles and Prophets; for all will agree so far as this, that Elijah, Jeremiah, the Baptist, and St. Paul are in their history and mode of life (I do not speak of measures of grace, no, nor of doctrine and conduct, for these are the points in dispute, but) in what is external and meets the eye (and this is no slight resemblance when things are viewed as a whole and from a distance)—these saintly and heroic men, I say, are more like a Dominican preacher, or a Jesuit missionary, or a Carmelite friar, more like St. Toribio, or St. Vincent Ferrer, or St. Francis Xavier, or St. Alphonso Liguori, than to any individuals, or to any classes of men, that can be found in other communions. And then, in addition, there is the high antecedent probability that Providence would watch over His own work, and would direct and ratify those developments of doctrine which were inevitable.

## 2.

If this is, on the whole, a true view of the general shape under which the existing body of developments commonly called Catholic present themselves before us, antecedently to our looking into the particular evidence on which they stand, I think we shall be at no loss to determine what both logical truth and duty prescribe to us as to our reception of them. It is very little to say that we should treat them as we are accustomed to treat other alleged facts and truths and the evidence for them, such as come to us with a fair presumption in their favour. Such are of every day's occurrence; and what is our behaviour towards them? We meet them not with suspicion and criticism, but with a frank confidence. We do not in the first instance exercise our reason upon opinions which are received, but our faith. We do not begin with doubting; we take them on trust, and we put them on trial, and that not of set purpose, but spontaneously. We prove them by using them, by applying them to the subject matter, or the evidence, or the body of circumstances, to which they belong, as if they gave it its interpretation or its colour as a matter of course; and only when they fail, in the event, in illustrating phenomena or harmonizing facts do we discover that we must reject the doctrines or the statements which we had in the first instance taken for granted. Again, we take the evidence for them, whatever it be, as a whole, as forming a combined proof; and we interpret what is obscure in separate portions by such portions as are clear. Moreover, we bear with these in proportion to the strength of the antecedent probability in their favour, we are patient with difficulties in their application, with apparent objections to them drawn from other matters of fact, deficiency in their comprehensiveness, or want of neatness in their working, provided their claims on our attention are considerable.

### 3.

Thus most men take Newton's theory of gravitation for granted, because it is generally received, and use it without rigidly testing it first, each for himself (as it can be tested) by phenomena; and if phenomena are found which it does not satisfactorily solve, this does not trouble us, for a way there must be of explaining them, consistently with that theory, though it does not occur to ourselves. Again, if we found a concise or obscure passage in one of Cicero's letters to Atticus, we should not scruple to admit as its true explanation a more explicit statement in his *Ad Familiares*. Æschylus is illustrated by Sophocles in point of language, and Thucydides by Aristophanes in point of history. Horace, Persius, Suetonius, Tacitus, and Juvenal may be made to throw light upon each other. Even Plato may gain a commentator in Plotinus, and St. Anselm is interpreted by St. Thomas. Two writers, indeed, may be already known to differ, and then we do not join them together as fellow witnesses to common truths; Luther has taken on himself to explain St. Augustine, and Voltaire, Pascal, without persuading the world that they have a claim to do so; but in no case do we begin with asking whether a comment does not disagree with its text, when there is a prima facie congruity between them. We elucidate the text by the comment, though, or rather because, the comment is fuller and more explicit than the text.

### 4.

Thus too we deal with Scripture, when we have to interpret the prophetical text and the types of the Old Testament. The event which is the development is also the interpretation of the prediction; it provides a fulfilment by imposing a meaning. And we accept certain events as the fulfilment of prophecy from the broad correspondence of the one with the other, in spite of many incidental difficulties. The difficulty, for instance, in accounting for the fact that the dispersion of the Jews followed upon their keeping, not their departing from their Law, does not hinder us from insisting on their present state as an argument against the infidel. Again, we readily submit our reason on competent authority, and accept certain events as an accomplishment of predictions which seem very far removed from them; as in the passage, "Out of Egypt have I called My Son." Nor do we find a difficulty when St. Paul appeals to a text of the Old Testament, which stands otherwise in our Hebrew copies; as the words, "A body hast Thou prepared Me." We receive such difficulties on faith, and leave them to take care of themselves. Much less do we consider mere fulness in the interpretation, or definiteness, or again strangeness, as a sufficient reason for depriving the text, or the action to which it is applied, of the advantage of such interpretation. We make it no objection that the words themselves come short of it, or that the sacred writer did not contemplate it, or that a previous fulfilment satisfies it. A reader who came to the inspired text by himself, beyond the influence of that traditional acceptation which happily encompasses it, would be surprised to be told that the Prophet's words, "A virgin shall conceive," etc., or "Let all the Angels of God worship Him," refer to our Lord; but assuming the intimate connexion between Judaism and Christianity, and the inspiration of the New Testament, we do not scruple to believe it. We rightly feel that it is no prejudice to our receiving the prophecy of Balaam in its Christian meaning that it is adequately fulfilled in David; or the history of Jonah that it is poetical in character and has a moral in itself like an apologue; or the meeting of Abraham and Melchizedek that it is too brief and simple to mean any great thing, as St. Paul interprets it.

### 5.

Butler corroborates these remarks, when speaking of the particular evidence for Christianity. "The obscurity or unintelligibleness," he says, "of one part of a prophecy does not in any degree invalidate the proof of foresight, arising from the appearing completion of those other parts which are understood. For the case is evidently the same as if those parts, which are not understood, were lost, or not written at all, or written in an unknown tongue. Whether this observation be commonly attended to or not, it is so evident that one can scarce bring one's self to set down an instance in common matters to exemplify it."[1] He continues, "Though a man should be incapable, for want of learning, or opportunities of inquiry, or from not having turned his

---

[1] Anal. ii. 7.

studies this way, even so much as to judge whether particular prophecies have been throughout completely fulfilled; yet he may see, in general, that they have been fulfilled to such a degree, as, upon very good ground, to be convinced of foresight more than human in such prophecies, and of such events being intended by them. For the same reason also, though, by means of the deficiencies in civil history, and the different accounts of historians, the most learned should not be able to make out to satisfaction that such parts of the prophetic history have been minutely and throughout fulfilled; yet a very strong proof of foresight may arise from that general completion of them which is made out; as much proof of foresight, perhaps, as the Giver of prophecy intended should ever be afforded by such parts of prophecy."

### 6.

He illustrates this by the parallel instance of fable and concealed satire. "A man might be assured that he understood what an author intended by a fable or parable, related without any application or moral, merely from seeing it to be easily capable of such application, and that such a moral might naturally be deduced from it. And he might be fully assured that such persons and events were intended in a satirical writing, merely from its being applicable to them. And, agreeably to the last observation, he might be in a good measure satisfied of it, though he were not enough informed in affairs, or in the story of such persons, to understand half the satire. For his satisfaction, that he understood the meaning, the intended meaning, of these writings, would be greater or less, in proportion as he saw the general turn of them to be capable of such application, and in proportion to the number of particular things capable of it." And he infers hence, that if a known course of events, or the history of a person as our Lord, is found to answer on the whole to the prophetical text, it becomes fairly the right interpretation of that text, in spite of difficulties in detail. And this rule of interpretation admits of an obvious application to the parallel case of doctrinal passages, when a certain creed, which professes to have been derived from Revelation, comes recommended to us on strong antecedent grounds and presents no strong opposition to the sacred text.

The same author observes that the first fulfilment of a prophecy is no valid objection to a second, when what seems like a second has once taken place; and, in like manner, an interpretation of doctrinal texts may be literal, exact, and sufficient, yet in spite of all this may not embrace what is really the full scope of their meaning; and that fuller scope, if it so happen, may be less satisfactory and precise, as an interpretation, than their primary and narrow sense. Thus, if the Protestant interpretation of the sixth chapter of St. John were true and sufficient for its letter (which of course I do not grant) that would not hinder the Roman, which at least is quite compatible with the text, being the higher sense and the only rightful. In such cases the justification of the larger and higher interpretation lies in some antecedent probability, such as Catholic consent; and the ground of the narrow is the context, and the rules of grammar; and, whereas the argument of the critical commentator is that the sacred text *need not* mean more than the letter, those who adopt a deeper view of it maintain, as Butler in the case of prophecy, that we have no warrant for putting a limit to the sense of words which are not human but divine.

## 7.

Now it is but a parallel exercise of reasoning to interpret the previous history of a doctrine by its later development, and to consider that it contains the later *in posse* and in the divine intention; and the grudging and jealous temper which refuses to enlarge the sacred text for the fulfilment of prophecy is the very same that will occupy itself in carping at the Antenicene testimonies for Nicene or medieval doctrines and usages. When "I and My Father are One" is urged in proof of our Lord's unity with the Father, heretical disputants do not see why the words must be taken to denote more than a unity of will. When "This is My Body" is alleged as a warrant for the change of the Bread into the Body of Christ, they explain away the words into a figure, because such is their most obvious interpretation. And, in like manner, when Roman Catholics urge St. Gregory's invocations, they are told that these are but rhetorical; or St. Clement's allusion to Purgatory, that perhaps it was Platonism; or Origen's language about praying to Angels and the merits of Martyrs, that it is but an instance of his heterodoxy; or St. Cyprian's exaltation of the *Cathedra Petri*, that he need not be contemplating more than a figurative or abstract see; or the general testimony to the spiritual authority of Rome in primitive times, that it arose from her temporal greatness; or Tertullian's language about Tradition and the Church, that he took a lawyer's view of those subjects; whereas the early condition, and the evidence, of each doctrine respectively, ought consistently to be interpreted by means of that development which was ultimately attained.

## 8.

Moreover, since, as above shown, the doctrines all together make up one integral religion, it follows that the several evidences which respectively support those doctrines belong to a whole, and must be thrown into a common stock, and all are available in the defence of any. A collection of weak evidences makes up a strong evidence; again, one strong argument imparts cogency to collateral arguments which are in themselves weak. For instance, as to the miracles, whether of Scripture or the Church, "the number of those which carry with them their own proof now, and are believed for their own sake, is small, and they furnish the grounds on which we receive the rest."[2] Again, no one would fancy it necessary, before receiving St. Matthew's Gospel, to find primitive testimony in behalf of every chapter and verse; when only part is proved to have been in existence in ancient times, the whole is proved, because that part is but part of a whole; and when the whole is proved, it may shelter such parts as for some incidental reason have less evidence of their antiquity. Again, it would be enough to show that St. Augustine knew the Italic version of the Scriptures, if he quoted it once or twice. And, in like manner, it will be generally admitted that the proof of a Second Person in the Godhead lightens greatly the burden of proof necessary for belief in a Third Person; and that, the Atonement being in some sort a correlative of eternal punishment, the evidence for the former doctrine virtually increases the evidence for the latter. And so a Protestant controversialist would feel that it told little, except as an omen of victory, to reduce an opponent to a denial of Transubstantiation, if he still adhered firmly to the Invocation of Saints, Purgatory, the Seven Sacraments, and the doctrine of merit; and little too for one of his own party to condemn the adoration of the Host, the supremacy of Rome, the acceptableness of celibacy, auricular confession, communion under one kind, and tradition, if he was zealous for the doctrine of the Immaculate Conception.

## 9.

The principle on which these remarks are made has the sanction of some of the deepest of English divines. Bishop Butler, for instance, who has so often been quoted here, thus argues in behalf of Chris-

[2] On Miracles, Essay ii. 111.

tianity itself, though confessing at the same time the disadvantage which in consequence the revealed system lies under. "Probable proofs," he observes, "by being added, not only increase the evidence, but multiply it. Nor should I dissuade any one from setting down what he thought made for the contrary side. . . . The truth of our religion, like the truth of common matters, is to be judged by all the evidence taken together. And unless the whole series of things which may be alleged in this argument, and every particular thing in it, can reasonably be supposed to have been by accident (for here the stress of the argument for Christianity lies), then is the truth of it proved; in like manner, as if, in any common case, numerous events acknowledged were to be alleged in proof of any other event disputed, the truth of the disputed event would be proved, not only if any one of the acknowledged ones did of itself clearly imply it, but though no one of them singly did so, if the whole of the acknowledged events, taken together, could not in reason be supposed to have happened, unless the disputed one were true.

"It is obvious how much advantage the nature of this evidence gives to those persons who attack Christianity, especially in conversation. For it is easy to show, in a short and lively manner, that such and such things are liable to objection, that this and another thing is of little weight in itself; but impossible to show, in like manner, the united force of the whole argument in one view."[3]

In like manner, Mr. Davison condemns that "vicious manner of reasoning" which represents "any insufficiency of the proof, in its several branches, as so much objection"; which manages "the inquiry so as to make it appear that, if the divided arguments be inconclusive one by one, we have a series of exceptions to the truths of religion instead of a train of favourable presumptions, growing stronger at every step. The disciple of Scepticism is taught that he cannot fully rely on this or that motive of belief, that each of them is insecure, and the conclusion is put upon him that they ought to be discarded one after another, instead of being connected and combined."[4] No work perhaps affords more specimens in a short compass of the breach of the principle of reasoning inculcated in these passages, than Barrow's Treatise on the Pope's Supremacy.

[3] Anal. ii. 7.
[4] On Prophecy, i. p. 28.

## 10.

The remarks of these two writers relate to the duty of combining doctrines which belong to one body, and evidences which relate to one subject; and few persons would dispute it in the abstract. The application which has been here made of the principle is this—that where a doctrine comes recommended to us by strong presumptions of its truth, we are bound to receive it unsuspiciously, and use it as a key to the evidences to which it appeals, or the facts which it professes to systematize, whatever may be our eventual judgment about it. Nor is it enough to answer that the voice of our particular Church, denying this so-called Catholicism, is an antecedent probability which outweighs all others and claims our prior obedience, loyally and without reasoning, to its own interpretation. This may excuse individuals certainly, in beginning with doubt and distrust of the Catholic developments, but it only shifts the blame to the particular Church, Anglican or other, which thinks itself qualified to enforce so peremptory a judgment against the one and only successor, heir, and representative of the Apostolic college.

## SECTION II

### STATE OF THE EVIDENCE

Bacon is celebrated for destroying the credit of a method of reasoning much resembling that which it has been the object of this chapter to recommend. "He who is not practised in doubting," he says, "but forward in asserting and laying down such principles as he takes to be approved, granted and manifest, and, according to the established truth thereof, receives or rejects everything, as squaring with or proving contrary to them, is only fitted to mix and confound things with words, reason with madness, and the world with fable and fiction, but not to interpret the works of nature."[5] But he was aiming at the application of these modes of reasoning to what should be strict investigation, and that in the province of physics; and this he might well censure, without attempting (what is impossible) to banish them from history, ethics, and religion. Physical facts are present; they are submitted to the

[5] Aphor. 5, vol. iv. p. xi. ed. 1815.

senses, and the senses may be satisfactorily tested, corrected, and verified. To trust to anything but sense in a matter of sense is irrational; why are the senses given us but to supersede less certain, less immediate informants? We have recourse to reason or authority to determine facts when the senses fail us; but with the senses we begin. We deduce, we form inductions, we abstract, we theorize from facts; we do not begin with surmise and conjecture, much less do we look to the tradition of past ages, or the decree of foreign teachers, to determine matters which are in our hands and under our eyes.

But it is otherwise with history, the facts of which are not present; it is otherwise with ethics, in which phenomena are more subtle, closer, and more personal to individuals than other facts, and not referable to any common standard by which all men can decide upon them. In such sciences, we cannot rest upon mere facts, if we would, because we have not got them. We must do our best with what is given us, and look about for aid from any quarter; and in such circumstances the opinions of others, the traditions of ages, the prescriptions of authority, antecedent auguries, analogies, parallel cases, these and the like, not indeed taken at random, but, like the evidence from the senses, sifted and scrutinized, obviously become of great importance.

## 2.

And, further, if we proceed on the hypothesis that a merciful Providence has supplied us with means of gaining such truth as concerns us, in different subject matters, though with different instruments, then the simple question is what those instruments are which are proper to a particular case. If they are of the appointment of a Divine Protector, we may be sure that they will lead to the truth, whatever they are. The less exact methods of reasoning may do His work as well as the more perfect, if He blesses them. He may bless antecedent probabilities in ethical inquiries, who blesses experience and induction in the art of medicine.

And if it is reasonable to consider medicine, or architecture, or engineering, in a certain sense, divine arts, as being divinely ordained means of our receiving divine benefits, much more may ethics be called divine; while as to religion, it directly professes to be the method of recommending ourselves to Him and learning His will. If then it be His gracious purpose that we should learn it, the means He gives for learning it, be they promising or not to human eyes, are sufficient because they are His. And what they are at this particular time, or to this person, depends on His disposition. He may have imposed simple prayer and obedience on some men as the instrument of their attaining to the mysteries and precepts of Christianity. He may lead others through the written word, at least for some stages of their course; and if the formal basis on which He has rested His revelations be, as it is, of an historical and philosophical character, then antecedent probabilities, subsequently corroborated by facts, will be sufficient, as in the parallel case of other history, to bring us safely to the matter, or at least to the organ, of those revelations.

### 3.

Moreover, in subjects which belong to moral proof, such, I mean, as history, antiquities, political science, ethics, metaphysics, and theology, which are pre-eminently such, and especially in theology and ethics, antecedent probability may have a real weight and cogency which it cannot have in experimental science; and a mature politician or divine may have a power of reaching matters of fact in consequence of his peculiar habits of mind which is seldom given in the same degree to physical inquirers, who, for the purposes of this particular pursuit, are very much on a level. And this last remark at least is confirmed by Lord Bacon, who confesses, "Our method of discovering the sciences does not much depend upon subtlety and strength of genius, but lies level to almost every capacity and understanding";[6] though surely sciences there are in which genius is everything and rules all but nothing.

### 4.

It will be a great mistake then to suppose that because this eminent philosopher condemned presumption and prescription in inquiries into facts which are external to us, present with us, and common to us all, therefore authority, tradition, verisimilitude, analogy, and the like, are mere "idols of the den" or "of the theatre" in history or ethics. Here we may oppose to him an author in his own line as great as he is: "Experience," says Bacon, "is by far the best demonstration, provided it dwell in the experiment; for the transferring of it to other things judged alike is very fallacious, unless done with great exactness and regularity."[7] Niebuhr explains or corrects him: "Instances are not

[6]Nov. Org. i. 2, § 26, vol. iv. p. 29.
[7]Nov. Org. § 70, p. 44.

arguments," he grants, when investigating an obscure question of Roman history—"instances are not arguments, but in history are scarcely of less force; above all, where the parallel they exhibit is in the progressive development of institutions."[8] Here this sagacious writer recognizes the true principle of historical logic while he exemplifies it.

The same principle is involved in the well-known maxim of Aristotle that "it is much the same to admit the probabilities of a mathematician, and to look for demonstration from an orator." In all matters of human life, presumption verified by instances, is our ordinary instrument of proof and, if the antecedent probability is great, it almost supersedes instances. Of course, as is plain, we may err grievously in the antecedent view which we start with, and in that case, our conclusions may be wide of the truth; but that only shows that we had no right to assume a premise which was untrustworthy, not that our reasoning was faulty.

## 5.

I am speaking of the process itself, and its correctness is shown by its general adoption. In religious questions a single text of Scripture is all-sufficient with most people, whether the well disposed or the prejudiced, to prove a doctrine or a duty in cases when a custom is established or a tradition is strong. "Not forsaking the assembling of ourselves together" is sufficient for establishing social, public, nay, Sunday worship. "Where the tree falleth, there shall it lie" shows that our probation ends with life. "Forbidding to marry" determines the Pope to be the man of sin. Again, it is plain that a man's after course for good or bad brings out the passing words or obscure actions of previous years. Then, on a retrospect, we use the event as a presumptive interpretation of the past, of those past indications of his character which, considered as evidence, were too few and doubtful to bear insisting on at the time, and would have seemed ridiculous had we attempted to do so. And the antecedent probability is even found to triumph over contrary evidence, as well as to sustain what agrees with it. Every one may know of cases in which a plausible charge against an individual was borne down at once by weight of character, though that character was incommensurate of course with the circumstances which gave rise to suspicion, and had no direct neutralizing force to destroy it. On the other hand, it is sometimes said, and even if not

---

[8] Hist. of Rome, vol. i. p. 345, ed. 1828.

literally true will serve in illustration, that not a few of those who are put on trial in our criminal courts are not legally guilty of the particular crime on which a verdict is found against them, being convicted not so much upon the particular evidence as on the presumption arising from their want of character and the memory of their former offences. Nor is it in slight matters only or unimportant that we thus act. Our dearest interests, our personal welfare, our property, our health, our reputation, we freely hazard, not on proof, but on a simple probability, which is sufficient for our conviction, because prudence dictates to us so to take it. We must be content to follow the law of our being in religious matters as well as in secular.

### 6.

But there is more to say on the subordinate position which direct evidence holds among the *motiva* of conviction in most matters. It is no paradox to say that there is a certain scantiness, nay an absence of evidence, which may even tell in favour of statements which require to be made good. There are indeed cases in which we cannot discover the law of silence or deficiency, which are then simply unaccountable. Thus Lucian, for whatever reason, hardly notices Roman authors or affairs.[9] Maximus Tyrius, who wrote several of his works at Rome, nevertheless makes no reference to Roman history. Paterculus, the historian, is mentioned by no ancient writer except Priscian. What is more to our present purpose, Seneca, Pliny the elder, and Plutarch are altogether silent about Christianity; and perhaps Epictetus also, and the Emperor Marcus. The Jewish Mishna, too, compiled about A.D. 180, is silent about Christianity; and the Jerusalem and Babylonish Talmuds almost so, though the one was complied about A.D. 300 and the other A.D. 500.[10] Eusebius again, is very uncertain in his notice of facts: he does not speak of St. Methodius, nor of St. Anthony, nor of the martyrdom of St. Perpetua, nor of the miraculous powers of St. Gregory Thaumaturgus; and he mentions Constantine's luminous cross, not in his Ecclesiastical History, where it would naturally find a place, but in his life of the Emperor. Moreover, those who receive that wonderful occurrence, which is, as one who rejects it allows,[11] "so inexplicable to the historical inquirer," have to explain the difficulty of

[9]Lardner's Heath. Test. p. 22.
[10]Paley's Evid. p. i. prop. 1, 7.
[11]Milman, Christ. vol. ii. p. 352.

the universal silence on the subject of all the Fathers of the fourth and fifth centuries, excepting Eusebius.

In like manner, Scripture has its unexplained omissions. No religious school finds its own tenets and usages on the surface of it. The remark applies also to the very context of Scripture, as in the obscurity which hangs over Nathanael or the Magdalen. It is a remarkable circumstance that there is no direct intimation all through Scripture that the Serpent mentioned in the temptation of Eve was the evil spirit, till we come to the vision of the Woman and Child, and their adversary, the Dragon, in the twelfth chapter of the Apocalypse.

## 7.

Omissions, thus absolute and singular, when they occur in the evidence of facts or doctrines, are of course difficulties; on the other hand, not unfrequently they admit of explanation. Silence may arise from the very notoriety of the facts in question, as in the case of the seasons, the weather, or other natural phenomena; or from their sacredness, as the Athenians would not mention the mythological Furies; or from external constraint, as the omission of the statues of Brutus and Cassius in the procession. Or it may proceed from fear or disgust, as on the arrival of unwelcome news; or from indignation, or hatred, or contempt, or perplexity, as Josephus is silent about Christianity, and Eusebius passes over the death of Crispus in his life of Constantine; or from other strong feeling, as implied in the poet's sentiment, "Give sorrow words"; or from policy or other prudential motive, or propriety, as Queen's Speeches do not mention individuals, however influential in the political world, and newspapers after a time were silent about the cholera. Or again, from the natural and gradual course which the fact took, as in the instance of inventions and discoveries, the history of which is on this account often obscure; or from loss of documents or other direct testimonies, as we should not look for theological information in a treatise on geology.

## 8.

Again, it frequently happens that omissions proceed on some law, as the varying influence of an external cause; and then, so far from being a perplexity, they may even confirm such evidence as occurs, by becoming, as it were, its correlative. For instance, an obstacle may be assignable, person, or principle, or accident, which ought, if it exists, to reduce or distort the indications of a fact to that very point, or in that very direction, or with the variations, or in the order and succession, which do occur in its actual history. At first sight it might be a suspicious circumstance that but one or two manuscripts of some celebrated document were forthcoming; but if it were known that the sovereign power had exerted itself to suppress and destroy it at the time of its publication, and that the extant manuscripts were found just in those places where history witnessed to the failure of the attempt, the coincidence would be highly corroborative of that evidence which alone remained.

Thus it is possible to have too much evidence; that is, evidence so full or exact as to throw suspicion over the case for which it is adduced. The genuine Epistles of St. Ignatius contain none of those ecclesiastical terms, such as "priest" or "see," which are so frequent afterwards; and they quote Scripture sparingly. The interpolated epistles quote it largely; that is, they are too Scriptural to be Apostolic. Few persons, again, who are acquainted with the primitive theology but will be sceptical at first reading of the authenticity of such works as the longer Creed of St. Gregory Thaumaturgus, or St. Hippolytus contra Beronem, from the precision of the theological language, which is unsuitable to the Antenicene period.

### 9.

The influence of circumstances upon the expression of opinion or testimony supplies another form of the same law of omission. "I am ready to admit," says Paley, "that the ancient Christian advocates did not insist upon the miracles in argument so frequently as I should have done. It was their lot to contend with notions of magical agency, against which the mere production of the facts was not sufficient for the convincing of their adversaries; I do not know whether they themselves thought it quite decisive of the controversy. But since it is proved, I conceive with certainty, that the sparingness with which they appealed to miracles was owing neither to their ignorance nor their doubt of the facts, it is at any rate an objection, not to the truth of the history, but to the judgment of its defenders."[12] And, in like manner, Christians were not likely to entertain the question of the abstract allowableness of images in the Catholic ritual, with the actual superstitions and immoralities of paganism before their eyes. Nor were they

[12] Evidences, iii. 5.

likely to determine the place of the Blessed Mary in our reverence before they had duly secured, in the affections of the faithful, the supreme glory and worship of God Incarnate, her Eternal Lord and Son. Nor would they recognize Purgatory as a part of the Dispensation, till the world had flowed into the Church, and a habit of corruption had been largely superinduced. Nor could ecclesiastical liberty be asserted till it had been assailed. Nor would a Pope arise but in proportion as the Church was consolidated. Nor would monachism be needed while martyrdoms were in progress. Nor could St. Clement give judgment on the doctrine of Berengarius, nor St. Dionysius refute the Ubiquists, nor St. Irenæus denounce the Protestant view of Justification, nor St. Cyprian draw up a theory of toleration. There is "a time for every purpose under the heaven"; "a time to keep silence and a time to speak."

## 10.

Sometimes when the want of evidence for a series of facts or doctrines is unaccountable, an unexpected explanation or addition in the course of time is found as regards a portion of them, which suggests a ground of patience as regards the historical obscurity of the rest. Two instances are obvious to mention of an accidental silence of clear primitive testimony as to important doctrines, and its removal. In the number of the articles of Catholic belief which the Reformation especially resisted were the Mass and the sacramental virtue of Ecclesiastical Unity. Since the date of that movement, the shorter Epistles of St. Ignatius have been discovered, and the early liturgies verified; and this with most men has put an end to the controversy about those doctrines. The good fortune which has happened to them may happen to others; and though it does not, yet that it has happened to them is to those others a sort of compensation for the obscurity in which their early history continues to be involved.

## 11.

I may seem in these remarks to be preparing the way for a broad admission of the absence of any sanction in primitive Christianity in behalf of its medieval form, but I do not make them with this intention. Not from misgivings of this kind, but from the claims of a sound logic, I think it right to insist, that, whatever early testimonies I may bring in support of later developments of doctrine, are in great measure brought *ex abundante*, a matter of grace, not of compulsion. The *onus probandi* is with those who assail a teaching which is, and has long been, in possession. As for positive evidence in our behalf, they must take what they can get, if they cannot get as much as they might wish, inasmuch as antecedent probabilities, as I have said, go so very far towards dispensing with it. It is a first strong point that, in an idea such as Christianity, developments cannot but be, and those surely divine, because it is divine; a second that, if so, they are those very ones which exist, because there are no others; and a third point is the fact that they are found just there, where true developments ought to be found—namely, in the historic seats of Apostolical teaching and in the authoritative homes of immemorial tradition.

## 12.

And if it be said in reply that the difficulty of admitting these developments of doctrine lies not merely in the absence of early testimony for them but in the actual existence of distinct testimony against them—or, as Chillingworth says, in "Popes against Popes, Councils against Councils"—I answer, of course this will be said; but let the fact of this objection be carefully examined, and its value reduced to its true measure before it is used in argument. I grant that there are "bishops against bishops in Church history, Fathers against Fathers, Fathers against themselves," for such differences in individual writers are consistent with, or rather are involved in the very idea of doctrinal development, and consequently are no real objection to it; the one essential question is whether the recognized organ of teaching, the Church herself, acting through Pope or Council as the oracle of heaven, has ever contradicted her own enunciations. If so, the hypothesis which I am advocating is at once shattered; but till I have positive and distinct evidence of the fact, I am slow to give credence to the existence of so great an improbability.

# CHAPTER IV

# INSTANCES IN ILLUSTRATION

It follows now to inquire how much evidence is actually producible for those large portions of the present Creed of Christendom which have not a recognized place in the primordial idea and the historical outline of the religion, yet which come to us with certain antecedent considerations strong enough in reason to raise the effectiveness of that evidence to a point disproportionate, as I have allowed, to its intrinsic value. In urging these considerations here, of course I exclude for the time the force of the Church's claim of infallibility in her acts, for which so much can be said, but I do not exclude the logical cogency of those acts considered as testimonies to the faith of the times before them.

My argument then is this: that, from the first age of Christianity, its teaching looked towards those ecclesiastical dogmas, afterwards recognized and defined with (as time went on) more or less determinate advance in the direction of them; till at length that advance became so pronounced as to justify their definition and to bring it about, and to place them in the position of rightful interpretations and keys of the remains and the records in history of the teaching which had so terminated.

## 2.

This line of argument is not unlike that which is considered to constitute a sufficient proof of truths in physical science. An instance of this is furnished us in a work on mechanics of the past generation, by a writer of name, and his explanation of it will serve as an introduction to our immediate subject. After treating of the laws of motion, he goes on to observe, "These laws are the simplest principles to which motion can be reduced, and upon them the whole theory depends. They are not indeed self-evident, nor do they admit of accurate proof by experiment, on account of the great nicety required in adjusting the instruments and making the experiments; and on account of the effects of friction, and the air's resistance, which cannot entirely be removed. They are, however, constantly, and invariably, suggested to our senses, and they agree with experiment as far as experiment can go; and the more accurately the experiments are made, and the greater care we take to remove all those impediments which tend to render the conclusions erroneous, the more nearly do the experiments coincide with these laws."[1] And thus a converging evidence in favour of certain doctrines may, under circumstances, be as clear a proof of their Apostolical origin as can be reached practically from the *Quod semper, quod ubique, quod ab omnibus.*

In such a method of proof there is, first, an imperfect, secondly, a growing evidence, thirdly, in consequence a delayed inference and judgment, fourthly, reasons producible to account for the delay.

## SECTION I

### INSTANCES CURSORILY NOTICED

### 1.

### 1. Canon of the New Testament

As regards the New Testament, Catholics and Protestants receive the same books as canonical and inspired; yet among those books some are to be found which certainly have no right there if, following the rule of Vincentius, we receive nothing as of divine authority but what has been received always and everywhere. The degrees of evidence are very various for one book and another. "It is confessed," says Less, "that not all the Scriptures of our New Testament have been received with universal consent as genuine works of the Evangelists and Apostles. But that man must have predetermined to oppose the most palpable truths, and must reject all history, who will not confess that the *greater* part of the New Testament has been universally received as authentic, and that the remaining books have been acknowledged as such by the *majority* of the ancients."[2]

### 2.

For instance, as to the Epistle of St. James. It is true, it is contained in the old Syriac version in the second century; but Origen, in the third

---

[1] Wood's Mechanics, p. 31.
[2] Authent. N. T. Tr. p. 237.

century, is the first writer who distinctly mentions it among the Greeks; and it is not quoted by name by an Latin till the fourth. St. Jerome speaks of its gaining credit "by degrees, in process of time." Eusebius says no more than that it had been, up to his time, acknowledged by the majority; and he classes it with the Shepherd of St. Hermas and the Epistle of St. Barnabas.[3]

Again: "The Epistle to the Hebrews, though received in the East, was not received in the Latin Churches till St. Jerome's time. St. Irenæus either does not affirm, or denies that it is St. Paul's. Tertullian ascribes it to St. Barnabas. Caius excludes it from his list. St. Hippolytus does not receive it. St. Cyprian is silent about it. It is doubtful whether St. Optatus received it."[4]

Again, St. Jerome tells us, that in his day, towards A.D. 400, the Greek Church rejected the Apocalypse but the Latin received it.

Again: "The New Testament consists of twenty-seven books in all, though of varying importance. Of these, fourteen are not mentioned at all till from eighty to one hundred years after St. John's death, in which number are the Acts, the Second to the Corinthians, the Galatians, the Colossians, the Two to the Thessalonians, and St. James. Of the other thirteen, five, viz., St. John's Gospel, the Philippians, the First to Timothy, the Hebrews, and the First of St. John are quoted but by one writer during the same period."[5]

## 3.

On what ground, then, do we receive the Canon as it comes to us but on the authority of the Church of the fourth and fifth centuries? The Church at that era decided—not merely bore testimony, but passed a judgment on former testimony—decided, that certain books were of authority. And on what ground did she so decide? on the ground that hitherto a decision had been impossible, in an age of persecution, from want of opportunities for research, discussion, and testimony, from the private or the local character of some of the books, and from misapprehension of the doctrine contained in others. Now, however, facilities were at length given for deciding once for all on what had been in suspense and doubt for three centuries. On this

[3] According to Less.
[4] Tracts for the Times, No. 85, p. 78 [Discuss. iii. 6, p. 207].
[5] Ibid. p. 209. These results are taken from Less, and are practically accurate.

subject I will quote another passage from the same Tract: "We depend upon the fourth and fifth centuries thus:-As to Scripture, former centuries do not speak distinctly, frequently, or unanimously, except of some chief books, as the Gospels; but we see in them, as we believe, an ever-growing tendency and approximation to that full agreement which we find in the fifth. The testimony given at the latter date is the limit to which all that has been before said converges. For instance, it is commonly said, *Exceptio probat regulam*; when we have reason to think that a writer or an age *would* have witnessed so and so, *but for* this or that, and that this or that were mere accidents of his position, then he or it may be said to *tend towards* such testimony. In this way the first centuries tend towards the fifth. Viewing the matter as one of moral evidence, we seem to see in the testimony of the fifth the very testimony which every preceding century gave, accidents excepted, such as the present loss of documents once extant, or the then existing misconceptions which want of intercourse between the Churches occasioned. The fifth century acts as a comment on the obscure text of the centuries before it, and brings out a meaning, which with the help of the comment any candid person sees really to be theirs."[6]

4.

*2. Original Sin*

I have already remarked upon the historical fact, that the recognition of Original Sin, considered as the consequence of Adam's fall, was, both as regards general acceptance and accurate understanding, a gradual process, not completed till the time of Augustine and Pelagius. St. Chrysostom lived close up to that date, but there are passages in his works, often quoted which we should not expect to find worded as they stand if they had been written fifty years later. It is commonly, and reasonably, said in explanation that the fatalism, so prevalent in various shapes pagan and heretical, in the first centuries, was an obstacle to an accurate apprehension of the consequences of the fall, as the presence of the existing idolatry was to the use of images. If this be so, we have here an instance of a doctrine held back for a time by circumstances, yet in the event forcing its way into its normal shape, and at length authoritatively fixed in it, that is, of a doctrine held implicitly, then asserting itself, and at length fully developed.

[6]No. 85 [Discuss. p. 236].

### 5.

### *3. Infant Baptism*

One of the passages of St. Chrysostom to which I might refer is this, "We baptize infants, though they are not defiled with sin, that they may receive sanctity, righteousness, adoption, heirship, brotherhood with Christ, and may become His members." (*Aug. contr. Jul.* i. 21.) This at least shows that he had a clear view of the importance and duty of infant baptism, but such was not the case even with Saints in the generation immediately before him. As is well known, it was not unusual in that age of the Church for those who might be considered catechumens to delay their baptism, as Protestants now delay reception of the Holy Eucharist. It is difficult for us at this day to enter into the assemblage of motives which led to this postponement; to a keen sense and awe of the special privileges of baptism which could only once be received, other reasons would be added—reluctance to being committed to a strict rule of life, and to making a public profession of religion, and to joining in a specially intimate fellowship or solidarity with strangers. But so it was in matter of fact, for reasons good or bad, that infant baptism, which is a fundamental rule of Christian duty with us, was less earnestly insisted on in early times.

### 6.

Even in the fourth century St. Gregory Nazianzen, St. Basil, and St. Augustine, having Christian mothers, still were not baptized till they were adults. St. Gregory's mother dedicated him to God immediately on his birth; and again when he had come to years of discretion, with the rite of taking the gospels into his hands by way of consecration. He was religiously minded from his youth, and had devoted himself to a single life. Yet his baptism did not take place till after he had attended the schools of Cæsarea, Palestine, and Alexandria, and was on his voyage to Athens. He had embarked during the November gales, and for twenty days his life was in danger. He presented himself for baptism as soon as he got to land. St. Basil was the son of Christian confessors on both father's and mother's side. His grandmother Macrina, who brought him up, had for seven years lived with her husband in the woods of Pontus during the Decian persecution. His father was said to have wrought miracles; his mother, an orphan of great beauty of person, was forced from her unprotected state to abandon the hope of a single life, and was conspicuous in matrimony for her care of strangers and the poor, and for her offerings to the churches. How religiously she brought up her children is shown by the singular blessing that four out of ten have since been canonized as Saints. St. Basil was one of these; yet the child of such parents was not baptized till he had come to man's estate—till, according to the Benedictine Editor, his twenty-first, and perhaps his twenty-ninth, year. St. Augustine's mother, who is herself a Saint, was a Christian when he was born, though his father was not. Immediately on his birth, he was made a catechumen; in his childhood he fell ill and asked for baptism. His mother was alarmed, and was taking measures for his reception into the Church, when he suddenly got better, and it was deferred. He did not receive baptism till the age of thirty-three, after he had been for nine years a victim of Manichæan error. In like manner, St. Ambrose, though brought up by his mother and holy nuns, one of them his own sister St. Marcellina, was not baptized till he was chosen bishop at the age of about thirty-four, nor his brother St. Satyrus till about the same age, after the serious warning of a shipwreck. St. Jerome too, though educated at Rome, and so far under religious influences, as, with other boys, to be in the observance of Sunday, and of devotions in the catacombs, had no friend to bring him to baptism till he had reached man's estate and had travelled.

### 7.

Now how are the modern sects, which protest against infant baptism, to be answered by Anglicans with this array of great names in their favour? By the later rule of the Church surely; by the dicta of some later Saints, as by St. Chrysostom; by one or two inferences from Scripture; by an argument founded on the absolute necessity of Baptism for salvation—sufficient reasons certainly, but impotent to reverse the fact that neither in Dalmatia nor in Cappadocia, neither in Rome, nor in Africa was it then imperative on Christian parents, as it is now, to give baptism to their young children. It was on retrospect and after the truths of the Creed had sunk into the Christian mind, that the authority of such men as St. Cyprian, St. Chrysostom, and St. Augustine brought round the *orbis terrarum* to the conclusion, which the infallible Church confirmed, that observance of the rite was the rule, and the non-observance the exception.

8.

### 4. Communion in One Kind

In the beginning of the fifteenth century, the Council of Constance pronounced that "though in the primitive Church the Sacrament" of the Eucharist "was received by the faithful under each kind, yet the custom has been reasonably introduced, for the avoiding of certain dangers and scandals, that it should be received by the consecrators under each kind, and by the laity only under the kind of Bread; since it is most firmly to be believed, and in no wise doubted, that the whole Body and Blood of Christ is truly contained as well under the kind of Bread as under the kind of Wine."

Now the question is whether the doctrine here laid down, and carried into effect in the usage here sanctioned, was entertained by the early Church, and may be considered a just development of its principles and practices. I answer that, starting with the presumption that the Council has ecclesiastical authority, which is the point here to be assumed, we shall find quite enough for its defence, and shall be satisfied to decide in the affirmative; we shall readily come to the conclusion that Communion under either kind is lawful, each kind conveying the full gift of the Sacrament.

For instance, Scripture affords us two instances of what may reasonably be considered the administration of the form of bread without that of wine; viz., our Lord's own example towards the two disciples at Emmaus, and St. Paul's action at sea during the tempest. Moreover, St. Luke speaks of the first Christians as continuing in the "*breaking of bread*, and in prayer," and of the first day of the week "when they came together to *break bread*."

And again, in the sixth chapter of St. John, our Lord says absolutely, "He that eateth Me, even he shall live by Me." And, though He distinctly promises that we shall have it granted to us to drink His blood, as well as to eat His flesh; nevertheless, not a word does He say to signify that, as He is the Bread from Heaven and the living Bread, so He is the heavenly, living Wine also. Again, St. Paul says that "whosoever shall eat this Bread *or* drink this Cup of the Lord unworthily, shall be guilty of the Body and Blood of the Lord."

Many of the types of the Holy Eucharist, as far as they go, tend to the same conclusion; as the Manna, to which our Lord referred, the Paschal Lamb, the Shewbread, the sacrifices from which the blood was poured out, and the miracle of the loaves, which are figures of the bread alone; while the water from the rock, and the Blood from our Lord's side correspond to the wine without the bread. Others are representations of both kinds; as Melchizedek's feast, and Elijah's miracle of the meal and oil.

## 9.

And, further, it certainly was the custom in the early Church, under circumstances, to communicate in one kind, as we learn from St. Cyprian, St. Dionysius, St. Basil, St. Jerome, and others. For instance, St. Cyprian speaks of the communion of an infant under wine, and of a woman under bread; and St. Ambrose speaks of his brother in shipwreck folding the consecrated bread in a handkerchief, and placing it round his neck; and the monks and hermits in the desert can hardly be supposed to have been ordinarily in possession of consecrated wine as well as bread. From the following letter of St. Basil, it appears that not only the monks but the whole laity of Egypt ordinarily communicated in bread only. He seems to have been asked by his correspondent whether in time of persecution it was lawful, in the absence of priest or deacon, to take the communion "in one's own *hand*," that is, of course, the bread; he answers that it may be justified by the following parallel cases, in mentioning which he is altogether silent about the cup. "It is plainly no fault," he says, "for long custom supplies instances enough to sanction it. For all the monks in the desert, where there is no priest, keep the communion at home, and partake it from themselves. In Alexandria too, and in Egypt, each of the laity, for the most part, has the Communion in his house, and, when he will, he partakes it by means of himself. For when once the priest has celebrated the Sacrifice and given it, he who takes it as a whole together, and then partakes of it daily, reasonably ought to think that he partakes and receives from him who has given it."[7] It should be added, that in the beginning of the letter he may be interpreted to speak of communion in both kinds, and to say that it is "good and profitable."

Here we have the usage of Pontus, Egypt, Africa, and Milan. Spain may be added, if a late author is right in his view of the meaning of a Spanish canon;[8] and Syria as well as Egypt, at least

---

[7] Ep. 93. I have thought it best to give an over-literal translation.

[8] Vid. Concil. Bracar. ap. Aguirr. Conc. Hisp. t. ii. p. 676. "That the cup was not administered at the same time is not so clear; but from the tenor of this first Canon in the Acts of the Third Council of Braga, which condemns the notion that the Host should be steeped in the chalice, we have no doubt

at a later date, since Nicephorus[9] tells us that the Acephali, having no bishops, kept the bread which their last priests had consecrated, and dispensed crumbs of it every year at Easter for the purposes of Communion.

## 10.

But it may be said that after all it is so very hazardous and fearful a measure actually to withdraw from Christians one half of the Sacrament that, in spite of these precedents, some direct warrant is needed to reconcile the mind to it. There might have been circumstances which led St. Cyprian, or St. Basil, or the Apostolical Christians before them to curtail it, about which we know nothing. It is not therefore safe in us, because it was safe in them. Certainly a warrant is necessary; and just such a warrant is the authority of the Church. If we can trust her implicitly, there is nothing in the state of the evidence to form an objection to her decision in this instance, and in proportion as we find we can trust her does our difficulty lessen. Moreover, children, not to say infants, were at one time admitted to the Eucharist, at least to the cup; on what authority are they now excluded from cup and bread also? St. Augustine considered the usage to be of Apostolical origin; and it continued in the West down to the twelfth century; it continues in the East among Greeks, Russo-Greeks, and the various Monophysite Churches to this day, and that on the ground of its almost universality in the primitive Church.[10] Is it a greater innovation to suspend the cup, than to cut off children from Communion altogether? Yet we acquiesce in the latter deprivation without a scruple. It is safer to acquiesce with than without an authority; safer with the belief that the Church is the pillar and ground of the truth than with the belief that in so great a matter she is likely to err.

---

that the wine was withheld from the laity. Whether certain points of doctrine are or are not found in the Scriptures is no concern of the historian; all that he has to do is religiously to follow his guides, to suppress or distrust nothing through partiality."—*Dunham, Hist. of Spain and Port.* vol. i. p. 204. If *pro complemento communionis* in the Canon merely means "for the Cup," at least the Cup is spoken of as a complement; the same view is contained in the "confirmation of the Eucharist," as spoken of in St. Germain's life. Vid. Lives of Saints, No. 9, p. 28.

[9]Niceph. Hist. xviii. 45. Renaudot, however, tells us of two bishops at the time when the schism was at length healed. Patr. Al. Jac. p. 248. However, these had been consecrated by priests, p. 145.

[10]Vid. Bing. Ant. xv. 4, § 7; and Fleury, Hist. xxvi. 50, note 9.

## 11.

### 5. The Homoousion

The next instance I shall take is from the early teaching on the subject of our Lord's Consubstantiality and Coeternity.

In the controversy carried on by various learned men in the seventeenth and following century, concerning the statements of the early Fathers on this subject, the one party determined the patristic theology by the literal force of the separate expressions or phrases used in it, or by the philosophical opinions of the day; the other by the doctrine of the Catholic Church, as afterwards authoritatively declared. The one party argued that those Fathers *need not* have meant more than what was afterwards considered heresy; the other answered that there is *nothing to prevent* their meaning more. Thus the position which Bull maintains seems to be nothing beyond this, that the Nicene Creed is a natural key for interpreting the body of Antenicene theology. His very aim is to explain difficulties; now the notion of difficulties and their explanation implies a rule to which they are apparent exceptions, and in accordance with which they are to be explained. Nay, the title of his work, which is a "Defence of the Creed of Nicæa," shows that he is not investigating what is true and what false, but explaining and justifying a foregone conclusion, as sanctioned by the testimony of the great Council. Unless the statements of the Fathers had suggested difficulties, his work would have had no object. He allows that their language is not such as they would have used after the Creed had been imposed; but he says in effect that, if we will but take it in our hands and apply it equitably to their writings, we shall bring out and harmonize their teaching, clear their ambiguities, and discover their anomalous statements to be few and insignificant. In other words, he begins with a presumption, and shows how naturally facts close round it and fall in with it, if we will but let them. He does this triumphantly, yet he has an arduous work; out of about thirty writers whom he reviews, he has, for one cause or other to "explain piously" nearly twenty.

## SECTION II

### OUR LORD'S INCARNATION AND THE DIGNITY OF HIS BLESSED MOTHER AND OF ALL SAINTS

Bishop Bull's controversy had regard to Antenicene writers only, and to little more than to the doctrine of the Divine Son's consubstantiality and coeternity; and, as being controversy, it necessarily narrows and dries up a large and fertile subject. Let us see whether, treated historically, it will not present itself to us in various aspects which may rightly be called developments, as coming into view, one out of another, and following one after another by a natural order of succession.

### 2.

First then, that the language of the Antenicene Fathers, on the subject of our Lord's Divinity, may be far more easily accommodated to the Arian hypothesis than can the language of the Postnicene, is agreed on all hands. Thus St. Justin speaks of the Son as subservient to the Father in the creation of the world, as seen by Abraham, as speaking to Moses from the bush, as appearing to Joshua before the fall of Jericho,[11] as Minister and Angel, and as numerically distinct from the Father. Clement, again, speaks of the Word[12] as the "Instrument of God," "close to the Sole Almighty"; "ministering to the Omnipotent Father's will";[13] "an energy, so to say, or operation of the Father," and "constituted by His will as the cause of all good."[14] Again, the Council of Antioch, which condemned Paul of Samosata, says that He "appears to the Patriarchs and converses with them, being testified sometimes to be an Angel, at other times Lord, at others God"; that, while "it is impious to think that the God of all is called an Angel, the Son is the Angel of the Father."[15] Formal proof, however, is unnecessary; had

[11] Kaye's Justin, p. 59, etc.
[12] Kaye's Clement, p. 335.
[13] p. 341.
[14] Ib. 342.
[15] Reliqu. Sacr. t. ii. p. 469, 470.

not the fact been as I have stated it, neither Sandius would have professed to differ from the Postnicene Fathers, nor would Bull have had to defend the Antenicene.

### 3.

One principal change which took place, as time went on, was the following: the Antenicene Fathers, as in some of the foregoing extracts, speak of the Angelic visions in the Old Testament as if they were appearances of the Son; but St. Augustine introduced the explicit doctrine, which has been received since his date, that they were simply Angels through whom the Omnipresent Son manifested Himself. This indeed is the only interpretation which the Antenicene statements admitted, as soon as reason began to examine what they did mean. They could not mean that the Eternal God could really be seen by bodily eyes; if anything was seen, that must have been some created glory or other symbol, by which it pleased the Almighty to signify His Presence. What was heard was a sound, as external to His Essence, and as distinct from His Nature, as the thunder or the voice of the trumpet which pealed along Mount Sinai; what it was had not come under discussion till St. Augustine; both question and answer were alike undeveloped. The earlier Fathers spoke as if there were no medium interposed between the Creator and the creature, and so they seemed to make the Eternal Son the medium; what it really was they had not determined. St. Augustine ruled, and his ruling has been accepted in later times, that it was not a mere atmospheric phenomenon, or an impression on the senses, but the material form proper to an Angelic presence, or the presence of an Angel in that material garb in which blessed Spirits do ordinarily appear to men. Henceforth the Angel in the bush, the voice which spoke with Abraham, and the man who wrestled with Jacob were not regarded as the Son of God, but as Angelic ministers whom He employed and through whom He signified His presence and His will. Thus the tendency of the controversy with the Arians was to raise our view of our Lord's mediatorial acts, to impress them on us in their divine rather than their human aspect, and to associate them more intimately with the ineffable glories which surround the Throne of God. The Mediatorship was no longer regarded in itself, in that prominently subordinate place which it had once occupied in the thoughts of Christians, but as an office assumed by One, who though having become man in order to bear it, was still

God.[16] Works and attributes, which had hitherto been assigned to the Economy or to the Sonship, were now simply assigned to the Manhood. A tendency was also elicited, as the controversy proceeded, to contemplate our Lord more distinctly in His absolute perfections than in His relation to the First Person of the Blessed Trinity. Thus, whereas the Nicene Creed speaks of the "Father Almighty," and "His Only-begotten Son, our Lord, God from God, Light from Light, Very God from Very God," and of the Holy Ghost, "the Lord and Giver of Life," we are told in the Athanasian of "the Father Eternal, the Son Eternal, and the Holy Ghost Eternal," and that "none is afore or after other, none is greater or less than another."

### 4.

The Apollinarian and Monophysite controversy, which followed in the course of the next century, tended towards a development in the same direction. Since the heresies, which were in question, maintained, at least virtually, that our Lord was not man, it was obvious to insist on the passages of Scripture which describe His created and subservient nature, and this had the immediate effect of interpreting of His manhood texts which had hitherto been understood more commonly of His Divine Sonship. Thus, for instance, "My Father is greater than I," which had been understood even by St. Athanasius of our Lord as God, is applied by later writers more commonly to His humanity; and in this way the doctrine of His subordination to the Eternal Father, which formed so prominent a feature in Antenicene theology, comparatively fell into the shade.

### 5.

And coincident with these changes, a most remarkable result is discovered. The Catholic polemic, in view of the Arian and Monophysite errors, being of this character, became the natural introduction to the *cultus Sanctorum*; for in proportion as texts descriptive of created mediation ceased to belong to our Lord, so was a room opened for created mediators. Nay, as regards the instance of angelic appearances itself, as St. Augustine explained them, if those appearances were

---

[16]This subject is more exactly and carefully treated in Tracts Theol. and Eccles. pp. 192–226.

creatures, certainly creatures were worshipped by the Patriarchs, not indeed in themselves,[17] but as the token of a Presence greater than themselves. When "Moses hid his face, for he was afraid to look upon God," he hid his face before a creature; when Jacob said, "I have seen God face to face and my life is preserved," the Son of God was there, but what he saw, what he wrestled with, was an Angel. When "Joshua fell on his face to the earth and did worship before the captain of the Lord's host, and said unto him, What saith my Lord unto his servant?" what was seen and heard was a glorified creature, if St. Augustine is to be followed; and the Son of God was in him.

And there were plain precedents in the Old Testament for the lawfulness of such adoration. When "the people saw the cloudy pillar stand at the tabernacle-door," "all the people rose up and worshipped, every man in his tent-door."[18] When Daniel too saw "a certain man clothed in linen" "there remained no strength" in him, for his "comeliness was turned" in him "into corruption." He fell down on his face, and next remained on his knees and hands, and at length "stood trembling," and said "O my Lord, by the vision my sorrows are turned upon me, and I have retained no strength. For how can the servant of this my Lord talk with this my Lord?"[19] It might be objected perhaps to this argument that a worship which was allowable in an elementary system might be unlawful when "grace and truth" had come "through Jesus Christ"; but then it might be retorted surely that that elementary system had been emphatically opposed to all idolatry, and had been minutely jealous of everything which might approach to favouring it. Nay, the very prominence given in the Pentateuch to the doctrine of a Creator, and the comparative silence concerning the Angelic creation, and the prominence given to the Angelic creation in the later Prophets, taken together, were a token both of that jealousy, and of its cessation, as time went on. Nor can anything be concluded from St. Paul's censure of Angel worship, since the sin which he is denouncing was that of "not holding the Head," and of worshipping creatures *instead* of the Creator as the source of good. The same explanation avails for passages like those in St. Athanasius and Theodoret, in which the worship of Angels is discountenanced.

[17] They also had a *cultus* in themselves, and specially when a greater Presence did *not* overshadow them. Vid. Via Med. vol. ii. art. iv. 8, note 1.

[18] Exod. xxxiii. 10.

[19] Dan. x. 5–17.

## 6.

The Arian controversy had led to another development, which confirmed by anticipation the *cultus* to which St. Augustine's doctrine pointed. In answer to the objection urged against our Lord's supreme Divinity from texts which speak of His exaltation, St. Athanasius is led to insist forcibly on the benefits which have accrued to man through it. He says that, in truth, not Christ but that human nature which He had assumed was raised and glorified in Him. The more plausible was the heretical argument against His Divinity from those texts, the more emphatic is St. Athanasius's exaltation of our regenerate nature by way of explaining them. But intimate indeed must be the connexion between Christ and His brethren, and high their glory, if the language which seemed to belong to the Incarnate Word really belonged to them. Thus the pressure of the controversy elicited and developed a truth, which till then was held indeed by Christians, but less perfectly realized and not publicly recognized. The sanctification, or rather the deification of the nature of man, is one main subject of St. Athanasius's theology. Christ, in rising, raises His Saints with Him to the right hand of power. They become instinct with His life, of one body with His flesh, divine sons, immortal kings, gods. He is in them, because He is in human nature; and He communicates to them that nature, deified by becoming His, that them It may deify. He is in them by the Presence of His Spirit, and in them He is seen. They have those titles of honour by participation which are properly His. Without misgiving we may apply to them the most sacred language of Psalmists and Prophets. "Thou art a Priest for ever" may be said of St. Polycarp or St. Martin as well as of their Lord. "He hath dispersed abroad, he hath given to the poor" was fulfilled in St. Laurence. "I have found David My servant," first said typically of the King of Israel, and belonging really to Christ, is transferred back again by grace to His Vicegerents upon earth. "I have given thee the nations for thine inheritance" is the prerogative of Popes; "Thou hast given him his heart's desire" the record of a martyr; "thou hast loved righteousness and hated iniquity" the praise of Virgins.

## 7.

"As Christ," says St. Athanasius, "died, and was exalted as man, so, as man, is He said to take what, as God, He ever had, in order that even this so high a grant of grace might reach to us. For the Word did not suffer loss in receiving a body, that He should seek to receive a grace, but rather He deified that which He put on, nay, gave it graciously to the race of man. . . . For it is the Father's glory, that man, made and then lost, should be found again; and, when done to death, that he should be made alive, and should become God's temple. For whereas the powers in heaven, both Angels and Archangels, were ever worshipping the Lord, as they are now too worshipping Him in the Name of Jesus, this is our grace and high exaltation, that, even when He became man, the Son of God is worshipped, and the heavenly powers are not startled at seeing all of us, who are of one body with Him, introduced into their realms."[20] In this passage it is almost said that the glorified Saints will partake in the homage paid by Angels to Christ, the True Object of all worship; and at least a reason is suggested to us by it for the Angel's shrinking in the Apocalypse from the homage of St. John, the Theologian and Prophet of the Church.[21] But St. Athanasius proceeds still more explicitly, "In that the Lord, even when come in human body and called Jesus, was worshipped and believed to be God's Son, and that through Him the Father is known, it is plain, as has been said, that, *not the Word*, considered as the Word, received this so great grace, *but we*. For, because of our relationship to His Body, we too have become God's temple, and in consequence have been made God's sons, so that *even in us the Lord is now worshipped*, and beholders report, as the Apostle says, that 'God is in them of a truth.' "[22] It appears to be distinctly stated in this passage that those who are formally recognized as God's adopted sons in Christ are fit objects of worship on account of Him who is in them; a doctrine which both interprets and accounts for the invocation of Saints, the *cultus* of relics, and the religious veneration in which even the living have sometimes been held, who, being saintly, were distinguished by miraculous gifts.[23] Worship then is the necessary correlative of glory; and in the same sense in which created natures can share in the Creator's incommunicable glory are they also allowed a share of that worship which is His property alone.

[20] Athan. Orat. i. 42, Oxf. tr.
[21] Vid. supr. p. 149, note 17.
[22] Athan. ibid.
[23] And so Eusebius, in his Life of Constantine: "The all-holy choir of God's perpetual virgins, he was used almost to worship (σέβων), believing that that God, to whom they had consecrated themselves, was an inhabitant in the souls of such." Vit. Const. iv. 28.

## 8.

There was one other subject on which the Arian controversy had a more intimate, though not an immediate influence. Its tendency to give a new interpretation to the texts which speak of our Lord's subordination has already been noticed; such as admitted of it were henceforth explained more prominently of His manhood than of His Mediatorship or His Sonship. But there were other texts which did not admit of this interpretation, and which, without ceasing to belong to Him, might seem more directly applicable to a creature than to the Creator. He indeed was really the "Wisdom in whom the Father eternally delighted," yet it would be but natural, if, under the circumstances of Arian misbelief, theologians looked out for other than the Eternal Son to be the immediate object of such descriptions. And thus the controversy opened a question which it did not settle. It discovered a new sphere, if we may so speak, in the realms of light, to which the Church had not yet assigned its inhabitant. Arianism had admitted that our Lord was both the God of the Evangelical Covenant and the actual Creator of the Universe; but even this was not enough, because it did not confess Him to be the One, Everlasting, Infinite, Supreme Being, but as one who was made by the Supreme. It was not enough in accordance with that heresy to proclaim Him as having an ineffable origin before all worlds; not enough to place Him high above all creatures as the type of all the works of God's Hands; not enough to make Him the King of all Saints, the Intercessor for man with God, the Object of worship, the Image of the Father; not enough, because it was not all, and between all and anything short of all there was an infinite interval. The highest of creatures is levelled with the lowest in comparison of the One Creator Himself. That is, the Nicene Council recognized the eventful principle that, while we believe and profess any being to be made of a created nature, such a being is really no God to us, though honoured by us with whatever high titles and with whatever homage. Arius or Asterius did all but confess that Christ was the Almighty; they said much more than St. Bernard or St. Alphonso have since said of the Blessed Mary; yet they left Him a creature and were found wanting. Thus there was "a wonder in heaven": a throne was seen, far above all other created powers, mediatorial, intercessory; a title archetypal; a crown bright as the morning star; a glory issuing from the Eternal Throne; robes pure as the heavens; and a sceptre over all; and who was the predestined heir of that Majesty? Since it was not high enough for the Highest, who was that Wisdom, and what was her name, "the Mother of fair love, and fear, and holy hope," "exalted like a palm-tree in Engaddi, and a rose-plant in Jericho," "created from the beginning before the world" in God's everlasting counsels, and "in Jerusalem her power"? The vision is found in the Apocalypse, a Woman clothed with the sun, and the moon under her feet, and upon her head a crown of twelve stars. The votaries of Mary do not exceed the true faith unless the blasphemers of her Son came up to it. The Church of Rome is not idolatrous, unless Arianism is orthodoxy.

## 9.

I am not stating conclusions which were drawn out in the controversy, but of premises which were laid, broad and deep. It was then shown, it was then determined, that to exalt a creature was no recognition of its divinity. Nor am I speaking of the Semi-Arians, who, holding our Lord's derivation from the Substance of the Father, yet denying His Consubstantiality, really did lie open to the charge of maintaining two Gods, and present no parallel to the defenders of the prerogatives of St. Mary. But I speak of the Arians who taught that the Son's Substance was created; and concerning them it is true that St. Athanasius's condemnation of their theology is a vindication of the Medieval. Yet it is not wonderful, considering how Socinians, Sabellians, Nestorians, and the like, abound in these days, without their even knowing it themselves, if those who never rise higher in their notions of our Lord's Divinity, than to consider Him a man singularly inhabited by a Divine Presence, that is, a Catholic Saint—if such men should mistake the honour paid by the Church to the human Mother for that very honour which, and which alone, is worthy of her Eternal Son.

## 10.

I have said that there was in the first ages no public and ecclesiastical recognition of the place which St. Mary holds in the Economy of Grace; this was reserved for the fifth century, as the definition of our Lord's proper Divinity had been the work of the fourth. There was a controversy contemporary with those already mentioned, I mean the Nestorian, which brought out the complement of the development, to which they had been subservient; and which, if I may so speak, supplied the subject of that august proposition of which Arianism had provided the predicate. In order to do honour to Christ, in order to

defend the true doctrine of the Incarnation, in order to secure a right
faith in the manhood of the Eternal Son, the Council of Ephesus
determined the Blessed Virgin to be the Mother of God. Thus all
heresies of that day, though opposite to each other, tended in a most
wonderful way to her exaltation; and the School of Antioch, the fountain of primitive rationalism, led the Church to determine first the
conceivable greatness of a creature, and then the incommunicable
dignity of the Blessed Virgin.

### 11.

But the spontaneous or traditional feeling of Christians had in great
measure anticipated the formal ecclesiastical decision. Thus the title
*Theotocos*, or Mother of God, was familiar to Christians from primitive times, and had been used, among other writers, by Origen, Eusebius, St. Alexander, St. Athanasius, St. Ambrose, St. Gregory
Nazianzen, St. Gregory Nyssen, and St. Nilus. She had been called
Ever-Virgin by others, as by St. Epiphanius, St. Jerome, and Didymus.
By others, "the Mother of all living," as being the antitype of Eve; for,
as St. Epiphanius observes, "in truth," not in shadow, "from Mary
was Life itself brought into the world, that Mary might bear things
living, and might become Mother of living things."[24] St. Augustine
says that all have sinned "except the Holy Virgin Mary, concerning
whom, for the honour of the Lord, I wish no question to be raised at
all, when we are treating of sins." "She was alone and wrought the
world's salvation," says St. Ambrose, alluding to her conception of
the Redeemer. She is signified by the pillar of the cloud which guided
the Israelites, according to the same Father; and she had "so great
grace, as not only to have virginity herself, but to impart it to those to
whom she came"; "the Rod out of the stem of Jesse," says St. Jerome,
and "the Eastern gate through which the High Priest alone goes in and
out, yet is ever shut"; the wise woman, says St. Nilus, who "hath clad
all believers, from the fleece of the Lamb born of her, with the clothing
of incorruption, and delivered them from their spiritual nakedness";
"the Mother of Life, of beauty, of majesty, the Morning Star," according to Antiochus; "the mystical new heavens," "the heavens carrying the Divinity," "the fruitful vine by whom we are translated
from death unto life," according to St. Ephraim; "the manna which is
delicate, bright, sweet, and virgin, which, as though coming from

[24]Hær. 78, 18.

heaven, has poured down on all the people of the Churches a food pleasanter than honey," according to St. Maximus.

St. Proclus calls her "the unsullied shell which contains the pearl of price," "the sacred shrine of sinlessness," "the golden altar of holocaust," "the holy oil of anointing," "the costly alabaster box of spikenard," "the ark gilt within and without," "the heifer whose ashes, that is, the Lord's Body taken from her, cleanses those who are defiled by the pollution of sin," "the fair bride of the Canticles," "the stay (στήριγμα) of believers," "the Church's diadem," "the expression of orthodoxy." These are oratorical expressions; but we use oratory on great subjects, not on small. Elsewhere he calls her "God's only bridge to man"; and elsewhere he breaks forth, "Run through all creation in your thoughts, and see if there be equal to, or greater than, the Holy Virgin Mother of God."

## 12.

Theodotus too, one of the Fathers of Ephesus, or whoever it is whose homilies are given to St. Amphilochius: "As debtors and God's well-affected servants, let us make confession to God the Word and to His Mother, of the gift of words, as far as we are able . . . Hail, Mother, clad in light, of the light which sets not; hail all-undefiled mother of holiness; hail most pellucid fountain of the life-giving stream!" After speaking of the Incarnation, he continues, "Such paradoxes doth the Divine Virgin Mother ever bring to us in her holy irradiations, for with her is the Fount of Life, and breasts of the spiritual and guileless milk; from which to suck the sweetness, we have even now earnestly run to her, not as in forgetfulness of what has gone before, but in desire of what is to come."

To St. Fulgentius is ascribed the following: "Mary became the window of heaven, for God through her poured the True Light upon the world; the heavenly ladder, for through her did God descend upon earth. . . . Come, ye virgins, to a Virgin, come ye who conceive to one who did conceive, ye who bear to one who bore, mothers to a Mother, ye who give suck to one who suckled, young women to the Young." Lastly, "Thou hast found grace," says St. Peter Chrysologus, "how much? he had said above, Full. And full indeed, which with full shower might pour upon and into the whole creation."[25]

[25] Aug. de Nat. et Grat. 42. Ambros. Ep. 1, 49, § 2. In Psalm 118, v. 3. de Instit. Virg. 50. Hier. in Is. xi. 1, contr. Pelag. ii. 4. Nil. Ep. i. p. 267. Antioch.

Such was the state of sentiment on the subject of the Blessed Virgin, which the Arian, Nestorian, and Monophysite heresies found in the Church; and on which the doctrinal decisions consequent upon them impressed a form and a consistency which has been handed on in the East and West to this day.

## SECTION III

### THE PAPAL SUPREMACY

I will take one instance more. Let us see how, on the principles which I have been laying down and defending, the evidence lies for the Pope's supremacy.

As to this doctrine the question is this, whether there was not from the first a certain element at work, or in existence, divinely sanctioned, which, for certain reasons, did not at once show itself upon the surface of ecclesiastical affairs, and of which events in the fourth century are the development; and whether the evidence of its existence and operation, which does occur in the earlier centuries, be it much or little, is not just such as ought to occur upon such an hypothesis.

### 2.

For instance, it is true St. Ignatius is silent in his Epistles on the subject of the Pope's authority; but if in fact that authority could not

---

ap. Cyr. de Rect. Fid. p. 49. Ephr. Opp. Syr. t. 3, p. 607. Max, Hom. 45. Procl. Orat. vi. pp. 225–28, p. 60, p. 179, 180, ed. 1630. Theodot. ap. Amphiloch. pp. 39, etc. Fulgent. Serm. 3, p. 125. Chrysol. Serm. 142. A striking passage from another Sermon of the last-mentioned author, on the words "She cast in her mind what manner of salutation," etc., may be added: "Quantus sit Deus satis ignorat ille, qui hujus Virginis mentem non stupet, animum non miratur. Pavet cœlum, tremunt Angeli, creatura non sustinet, natura non sufficit; et una puella sic Deum in sui pectoris capit, recipit, oblectat hospitio, ut pacem terris, cœlis gloriam, salutem perditis, vitam mortuis, terrenis cum cœlestibus parentelam, ipsius Dei cum carne commercium pro ipsâ domûs exigat pensione, pro ipsius uteri mercede conquirat," etc. ["One who fails to marvel at the character and attitude of this virgin has little appreciation of the greatness of God. Heaven is struck with awe and angels tremble; creation cannot sustain it nor can nature suffice. Yet a girl so welcomes God into her bosom, receives and entertains him, that her lodging's recompense, the wages of her womb are peace on earth and glory in heaven, rescue for the be in active operation then, such silence is not so difficult to account for as the silence of Seneca or Plutarch about Christianity itself, or of Lucian about the Roman people. St. Ignatius directed his doctrine according to the need. While Apostles were on earth, there was the display neither of bishop nor Pope; their power had no prominence, as being exercised by Apostles. In course of time, first the power of the bishop displayed itself, and then the power of the Pope. When the Apostles were taken away, Christianity did not at once break into portions; yet separate localities might begin to be the scene of internal dissensions, and a local arbiter in consequence would be wanted. Christians at home did not yet quarrel with Christians abroad; they quarrelled at home among themselves. St. Ignatius applied the fitting remedy. The *Sacramentum Unitatis* was acknowledged on all hands; the mode of fulfilling and the means of securing it would vary with the occasion; and the determination of its essence, its seat, and its laws would be a gradual supply for a gradual necessity.

### 3.

This is but natural, and is parallel to instances which happen daily, and may be so considered without prejudice to the divine right whether of the Episcopate or of the Papacy. It is a common occurrence for a quarrel and a lawsuit to bring out the state of the law, and then the most unexpected results often follow. St. Peter's prerogative would remain a mere letter till the complication of ecclesiastical matters became the cause of ascertaining it. While Christians were "of one heart and one soul," it would be suspended; love dispenses with laws. Christians knew that they must live in unity, and they were in unity; in what that unity consisted, how far they could proceed, as it were, in bending it, and what at length was the point at which it broke, was an irrelevant as well as unwelcome inquiry. Relatives often live together in happy ignorance of their respective rights and properties, till a father or a husband dies; and then they find themselves against their will in separate interests, and on divergent courses, and dare not move without legal advisers. Again, the case is conceivable of a corporation or an academical body going on for centuries in the performance of the routine business which came in its way, and preserving a good under-

---

lost, life for the dead, kinship of heavenly with earthly things, and intercourse of God himself with flesh."] Serm. 140. [St. Basil, St. Chrysostom, and St. Cyril of Alexandria sometimes speak, it is true, in a different tone; on this subject vid. "Letter to Dr. Pusey," Note iii., Diff. of Angl. vol. 2.]

standing between its members, with statutes almost a dead letter and no precedents to explain them, and the rights of its various classes and functions undefined—then of its being suddenly thrown back by the force of circumstances upon the question of its formal character as a body politic, and in consequence developing in the relation of governors and governed. The *regalia Petri* might sleep, as the power of a chancellor has slept; not as an obsolete, for they never had been carried into effect, but as a mysterious privilege which was not understood; as an unfulfilled prophecy. For St. Ignatius to speak of popes when it was a matter of bishops, would have been like sending an army to arrest a housebreaker. The bishop's power indeed was from God, and the Pope's could be no more; he, as well as the Pope, was our Lord's representative, and had a sacramental office, but I am speaking, not of the intrinsic sanctity or divinity of such an office, but of its duties.

### 4.

When the Church, then, was thrown upon her own resources, first local disturbances gave exercise to bishops, and next ecumenical disturbances gave exercise to Popes; and whether communion with the Pope was necessary for Catholicity would not and could not be debated till a suspension of that communion had actually occurred. It is not a greater difficulty that St. Ignatius does not write to the Asian Greeks about Popes than that St. Paul does not write to the Corinthians about bishops. And it is a less difficulty that the Papal supremacy was not formally acknowledged in the second century than that there was no formal acknowledgment on the part of the Church of the doctrine of the Holy Trinity till the fourth. No doctrine is defined till it is violated.

And, in like manner, it was natural for Christians to direct their course in matters of doctrine by the guidance of mere floating, and, as it were, endemic tradition, while it was fresh and strong; but in proportion as it languished, or was broken in particular places, did it become necessary to fall back upon its special homes, first the Apostolic sees, and then the See of St. Peter.

### 5.

Moreover, an international bond and a common authority could not be consolidated, were it ever so certainly provided, while persecutions lasted. If the Imperial power checked the development of Councils, it availed also for keeping back the power of the Papacy. The Creed, the Canon, in like manner, both remained undefined. The Creed, the Canon, the Papacy, Ecumenical Councils, all began to form, as soon as the Empire relaxed its tyrannous oppression of the Church. And as it was natural that her monarchical power should display itself when the Empire became Christian, so was it natural also that further developments of that power should take place when that Empire fell. Moreover, when the power of the Holy See began to exert itself, disturbance and collision would be the necessary consequence. Of the Temple of Solomon it was said that "neither hammer, nor axe, nor any tool of iron was heard in the house, while it was in building." This is a type of the Church above; it was otherwise with the Church below, whether in the instance of Popes or Apostles. In either case, a new power had to be defined; as St. Paul had to plead, nay, to strive for his apostolic authority, and enjoined St. Timothy, as Bishop of Ephesus, to let no man despise him: so Popes too have not therefore been ambitious because they did not establish their authority without a struggle. It was natural that Polycrates should oppose St. Victor; and natural too that St. Cyprian should both extol the See of St. Peter, yet resist it when he thought it went beyond its province. And at a later day it was natural that Emperors should rise in indignation against it; and natural, on the other hand, that it should take higher ground with a younger power than it had taken with an elder and time-honoured.

## 6.

We may follow Barrow here without reluctance, except in his imputation of motives.

"In the first times," he says, "while the Emperors were pagans, their [the Popes'] pretences were suited to their condition, and could not soar high; they were not then so mad as to pretend to any temporal power, and a pittance of spiritual eminency did content them."

Again: "The state of the most primitive Church did not well admit such an universal sovereignty. For that did consist of small bodies incoherently situated, and scattered about in very distant places, and consequently unfit to be modelled into one political society, or to be governed by one head, especially considering their condition under persecution and poverty. What convenient resort for direction or justice could a few distressed Christians in Egypt, Ethiopia, Parthia, India, Mesopotamia, Syria, Armenia, Cappadocia, and other parts, have to Rome!"

Again: "Whereas no point avowed by Christians could be so apt to raise offence and jealousy in pagans against our religion as this, which setteth up a power of so vast extent and huge influence; whereas no novelty could be more surprising or startling than the creation of an universal empire over the consciences and religious practices of men; whereas also this doctrine could not be but very conspicuous and glaring in ordinary practice, it is prodigious that all pagans should not loudly exclaim against it," that is, on the supposition that the Papal power really was then in actual exercise.

And again: "It is most prodigious that, in the disputes managed by the Fathers against heretics, the Gnostics, Valentinians, etc., they should not, even in the first place, allege and urge the sentence of the universal pastor and judge, as a most evidently conclusive argument, as the most efficacious and compendious method of convincing and silencing them."

Once more: "Even Popes themselves have shifted their pretences, and varied in style, according to the different circumstances of time, and their variety of humours, designs, interests. In time of prosperity, and upon advantage, when they might safely do it, any Pope almost would talk high and assume much to himself; but when they were low, or stood in fear of powerful contradiction, even the boldest Popes would speak submissively or moderately."[26]

On the whole, supposing the power to be divinely bestowed, yet in the first instance more or less dormant, a history could not be traced out more probable, more suitable to that hypothesis, than the actual course of the controversy which took place age after age upon the Papal supremacy.

## 7.

It will be said that all this is a theory. Certainly it is: it is a theory to account for facts as they lie in the history, to account for so much being told us about the Papal authority in early times, and not more; a theory to reconcile what is and what is not recorded about it; and, which is the principal point, a theory to connect the words and acts of the Antenicene Church with that antecedent probability of a monarchical principle in the Divine Scheme, and that actual exemplification of it in the fourth century, which forms their presumptive interpretation. All depends on the strength of that presumption. Supposing there be otherwise good reason for saying that the Papal supremacy is part

[26] Pope's Suprem. ed. 1836, pp. 26, 27, 157, 171, 222.

of Christianity, there is nothing in the early history of the Church to contradict it.

## 8.

It follows to inquire in what this presumption consists? It has, as I have said, two parts, the antecedent probability of a Popedom, and the actual state of the Postnicene Church. The former of these reasons has unavoidably been touched upon in what has preceded. It is the absolute need of a monarchical power in the Church which is our ground for anticipating it. A political body cannot exist without government, and the larger is the body the more concentrated must the government be. If the whole of Christendom is to form one Kingdom, one head is essential; at least this is the experience of eighteen hundred years. As the Church grew into form, so did the power of the Pope develop; and wherever the Pope has been renounced, decay and division have been the consequence. We know of no other way of preserving the *Sacramentum Unitatis* but a centre of unity. The Nestorians have had their "Catholicus"; the Lutherans of Prussia have their general superintendent; even the Independents, I believe, have had an overseer in their missions. The Anglican Church affords an observable illustration of this doctrine. As her prospects have opened and her communion extended, the See of Canterbury has become the natural centre of her operations. It has at the present time jurisdiction in the Mediterranean, at Jerusalem, in Hindustan, in North America, at the Antipodes. It has been the organ of communication, when a Prime Minister would force the Church to a redistribution of her property, or a Protestant sovereign abroad would bring her into friendly relations with his own communion. Eyes have been lifted up thither in times of perplexity; thither have addresses been directed and deputations sent. Thence issue the legal decisions, or the declarations in Parliament, or the letters, or the private interpositions, which shape the fortunes of the Church and are the moving influence within her separate dioceses. It must be so; no Church can do without its Pope. We see before our eyes the centralizing process by which the See of St. Peter became the sovereign head of Christendom.

If such be the nature of the case, it is impossible, if we may so speak reverently, that an Infinite Wisdom, which sees the end from the beginning, in decreeing the rise of an universal Empire, should not have decreed the development of a sovereign ruler.

Moreover, all this must be viewed in the light of the general probability, so much insisted on above, that doctrine cannot but develop as time proceeds and need arises, and that its developments are parts of the Divine system, and that therefore it is lawful, or rather necessary, to interpret the words and deeds of the earlier Church by the determinate teaching of the later.

### 9.

And, on the other hand, as the counterpart of these anticipations, we are met by certain announcements in Scripture, more or less obscure and needing a comment, and claimed by the Papal See as having their fulfilment in itself. Such are the words, "Thou art Peter, and upon this rock I will build My Church; and the gates of hell shall not prevail against it, and I will give unto Thee the Keys of the Kingdom of Heaven." Again: "Feed My lambs, feed My sheep." And "Satan hath desired to have you; I have prayed for thee, and when thou art converted, strengthen thy brethren." Such, too, are various other indications of the Divine purpose as regards St. Peter, too weak in themselves to be insisted on separately, but not without a confirmatory power; such as his new name, his walking on the sea, his miraculous draught of fishes on two occasions, our Lord's preaching out of his boat, and His appearing first to him after His resurrection.

It should be observed, moreover, that a similar promise was made by the patriarch Jacob to Judah: "Thou art he whom thy brethren shall praise: the sceptre shall not depart from Judah till Shiloh come"; yet this promise was not fulfilled for perhaps eight hundred years, during which long period we hear little or nothing of the tribe descended from him. In like manner, "On this rock I will build My Church," "I give unto thee the Keys," "Feed My sheep," are not precepts merely, but prophecies and promises, promises to be accomplished by Him who made them, prophecies to be fulfilled according to the need, and to be interpreted by the event—by the history, that is, of the fourth and fifth centuries, though they had a partial fulfilment even in the preceding period, and a still more noble development in the middle ages.

### 10.

A partial fulfilment, or at least indications of what was to be, there certainly were in the first age. Faint one by one, at least they are various, and are found in writers of many times and countries, and thereby illustrative of each other, and forming a body of proof. Thus St. Clement, in the name of the Church of Rome, writes to the Corinthians when they were without a bishop; St. Ignatius of Antioch addresses the Roman Church, out of the Churches to which he writes, as "the Church, which has in dignity the first seat, of the city of the Romans,"[27] and implies that it was too high for his directing as being the Church of St. Peter and St. Paul. St. Polycarp of Smyrna has recourse to the Bishop of Rome on the question of Easter; the heretic Marcion, excommunicated in Pontus, betakes himself to Rome; Soter, Bishop of Rome, sends alms, according to the custom of his Church, to the Churches throughout the empire, and, in the words of Eusebius, "affectionately exhorted those who came to Rome, as a father his children"; the Montanists from Phrygia come to Rome to gain the countenance of its bishop; Praxeas, from Asia, attempts the like, and for a while is successful; St. Victor, Bishop of Rome, threatens to excommunicate the Asian Churches; St. Irenaeus speaks of Rome as "the greatest Church, the most ancient, the most conspicuous, and founded and established by Peter and Paul," appeals to its tradition, not in contrast indeed, but in preference to that of other Churches, and declares that "to this Church, every Church, that is, the faithful from every side must resort" or "must agree with it, *propter potiorem principalitatem.*" "O Church, happy in its position," says Tertullian, "into which the Apostles poured out, together with their blood, their whole doctrine"; and elsewhere, though in indignation and bitter mockery, he calls the Pope "the Pontifex Maximus, the Bishop of Bishops." The presbyters of St. Dionysius, Bishop of Alexandria, complain of his doctrine to St. Dionysius of Rome; the latter expostulates with him, and he explains. The Emperor Aurelian leaves "to the Bishops of Italy and of Rome" the decision, whether or not Paul of Samosata shall be dispossessed of the see-house at Antioch; St. Cyprian speaks of Rome as "the See of Peter and the principal Church, whence the unity of the priesthood took its rise . . . whose faith has been commended by the Apostles, to whom faithlessness can have no access"; St. Stephen refuses to receive St. Cyprian's deputation and separates himself from various Churches of the East; Fortunatus and Felix, deposed by St. Cyprian, have recourse to Rome; Basilides, deposed in Spain, betakes himself to Rome, and gains the ear of St. Stephen.

[27] ἥτις καὶ προκάθηται ἐν τόπῳ χωρίου Ῥωμαίων.

## 11.

St. Cyprian had his quarrel with the Roman See, but it appears he allows to it the title of the "Cathedra Petri," and even Firmilian is a witness that Rome claimed it. In the fourth and fifth centuries this title and its logical results became prominent. Thus St. Julius (A.D. 342) remonstrated by letter with the Eusebian party for "proceeding on their own authority as they pleased," and then, as he says, "desiring to obtain our concurrence in their decisions, though we never condemned [Athanasius]. Not so have the constitutions of Paul, not so have the traditions of the Fathers directed; this is another form of procedure, a novel practice. . . . For what we have received from the blessed Apostle Peter, that I signify to you; and I should not have written this, as deeming that these things are manifest unto all men, had not these proceedings so disturbed us."[28] St. Athanasius, by preserving this protest, has given it his sanction. Moreover, it is referred to by Socrates; and his account of it has the more force, because he happens to be incorrect in the details, and therefore did not borrow it from St. Athanasius: "Julius wrote back," he says, "that they acted against the Canons, because they had not called him to the Council, the Ecclesiastical Canon commanding that the Churches ought not to make Canons beside the will of the Bishop of Rome."[29] And Sozomen: "It was a sacerdotal law, to declare invalid whatever was transacted beside the will of the Bishop of the Romans."[30] On the other hand, the heretics themselves, whom St. Julius withstands, are obliged to acknowledge that Rome was "the School of the Apostles and the Metropolis of orthodoxy from the beginning"; and two of their leaders (Western bishops indeed) some years afterwards recanted their heresy before the Pope in terms of humble confession.

## 12.

Another Pope, St. Damasus, in his letter addressed to the Eastern bishops against Apollinaris (A.D. 382), calls those bishops his sons. "In that your charity pays the due reverence to the Apostolical See, ye profit yourselves the most, most honoured sons. For if, placed as we are in that Holy Church, in which the Holy Apostle sat and taught,

[28] Athan. Hist. Tracts. Oxf. tr. p. 56.
[29] Hist. ii. 17.
[30] Hist. iii. 10.

how it becometh us to direct the helm to which we have succeeded, we nevertheless confess ourselves unequal to that honour; yet do we therefore study as we may, if so be we may be able to attain to the glory of his blessedness."[31] "I speak," says St. Jerome to the same St. Damasus, "with the successor of the fisherman and the disciple of the Cross. I, following no one as my chief but Christ, am associated in communion with thy blessedness, that is, with the See of Peter. I know that on that rock the Church is built. Whosoever shall eat the Lamb outside this House is profane; if a man be not in the Ark of Noe, he shall perish when the flood comes in its power."[32] St. Basil entreats St. Damasus to send persons to arbitrate between the Churches of Asia Minor, or at least to make a report on the authors of their troubles, and name the party with which the Pope should hold communion. "We are in no wise asking anything new," he proceeds, "but what was customary with blessed and religious men of former times, and especially with yourself. For we know, by tradition of our fathers of whom we have inquired, and from the information of writings still preserved among us, that Dionysius, that most blessed Bishop, while he was eminent among you for orthodoxy and other virtues, sent letters of visitation to our Church at Cæsarea, and of consolation to our fathers, with ransomers of our brethren from captivity." In like manner, Ambrosiaster, a Pelagian in his doctrine, which here is not to the purpose, speaks of the "Church being God's house, whose ruler at this time is Damasus."[33]

### 13.

"We bear," says St. Siricius, another Pope (A.D. 385), "the burden of all who are laden; yea, rather the blessed Apostle Peter beareth them in us, who, as we trust, in all things protects and defends us the heirs of his government."[34] And he in turn is confirmed by St. Optatus. "You cannot deny your knowledge," says the latter to Parmenian, the Donatist, "that, in the city Rome, on Peter first hath an Episcopal See been conferred, in which Peter sat, the head of all the Apostles, . . . in which one See unity might be preserved by all, lest the other Apostles should support their respective Sees; in order that he might be at once a schismatic and a sinner, who against that one See (*singularem*) placed

[31] Theod. Hist. v. 10.
[32] Coustant, Epp. Pont. p. 546.
[33] In 1 Tim. iii. 14, 15.
[34] Coustant, p. 624.

a second. Therefore that one See (*unicam*), which is the first of the Church's prerogatives, Peter filled first; to whom succeeded Linus; to Linus, Clement; to Clement, etc., etc. . . . to Damasus, Siricius, who at this day is associated with us (*socius*), together with whom the whole world is in accordance with us, in the one bond of communion, by the intercourse of letters of peace."[35]

Another Pope: "Diligently and congruously do ye consult the *arcana* of the Apostolical dignity," says St. Innocent to the Council of Milevis (A.D. 417), "the dignity of him on whom, beside those things which are without, falls the care of all the Churches; following the form of the ancient rule, which you know, as well as I, has been preserved always by the whole world."[36] Here the Pope appeals, as it were, to the Rule of Vincentius; while St. Augustine bears witness that he did not outstep his prerogative, for, giving an account of this and another letter, he says, "He [the Pope] answered us as to all these matters as it was religious and becoming in the Bishop of the Apostolic See."[37]

Another Pope: "We have especial anxiety about all persons," says St. Celestine (A.D. 425), to the Illyrian bishops, "on whom, in the holy Apostle Peter, Christ conferred the necessity of making all men our care, when He gave him the Keys of opening and shutting." And St. Prosper, his contemporary, confirms him, when he calls Rome "the seat of Peter, which, being made to the world the head of pastoral honour, possesses by religion what it does not possess by arms"; and Vincent of Lerins, when he calls the Pope "the head of the world."[38]

## 14.

Another Pope: "Blessed Peter," says St. Leo (A.D. 440), "hath not deserted the helm of the Church which he had assumed . . . His power lives and his authority is pre-eminent in his See."[39] "That immoveableness, which, from the Rock Christ, he, when made a rock, received, has been communicated also to his heirs."[40] And as St. Athanasius and the Eusebians, by their contemporary testimonies, confirm St. Julius; and St. Jerome, St. Basil; and Ambrosiaster, St. Damasus; and St.

[35] Hist. ii. 3.
[36] Coustant, pp. 896, 1064.
[37] Ep. 186, 2.
[38] De Ingrat. 2. Common. 41.
[39] Serm. De Natal. iii. 3.
[40] Ibid. v. 4.

Optatus, St. Siricius; and St. Augustine, St. Innocent; and St. Prosper and St. Vincent, St. Celestine; so do St. Peter Chrysologus, and the Council of Chalcedon confirm St. Leo. "Blessed Peter," says Chrysologus, "who lives and presides in his own See, supplies truth of faith to those who seek it."[41] And the Ecumenical Council of Chalcedon, addressing St. Leo respecting Dioscorus, Bishop of Alexandria: "He extends his madness even against him to whom the custody of the vineyard has been committed by the Saviour, that is, against thy Apostolical holiness."[42] But the instance of St. Leo will occur again in a later chapter.

## 15.

The acts of the fourth century speak as strongly as its words. We may content ourselves here with Barrow's admissions:

"The Pope's power," he says, "was much amplified by the importunity of persons condemned or extruded from their places, whether upon just accounts, or wrongfully, and by faction; for they, finding no other more hopeful place of refuge and redress, did often apply to him: for what will not men do, whither will not they go in straits? Thus did Marcion go to Rome, and sue for admission to communion there. So Fortunatus and Felicissimus in St. Cyprian, being condemned in Afric, did fly to Rome for shelter; of which absurdity St. Cyprian doth so complain. So likewise Martianus and Basilides in St. Cyprian, being outed of their Sees for having lapsed from the Christian profession, did fly to Stephen for succour, to be restored. So Maximus, the Cynic, went to Rome, to get a confirmation of his election at Constantinople. So Marcellus, being rejected for heterodoxy, went thither to get attestation to his orthodoxy, of which St. Basil complaineth. So Apiarus, being condemned in Afric for his crimes, did appeal to Rome. And, on the other side, Athanasius being with great partiality condemned by the Synod of Tyre; Paulus and other bishops being extruded from their sees for orthodoxy; St. Chrysostom being condemned and expelled by Theophilus and his complices; Flavianus being deposed by Dioscorus and the Ephesine synod; Theodoret being condemned by the same; did cry out for help to Rome. Chelidonius, Bishop of Besançon, being deposed by Hilarius of Arles for crime, did fly to Pope Leo."

Again: "Our adversaries do oppose some instances of popes med-

---

[41] Ep. ad Eutych. fin.
[42] Concil. Hard. t. ii. p. 656.

dling in the constitution of bishops; as, Pope Leo I. saith, that Anatolius did 'by the favour of his assent obtain the bishopric of Constantinople.' The same Pope is alleged as having confirmed Maximus of Antioch. The same doth write to the Bishop of Thessalonica, his vicar, that he should 'confirm the elections of bishops by his authority.' He also confirmed Donatus, an African bishop: 'We will that Donatus preside over the Lord's flock, upon condition that he remember to send us an account of his faith.' . . . Pope Damasus did confirm the ordination of Peter Alexandrinus."

### 16.

And again: "The Popes indeed in the fourth century began to practise a fine trick, very serviceable to the enlargement of their power; which was to confer on certain bishops, as occasion served, or for continuance, the title of their vicar or lieutenant, thereby pretending to impart authority to them; whereby they were enabled for performance of divers things, which otherwise by their own episcopal or metropolitical power they could not perform. By which device they did engage such bishops to such a dependence on them, whereby they did promote the papal authority in provinces, to the oppression of the ancient rights and liberties of bishops and synods, doing what they pleased under pretence of this vast power communicated to them; and for fear of being displaced, or out of affection to their favourer, doing what might serve to advance the papacy. Thus did Pope Celestine constitute Cyril in his room. Pope Leo appointed Anatolius of Constantinople; Pope Felix, Acacius of Constantinople. . . . Pope Simplicius to Zeno, Bishop of Seville: 'We thought it convenient that you should be held up by the vicariat authority of our see.' So did Siricius and his successors constitute the bishops of Thessalonica to be their vicars in the diocese of Illyricum, wherein being then a member of the western empire they had caught a special jurisdiction; to which Pope Leo did refer in those words, which sometimes are impertinently alleged with reference to all bishops, but concern only Anastasius, Bishop of Thessalonica: 'We have entrusted thy charity to be in our stead; so that thou art called into part of the solicitude, not into plenitude of the authority.' So did Pope Zosimus bestow a like pretence of vicarious power upon the Bishop of Arles, which city was the seat of the temporal exarch in Gaul."[43]

[43] Barrow on the Supremacy, ed. 1836, pp. 263, 331, 384.

## 17.

More ample testimony for the Papal supremacy, as now professed by Roman Catholics, is scarcely necessary than what is contained in these passages; the simple question is, whether the clear light of the fourth and fifth centuries may be fairly taken to interpret to us the dim, though definite, outlines traced in the preceding.

# PART II

*Doctrinal Developments Viewed Relatively to Doctrinal Corruptions*

# CHAPTER V

# GENUINE DEVELOPMENTS
# CONTRASTED WITH CORRUPTIONS

I have been engaged in drawing out the positive and direct argument in proof of the intimate connexion, or rather oneness, with primitive Apostolic teaching, of the body of doctrine known at this day by the name of Catholic, and professed substantially both by Eastern and Western Christendom. That faith is undeniably the historical continuation of the religious system, which bore the name of Catholic in the eighteenth century, in the seventeenth, in the sixteenth, and so back in every preceding century, till we arrive at the first—undeniably the successor, the representative, the heir of the religion of Cyprian, Basil, Ambrose, and Augustine. The only question that can be raised is whether the said Catholic faith, as now held, is logically, as well as historically, the representative of the ancient faith. This then is the subject, to which I have as yet addressed myself, and I have maintained that modern Catholicism is nothing else but simply the legitimate growth and complement, that is, the natural and necessary development, of the doctrine of the early church, and that its divine authority is included in the divinity of Christianity.

### 2.

So far I have gone, but an important objection presents itself for distinct consideration. It may be said in answer to me that it is not enough that a certain large system of doctrine, such as that which goes by the name of Catholic, should admit of being referred to beliefs, opinions, and usages which prevailed among the first Christians, in order to my having a logical right to include a reception of the later teaching in the reception of the earlier; that an intellectual development may be in one sense natural, and yet untrue to its original, as diseases come of nature, yet are the destruction, or rather the negation of health; that the causes which stimulate the growth of ideas may also disturb and deform them; and that Christianity might indeed have been intended by its Divine Author for a wide expansion of the ideas proper to it, and yet this great benefit hindered by the evil birth of cognate errors which acted as its counterfeit; in a word, that what I have called developments in the Roman Church are nothing more or less than what used to be called her corruptions; and that new names do not destroy old grievances.

This is what may be said, and I acknowledge its force: it becomes necessary in consequence to assign certain characteristics of faithful developments, which none but faithful developments have, and the presence of which serves as a test to discriminate between them and corruptions. This I at once proceed to do, and I shall begin by determining what a corruption is, and why it cannot rightly be called, and how it differs from, a development.

## 3.

To find then what a corruption or perversion of the truth is, let us inquire what the word means, when used literally of material substances. Now it is plain, first of all, that a corruption is a word attaching to organized matters only; a stone may be crushed to powder, but it cannot be corrupted. Corruption, on the contrary, is the breaking up of life preparatory to its termination. This resolution of a body into its component parts is the stage before its dissolution; it begins when life has reached its perfection, and it is the sequel, or rather the continuation, of that process towards perfection, being at the same time the reversal and undoing of what went before. Till this point of regression is reached, the body has a function of its own, and a direction and aim in its action, and a nature with laws; these it is now losing, and the traits and tokens of former years; and with them its vigour and powers of nutrition, of assimilation, and of self-reparation.

## 4.

Taking this analogy as a guide, I venture to set down seven Notes of varying cogency, independence, and applicability, to discriminate healthy developments of an idea from its state of corruption and decay, as follows: There is no corruption if it retains one and the same type, the same principles, the same organization; if its beginnings anticipate its subsequent phases, and its later phenomena protect and subserve its earlier; if it has a power of assimilation and revival, and a vigorous action from first to last. On these tests I shall now enlarge, nearly in the order in which I have enumerated them.

## SECTION I

### FIRST NOTE OF A GENUINE DEVELOPMENT:
### PRESERVATION OF TYPE

This is readily suggested by the analogy of physical growth, which is such that the parts and proportions of the developed form, however altered, correspond to those which belong to its rudiments. The adult animal has the same make as it had on its birth; young birds do not grow into fishes, nor does the child degenerate into the brute, wild or domestic, of which he is by inheritance lord. Vincentius of Lerins adopts this illustration in distinct reference to Christian doctrine. "Let the soul's religion," he says, "imitate the law of the body, which, as years go on, develops indeed and opens out its due proportions, and yet remains identically what it was. Small are a baby's limbs, a youth's are larger, yet they are the same."[1]

### 2.

In like manner every calling or office has its own type, which those who fill it are bound to maintain; and to deviate from the type in any material point is to relinquish the calling. Thus both Chaucer and Goldsmith have drawn pictures of a true parish priest; these differ in details, but on the whole they agree together, and are one in such sense, that sensuality, or ambition, must be considered a forfeiture of that high title. Those magistrates, again, are called "corrupt" who are guided in their judgments by love of lucre or respect of persons, for the administration of justice is their essential function. Thus collegiate or monastic bodies lose their claim to their endowments or their buildings, as being relaxed and degenerate, if they neglect their statutes or their Rule. Thus, too, in political history, a mayor of the palace, such as he became in the person of Pepin, was no faithful development of the office he filled as originally intended and established.

[1] Commonit. 29.

### 3.

In like manner, it has been argued by a late writer, whether fairly or not does not interfere with the illustration, that the miraculous vision and dream of the Labarum could not have really taken place, as reported by Eusebius, because it is counter to the original type of Christianity. "For the first time," he says, on occasion of Constantine's introduction of the standard into his armies, "the meek and peaceful Jesus became a God of battle, and the Cross, the holy sign of Christian Redemption, a banner of bloody strife. . . . This was the first advance to the military Christianity of the Middle Ages, a modification of the pure religion of the Gospel, if directly opposed to its genuine principles, still apparently indispensable to the social progress of men."[2]

On the other hand, a popular leader may go through a variety of professions, he may court parties and break with them, he may contradict himself in words, and undo his own measures, yet there may be a steady fulfilment of certain objects, or adherence to certain plain doctrines, which gives a unity to his career, and impresses on beholders an image of directness and large consistency which shows a fidelity to his type from first to last.

### 4.

However, as the last instances suggest to us, this unity of type, characteristic as it is of faithful developments, must not be pressed to the extent of denying all variation, nay, considerable alteration of proportion and relation, as time goes on, in the parts or aspects of an idea. Great changes in outward appearance and internal harmony occur in the instance of the animal creation itself. The fledged bird differs much from its rudimental form in the egg. The butterfly is the development, but not in any sense the image, of the grub. The whale claims a place among mammalia, though we might fancy that, as in the child's game of catscradle, some strange introsusception had been permitted, to make it so like, yet so contrary, to the animals with which it is itself classed. And, in like manner, if beasts of prey were once in paradise, and fed upon grass, they must have presented bodily phenomena very different from the structure of muscles, claws, teeth, and viscera which now fit them for a carnivorous existence. Eutychius, Patriarch of Constantinople, on his death-bed, grasped his own hand

[2] Milman, Christ.

and said, "I confess that in this flesh we shall all rise again"; yet flesh and blood cannot inherit the kingdom of God, and a glorified body has attributes incompatible with its present condition on earth.

### 5.

More subtle still and mysterious are the variations which are consistent or not inconsistent with identity in political and religious developments. The Catholic doctrine of the Holy Trinity has ever been accused by heretics of interfering with that of the Divine Unity out of which it grew, and even believers will at first sight consider that it tends to obscure it. Yet Petavius says, "I will affirm, what perhaps will surprise the reader, that that distinction of Persons which, in regard to *proprietates* is in reality most great, is so far from disparaging the Unity and Simplicity of God that this very real distinction especially avails for the doctrine that God is One and most Simple."[3]

Again, Arius asserted that the Second Person of the Blessed Trinity was not able to comprehend the First, whereas Eunomius's characteristic tenet was in an opposite direction, viz., that not only the Son, but that all men could comprehend God; yet no one can doubt that Eunomianism was a true development, not a corruption of Arianism.

The same man may run through various philosophies or beliefs which are in themselves irreconcilable without inconsistency, since in him they may be nothing more than accidental instruments or expressions of what he is inwardly from first to last. The political doctrines of the modern Tory resemble those of the primitive Whig; yet few will deny that the Whig and Tory characters have each a discriminating type. Calvinism has changed into Unitarianism: yet this need not be called a corruption, even if it be not, strictly speaking, a development; for Harding, in controversy with Jewell, surmised the coming change three centuries since, and it has occurred not in one country but in many.

### 6.

The history of national character supplies an analogy, rather than an instance strictly in point; yet there is so close a connexion between the development of minds and of ideas that it is allowable to refer to it here. Thus we find England of old the most loyal supporter, and

---

[3] De Deo, ii. 4, § 8.

England of late the most jealous enemy, of the Holy See. As great a change is exhibited in France, once the eldest born of the Church and the flower of her knighthood, now democratic and lately infidel. Yet, in neither nation, can these great changes be well called corruptions.

Or again, let us reflect on the ethical vicissitudes of the chosen people. How different is their grovelling and cowardly temper on leaving Egypt from the chivalrous spirit, as it may be called, of the age of David or, again, from the bloody fanaticism which braved Titus and Hadrian! In what contrast is that impotence of mind which gave way at once, and bowed the knee, at the very sight of a pagan idol, with the stern iconoclasm and bigoted nationality of later Judaism! How startling the apparent absence of what would be called talent in this people during their supernatural Dispensation, compared with the gifts of mind which various witness assign to them now!

### 7.

And, in like manner, ideas may remain, when the expression of them is indefinitely varied; and we cannot determine whether a professed development is truly such or not, without some further knowledge than an experience of the mere fact of this variation. Nor will our instinctive feelings serve as a criterion. It must have been an extreme shock to St. Peter to be told he must slay and eat beasts, unclean as well as clean, though such a command was implied already in that faith which he held and taught; a shock, which a single effort, or a short period, or the force of reason would not suffice to overcome. Nay, it may happen that a representation which varies from its original may be felt as more true and faithful than one which has more pretensions to be exact. So it is with many a portrait which is not striking: at first look, of course, it disappoints us; but when we are familiar with it, we see in it what we could not see at first, and prefer it, not to a perfect likeness, but to many a sketch which is so precise as to be a caricature.

### 8.

On the other hand, real perversions and corruptions are often not so unlike externally to the doctrine from which they come as are changes which are consistent with it and true developments. When Rome changed from a republic to an empire, it was a real alteration of polity, or what may be called a corruption; yet in appearance the

change was small. The old offices or functions of government remained: it was only that the Imperator, or Commander in Chief,
concentrated them in his own person. Augustus was Consul and Tribune, Supreme Pontiff and Censor, and the Imperial rule was, in the
words of Gibbon, "an absolute monarchy disguised by the forms of a
commonwealth." On the other hand, when the dissimulation of Augustus was exchanged for the ostentation of Diocletian, the real alteration of constitution was trivial, but the appearance of change was
great. Instead of plain Consul, Censor, and Tribune, Diocletian became
Dominus or King, assumed the diadem, and threw around him the
forms of a court.

Nay, one cause of corruption in religion is the refusal to follow the
course of doctrine as it moves on, and an obstinacy in the notions of
the past. Certainly: as we see conspicuously in the history of the chosen
race. The Samaritans who refused to add the Prophets to the Law, and
the Sadducees who denied a truth which was covertly taught in the
Book of Exodus, were in appearance only faithful adherents to the
primitive doctrine. Our Lord found His people precisians in their
obedience to the letter; He condemned them for not being led on to
its spirit, that is, to its developments. The Gospel is the development
of the Law; yet what difference seems wider than that which separates
the unbending rule of Moses from the "grace and truth" which "came
by Jesus Christ?" Samuel had of old time fancied that the tall Eliab
was the Lord's anointed; and Jesse had thought David only fit for the
sheepcote; and when the Great King came, He was "as a root out of
a dry ground"; but strength came out of weakness, and out of the
strong sweetness.

So it is in the case of our friends; the most obsequious are not always
the truest, and seeming cruelty is often genuine affection. We know
the conduct of the three daughters in the drama towards the old king.
She who had found her love "more richer than her tongue," and could
not "heave her heart into her mouth," was in the event alone true to
her father.

## 9.

An idea then does not always bear about it the same external image;
this circumstance, however, has no force to weaken the argument for
its substantial identity, as drawn from its external sameness, when
such sameness remains. On the contrary, for that very reason, *unity
of type* becomes so much the surer guarantee of the healthiness and

soundness of developments, when it is persistently preserved in spite of their number or importance.


## SECTION II

### SECOND NOTE: CONTINUITY OF PRINCIPLES

As in mathematical creations figures are formed on distinct formulæ, which are the laws under which they are developed, so it is in ethical and political subjects. Doctrines expand variously according to the mind, individual or social, into which they are received; and the peculiarities of the recipient are the regulating power, the law, the organization, or, as it may be called, the form of the development. The life of doctrines may be said to consist in the law or principle which they embody.

Principles are abstract and general, doctrines relate to facts; doctrines develop, and principles at first sight do not; doctrines grow and are enlarged, principles are permanent; doctrines are intellectual, and principles are more immediately ethical and practical. Systems live in principles and represent doctrines. Personal responsibility is a principle, the Being of a God is a doctrine; from that doctrine all theology has come in due course, whereas that principle is not clearer under the Gospel than in paradise, and depends, not on belief in an Almighty Governor, but on conscience.

Yet the difference between the two sometimes merely exists in our mode of viewing them; and what is a doctrine in one philosophy is a principle in another. Personal responsibility may be made a doctrinal basis, and develop into Arminianism or Pelagianism. Again, it may be discussed whether infallibility is a principle or a doctrine of the Church of Rome, and dogmatism a principle or doctrine of Christianity. Again, consideration for the poor is a doctrine of the Church considered as a religious body, and a principle when she is viewed as a political power.

Doctrines stand to principles, as the definitions to the axioms and postulates of mathematics. Thus the fifteenth and seventeenth propositions of Euclid's Book I. are developments, not of the three first axioms, which are required in the proof, but of the definition of a right angle. Perhaps the perplexity, which arises in the mind of a beginner, on learning the early propositions of the second book, arises from these being more prominently exemplifications of axioms than developments of definitions. He looks for developments from the definition of the rectangle, and finds but various particular cases of the general truth, that "the whole is equal to its parts."

## 2.

It might be expected that the Catholic principles would be later in development than the Catholic doctrines, inasmuch as they lie deeper in the mind, and are assumptions rather than objective professions. This has been the case. The Protestant controversy has mainly turned, or is turning, on one or other of the principles of Catholicity; and to this day the rule of Scripture interpretation, the doctrine of Inspiration, the relation of faith to reason, moral responsibility, private judgment, inherent grace, the seat of infallibility, remain, I suppose, more or less undeveloped, or, at least, undefined, by the Church.

Doctrines stand to principles, if it may be said without fancifulness, as fecundity viewed relatively to generation, though this analogy must not be strained. Doctrines are developed by the operation of principles, and develop variously according to those principles. Thus a belief in the transitiveness of worldly goods leads the Epicurean to enjoyment, and the ascetic to mortification; and, from their common doctrine of the sinfulness of matter, the Alexandrian Gnostics became sensualists, and the Syrian devotees. The same philosophical elements, received into a certain sensibility or insensibility to sin and its consequences, leads one mind to the Church of Rome; another to what, for want of a better word, may be called Germanism.

Again, religious investigation sometimes is conducted on the principle that it is a duty "to follow and speak the truth," which really means that it is no duty to fear error, or to consider what is safest, or to shrink from scattering doubts, or to regard the responsibility of misleading; and thus it terminates in heresy or infidelity, without any blame to religious investigation in itself.

Again, to take a different subject, what constitutes a chief interest of dramatic compositions and tales, is to use external circumstances, which may be considered their law of development, as a means of bringing out into different shapes, and showing under new aspects, the personal peculiarities of character, according as either those circumstances or those peculiarities vary in the case of the personages introduced.

## 3.

Principles are popularly said to develop when they are but exemplified; thus the various sects of Protestantism, unconnected as they are with each other, are called developments of the principle of private judgment, of which really they are but applications and results.

A development, to be faithful, must retain both the doctrine and the principle with which it started. Doctrine without its correspondent principle remains barren, if not lifeless, of which the Greek Church seems an instance; or it forms those hollow professions which are familiarly called "shams," as a zeal for an established Church and its creed on merely conservative or temporal motives. Such, too, was the Roman Constitution between the reigns of Augustus and Diocletian.

On the other hand, principle without its corresponding doctrine may be considered as the state of religious minds in the heathen world, viewed relatively to Revelation; that is, of the "children of God who are scattered abroad."

Pagans may have, heretics cannot have, the same principles as Catholics; if the latter have the same, they are not real heretics, but in ignorance. Principle is a better test of heresy than doctrine. Heretics are true to their principles, but change to and fro, backwards and forwards, in opinion; for very opposite doctrines may be exemplifications of the same principle. Thus the Antiochenes and other heretics sometimes were Arians, sometimes Sabellians, sometimes Nestorians, sometimes Monophysites, as if at random, from fidelity to their common principle, that there is no mystery in theology. Thus Calvinists become Unitarians from the principle of private judgment. The doctrines of heresy are accidents and soon run to an end; its principles are everlasting.

This, too, is often the solution of the paradox, "Extremes meet," and of the startling reactions which take place in individuals; viz., the presence of some one principle or condition, which is dominant in their minds from first to last. If one of two contradictory alternatives be necessarily true on a certain hypothesis, then the denial of the one leads, by mere logical consistency and without direct reasons, to a reception of the other. Thus the question between the Church of Rome and Protestantism falls in some minds into the proposition, "Rome is either the pillar and ground of the Truth or she is Anti-christ"; in proportion, then, as they revolt from considering her the latter are they compelled to receive her as the former. Hence, too, men may pass from infidelity to Rome, and from Rome to infidelity, from a conviction in both courses that there is no tangible intellectual position between the two.

Protestantism, viewed in its more Catholic aspect, is doctrine without active principle; viewed in its heretical, it is active principle without doctrine. Many of its speakers, for instance, use eloquent and glowing language about the Church and its characteristics; some of them do not realize what they say, but use high words and general statements about "the faith," and "primitive truth," and "schism," and "heresy," to which they attach no definite meaning; while others speak of "unity," "universality," and "Catholicity," and use the words in their own sense and for their own ideas.

### 4.

The science of grammar affords another instance of the existence of special laws in the formation of systems. Some languages have more elasticity than others, and greater capabilities; and the difficulty of explaining the fact cannot lead us to doubt it. There are languages, for instance, which have a capacity for compound words, which, we cannot tell why, is in matter of fact denied to others. We feel the presence of a certain character or genius in each, which determines its path and its range; and to discover and enter into it is one part of refined scholarship. And when particular writers, in consequence perhaps of some theory, tax a language beyond its powers, the failure is conspicuous. Very subtle, too, and difficult to draw out, are the principles on which depends the formation of proper names in a particular people. In works of fiction, names or titles, significant or ludicrous, must be invented for the characters introduced; and some authors excel in their fabrication, while others are equally unfortunate. Foreign novels, perhaps, attempt to frame English surnames, and signally fail; yet what every one feels to be the case, no one can analyze: that is, our surnames are constructed on a law which is only exhibited in particular instances, and which rules their formation on certain, though subtle, determinations.

And so in philosophy, the systems of physics or morals, which go by celebrated names, proceed upon the assumption of certain conditions which are necessary for every stage of their development. The Newtonian theory of gravitation is based on certain axioms; for instance, that the fewest causes assignable for phenomena are the true ones: and the application of science to practical purposes depends upon the hypothesis that what happens today will happen tomorrow.

And so in military matters, the discovery of gunpowder developed the science of attack and defence in a new instrumentality. Again, it is said that when Napoleon began his career of victories, the enemy's generals pronounced that his battles were fought against rule, and that he ought not to be victorious.

### 5.

So states have their respective policies, on which they move forward, and which are the conditions of their well-being. Thus it is sometimes said that the true policy of the American Union, or the law of its prosperity, is not the enlargement of its territory but the cultivation of its internal resources. Thus Russia is said to be weak in attack, strong in defence, and to grow, not by the sword, but by diplomacy. Thus Islamism is said to be the form or life of the Ottoman, and Protestant-ism of the British Empire, and the admission of European ideas into the one, or of Catholic ideas into the other, to be the destruction of the respective conditions of their power. Thus Augustus and Tiberius governed by dissimulation; thus Pericles in his "Funeral Oration" draws out the principles of the Athenian commonwealth, viz., that it is carried on not by formal and severe enactments but by the ethical character and spontaneous energy of the people.

The political principles of Christianity, if it be right to use such words of a divine polity, are laid down for us in the Sermon on the Mount. Contrariwise to other empires, Christians conquer by yielding; they gain influence by shrinking from it; they possess the earth by renouncing it. Gibbon speaks of "the vices of the clergy" as being "to a philosophic eye far less dangerous than their virtues."[4]

Again, as to Judaism, it may be asked on what law it developed; that is, whether Mahometanism may not be considered as a sort of Judaism, as formed by the presence of a different class of influences. In this contrast between them, perhaps it may be said that the expecta-tion of a Messiah was the principle or law which expanded the ele-ments, almost common to Judaism with Mahometanism, into their respective characteristic shapes.

One of the points of discipline to which Wesley attached most importance was that of preaching early in the morning. This was his principle. In Georgia, he began preaching at five o'clock every day, winter and summer. "Early preaching," he said, "is the glory of the

[4] ch. xlix.

Methodists; whenever this is dropt, they will dwindle away into nothing, they have lost their first love, they are a fallen people."


### 6.

Now, these instances show, as has been incidentally observed of
some of them, that the destruction of the special laws or principles of
a development is its corruption. Thus, as to nations, when we talk of
the spirit of a people being lost, we do not mean that this or that act
has been committed, or measure carried, but that certain lines of
thought or conduct by which it has grown great are abandoned. Thus
the Roman poets consider their state in course of ruin because its *prisci
mores* and *pietas* were failing. And so we speak of countries or persons
as being in a false position, when they take up a course of policy, or
assume a profession, inconsistent with their natural interests or real
character. Judaism, again, was rejected when it rejected the Messiah.

Thus the *continuity* or *the alteration of the principles* on which an
idea has developed is a second mark of discrimination between a true
development and a corruption.


## SECTION III

### THIRD NOTE: POWER OF ASSIMILATION

In the physical world, whatever has life is characterized by growth,
so that in no respect to grow is to cease to live. It grows by taking into
its own substance external materials; and this absorption or assimilation is completed when the materials appropriated come to belong to
it or enter into its unity. Two things cannot become one, except there
be a power of assimilation in one or the other. Sometimes assimilation
is effected only with an effort; it is possible to die of repletion, and
there are animals who lie torpid for a time under the contest between
the foreign substance and the assimilating power. And different food
is proper for different recipients.

This analogy may be taken to illustrate certain peculiarities in the
growth or development in ideas, which were noticed in the first chapter. It is otherwise with mathematical and other abstract creations,
which, like the soul itself, are solitary and self-dependent; but doctrines
and views which relate to man are not placed in a void, but in the

crowded world, and make way for themselves by interpenetration, and develop by absorption. Facts and opinions, which have hitherto been regarded in other relations and grouped round other centres, henceforth are gradually attracted to a new influence and subjected to a new sovereign. They are modified, laid down afresh, thrust aside, as the case may be. A new element of order and composition has come among them; and its life is proved by this capacity of expansion, without disarrangement or dissolution. An eclectic, conservative, assimilating, healing, moulding process, a unitive power, is of the essence, and a third test, of a faithful development.

## 2.

Thus, a power of development is a proof of life, not only in its essay, but especially in its success; for a mere formula either does not expand or is shattered in expanding. A living idea becomes many, yet remains one.

The attempt at development shows the presence of a principle, and its success the presence of an idea. Principles stimulate thought, and an idea concentrates it.

The idea never was that throve and lasted, yet, like mathematical truth, incorporated nothing from external sources. So far from the fact of such incorporation implying corruption, as is sometimes supposed, development is a process of incorporation. Mahometanism may be in external developments scarcely more than a compound of other theologies, yet no one would deny that there has been a living idea somewhere in a religion which has been so strong, so wide, so lasting a bond of union in the history of the world. Why it has not continued to develop after its first preaching, if this be the case, as it seems to be, cannot be determined without a greater knowledge of that religion, and how far it is merely political, how far theological, than we commonly possess.

## 3.

In Christianity, opinion, while a raw material, is called philosophy or scholasticism; when a rejected refuse, it is called heresy.

Ideas are more open to an external bias in their commencement than afterwards; hence the great majority of writers who consider the medieval Church corrupt trace its corruption to the first four centuries, not to what are called the Dark Ages.

That an idea more readily coalesces with these ideas than with those does not show that it has been unduly influenced, that is, corrupted by them, but that it has an antecedent affinity to them. At least it shall be assumed here that, when the Gospels speak of virtue going out of our Lord, and of His healing with the clay which His lips had moistened, they afford instances not of a perversion of Christianity, but of affinity to notions which were external to it; and that St. Paul was not biassed by Orientalism, though he said, after the manner of some Eastern sects, that it was "excellent not to touch a woman."

### 4.

Thus in politics, too, ideas are sometimes proposed, discussed, rejected, or adopted, as it may happen, and sometimes they are shown to be unmeaning and impossible; sometimes they are true, but partially so, or in subordination to other ideas, with which, in consequence, they are as wholes or in part incorporated, as far as these have affinities to them, the power to incorporate being thus recognized as a property of life. Mr. Bentham's system was an attempt to make the circle of legal and moral truths developments of certain principles of his own; those principles of his may, if it so happen, prove unequal to the weight of truths which are eternal, and the system founded on them may break into pieces; or again, a state may absorb certain of them, for which it has affinity, that is, it may develop in Benthamism, yet remain in substance what it was before. In the history of the French Revolution we read of many middle parties, who attempted to form theories of constitutions short of those which they would call extreme, and successively failed from the want of power or reality in their characteristic ideas. The Semi-Arians attempted a middle way between orthodoxy and heresy, but could not stand their ground; at length part fell into Macedonianism, and part joined the Church.

### 5.

The stronger and more living is an idea, that is, the more powerful hold it exercises on the minds of men, the more able is it to dispense with safeguards, and trust to itself against the danger of corruption. As strong frames exult in their agility, and healthy constitutions throw off ailments, so parties or schools that live can afford to be rash, and will sometimes be betrayed into extravagances, yet are brought right by their inherent vigour. On the other hand, unreal systems are commonly decent externally. Forms, subscriptions, or articles of religion are indispensable when the principle of life is weakly. Thus Presbyterianism has maintained its original theology in Scotland where legal subscriptions are enforced, while it has run into Arianism or Unitarianism where that protection is away. We have yet to see whether the Free Kirk can keep its present theological ground. The Church of Rome can consult expedience more freely than other bodies, as trusting to her living tradition, and is sometimes thought to disregard principle and scruple, when she is but dispensing with forms. Thus Saints are often characterized by acts which are no pattern for others; and the most gifted men are, by reason of their very gifts, sometimes led into fatal inadvertences. Hence vows are the wise defence of unstable virtue, and general rules the refuge of feeble authority.

And so much may suffice on the *unitive power* of faithful developments, which constitutes their third characteristic.

## SECTION IV

### FOURTH NOTE: LOGICAL SEQUENCE

Logic is the organization of thought, and, as being such, is a security for the faithfulness of intellectual developments; and the necessity of using it is undeniable as far as this, that its rules must not be transgressed. That it is not brought into exercise in every instance of doctrinal development is owing to the varieties of mental constitution, whether in communities or in individuals, with whom great truths or seeming truths are lodged. The question indeed may be asked whether a development can be other in any case than a logical operation; but, if by this is meant a conscious reasoning from premises to conclusion, of course the answer must be in the negative. An idea under one or other of its aspects grows in the mind by remaining there; it becomes familiar and distinct, and is viewed in its relations; it leads to other aspects, and these again to others, subtle, recondite, original, according to the character, intellectual and moral, of the recipient; and thus a body of thought is gradually formed without his recognizing what is going on within him. And all this while, or at least from time to time, external circumstances elicit into formal statement the thoughts which are coming into being in the depths of his mind; and soon he has to begin to defend them; and then again a further process must take place, of analyzing his statements and ascertaining their dependence one on another. And thus he is led to regard as consequences, and to trace to principles, what hitherto he has discerned by a moral perception, and adopted on sympathy; and logic is brought in to arrange and inculcate what no science was employed in gaining.

And so in the same way, such intellectual processes, as are carried on silently and spontaneously in the mind of a party or school, of necessity come to light at a later date, and are recognized, and their issues are scientifically arranged. And then logic has the further function of propagation; analogy, the nature of the case, antecedent probability, application of principles, congruity, expedience being some of the methods of proof by which the development is continued from mind to mind and established in the faith of the community.

Yet even then the analysis is not made on a principle, or with any view to its whole course and finished results. Each argument is brought for an immediate purpose; minds develop step by step, without looking behind them or anticipating their goal, and without either intention or promise of forming a system. Afterwards, however, this logical character which the whole wears becomes a test that the process has been a true development, not a perversion or corruption, from its evident naturalness; and in some cases from the gravity, distinctness, precision, and majesty of its advance, and the harmony of its proportions, like the tall growth, and graceful branching, and rich foliage, of some vegetable production.

## 2.

The process of development, thus capable of a logical expression, has sometimes been invidiously spoken of as rationalism and contrasted with faith. But, though a particular doctrine or opinion which is subjected to development may happen to be rationalistic, and, as is the original, such are its results: and though we may develop erroneously, that is, reason incorrectly, yet the developing itself as little deserves that imputation in any case, as an inquiry into an historical fact, which we do not thereby make but ascertain—for instance, whether or not St. Mark wrote his Gospel with St. Matthew before him, or whether Solomon brought his merchandise from Tartessus or some Indian port. Rationalism is the exercise of reason instead of faith in matters of faith; but one does not see how it can be faith to adopt the premises, and unbelief to accept the conclusion.

At the same time it may be granted that the spontaneous process which goes on within the mind itself is higher and choicer than that which is logical; for the latter, being scientific, is common property, and can be taken and made use of by minds who are personally strangers, in any true sense, both to the ideas in question and to their development.

### 3.

Thus, the holy Apostles would without words know all the truths concerning the high doctrines of theology, which controversialists after them have piously and charitably reduced to formulae, and developed through argument. Thus, St. Justin or St. Irenæus might be without any digested ideas of Purgatory or Original Sin, yet have an intense feeling, which they had not defined or located, both of the fault of our first nature and the responsibilities of our nature regenerate. Thus St. Antony said to the philosophers who came to mock him, "He whose mind is in health does not need letters"; and St. Ignatius Loyola, while yet an unlearned neophyte, was favoured with transcendent perceptions of the Holy Trinity during his penance at Manresa. Thus St. Athanasius himself is more powerful in statement and exposition than in proof; while in Bellarmine we find the whole series of doctrines carefully drawn out, duly adjusted with one another, and exactly analyzed one by one.

The history of empires and of public men supplies so many instances of logical development in the field of politics, that it is needless to do more than to refer to one of them. It is illustrated by the words of Jeroboam, "Now shall this kingdom return to the house of David, if this people go up to do sacrifice in the house of the Lord at Jerusalem ... Wherefore the king took counsel and made two calves of gold, and said unto them, Behold thy gods, O Israel." Idolatry was a duty of kingcraft with the schismatical kingdom.

### 4.

A specimen of logical development is afforded us in the history of Lutheranism as it has of late years been drawn out by various English writers. Luther started on a double basis, his dogmatic principle being contradicted by his right of private judgment, and his sacramental by his theory of justification. The sacramental element never showed signs of life; but on his death, that which he represented in his own person as a teacher, the dogmatic, gained the ascendancy; and "every expression of his upon controverted points became a norm for the party, which, at all times the largest, was at last coextensive with the Church itself. This almost idolatrous veneration was perhaps increased by the selection of declarations of faith, of which the substance on the whole was his, for the symbolical books of his Church."[5] Next a reaction took place; private judgment was restored to the supremacy. Calixtus put reason, and Spener the so-called religion of the heart, in the place of dogmatic correctness. Pietism for the time died away; but rationalism developed in Wolf, who professed to prove all the orthodox doctrines, by a process of reasoning, from premises level with the reason. It was soon found that the instrument which Wolf had used for orthodoxy could as plausibly be used against it; in his hands it had proved the Creed; in the hands of Semler, Ernesti, and others, it disproved the authority of Scripture. What was religion to be made to consist in now? A sort of philosophical pietism followed; or rather Spener's pietism and the original theory of justification were analyzed more thoroughly, and issued in various theories of pantheism, which from the first was at the bottom of Luther's doctrine and personal character. And this appears to be the state of Lutheranism at present, whether we view it in the philosophy of Kant, in the open infidelity of Strauss, or in the religious professions of the new Evangelical Church of Prussia. Applying this instance to the subject which it has been here brought to illustrate, I should say that the equable and orderly march and natural succession of views, by which the creed of Luther has been changed into the infidel or heretical philosophy of his present representatives, is a proof that that change is no perversion or corruption, but a faithful development of the original idea.

## 5.

This is but one out of many instances with which the history of the Church supplies us. The fortunes of a theological school are made, in a later generation, the measure of the teaching of its founder. The great Origen after his many labours died in peace; his immediate pupils were Saints and rulers in the Church; he has the praise of St. Athanasius, St. Basil, and St. Gregory Nazianzen, and furnishes materials to St. Ambrose and St. Hilary; yet, as time proceeded, a definite heterodoxy was the growing result of his theology, and at length, three hundred years after his death, he was condemned, and, as has generally been

---

[5] Pusey on German Rationalism, p. 21, note.

considered, in an Ecumenical Council.[6] "Diodorus of Tarsus," says Tillemont, "died at an advanced age, in the peace of the Church, honoured by the praises of the greatest saints, and crowned with a glory, which, having ever attended him through life, followed him after his death";[7] yet St. Cyril of Alexandria considers him and Theodore of Mopsuestia the true authors of Nestorianism, and he was placed in the event by the Nestorians among their Saints. Theodore himself was condemned after his death by the same Council which is said to have condemned Origen, and is justly considered the chief rationalizing doctor of antiquity; yet he was in the highest repute in his day, and the Eastern Synod complains, as quoted by Facundus, that "Blessed Theodore, who died so happily, who was so eminent a teacher for five and forty years, and overthrew every heresy, and in his lifetime experienced no imputation from the orthodox, now after his death so long ago, after his many conflicts, after his ten thousand books composed in refutation of errors, after his approval in the sight of priests, emperors, and people, runs the risk of receiving the reward of heretics, and of being called their chief."[8] There is a certain continuous advance and determinate path which belong to the history of a doctrine, policy, or institution, and which impress upon the common sense of mankind, that what it ultimately becomes is the issue of what it was at first. This sentiment is expressed in the proverb, not limited to Latin, *Exitus acta probat*; and is sanctioned by Divine wisdom when, warning us against false prophets, it says, "Ye shall know them by their fruits."

A doctrine, then, professed in its mature years by a philosophy or religion is likely to be a true development, not a corruption, in proportion as it seems to be the *logical issue* of its original teaching.

## SECTION V

### FIFTH NOTE: ANTICIPATION OF ITS FUTURE

Since, when an idea is living, that is, influential and effective, it is sure to develop according to its own nature, and the tendencies, which

---

[6]Halloix, Valesius, Lequien, Gieseler, Döllinger, etc., say that he was condemned, not in the fifth Council, but in the Council under Mennas.

[7]Mem. Eccl. tom. viii. p. 562.

[8]Def. Tr. Cap. viii. init.

are carried out on the long run, may under favourable circumstances show themselves early as well as late, and logic is the same in all ages, instances of a development which is to come, though vague and isolated, may occur from the very first, though a lapse of time be necessary to bring them to perfection. And since developments are in great measure only aspects of the idea from which they proceed, and all of them are natural consequences of it, it is often a matter of accident in what order they are carried out in individual minds; and it is in no wise strange that here and there definite specimens of advanced teaching should very early occur, which in the historical course are not found till a late day. The fact, then, of such early or recurring intimations of tendencies which afterwards are fully realized is a sort of evidence that those later and more systematic fulfilments are only in accordance with the original idea.

## 2.

Nothing is more common, for instance, than accounts or legends of the anticipations, which great men have given in boyhood of the bent of their minds, as afterwards displayed in their history; so much so that the popular expectation has sometimes led to the invention of them. The child Cyrus mimics a despot's power, and St. Athanasius is elected bishop by his playfellows.

It is noticeable that in the eleventh century, when the Russians were but pirates upon the Black Sea, Constantinople was their aim; and that a prophecy was in circulation in that city that they should one day gain possession of it.

In the reign of James the First, we have an observable anticipation of the system of influence in the management of political parties, which was developed by Sir R. Walpole a century afterwards. This attempt is traced by a living writer to the ingenuity of Lord Bacon. "He submitted to the King that there were expedients for more judiciously managing a House of Commons; . . . that much might be done by forethought towards filling the House with well-affected persons, winning or blinding the lawyers . . . and drawing the chief constituent bodies of the assembly, the country gentlemen, the merchants, the courtiers, to act for the King's advantage; that it would be expedient to tender voluntarily certain graces and modifications of the King's prerogative," etc.[9] The writer adds, "This circumstance, like several others in the present

[9] Hallam's Const. Hist. ch. vi. p. 461.

reign, is curious, as it shows the rise of a systematic parliamentary influence, which was one day to become the mainspring of government."

### 3.

Arcesilas and Carneades, the founders of the later Academy, are known to have innovated on the Platonic doctrine by inculcating a universal scepticism; and they did this, as if on the authority of Socrates, who had adopted the method of *ironia* against the Sophists, on their professing to know everything. This, of course, was an insufficient plea. However, could it be shown that Socrates did on one or two occasions evidence deliberate doubts on the great principles of theism or morals, would any one deny that the innovation in question had grounds for being considered a true development, not a corruption?

It is certain that, in the idea of Monachism, prevalent in ancient times, manual labour had a more prominent place than study; so much so that De Rancé, the celebrated Abbot of La Trappe, in controversy with Mabillon, maintained his ground with great plausibility against the latter's apology for the literary occupations for which the Benedictines of France are so famous. Nor can it be denied that the labours of such as Mabillon and Montfaucon are at least a development upon the simplicity of the primitive institution. And yet it is remarkable that St. Pachomius, the first author of a monastic rule, enjoined a library in each of his houses, and appointed conferences and disputations three times a week on religious subjects, interpretation of Scripture, or points of theology. St. Basil, the founder of Monachism in Pontus, one of the most learned of the Greek Fathers, wrote his theological treatises in the intervals of agricultural labour. St. Jerome, the author of the Latin versions of Scripture, lived as a poor monk in a cell at Bethlehem. These, indeed, were but exceptions in the character of early Monachism; but they suggest its capabilities and anticipate its history. Literature is certainly not inconsistent with its idea.

### 4.

In the controversies with the Gnostics, in the second century, striking anticipations occasionally occur, in the works of their Catholic opponents, of the formal dogmatic teaching developed in the Church in the course of the Nestorian and Monophysite controversies in the fifth. On the other hand, Paul of Samosata, one of the first disciples of the

Syrian school of theology, taught a heresy sufficiently like Nestorianism, in which that school terminated, to be mistaken for it in later
times; yet for a long while after him the characteristic of the school
was Arianism, an opposite heresy.

Lutheranism has by this time become in most places almost simple
heresy or infidelity; it has terminated, if it has even yet reached its
limit, in a denial both of the Canon and the Creed, nay, of many
principles of morals. Accordingly the question arises, whether these
conclusions are in fairness to be connected with its original teaching
or are a corruption. And it is no little aid towards its resolution to find
that Luther himself at one time rejected the Apocalypse, called the
Epistle of St. James "*straminea*," condemned the word "Trinity," fell
into a kind of Eutychianism in his view of the Holy Eucharist, and in a
particular case sanctioned bigamy. Calvinism, again, in various distinct
countries, has become Socinianism, and Calvin himself seems to have
denied our Lord's Eternal Sonship and ridiculed the Nicene Creed.

Another evidence, then, of the faithfulness of an ultimate development is its *definite anticipation* at an early period in the history of the
idea to which it belongs.

## SECTION VI

### SIXTH NOTE: CONSERVATIVE ACTION UPON ITS PAST

As developments which are preceded by definite indications have a
fair presumption in their favour, so those which do but contradict and
reverse the course of doctrine which has been developed before them,
and out of which they spring, are certainly corrupt; for a corruption
is a development in that very stage in which it ceases to illustrate, and
begins to disturb, the acquisitions gained in its previous history.

It is the rule of creation, or rather of the phenomena which it
presents, that life passes on to its termination by a gradual, impercepti-
ble course of change. There is ever a maximum in earthly excellence,
and the operation of the same causes which made things great makes
them small again. Weakness is but the resulting product of power.
Events move in cycles; all things come round, "the sun ariseth and
goeth down, and hasteth to his place where he arose." Flowers first
bloom, and then fade; fruit ripens and decays. The fermenting process,
unless stopped at the due point, corrupts the liquor which it has cre-

ated. The grace of spring, the richness of autumn are but for a moment, and worldly moralists bid us *Carpe diem*, for we shall have no second opportunity. Virtue seems to lie in a mean, between vice and vice; and as it grew out of imperfection, so to grow into enormity. There is a limit to human knowledge, and both sacred and profane writers witness that overwisdom is folly. And in the political world states rise and fall, the instruments of their aggrandizement becoming the weapons of their destruction. And hence the frequent ethical maxims, such as, *Ne quid nimis, Medio tutissimus*, "vaulting ambition," which seem to imply that too much of what is good is evil.

So great a paradox of course cannot be maintained as that truth literally leads to falsehood, or that there can be an excess of virtue; but the appearance of things and the popular language about them will at least serve us in obtaining an additional test for the discrimination of a bona fide development of an idea from its corruption.

A true development, then, may be described as one which is conservative of the course of antecedent developments being really those antecedents and something besides them: it is an addition which illustrates, not obscures, corroborates, not corrects, the body of thought from which it proceeds; and this is its characteristic as contrasted with a corruption.

## 2.

For instance, a gradual conversion from a false to a true religion, plainly, has much of the character of a continuous process, or a development, in the mind itself, even when the two religions, which are the limits of its course, are antagonists. Now let it be observed, that such a change consists in addition and increase chiefly, not in destruction. "True religion is the summit and perfection of false religions; it combines in one whatever there is of good and true separately remaining in each. And in like manner the Catholic Creed is for the most part the combination of separate truths, which heretics have divided among themselves, and err in dividing. So that, in matter of fact, if a religious mind were educated in and sincerely attached to some form of heathenism or heresy, and then were brought under the light of truth, it would be drawn off from error into the truth, not by losing what it had, but by gaining what it had not, not by being unclothed, but by being 'clothed upon,' 'that mortality may be swallowed up of life.' That same principle of faith which attaches it at first to the wrong doctrine would attach it to the truth; and that portion of its original doctrine, which was to be cast off as absolutely false, would not be directly rejected, but indirectly, *in* the reception of the truth which is its opposite. True conversion is ever of a positive, not a negative character."[10]

Such too is the theory of the Fathers as regards the doctrines fixed by Councils, as is instanced in the language of St. Leo. "To be seeking for what has been disclosed, to reconsider what has been finished, to tear up what has been laid down, what is this but to be unthankful for what is gained?"[11] Vincentius of Lerins, in like manner, speaks of the development of Christian doctrine, as *profectus fidei non permutatio*.[12] And so as regards the Jewish Law, our Lord said that He came "not to destroy, but to fulfil."

### 3.

Mahomet is accused of contradicting his earlier revelations by his later, "which is a thing so well known to those of his sect that they all acknowledge it; and therefore when the contradictions are such as they cannot solve them, then they will have one of the contradictory places to be revoked. And they reckon in the whole Alcoran about a hundred and fifty verses which are thus revoked."[13]

Schelling, says Mr. Dewar, considers "that the time has arrived when an esoteric speculative Christianity ought to take the place of the exoteric empiricism which has hitherto prevailed." This German philosopher "acknowledges that such a project is opposed to the evident design of the Church, and of her earliest teachers."[14]

### 4.

When Roman Catholics are accused of substituting another Gospel for the primitive Creed, they answer that they hold, and can show that they hold, the doctrines of the Incarnation and Atonement as firmly as any Protestant can state them. To this it is replied that they do certainly profess them, but that they obscure and virtually annul them by their additions; that the *cultus* of St. Mary and the Saints is no development of the truth, but a corruption and a religious mischief to

[10] Tracts for the Times, No. 85, p. 73. [Discuss. p. 200; vid. also Essay on Assent, pp. 249–51.]
[11] Ep. 162.
[12] Ib. p. 309.
[13] Prideaux, Life of Mahomet, p. 90.
[14] German Protestantism, p. 176.

those doctrines of which it is the corruption, because it draws away the mind and heart from Christ. But they answer that, so far from this, it subserves, illustrates, protects the doctrine of our Lord's loving kindness and mediation. Thus the parties in controversy join issue on the common ground, that a developed doctrine which reverses the course of development which has preceded it, is no true development but a corruption; also, that what is corrupt acts as an element of unhealthiness towards what is sound. This subject, however, will come before us in its proper place by and by.

## 5.

Blackstone supplies us with an instance, in another subject matter, of a development which is justified by its utility when he observes that "when society is once formed, government results of course, as necessary to preserve and to keep that society in order."[15]

On the contrary, when the Long Parliament proceeded to usurp the executive, they impaired the popular liberties which they seemed to be advancing; for the security of those liberties depends on the separation of the executive and legislative powers, or on the enactors being subjects, not executors of the laws.

And in the history of ancient Rome, from the time that the privileges gained by the tribunes in behalf of the people became an object of ambition to themselves, the development had changed into a corruption.

And thus a sixth test of a true development is that it is of a *tendency conservative* of what has gone before it.

## SECTION VII

### SEVENTH NOTE: CHRONIC VIGOUR

Since the corruption of an idea, as far as the appearance goes, is a sort of accident or affection of its development, being the end of a course, and a transition state leading to a crisis, it is, as has been observed above, a brief and rapid process. While ideas live in men's minds, they are ever enlarging into fuller development; they will not

[15] Vol. i. p. 118.

be stationary in their corruption any more than before it; and dissolution is that further state to which corruption tends. Corruption cannot, therefore, be of long standing; and thus *duration* is another test of a faithful development.

*Si gravis, brevis; si longus, levis* is the Stoical topic of consolation under pain; and of a number of disorders it can even be said, The worse, the shorter.

Sober men are indisposed to change in civil matters, and fear reforms and innovations, lest, if they go a little too far, they should at once run on to some great calamities before a remedy can be applied. The chance of a slow corruption does not strike them. Revolutions are generally violent and swift; now, in fact, they are the course of a corruption.

## 2.

The course of heresies is always short; it is an intermediate state between life and death, or what is like death; or, if it does not result in death, it is resolved into some new, perhaps opposite, course of error, which lays no claim to be connected with it. And in this way indeed, but in this way only, an heretical principle will continue in life many years, first running one way, then another.

The abounding of iniquity is the token of the end approaching; the faithful in consequence cry out, How long? as if delay opposed reason as well as patience. Three years and a half are to complete the reign of Antichrist.

Nor is it any real objection that the world is ever corrupt, and yet, in spite of this, evil does not fill up its measure and overflow; for this arises from the external counteractions of truth and virtue, which bear it back; let the Church be removed, and the world will soon come to its end.

And so again, if the chosen people age after age became worse and worse, till there was no recovery, still their course of evil was continually broken by reformations, and was thrown back upon a less advanced stage of declension.

## 3.

It is true that decay, which is one form of corruption, is slow; but decay is a state in which there is no violent or vigorous action at all, whether of a conservative or a destructive character, the hostile influence being powerful enough to enfeeble the functions of life, but not to quicken its own process. And thus we see opinions, usages, and systems, which are of venerable and imposing aspect, but which have no soundness within them, and keep together from a habit of consistence, or from dependence on political institutions; or they become almost peculiarities of a country, or the habits of a race, or the fashions of society. And then, at length, perhaps, they go off suddenly and die out under the first rough influence from without. Such are the superstitions which pervade a population, like some ingrained dye or inveterate odour, and which at length come to an end, because nothing lasts for ever, but which run no course, and have no history; such was the established paganism of classical times, which was the fit subject of persecution, for its first breath made it crumble and disappear. Such apparently is the state of the Nestorian and Monophysite communions; such might have been the condition of Christianity had it been absorbed by the feudalism of the Middle Ages; such too is that Protestantism, or (as it sometimes calls itself) attachment to the Establishment, which is not unfrequently the boast of the respectable and wealthy among ourselves.

Whether Mahometanism external to Christendom, and the Greek Church within it, fall under this description is yet to be seen. Circumstances can be imagined which would even now rouse the fanaticism of the Moslem; and the Russian despotism does not meddle with the usages, though it may domineer over the priesthood, of the national religion.

Thus, while a corruption is distinguished from decay by its energetic action, it is distinguished from a development by its *transitory character*.

#### 4.

Such are seven out of various Notes, which may be assigned, of fidelity in the development of an idea. The point to be ascertained is the unity and identity of the idea with itself through all stages of its development from first to last, and these are seven tokens that it may rightly be accounted one and the same all along. To guarantee its own substantial unity, it must be seen to be one in type, one in its system of principles, one in its unitive power towards externals, one in its logical consecutiveness, one in the witness of its early phases to its later, one in the protection which its later extend to its earlier, and one in its union of vigour with continuance, that is, in its tenacity.

# CHAPTER VI

# APPLICATION OF THE SEVEN NOTES TO THE EXISTING DEVELOPMENTS OF CHRISTIAN DOCTRINE

## APPLICATION OF THE FIRST NOTE OF A TRUE DEVELOPMENT: PRESERVATION OF TYPE

Now let me attempt to apply the foregoing seven Notes of fidelity in intellectual developments to the instance of Christian doctrine. And first as to the Note of *identity of type*.

I have said above that, whereas all great ideas are found, as time goes on, to involve much which was not seen at first to belong to them, and have developments, that is, enlargements, applications, uses and fortunes, very various, one security against error and perversion in the process is the maintenance of the original type which the idea presented to the world at its origin, amid and through all its apparent changes and vicissitudes from first to last.

How does this apply to Christianity? What is its original type? and has that type been preserved in the developments commonly called Catholic which have followed, and in the Church which embodies and teaches them? Let us take it as the world now views it in its age; and let us take it as the world once viewed it in its youth; and let us see whether there be any great difference between the early and the later description of it. The following statement will show my meaning:

There is a religious communion claiming a divine commission, and holding all other religious bodies around it heretical or infidel; it is a well-organized, well-disciplined body; it is a sort of secret society, binding together its members by influences and by engagements which it is difficult for strangers to ascertain. It is spread over the known world; it may be weak or insignificant locally, but it is strong on the whole from its continuity; it may be smaller than all other religious bodies together, but is larger than each separately. It is a natural enemy to governments external to itself; it is intolerant and engrossing, and tends to a new modelling of society; it breaks laws, it divides families.

It is a gross superstition; it is charged with the foulest crimes; it is despised by the intellect of the day; it is frightful to the imagination of the many. And there is but one communion such.

Place this description before Pliny or Julian; place it before Frederick the Second or Guizot.[1] "Apparent diræ facies." Each knows at once, without asking a question, who is meant by it. One object, and only one, absorbs each item of the detail of the delineation.


## SECTION I

### THE CHURCH OF THE FIRST CENTURIES

The prima facie view of early Christianity, in the eyes of witnesses external to it, is presented to us in the brief but vivid descriptions given by Tacitus, Suetonius, and Pliny, the only heathen writers who distinctly mention it for the first hundred and fifty years.

Tacitus is led to speak of the religion, on occasion of the conflagration of Rome, which was popularly imputed to Nero. "To put an end to the report," he says, "he laid the guilt on others, and visited them with the most exquisite punishment, those, namely, who, held in abhorrence for their crimes (*per flagitia invisos*), were popularly called Christians. The author of that profession (*nominis*) was Christ, who, in the reign of Tiberius, was capitally punished by the Procurator, Pontius Pilate. The deadly superstition (*exitiabilis superstitio*), though checked for a while, broke out afresh; and that, not only throughout Judæa, the original seat of the evil, but through the City also, whither all things atrocious or shocking (*atrocia aut pudenda*) flow together from every quarter and thrive. At first, certain were seized who avowed it; then, on their report, a vast multitude were convicted, not so much of firing the City, as of hatred of mankind (*odio humani generis*)." After describing their tortures, he continues, "In consequence, though they were guilty, and deserved most signal punishment, they began to be pitied, as if destroyed not for any public object, but from the barbarity of one man."

Suetonius relates the same transactions thus: "Capital punishments were inflicted on the Christians, a class of men of a new and magical

---

[1] This juxtaposition of names has been strangely distorted by critics. In the intention of the author, Guizot matched with Pliny, not with Frederick.

superstition (*superstitionis novæ et maleficæ*)." What gives additional character to this statement is its context; for it occurs as one out of various police or sumptuary or domestic regulations which Nero made; such as "controlling private expenses, forbidding taverns to serve meat, repressing the contests of theatrical parties, and securing the integrity of wills."

When Pliny was Governor of Pontus, he wrote his celebrated letter to the Emperor Trajan, to ask advice how he was to deal with the Christians, whom he found there in great numbers. One of his points of hesitation was whether the very profession of Christianity was not by itself sufficient to justify punishment; "whether the name itself should be visited, though clear of flagitious acts (*flagitia*), or only when connected with them." He says, he had ordered for execution such as persevered in their profession, after repeated warnings, "as not doubting, whatever it was they professed, that at any rate contumacy and inflexible obstinacy ought to be punished." He required them to invoke the gods, to sacrifice wine and frankincense to the images of the Emperor, and to blaspheme Christ; "to which," he adds, "it is said no real Christian can be compelled." Renegades informed him that "the sum total of their offence or fault was meeting before light on an appointed day, and saying with one another a form of words (*carmen*) to Christ, as if to a god, and binding themselves by oath, (not to the commission of any wickedness, but) against the commission of theft, robbery, adultery, breach of trust, denial of deposits; that, after this they were accustomed to separate, and then to meet again for a meal, but eaten all together and harmless; however, that they had even left this off after his edicts enforcing the Imperial prohibition of *Hetæriæ* or Associations." He proceeded to put two women to the torture, but "discovered nothing beyond a bad and excessive superstition" (*superstitionem pravam et immodicam*), "the contagion" of which, he continues, "had spread through villages and country, till the temples were emptied of worshippers."

## 2.

In these testimonies, which will form a natural and convenient text for what is to follow, we have various characteristics brought before us of the religion to which they relate. It was a superstition, as all three writers agree; a bad and excessive superstition, according to Pliny; a magical superstition, according to Suetonius; a deadly superstition, according to Tacitus. Next, it was embodied in a society, and moreover a secret and unlawful society or *hetæria*; and it was a proselytizing society; and its very name was connected with "flagitious," "atrocious," and "shocking" acts.

### 3.

Now these few points, which are not all which might be set down, contain in themselves a distinct and significant description of Christianity; but they have far greater meaning when illustrated by the history of the times, the testimony of later writers, and the acts of the Roman government towards its professors. It is impossible to mistake the judgment passed on the religion by these three writers, and still more clearly by other writers and Imperial functionaries. They evidently associated Christianity with the oriental superstitions, whether propagated by individuals or embodied in a rite, which were in that day traversing the Empire, and which in the event acted so remarkable a part in breaking up the national forms of worship, and so in preparing the way for Christianity. This, then, is the broad view which the educated heathen took of Christianity; and if it had been very unlike those rites and curious arts in external appearance, they would not have confused it with them.

Changes in society are, by a providential appointment, commonly preceded and facilitated by the setting in of a certain current in men's thoughts and feelings in that direction towards which a change is to be made. And as lighter substances whirl about before the tempest and presage it, so words and deeds, ominous but not effective of the coming revolution, are circulated beforehand through the multitude, or pass across the field of events. This was specially the case with Christianity, as became its high dignity; it came heralded and attended by a crowd of shadows, shadows of itself, impotent and monstrous as shadows are, but not at first sight distinguishable from it by common spectators. Before the mission of the Apostles, a movement, of which there had been earlier parallels, had begun in Egypt, Syria, and the neighbouring countries tending to the propagation of new and peculiar forms of worship throughout the Empire. Prophecies were afloat that some new order of things was coming in from the East, which increased the existing unsettlement of the popular mind; pretenders made attempts to satisfy its wants, and old traditions of the Truth, embodied for ages in local or in national religions, gave to these attempts a doctrinal and ritual shape, which became an additional point of resemblance to that Truth which was soon visibly to appear.

## 4.

The distinctive character of the rites in question lay in their appealing to the gloomy rather than to the cheerful and hopeful feelings, and in their influencing the mind through fear. The notions of guilt and expiation, of evil and good to come, and of dealings with the invisible world, were in some shape or other pre-eminent in them, and formed a striking contrast to the classical polytheism, which was gay and graceful, as was natural in a civilized age. The new rites, on the other hand, were secret; their doctrine was mysterious; their profession was a discipline, beginning in a formal initiation, manifested in an association, and exercised in privation and pain. They were from the nature of the case proselytizing societies, for they were rising into power; nor were they local, but vagrant, restless, intrusive, and encroaching. Their pretensions to supernatural knowledge brought them into easy connexion with magic and astrology, which are as attractive to the wealthy and luxurious as the more vulgar superstitions to the populace.

## 5.

Such were the rites of Cybele, Isis, and Mithras; such the Chaldeans, as they were commonly called, and the Magi; they came from one part of the world, and during the first and second century spread with busy perseverance to the northern and western extremities of the empire.[2] Traces of the mysteries of Cybele, a Syrian deity, if the famous temple at Hierapolis was hers, have been found in Spain, in Gaul, and in Britain, as high up as the wall of Severus. The worship of Isis was the most widely spread of all the pagan deities; it was received in Ethiopia and in Germany, and even the name of Paris has been fancifully traced to it. Both worships, as well as the science of magic, had their colleges of priests and devotees, which were governed by a president, and in some places were supported by farms. Their processions passed from town to town, begging as they went and attracting proselytes. Apuleius describes one of them as seizing a whip, accusing himself of some offence, and scourging himself in public. These strollers, *circulatores* or *agyrtœ* in classical language, told fortunes, and distributed prophetical tickets to the ignorant people who consulted them. Also, they were learned in

---

[2]Vid. Muller de Hierarch. et Ascetic. Warburton, Div. Leg. ii. 4. Selder de Diis Syr. Acad. des Inscript. t. 3, hist. p. 296, t. 5, mem. p. 63, t. 10, mem. p. 267. Lucian. Pseudomant. Cod. Theod. ix. 16.

the doctrine of omens, of lucky and unlucky days, of the rites of expiation and of sacrifices. Such an *agyrtes* or itinerant was the notorious Alexander of Abonotichus, till he managed to establish himself in Pontus, where he carried on so successful an imposition that his fame reached Rome, and men in office and station entrusted him with their dearest political secrets. Such a wanderer, with a far more religious bearing and a high reputation for virtue, was Apollonius of Tyana, who professed the Pythagorean philosophy, claimed the gift of miracles, and roamed about preaching, teaching, healing, and prophesying from India and Alexandria to Athens and Rome. Another solitary proselytizer, though of an earlier time and of an avowed profligacy, had been the Sacrificulus, viewed with such horror by the Roman Senate, as introducing the infamous Bacchic rites into Rome. Such, again, were those degenerate children of a divine religion, who, in the words of their Creator and Judge, "compassed sea and land to make one proselyte," and made him "twofold more the child of hell than themselves."

## 6.

These vagrant religionists for the most part professed a severe rule of life, and sometimes one of fanatical mortification. In the mysteries of Mithras, the initiation[3] was preceded by fasting and abstinence, and a variety of painful trials; it was made by means of a baptism as a spiritual washing; and it included an offering of bread, and some emblem of a resurrection. In the Samothracian rites it had been a custom to initiate children; confession too of greater crimes seems to have been required, and would naturally be involved in others in the inquisition prosecuted into the past lives of the candidates for initiation. The garments of the converts were white; their calling was considered as a warfare (*militia*), and was undertaken with a *sacramentum*, or military oath. The priests shaved their heads and wore linen, and when they were dead were buried in a sacerdotal garment. It is scarcely necessary to refer to the mutilation inflicted on the priests of Cybele; one instance of their scourgings has been already mentioned; and Tertullian speaks of their high priest cutting his arms for the life of the Emperor Marcus.[4] The priests of Isis, in lamentation for Osiris, tore

---

[3] Acad. t. 16, mem. p. 27.
[4] Apol. 25. Vid. also Prudent. in hon. Romani, circ. fin. and Lucian de Deo Syr. 50.

their breasts with pine cones. This lamentation was a ritual observance, founded on some religious mystery: Isis lost Osiris, and the initiated wept in memory of her sorrow; the Syrian goddess had wept over dead Thammuz, and her mystics commemorated it by a ceremonial woe; in the rites of Bacchus, an image was laid on a bier at midnight,[5] which was bewailed in metrical hymns; the god was supposed to die, and then to revive. Nor was this the only worship which was continued through the night; while some of the rites were performed in caves.

## 7.

Only a heavenly light can give purity to nocturnal and subterraneous worship. Caves were at that time appropriated to the worship of the infernal gods. It was but natural that these wild religions should be connected with magic and its kindred arts; magic has at all times led to cruelty, and licentiousness would be the inevitable reaction from a temporary strictness. An extraordinary profession, when men are in a state of mere nature, makes hypocrites or madmen, and will in no long time be discarded except by the few. The world of that day associated together in one company, Isiac, Phrygian, Mithriac, Chaldean, wizard, astrologer, fortune-teller, itinerant, and, as was not unnatural, Jew. Magic was professed by the profligate Alexander, and was imputed to the grave Apollonius. The rites of Mithras came from the Magi of Persia; and it is obviously difficult to distinguish in principle the ceremonies of the Syrian Taurobolium from those of the Necyomantia in the Odyssey, or of Canidia in Horace. The Theodosian Code calls magic generally a "superstition"; and magic, orgies, mysteries, and "sabbathizings" were referred to the same "barbarous" origin. "Magical superstitions," the "rites of the Magi," the "promises of the Chaldeans," and the "Mathematici" are familiar to the readers of Tacitus. The Emperor Otho, an avowed patron of oriental fashions, took part in the rites of Isis, and consulted the Mathematici. Vespasian, who also consulted them, is heard of in Egypt as performing miracles at the suggestion of Serapis. Tiberius, in an edict, classes together "Egyptian and Jewish rites"; and Tacitus and Suetonius, in recording it, speak of the two religions together as "*ea superstitio.*"[6] Augustus had already associated them together as superstitions, and as unlawful, and that

[5] Vid. also the scene in Jul. Firm. p. 449.
[6] Tac. Ann. ii. 85; Sueton. Tiber. 36.

in contrast to others of a like foreign origin. "As to foreign rites (*peregrinæ ceremoniæ*)," says Suetonius, "as he paid more reverence to those which were old and enjoined, so did he hold the rest in contempt."[7] He goes on to say that, even on the judgment-seat, he had recognized the Eleusinian priests, into whose mysteries he had been initiated at Athens; "whereas, when travelling in Egypt, he had refused to see Apis, and had approved of his grandson Caligula's passing by Judæa without sacrificing at Jerusalem." Plutarch speaks of magic as connected with the mournful mysteries of Orpheus and Zoroaster, with the Egyptian and the Phrygian; and, in his treatise on superstition, he puts together in one clause, as specimens of that disease of mind, "covering oneself with mud, wallowing in the mire, sabbathizings, fallings on the face, unseemly postures, foreign adorations."[8] Ovid mentions in consecutive verses the rites of "Adonis lamented by Venus," "the Sabbath of the Syrian Jew," and the "Memphitic Temple of Io in her linen dress."[9] Juvenal speaks of the rites, as well as the language and the music, of the Syrian Orontes having flooded Rome; and, in his description of the superstition of the Roman women, he places the low Jewish fortune-teller between the pompous priests of Cybele and Isis, and the bloody witchcraft of the Armenian haruspex and the astrology of the Chaldeans.[10]

### 8.

The Christian, being at first accounted a kind of Jew, was even on that score included in whatever odium, and whatever bad associations, attended on the Jewish name. But in a little time his independence of the rejected people was clearly understood, as even the persecutions show; and he stood upon his own ground. Still his character did not change in the eyes of the world; for favour or for reproach, he was still associated with the votaries of secret and magical rites. The Emperor Hadrian, noted as he is for his inquisitive temper, and a partaker in so many mysteries,[11] still believed that the Christians of Egypt allowed themselves in the worship of Serapis. They are brought into connexion with the magic of Egypt in the history of what is commonly called the Thundering Legion, so far as this, that the rain which relieved the

[7] August. 93.
[8] De Superst. 3.
[9] De Art. Am. i. init.
[10] Sat. iii. vi.
[11] Tertul. Ap. 5.

Emperor's army in the field, and which the Church ascribed to the prayers of the Christian soldiers, is by Dio Cassius attributed to an Egyptian magician, who obtained it by invoking Mercury and other spirits. This war had been the occasion of one of the first recognitions which the state had conceded to the oriental rites, though statesmen and emperors, as private men, had long taken part in them. The Emperor Marcus had been urged by his fears of the Marcomanni to resort to these foreign introductions, and is said to have employed Magi and Chaldeans in averting an unsuccessful issue of the war. It is observable that, in the growing countenance which was extended to these rites in the third century, Christianity came in for a share. The chapel of Alexander Severus contained statues of Abraham, Orpheus, Apollonius, Pythagoras, and our Lord. Here indeed, as in the case of Zenobia's Judaism, an eclectic philosophy aided the comprehension of religions. But, immediately before Alexander, Heliogabalus, who was no philosopher, while he formally seated his Syrian idol in the Palatine, while he observed the mysteries of Cybele and Adonis, and celebrated his magic rites with human victims, intended also, according to Lampridius, to unite with his horrible superstition "the Jewish and Samaritan religions and the Christian rite, that so the priesthood of Heliogabalus might comprise the mystery of every worship."[12] Hence, more or less, the stories which occur in ecclesiastical history of the conversion or good-will of the emperors to the Christian faith, of Hadrian, Mammæa, and others, besides Heliogabalus and Alexander. Such stories might often mean little more than that they favoured it among other forms of oriental superstition.

### 9.

What has been said is sufficient to bring before the mind an historical fact, which indeed does not need evidence. Upon the established religions of Europe the East had renewed her encroachments, and was pouring forth a family of rites which in various ways attracted the attention of the luxurious, the political, the ignorant, the restless, and the remorseful. Armenian, Chaldee, Egyptian, Jew, Syrian, Phrygian, as the case might be, was the designation of the new hierophant; and magic, superstition, barbarism, jugglery were the names given to his rite by the world. In this company appeared Christianity. When then three well-informed writers call Christianity a superstition and a magi-

[12] Vit. Hel. 3.

cal superstition, they were not using words at random, or the language of abuse, but they were describing it in distinct and recognized terms as cognate to those gloomy, secret, odious, disreputable religions which were making so much disturbance up and down the empire.

### 10.

The impression made on the world by circumstances immediately before the rise of Christianity received a sort of confirmation upon its rise, in the appearance of the Gnostic and kindred heresies, which issued from the Church during the second and third centuries. Their resemblance in ritual and constitution to the oriental religions, sometimes their historical relationship, is undeniable; and certainly it is a singular coincidence that Christianity should be first called a magical superstition by Suetonius, and then should be found in the intimate company, and seemingly the parent, of a multitude of magical superstitions, if there was nothing in the religion itself to give rise to such a charge.

### 11.

The Gnostic family[13] suitably traces its origin to a mixed race, which had commenced its national history by associating Orientalism with Revelation. After the captivity of the ten tribes, Samaria was colonized by "men from Babylon and Cushan, and from Ava, and from Hamath, and from Sepharvaim," who were instructed at their own instance in "the manner of the God of the land," by one of the priests of the Church of Jeroboam. The consequence was that "they feared the Lord and served their own gods." Of this country was Simon, the reputed patriarch of the Gnostics; and he is introduced in the Acts of the Apostles as professing those magical powers which were so principal a characteristic of the oriental mysteries. His heresy, though broken into a multitude of sects, was poured over the world with a catholicity not inferior in its day to that of Christianity. St. Peter, who fell in with him originally in Samaria, seems to have encountered him again at Rome. At Rome, St. Polycarp met Marcion of Pontus, whose followers spread through Italy, Egypt, Syria, Arabia, and Persia; Valentinus preached his doctrines in Alexandria, Rome, and Cyprus; and we read of his disciples in Crete, Cæsarea, Antioch, and other parts of the

---

[13] Vid. Tillemont, Mem. and Lardner's Hist. Heretics.

East. Bardesanes and his followers were found in Mesopotamia. The Carpocratians are spoken of at Alexandria, at Rome, and in Cephallenia; the Basilidians spread through the greater part of Egypt; the Ophites were apparently in Bithynia and Galatia; the Cainites or Caians in Africa, and the Marcosians in Gaul. To these must be added several sects, which, though not strictly of the Gnostic stock, are associated with them in date, character, and origin—the Ebionites of Palestine, the Cerinthians, who rose in some part of Asia Minor, the Encratites and kindred sects, who spread from Mesopotamia to Syria, to Cilicia and other provinces of Asia Minor, and thence to Rome, Gaul, Aquitaine, and Spain; and the Montanists, who, with a town in Phrygia for their metropolis, reached at length from Constantinople to Carthage.

"When [the reader of Christian history] comes to the second century," says Dr. Burton, "he finds that Gnosticism, under some form or other, was professed in every part of the then civilized world. He finds it divided into schools, as numerously and as zealously attended as any which Greece or Asia could boast in their happiest days. He meets with names totally unknown to him before, which excited as much sensation as those of Aristotle or Plato. He hears of volumes having been written in support of this new philosophy, not one of which has survived to our own day."[14] Many of the founders of these sects had been Christians; others were of Jewish parentage; others were more or less connected in fact with the pagan rites to which their own bore so great a resemblance. Montanus seems even to have been a mutilated priest of Cybele; the followers of Prodicus professed to possess the secret books of Zoroaster; and the doctrine of dualism, which so many of the sects held, is to be traced to the same source. Basilides seems to have recognized Mithras as the Supreme Being, or the Prince of Angels, or the Sun, if Mithras is equivalent to Abraxas, which was inscribed upon his amulets: on the other hand, he is said to have been taught by an immediate disciple of St. Peter, and Valentinus by an immediate disciple of St. Paul. Marcion was the son of a Bishop of Pontus, Tatian a disciple of St. Justin Martyr.

## 12.

Whatever might be the history of these sects, and though it may be a question whether they can be properly called "superstitions," and

[14]Bampton Lect. 2.

though many of them numbered educated men among their teachers and followers, they closely resembled, at least in ritual and profession, the vagrant pagan mysteries which have been above described. Their very name of "Gnostic" implied the possession of a secret, which was to be communicated to their disciples. Ceremonial observances were the preparation, and symbolical rites the instrument, of initiation. Tatian and Montanus, the representatives of very distinct schools, agreed in making asceticism a rule of life. The followers of each of these sectaries abstained from wine; the Tatianites and Marcionites, from flesh; the Montanists kept three Lents in the year. All the Gnostic sects seem to have condemned marriage on one or other reason.[15] The Marcionites had three baptisms or more; the Marcosians had two rites of what they called redemption; the latter of these was celebrated as a marriage, and the room adorned as a marriage-chamber. A consecration to a priesthood then followed with anointing. An extreme unction was another of their rites, and prayers for the dead one of their observances. Bardesanes and Harmonius were famous for the beauty of their chants. The prophecies of Montanus were delivered, like the oracles of the heathen, in a state of enthusiasm or ecstasy. To Epiphanes, the son of Carpocrates, who died at the age of seventeen, a temple was erected in the island of Cephallenia, his mother's birthplace, where he was celebrated with hymns and sacrifices. A similar honour was paid by the Carpocratians to Homer, Pythagoras, Plato, Aristotle, as well as to the Apostles; crowns were placed upon their images, and incense burned before them. In one of the inscriptions found at Cyrene, about twenty years since, Zoroaster, Pythagoras, Epicurus, and others, are put together with our Lord, as guides of conduct. These inscriptions also contain the Carpocratian tenet of a community of women. I am unwilling to allude to the agapæ and communions of certain of these sects, which were not surpassed in profligacy by the pagan rites of which they were an imitation. The very name of Gnostic became an expression for the worst impurities, and no one dared eat bread with them, or use their culinary instruments or plates.

### 13.

These profligate excesses are found in connexion with the exercise of magic and astrology.[16] The amulets of the Basilidians are still extant

---

[15] Burton, Bampton Lect. note 61.
[16] Burton, Bampton Lect. note 44.

in great numbers, inscribed with symbols, some Christian, some with figures of Isis, Serapis, and Anubis, represented according to the gross indecencies of the Egyptian mythology.[17] St. Irenæus had already connected together the two crimes in speaking of the Simonians: "Their mystical priests," he says, "live in lewdness, and practise magic, according to the ability of each. They use exorcisms and incantations; love-potions too, and seductive spells; the virtue of spirits, and dreams, and all other curious arts, they diligently observe."[18] The Marcosians were especially devoted to these "curious arts," which are also ascribed to Carpocrates and Apelles. Marcion and others are reported to have used astrology. Tertullian speaks generally of the sects of his day: "Infamous are the dealings of the heretics with sorcerers very many, with mountebanks, with astrologers, with philosophers, to wit, such as are given to curious questions. They everywhere remember, 'Seek, and ye shall find.' "[19]

Such were the Gnostics; and to external and prejudiced spectators, whether philosophers, as Celsus and Porphyry, or the multitude, they wore an appearance sufficiently like the Church to be mistaken for her in the latter part of the Antenicene period, as she was confused with the pagan mysteries in the earlier.

## 14.

Of course it may happen that the common estimate concerning a person or a body is purely accidental and unfounded; but in such cases it is not lasting. Such were the calumnies of child-eating and impurity in the Christian meetings, which were almost extinct by the time of Origen, and which might arise from the world's confusing them with the pagan and heretical rites. But when it continues from age to age, it is certainly an index of a fact, and corresponds to definite qualities in the object to which it relates. In that case, even mistakes carry information; for they are cognate to the truth, and we can allow for them. Often what seems like a mistake is merely the mode in which the informant conveys his testimony, or the impression which a fact makes on him. Censure is the natural tone of one man in a case where praise is the natural tone of another; the very same character or action inspires one mind with enthusiasm, and another with contempt. What

---

[17] Montfaucon, Antiq. t. ii. part 2, p. 353.
[18] Hær. i. 20.
[19] De Præscr. 43.

to one man is magnanimity, to another is romance, and pride to a third, and pretence to a fourth, while to a fifth it is simply unintelligible; and yet there is a certain analogy in their separate testimonies which conveys to us what the thing is like and what it is not like. When a man's acknowledged note is superstition, we may be pretty sure we shall not find him an Academic or an Epicurean; and even words which are ambiguous, as "atheist," or "reformer," admit of a sure interpretation when we are informed of the speaker. In like manner, there is a certain general correspondence between magic and miracle, obstinacy and faith, insubordination and zeal for religion, sophistry and argumentative talent, craft and meekness, as is obvious. Let us proceed then in our contemplation of this reflection, as it may be called of primitive Christianity in the mirror of the world.

## 15.

All three writers, Tacitus, Suetonius, and Pliny, call it a "superstition"; this is no accidental imputation, but is repeated by a variety of subsequent writers and speakers. The charge of Thyestean banquets scarcely lasts a hundred years; but, while pagan witnesses are to be found, the Church is accused of superstition. The heathen disputant in Minucius calls Christianity, "*Vana et demens superstitio*." The lawyer Modestinus speaks, with an apparent allusion to Christianity, of "weak minds being terrified *superstitione numinis*." The heathen magistrate asks St. Marcellus, whether he and others have put away "vain superstitions," and worship the gods whom the emperors worship. The pagans in Arnobius speak of Christianity as "an execrable and unlucky religion, full of impiety and sacrilege, contaminating the rites instituted from of old with the superstition of its novelty." The anonymous opponent of Lactantius calls it, "*Impia et anilis superstitio*." Diocletian's inscription at Clunia was, as it declared, on occasion of "the total extinction of the superstition of the Christians, and the extension of the worship of the gods." Maximin, in his Letter upon Constantine's Edict, still calls it a superstition.[20]

## 16.

Now what is meant by the word thus attached by a consensus of heathen authorities to Christianity? At least, it cannot mean a religion

[20] Vid. Kortholt, in Plin. et Traj. Epp. p. 152. Comment. in Minuc. F. etc.

in which a man might think what he pleased, and was set free from all yokes, whether of ignorance, fear, authority, or priestcraft. When heathen writers call the oriental rites superstitions, they evidently use the word in its modern sense; it cannot surely be doubted that they apply it in the same sense to Christianity. But Plutarch explains for us the word at length, in his treatise which bears the name: "Of all kinds of fear," he says, "superstition is the most fatal to action and resource. He does not fear the sea who does not sail, nor war who does not serve, nor robbers who keeps at home, nor the sycophant who is poor, nor the envious if he is a private man, nor an earthquake if he lives in Gaul, nor thunder if he lives in Ethiopia; but he who fears the gods fears everything, earth, seas, air, sky, darkness, light, noises, silence, sleep. Slaves sleep and forget their masters; of the fettered doth sleep lighten the chain; inflamed wounds, ulcers cruel and agonizing, are not felt by the sleeping. Superstition alone has come to no terms with sleep; but in the very sleep of her victims, as though they were in the realms of the impious, she raises horrible spectres, and monstrous phantoms, and various pains, and whirls the miserable soul about, and persecutes it. They rise, and, instead of making light of what is unreal, they fall into the hands of quacks and conjurers, who say, 'Call the crone to expiate, bathe in the sea, and sit all day on the ground.' " He goes on to speak of the introduction of "uncouth names and barbarous terms" into "the divine and national authority of religion"; observes that, whereas slaves, when they despair of freedom, may demand to be sold to another master, superstition admits of no change of gods, since "the god cannot be found whom he will not fear, who fears the gods of his family and his birth, who shudders at the Saving and the Benignant, who has a trembling and dread at those from whom we ask riches and wealth, concord, peace, success of all good words and deeds." He says, moreover, that, while death is to all men an end of life, it is not so to the superstitious; for then "there are deep gates of hell to yawn, and headlong streams of at once fire and gloom are opened, and darkness with its many phantoms encompasses, ghosts presenting horrid visages and wretched voices, and judges and execu-tioners, and chasms and dens full of innumerable miseries."

Presently, he says, that in misfortune or sickness the superstitious man refuses to see physician or philosopher, and cries, "Suffer me, O man, to undergo punishment, the impious, the cursed, the hated of gods and spirits. The Atheist," with whom all along he is contrasting the superstitious disadvantageously, "wipes his tears, trims his hair, doffs his mourning; but how can you address, how help the superstitious? He sits apart in sackcloth or filthy rags; and often he strips himself and rolls in the mud, and tells out his sins and offences, as having eaten and drunken something, or walked some way which the divinity did not allow. . . . And in his best mood, and under the influence of a good-humoured superstition, he sits at home, with sacrifice and slaughter all round him, while the old crones hang on him as on a peg, as Bion says, any charm they fall in with." He continues, "What men like best are festivals, banquets at the temples, initiations, orgies, votive prayers, and adorations. But the superstitious wishes indeed, but is unable to rejoice. He is crowned and turns pale; he sacrifices and is in fear; he prays with a quivering voice, and burns incense with trembling hands, and altogether belies the saying of Pythagoras, that we are then in best case when we go to the gods; for superstitious men are in most wretched and evil case, approaching the houses or shrines of the gods as if they were the dens of bears, or the holes of snakes, or the caves of whales."

## 17.

Here we have a vivid picture of Plutarch's idea of the essence of superstition; it was the imagination of the existence of an unseen ever-present Master; the bondage of a rule of life, of a continual responsibility; obligation to attend to little things, the impossibility of escaping from duty, the inability to choose or change one's religion, an interference with the enjoyment of life, a melancholy view of the world, sense of sin, horror at guilt, apprehension of punishment, dread, self-abasement, depression, anxiety and endeavour to be at peace with heaven, and error and absurdity in the methods chosen for the purpose. Such too had been the idea of the Epicurean Velleius, when he shrunk with horror from the "*sempiternus dominus*" and "*curiosus Deus*" of the Stoics.[21] Such, surely, was the meaning of Tacitus, Suetonius, and Pliny. And hence of course the frequent reproach cast on Christians as credulous, weak-minded, and poor-spirited. The heathen objectors

---

[21]"Itaque imposuistis in cervicibus nostris sempiternum dominum, quem dies et noctes timeremus; quis enim non timeat omnia providentem et cogitantem et animadvertentem, et omnia ad se pertinere putantem, curiosum, et plenum negotii Deum?" ["So you have imposed on our necks an eternal master, to be feared night and day. Who would not be in dread of a god whose foresight, thought, and attention extended over absolutely everything? a god indifferent to nothing, ever diligent, and incessantly busy?"]—*Cic. de Nat. Deor.* i. 20.

in Minucius and Lactantius speak of their "old-woman's tales."[22] Celsus accuses them of "assenting at random and without reason," saying, "Do not inquire, but believe." "They lay it down," he says elsewhere, "Let no educated man approach, no man of wisdom, no man of sense; but if a man be unlearned, weak in intellect, an infant, let him come with confidence. Confessing that these are worthy of their God, they evidently desire, as they are able, to convert none but fools, and vulgar, and stupid, and slavish, women and boys." They "take in the simple, and lead him where they will." They address themselves to "youths, house-servants, and the weak in intellect." They "hurry away from the educated, as not fit subjects of their imposition, and inveigle the rustic."[23] "Thou," says the heathen magistrate to the Martyr Fructuosus, "who as a teacher dost disseminate a new fable, that fickle girls may desert the groves and abandon Jupiter, condemn, if thou art wise, the anile creed."[24]

## 18.

Hence the epithets of itinerant, mountebank, conjurer, cheat, sophist, sorcerer, heaped upon the teachers of Christianity; sometimes to account for the report or apparent truth of their miracles, sometimes to explain their success. Our Lord was said to have learned His miraculous power in Egypt; "wizard, mediciner, cheat, rogue, conjurer" were the epithets applied to Him by the opponents of Eusebius;[25] they "worship that crucified sophist," says Lucian;[26] "Paul, who surpasses all the conjurers and impostors who ever lived," is Julian's account of the Apostle. "You have sent through the whole world," says St. Justin to Trypho, "to preach that a certain atheistic and lawless sect has sprung from one Jesus, a Galilean cheat."[27] "We know," says Lucian, speaking of Chaldeans and Magicians, "the Syrian from Palestine, who is the sophist in these matters, how many lunatics, with eyes distorted and mouth in foam, he raises and sends away restored, ridding them from the evil at a great price."[28] "If any conjurer came to them, a man of skill and knowing how to manage matters," says the same writer,

[22] Min. c. 11. Lact. v. 1, 2. Vid. Arnob. ii. 8, etc.
[23] Origen, contr. Cels. i. 9, iii. 44, 50, vi. 44.
[24] Prudent. in hon. Fruct. 37.
[25] Evan. Dem. iii. 3, 4.
[26] Mort. Peregr. 13.
[27] c. 108.
[28] i.e. Philop. 16.

"he made money in no time, with a broad grin at the simple fellows."[29] The officer who had custody of St. Perpetua feared her escape from prison "by magical incantations."[30] When St. Tiburtius had walked barefoot on hot coals, his judge cried out that Christ had taught him magic. St. Anastasia was thrown into prison as a mediciner; the populace called out against St. Agnes, "Away with the witch," *Tolle magam, tolle maleficam.* When St. Bonosus and St. Maximilian bore the burning pitch without shrinking, Jews and Gentiles cried out, "*Isti magi et malefici.*" "What new delusion," says the heathen magistrate concerning St. Romanus, "has brought in these sophists to deny the worship of the gods? How doth this chief sorcerer mock us, skilled by his Thessalian charm *(carmine)* to laugh at punishment."[31]

Hence we gather the meaning of the word "*carmen*" as used by Pliny; when he speaks of the Christians "saying with one another a *carmen* to Christ as to a god," he meant pretty much what Suetonius expresses by the "*malefica superstitio.*"[32] And the words of the last-mentioned writer and Tacitus are still more exactly, and, I may say, singularly illustrated by clauses which occur in the Theodosian code; which seem to show that these historians were using formal terms and phrases to express their notion of Christianity. For instance, Tacitus says, "*Quos per flagitia invisos, vulgus Christianos appellabat*" ["those whom the public know as Christians, detested for the shameful things they do"]; and the Law against the Malefici and Mathematici in the Code speaks of those, "*Quos ob facinorum magnitudinem vulgus maleficos appellat*" ["those popularly identified as sorcerers because of the sheer magnitude of their wickedness"].[33] Again, Tacitus charges Christians with the "*odium humani generis*" ["hatred of the human race"]: this is the very characteristic of a practiser in magic; the Laws

[29] De Mort. Pereg. ibid.
[30] Ruin. Mart. pp. 100, 594, etc.
[31] Prud. in hon. Rom. vv. 404, 868.
[32] We have specimens of *carmina* ascribed to Christians in the Philopatris.
[33] Goth. in Cod. Th. t. 5, p. 120, ed. 1665. Again, "Qui malefici vulgi consuetudine nuncupantur" ["whom the public are accustomed to describe as sorcerers"]. Leg. 6. So Lactantius, "Magi et ii quos verè maleficos vulgus appellat" ["magicians, and those whom the public truly identify as sorcerers"]. Inst. ii. 17. "Quos et maleficos vulgus appellat" ["whom the public also call sorcerers"]. August. Civ. Dei, x. 19. "Quos vulgus mathematicos vocat" ["whom the public call astrologers"]. Hieron. in Dan. c. ii. Vid. Gothof. in loc. Other laws speak of those who were "maleficiorum labe polluti" ["stained with the pollution of witchcraft"], and of the "maleficiorum scabies" ["sorcerers' itch"].

call the Malefici, *"humani generis hostes"* ["enemies of the human race"], *"humani generis inimici"* ["adversaries of the human race"], *"naturae peregrini"* ["alien to nature"], *"communis salutis hostes"* ["enemies of the community's well-being"].[34]

### 19.

This also explains the phenomenon, which has created so much surprise to certain moderns—that a grave, well-informed historian like Tacitus should apply to Christians what sounds like abuse. Yet what is the difficulty, supposing that Christians were considered mathematici and magi, and these were the secret intriguers against established government, the allies of desperate politicians, the enemies of the established religion, the disseminators of lying rumours, the perpetrators of poisonings and other crimes? "Read this," says Paley, after quoting some of the most beautiful and subduing passages of St. Paul, "read this, and then think of *exitiabilis superstitio*"; and he goes on to express a wish "in contending with heathen authorities, to produce our books against theirs,"[35] as if it were a matter of books. Public men care very little for books; the finest sentiments, the most luminous philosophy, the deepest theology, inspiration itself move them but little; they look at facts, and care only for facts. The question was, What was the worth, what the tendency of the Christian body in the state? What Christians said, what they thought, was little to the purpose. They might exhort to peaceableness and passive obedience as strongly as words could speak; but what did they *do*, what was their political position? This is what statesmen thought of then, as they do now. What had men of the world to do with abstract proofs or first principles? a statesman measures parties, and sects, and writers by their bearing upon *him*; and he has a practised eye in this sort of judgment, and is not likely to be mistaken. " 'What is Truth?' said jesting Pilate." Apologies, however eloquent or true, availed nothing with the Roman magistrate against the sure instinct which taught him to dread Christianity. It was a dangerous enemy to any power not built upon itself; he felt it, and the event justified his apprehension.

---

[34] Tertullian too mentions the charge of "hostes principum Romanorum, populi, generis humani, Deorum, Imperatorum, legum, morum, naturae totius inimici" ["Enemies of Rome's leaders, of the people, of the human race, of gods, emperors, laws, customs, and the whole of nature."]. Apol. 2, 35, 38, ad. Scap. 4, ad. Nat. i. 17.

[35] Evid. part ii. ch. 4.

## 20.

We must not forget the well-known character of the Roman state in its dealings with its subjects. It had had from the first an extreme jealousy of secret societies; it was prepared to grant a large toleration and a broad comprehension, but, as is the case with modern governments, it wished to have jurisdiction and the ultimate authority in every movement of the body politic and social, and its civil institutions were based, or essentially depended, on its religion. Accordingly, every innovation upon the established paganism, except it was allowed by the law, was rigidly repressed. Hence the professors of low superstitions, of mysteries, of magic, of astrology, were the outlaws of society, and were in a condition analogous, if the comparison may be allowed, to smugglers or poachers among ourselves, or perhaps to burglars and highwaymen. The modern robber is sometimes made to ask in novels or essays why the majority of a people should bind the minority, and why he is amenable to laws which he does not enact; but the magistrate, relying on the power of the sword, wishes all men to gain a living indeed, and to prosper, but only in his own legally sanctioned ways, and he hangs or transports dissenters from his authority. The Romans applied this rule to religion. Lardner protests against Pliny's application of the words "contumacy and inflexible obstinacy" to the Christians of Pontus. "Indeed, these are hard words," he says, "very improperly applied to men who were open to conviction, and willing to satisfy others, if they might have leave to speak."[36] And he says, "It seems to me that Pliny acted very arbitrarily and unrighteously, in his treatment of the Christians in his province. What right had Pliny to act in this manner? by what law or laws did he punish [them] with death?"—but the Romans had ever burnt the sorcerer, and banished his consulters for life.[37] It was an ancient custom. And at mysteries they looked with especial suspicion, because, since the established religion did not include them in its provisions, they really did supply what may be called a demand of the age. The Greeks of an earlier day had naturalized among themselves the Eleusinian and other mysteries, which had come from Egypt and Syria, and had little to fear from a fresh invasion from the same quarter; yet even in Greece, as Plutarch tells us, the "*carmina*" of the itinerants of Cybele and Serapis threw the Pythian verses out of fashion, and henceforth the responses from

[36] Heathen Test. 9.
[37] Gothof. in Cod. Th. t. 5, p. 121.

the temple were given in prose. Soon the oracles altogether ceased. What would cause in the Roman mind still greater jealousy of Christianity was the general infidelity which prevailed among all classes as regards the mythological fables of Charon, Cerberus, and the realms of punishment.[38]

## 21.

We know what opposition had been made in Rome even to the philosophy of Greece; much greater would be the aversion of constitutional statesmen and lawyers to the ritual of barbarians. Religion was the Roman point of honour. "Spaniards might rival them in numbers," says Cicero, "Gauls in bodily strength, Carthaginians in address, Greeks in the arts, Italians and Latins in native talent, but the Romans surpassed all nations in piety and devotion."[39] It was one of their laws, "Let no one have gods by himself, nor worship in private new gods nor adventitious, unless added on public authority."[40] Lutatius,[41] at the end of the first Punic war, was forbidden by the senate to consult the *Sortes Prænestinæ* as being "*auspicia alienigena*." Some years afterwards the Consul took axe in hand, and commenced the destruction of the temples of Isis and Serapis. In the second Punic war, the senate had commanded the surrender of the *libri vaticini* or *precationes*, and any written art of sacrificing. When a secret confraternity was discovered, at a later date, the Consul spoke of the rule of their ancestors which forbade the forum, circus, and city to *Sacrificuli* and prophets, and burnt their books. In the next age banishment was inflicted on individuals who were introducing the worship of the Syrian Sabazius; and in the next the Iseion and Serapeion were destroyed a second time. Mæcenas in Dio advises Augustus to honour the gods according to the national custom, because the contempt of the country's deities leads to civil insubordination, reception of foreign laws, conspiracies, and secret meetings.[42] "Suffer no one," he adds, "to deny the gods or to practise sorcery." The civilian Julius Paulus lays it down as one of the leading principles of Roman law that those who introduce new or untried religions should be degraded, and if in the lower orders put to

[38] Cic. pro Cluent. 61. Gieseler transl. vol. i. p. 21, note 5. Acad. Inscr. t. 34, hist. p. 110.
[39] De Harusp. Resp. 9.
[40] De Legg. ii. 8.
[41] Acad. Inscr. ibid.
[42] Neander, Eccl. Hist. tr. vol. i. p. 81.

death.[43] In like manner, it is enacted in one of Constantine's laws that the haruspices should not exercise their art in private; and there is a law of Valentinian's against nocturnal sacrifices or magic. It is more immediately to our purpose that Trajan had been so earnest in his resistance to *hetæriæ* or secret societies, that, when a fire had laid waste Nicomedia, and Pliny proposed to him to incorporate a body of a hundred and fifty firemen in consequence,[44] he was afraid of the precedent and forbade it.

## 22.

What has been said will suggest another point of view in which the oriental rites were obnoxious to the government, viz., as being vagrant and proselytizing religions. If it tolerated foreign superstitions, this would be on the ground that districts or countries within its jurisdiction held them; to proselytize to a rite hitherto unknown, to form a new party, and to propagate it through the Empire—a religion not local but Catholic—was an offence against both order and reason. The state desired peace everywhere, and no change; "considering," according to Lactantius, "that they were rightly and deservedly punished who execrated the public religion handed down to them by their ancestors."[45]

It is impossible surely to deny that, in assembling for religious purposes, the Christians were breaking a solemn law, a vital principle of the Roman constitution; and this is the light in which their conduct was regarded by the historians and philosophers of the Empire. This was a very strong act on the part of the disciples of the great Apostle, who had enjoined obedience to the powers that be. Time after time they resisted the authority of the magistrate; and this is a phenomenon inexplicable on the theory of private judgment or of the voluntary principle. The justification of such disobedience lies simply in the necessity of obeying the higher authority of some divine law; but if Christianity were in its essence only private and personal, as so many now think, there was no necessity of their meeting together at all. If, on the other hand, in assembling for worship and holy communion, they were fulfilling an indispensable observance, Christianity has imposed a social law on the world, and formally enters the field of politics.

[43] Muller, p. 21, 22, 30. Tertull. Ox. tr. p. 12, note *p*.
[44] Gibbon, Hist. ch. 16, note 14.
[45] Epit. Instit. 55.

Gibbon says that, in consequence of Pliny's edict, "the prudence of the Christians suspended their agapæ; but it was *impossible* for them to omit the exercise of public worship."[46] We can draw no other conclusion.

## 23.

At the end of three hundred years, a more remarkable violation of law seems to have been admitted by the Christian body. It shall be given in the words of Dr. Burton; he has been speaking of Maximin's edict, which provided for the restitution of any of their lands or buildings which had been alienated from them. "It is plain," he says, "from the terms of this edict, that the Christians had for some time been in possession of property. It speaks of houses and lands which did not belong to individuals, but to the whole body. Their possession of such property could hardly have escaped the notice of the government; but it seems to have been held in direct violation of a law of Diocletian, which prohibited corporate bodies, or associations which were not legally recognized, from acquiring property. The Christians were certainly not a body recognized by law at the beginning of the reign of Diocletian, and it might almost be thought that this enactment was specially directed against them. But, like other laws which are founded upon tyranny, and are at variance with the first principles of justice, it is probable that this law about corporate property was evaded. We must suppose that the Christians had purchased lands and houses before the law was passed; and their disregard of the prohibition may be taken as another proof that their religion had now taken so firm a footing that the executors of the laws were obliged to connive at their being broken by so numerous a body."[47]

## 24.

No wonder that the magistrate who presided at the martyrdom of St. Romanus calls them in Prudentius "a rebel people";[48] that Galerius speaks of them as "a nefarious conspiracy"; the heathen in Minucius,

---

[46]Gibbon, ibid. Origen admits and defends the violation of the laws: οὐκ ἄλογον συνθήκας παρὰ τὰ νενομιομένα ποιεῖν, τὰς, ὑπὲρ ἀληθείας. ["not unreasonable to enter for the sake of truth into commitments prohibited by the law . . ."] c. Cels. i. 1.

[47]Hist. p. 418.

[48]In hon. Rom. 62. In Act. S. Cypr. 4, Tert. Apol. 10. etc.

as "men of a desperate faction"; that others make them guilty of sacrilege and treason, and call them by those other titles which, more closely resembling the language of Tacitus, have been noticed above. Hence the violent accusations against them as the destruction of the Empire, the authors of physical evils, and the cause of the anger of the gods.

"Men cry out," says Tertullian, "that the state is beset, that the Christians are in their fields, in their forts, in their islands. They mourn as for a loss that every sex, condition, and now even rank, is going over to this sect. And yet they do not by this very means advance their minds to the idea of some good therein hidden; they allow not themselves to conjecture more rightly, they choose not to examine more closely. The generality run upon a hatred of this name, with eyes so closed that in bearing favourable testimony to any one they mingle with it the reproach of the name. 'A good man Caius Seius, only he is a Christian.' So another, 'I marvel that that wise man Lucius Titius hath suddenly become a Christian.' No one reflecteth whether Caius be not therefore good and Lucius wise because a Christian, or therefore a Christian because wise and good. They praise that which they know, they revile that which they know not. Virtue is not in such account as hatred of the Christians. Now, then, if the hatred be of the name, what guilt is there in names? What charge against words? Unless it be that any word which is a name have either a barbarous or ill-omened, or a scurrilous or an immodest sound. If the Tiber cometh up to the walls, if the Nile cometh not up to the fields, if the heaven hath stood still, if the earth hath been moved, if there be any famine, if any pestilence, 'The Christians to the lions' is forthwith the word."[49]

### 25.

"Men of a desperate, lawless, reckless faction," says the heathen Cæcilius, in the passage above referred to, "who collect together out of the lowest rabble the thoughtless portion, and credulous women seduced by the weakness of their sex, and form a mob of impure conspirators, of whom nocturnal assemblies, and solemn fastings, and unnatural food, no sacred rite but pollution, is the bond. A tribe lurking and light-hating, dumb for the public, talkative in corners, they despise our temples as if graves, spit at our gods, deride our

---

[49] Apol. i. 3, 39, Oxf. tr.

religious forms; pitiable themselves, they pity, forsooth, our priests; half-naked themselves, they despise our honours and purple; monstrous folly and incredible impudence! . . . Day after day, their abandoned morals wind their serpentine course; over the whole world are those most hideous rites of an impious association growing into shape: . . . they recognize each other by marks and signs, and love each other almost before they recognize; promiscuous lust is their religion. Thus does their vain and mad superstition glory in crimes. . . . The writer who tells the story of a criminal capitally punished, and of the gibbet (*ligna feralia*) of the cross being their observance (*ceremonias*), assigns to them thereby an altar in keeping with the abandoned and wicked, that they may worship (*colant*) what they merit. . . . Why their mighty effort to hide and shroud whatever it is they worship (*colunt*), since things honest ever like the open day, and crimes are secret? Why have they no altars, no temples, no images known to us, never speak abroad, never assemble freely, were it not that what they worship and suppress is subject either of punishment or of shame? . . . What monstrous, what portentous notions do they fabricate! that that God of theirs, whom they can neither show nor see, should be inquiring diligently into the characters, the acts, nay the words and secret thoughts of all men; running to and fro, forsooth, and present everywhere, troublesome, restless, nay impudently curious they would have him; that is, if he is close at every deed, interferes in all places, while he can neither attend to each as being distracted through the whole, nor suffice for the whole as being engaged about each. Think too of their threatening fire, meditating destruction to the whole earth, nay the world itself with its stars! . . . Nor content with this mad opinion, they add and append their old wives' tales about a new birth after death, ashes and cinders, and by some strange confidence believe each other's lies. Poor creatures! consider what hangs over you after death, while you are still alive. Lo, the greater part of you, the better, as you say, are in want, cold, toil, hunger, and your God suffers it; but I omit common trials. Lo, threats are offered to you, punishments, torments; crosses to be undergone now, not worshipped (*adorandæ*); fires too which ye predict and fear; where is that God who can recover, but cannot preserve your life? The answer of Socrates, when he was asked about heavenly matters, is well known, 'What is above us does not concern us.' My opinion also is, that points which are doubtful, as are the points in question, must be left; nor, when so many and such great men are in controversy on the subject, must judgment be rashly and audaciously given on either side, lest the consequence be either anile superstition or the overthrow of all religion."

## 26.

Such was Christianity in the eyes of those who witnessed its rise and propagation—one of a number of wild and barbarous rites which were pouring in upon the Empire from the ancient realms of superstition, and the mother of a progeny of sects which were faithful to the original they had derived from Egypt or Syria; a religion unworthy of an educated person, as appealing not to the intellect, but to the fears and weaknesses of human nature, and consisting not in the rational and cheerful enjoyment, but in a morose rejection of the gifts of Providence; a horrible religion, as inflicting or enjoining cruel sufferings, and monstrous and loathsome in its very indulgence of the passions; a religion leading by reaction to infidelity; a religion of magic, and of the vulgar arts, real and pretended, with which magic was accompanied; a secret religion which dared not face the day; an itinerant, busy, proselytizing religion, forming an extended confederacy against the state, resisting its authority and breaking its laws. There may be some exceptions to this general impression, such as Pliny's discovery of the innocent and virtuous rule of life adopted by the Christians of Pontus; but this only proves that Christianity was not in fact the infamous religion which the heathen thought it; it did not reverse their general belief to that effect.

## 27.

Now it must be granted that, in some respects, this view of Christianity depended on the times, and would alter with their alteration. When there was no persecution, martyrs could not be obstinate, and when the Church was raised aloft in high places, it was no longer in caves. Still, I believe, it continued substantially the same in the judgment of the world external to it, while there was an external world to judge of it. "They thought it enough," says Julian in the fourth century, of our Lord and His Apostles, "to deceive women, servants, and slaves, and by their means wives and husbands." "A human fabrication," says he elsewhere, "put together by wickedness, having nothing divine in it, but making a perverted use of the fable-loving, childish, irrational part of the soul, and offering a set of wonders to create belief." "Miserable men," he says elsewhere, "you refuse to worship the ancile, yet you worship the wood of the cross, and sign it on your foreheads, and fix it on your doors. Shall one for this hate the intelligent among you, or pity the less understanding, who in following you have gone to such an excess of perdition as to leave the everlasting gods and go over to a dead Jew?" He speaks of their adding other dead men to Him who died so long ago. "You have filled all places with sepulchres and monuments, though it is nowhere told you in your religion to haunt the tombs and to attend upon them." Elsewhere he speaks of their "leaving the gods for corpses and relics." On the other hand, he attributes the growth of Christianity to its humanity towards strangers, care in burying the dead, and pretended religiousness of life. In another place he speaks of their care of the poor.[50]

Libanius, Julian's preceptor in rhetoric, delivers the same testimony, as far as it goes. He addressed his Oration for the Temples to a Christian Emperor, and would in consequence be guarded in his language; however it runs in one direction. He speaks of "those black-habited men," meaning the monks, "who eat more than elephants, and by the number of their potations trouble those who send them drink in their chantings, and conceal this by paleness artificially acquired." They "are in good condition out of the misfortunes of others, while they pretend to serve God by hunger." Those whom they attack "are like bees, they like drones." I do not quote this passage to prove that there were monks in Libanius's days, which no one doubts, but to show his impression of Christianity, as far as his works betray it.

Numantian, in the same century, describes in verse his voyage from Rome to Gaul: one book of the poem is extant; he falls in with Christianity on two of the islands which lie in his course. He thus describes them as found on one of these: "The island is in a squalid state, being full of light-haters. They call themselves monks, because they wish to live alone without witness. They dread the gifts, from fearing the reverses, of fortune. Thus Homer says that melancholy was the cause of Bellerophon's anxiety; for it is said that after the wounds of grief mankind displeased the offended youth." He meets on the other island a Christian, whom he had known, of good family and fortune, and happy in his marriage, who "impelled by the Furies had left men and gods, and, credulous exile, was living in base concealment. Is not this herd," he continues, "worse than Circean poison? Then bodies were changed, now minds."

[50] Julian ap. Cyril, pp. 39, 194, 206, 335. Epp. pp. 305, 429, 438, ed. Spanh.

## 28.

In the Philopatris, which is the work of an author of the fourth century,[51] Critias is introduced pale and wild. His friend asks him if he has seen Cerberus or Hecate; and he answers that he has heard a rigmarole from certain "thrice-cursed sophists"; which he thinks would drive him mad if he heard it again, and was nearly sending him headlong over some cliff as it was. He retires for relief with his inquirer to a pleasant place, shadowed by planes, where swallows and nightingales are singing, and a quiet brook is purling. Triephon, his friend, expresses a fear lest he has heard some incantation, and is led by the course of the dialogue, before his friend tells his tale, to give some account of Christianity, being himself a Christian. After speaking of the creation, as described by Moses, he falls at once upon that doctrine of a particular providence which is so distasteful to Plutarch, Velleius in Cicero, and Cæcilius, and generally to unbelievers. "He is in heaven," he says, "looking at just and unjust, and causing actions to be entered in books; and He will recompense all on a day which He has appointed." Critias objects that he cannot make this consistent with the received doctrine about the Fates, "even though he has perhaps been carried aloft with his master, and initiated in unspeakable mysteries." He also asks if the deeds of the Scythians are written in heaven; for if so, there must be many scribes there. After some more words, in course of which, as in the earlier part of the dialogue, the doctrine of the Holy Trinity is introduced, Critias gives an account of what befell him. He says, he fell in with a crowd in the streets; and, while asking a friend the cause of it, others joined them (Christians or monks), and a conversation ensues, part of it corrupt or obscure, on the subject, as Gesner supposes, of Julian's oppression of the Christians, especially of the clergy. One of these interlocutors is a wretched old man, whose "phlegm is paler than death"; another has "a rotten cloke on, and no covering on head or feet," who says he has been told by some ill-clad person from the mountains, with a shorn crown, that in the theatre was a name hieróglyphically written of one who would flood the highway with gold. On his laughing at the story, his friend Crato, whom he had joined, bids him be silent, using a Pythagorean word; for he has "most excellent matters to initiate him into, and that the prediction is no dream but true," and will be fulfilled in August, using the Egyptian name of the month. He attempts to leave them in

---

[51] Niebuhr ascribes it to the beginning of the tenth.

disgust, but Crato pulls him back "at the instigation of that old demon." He is in consequence persuaded to go "to those conjurers," who, says Crato, would "initiate in all mysteries." He finds, in a building which is described in the language used by Homer of the Palace of Menelaus, "not Helen, no, but men pale and downcast," who ask, whether there was any bad news; "for they seemed," he says, "wishing the worst; and rejoicing in misfortune, as the Furies in the theatres." On their asking him how the city and the world went on, and his answering that things went on smoothly and seemed likely to do so still, they frown, and say that "the city is in travail with a bad birth." "You, who dwell aloft," he answers, "and see everything from on high, doubtless have a keen perception in this matter; but tell me, how is the sky? will the Sun be eclipsed? will Mars be in quadrature with Jupiter? etc."; and he goes on to jest upon their celibacy. On their persisting in prophesying evil to the state, he says, "This evil will fall on your own head, since you are so hard upon your country; for not as high-flyers have ye heard this, nor are ye adepts in the restless astrological art, but if divinations and conjurings have seduced you, double is your stupidity; for they are the discoveries of old women and things to laugh at." The interview then draws to an end; but more than enough has been quoted already to show the author's notion of Christianity.

## 29.

Such was the language of paganism after Christianity had for fifty years been exposed to the public gaze; after it had been before the world for fifty more, St. Augustine had still to defend it against the charge of being the cause of the calamities of the Empire. And for the charge of magic, when the Arian bishops were in formal disputations with the Catholic, before Gungebald, Burgundian King of France, at the end of the fifth century, we find still that they charged the Catholics with being "praestigiatores,"* and worshipping a number of gods; and when the Catholics proposed that the king should repair to the shrine of St. Justus, where both parties might ask him concerning their respective faiths, the Arians cried out that "they would not seek enchantments like Saul, for Scripture was enough for them, which was more powerful than all bewitchments."[52] This was said, not against

* "Tricksters"
[52] Sirm. Opp. ii. p. 225, ed. Ven.

strangers of whom they knew nothing, as Ethelbert might be suspicious of St. Augustine and his brother missionaries, but against a body of men who lived among them.

I do not think it can be doubted then that, had Tacitus, Suetonius, and Pliny, Celsus, Prophyry, and the other opponents of Christianity lived in the fourth century, their evidence concerning Christianity would be very much the same as it has come down to us from the centuries before it. In either case, a man of the world and a philosopher would have been disgusted at the gloom and sadness of its profession, its mysteriousness, its claim of miracles, the want of good sense imputable to its rule of life, and the unsettlement and discord it was introducing into the social and political world.

## 30.

On the whole then I conclude as follows: if there is a form of Christianity now in the world which is accused of gross superstition, of borrowing its rites and customs from the heathen, and of ascribing to forms and ceremonies an occult virtue; a religion which is considered to burden and enslave the mind by its requisitions, to address itself to the weak-minded and ignorant, to be supported by sophistry and imposture, and to contradict reason and exalt mere irrational faith; a religion which impresses on the serious mind very distressing views of the guilt and consequences of sin, sets upon the minute acts of the day, one by one, their definite value for praise or blame, and thus casts a grave shadow over the future; a religion which holds up to admiration the surrender of wealth, and disables serious persons from enjoying it if they would; a religion, the doctrines of which, be they good or bad, are to the generality of men unknown; which is considered to bear on its very surface signs of folly and falsehood so distinct that a glance suffices to judge of it, and that careful examination is preposterous; which is felt to be so simply bad, that it may be calumniated at hazard and at pleasure, it being nothing but absurdity to stand upon the accurate distribution of its guilt among its particular acts, or painfully to determine how far this or that story concerning it is literally true, or what has to be allowed in candour, or what is improbable, or what cuts two ways, or what is not proved, or what may be plausibly defended; a religion such, that men look at a convert to it with a feeling which no other denomination raises except Judaism, Socialism, or Mormonism, viz., with curiosity, suspicion, fear, disgust, as the case may be, as if something strange had befallen him, as if he had had an initiation into a mystery, and had come into communion with dreadful influences, as if he were now one of a confederacy which claimed him, absorbed him, stripped him of his personality, reduced him to a mere organ or instrument of a whole; a religion which men hate as proselytizing, anti-social, revolutionary, as dividing families, separating chief friends, corrupting the maxims of government, making a mock at law, dissolving the empire, the enemy of human nature, and a "conspirator against its rights and privileges";[53] a religion which they consider the champion and instrument of darkness, and a pollution calling down upon the land the anger of heaven; a religion which they associate with intrigue and conspiracy, which they speak about in whispers, which they detect by anticipation in whatever goes wrong, and to which they impute whatever is unaccountable; a religion, the very name of which they cast out as evil, and use simply as a bad epithet, and which from the impulse of self-preservation they would persecute if they could—if there be such a religion now in the world, it is not unlike Christianity as that same world viewed it, when first it came forth from its Divine Author.[54]

# SECTION II

## THE CHURCH OF THE FOURTH CENTURY

Till the Imperial government had become Christian, and heresies were put down by the arm of power, the face of Christendom presented

[53] Proph. Office, p. 132 [Via Med. vol. i. p. 109].

[54] Since the publication of this volume in 1845, a writer in a Conservative periodical of great name has considered that no happier designation could be bestowed upon us than that which heathen statesmen gave to the first Christians, "enemies of the human race." What a remarkable witness to our identity with the Church of St. Paul ("a pestilent fellow, and a mover of sedition throughout the world"), of St. Ignatius, St. Polycarp, and the other Martyrs! In this matter, Conservative politicians join with Liberals, and with the movement parties in Great Britain, France, Germany, and Italy, in their view of our religion.

"The Catholics," says the *Quarterly Review* for January, 1873, pp. 181–82, "wherever they are numerous and powerful in a Protestant nation, *compel* (sic) as it were by a law of their being, that nation to treat them with stern repression and control. . . . Catholicism, if it be true to itself, and its mission, *cannot* (sic) . . . wherever and whenever the opportunity is afforded it, abstain from claiming, working for, and grasping that supremacy and paramount much the same appearance all along as on the first propagation of the religion. What Gnosticism, Montanism, Judaism and, I may add, the oriental mysteries were to the nascent Church, as described in the foregoing section, such were the Manichean, Donatist, Apollinarian, and contemporary sects afterwards. The Church in each place looked at first sight as but one out of a number of religious communions, with little of a very distinctive character except to the careful inquirer. Still there were external indications of essential differences within; and, as we have already compared it in the first centuries, we may now contrast it in the fourth, with the rival religious bodies with which it was encompassed.

## 2.

How was the man to guide his course who wished to join himself to the doctrine and fellowship of the Apostles in the times of St. Athanasius, St. Basil, and St. Augustine? Few indeed were the districts in the *orbis terrarum*, which did not then, as in the Antenicene era, present a number of creeds and communions for his choice. Gaul indeed is said at that era to have been perfectly free from heresies; at least none are mentioned as belonging to that country in the Theodosian Code. But in Egypt, in the early part of the fourth century, the Meletian schism numbered one-third as many bishops as were contained in the whole Patriarchate. In Africa, towards the end of it, while the Catholic bishops amounted in all to 466, the Donatists rivalled them with as many as four hundred. In Spain Priscillianism was spread from the Pyrenees to the ocean. It seems to have been the religion of the population in the province of Gallicia, while its author Priscillian, whose death had been contrived by the Ithacians, was honoured as a Martyr. The Manichees, hiding themselves under a variety of names in different localities, were not in the least flourishing condition at Rome. Rome and Italy were the seat of the Marcionites. The Origenists, too, are mentioned by St. Jerome as "bringing a cargo of blasphemies into the port of Rome." And Rome was the seat of a Novatian, a Donatist, and a Luciferian bishop, in addition to the legitimate

---

influence and control, which it conscientiously believes to be its inalienable and universal due. . . . By the force of circumstances, by the inexorable logic of its claims, it must be the intestine foe or the disturbing element of every state in which it does not bear sway; and . . . it must now stand out in the estimate of all Protestants, Patriots and Thinkers" (philosophers and historians, as Tacitus?) "as the *hostis humani generis* (sic), etc."

occupant of the See of St. Peter. The Luciferians, as was natural under the circumstances of their schism, were sprinkled over Christendom from Spain to Palestine, and from Treves to Lybia; while in its parent country Sardinia, as a centre of that extended range, Lucifer seems to have received the honours of a Saint.

When St. Gregory Nazianzen began to preach at Constantinople, the Arians were in possession of its hundred churches; they had the populace in their favour, and, after their legal dislodgment, edict after edict was ineffectually issued against them. The Novatians too abounded there, and the Sabbatians, who had separated from them, had a church, where they prayed at the tomb of their founder. Moreover, Apollinarians, Eunomians, and Semi-Arians, mustered in great numbers at Constantinople. The Semi-Arian bishops were as popular in the neighbouring provinces, as the Arian doctrine in the capital. They had possession of the coast of the Hellespont and Bithynia; and were found in Phrygia, Isauria, and the neighbouring parts of Asia Minor. Phrygia was the headquarters of the Montanists, and was overrun by the Messalians, who had advanced thus far from Mesopotamia, spreading through Syria, Lycaonia, Pamphylia, and Cappadocia in their way. In the lesser Armenia, the same heretics had penetrated into the monasteries. Phrygia, too, and Paphlagonia were the seat of the Novatians, who besides were in force at Nicaea and Nicomedia, were found in Alexandria, Africa, and Spain, and had a bishop even in Scythia. The whole tract of country from the Hellespont to Cilicia had nearly lapsed into Eunomianism, and the tract from Cilicia as far as Phœnicia into Apollinarianism. The disorders of the Church of Antioch are well known: an Arian succession, two orthodox claimants, and a bishop of the Apollinarians. Palestine abounded in Origenists, if at that time they may properly be called a sect; Palestine, Egypt, and Arabia were overrun with Marcionites; Osrhoëne was occupied by the followers of Bardesanes and Harmonius, whose hymns so nearly took the place of national tunes that St. Ephrem found no better way of resisting the heresy than setting them to fresh words. Theodoret in Comagene speaks in the next century of reclaiming eight villages of Marcionites, one of Eunomians, and one of Arians.

## 3.

These sects were of very various character. Learning, eloquence, and talent were the characteristics of the Apollinarians, Manichees, and Pelagians; Tichonius the Donatist was distinguished in Biblical interpretation; the Semi-Arian and Apollinarian leaders were men of grave and correct behaviour; the Novatians had sided with the Orthodox during the Arian persecution; the Montanists and Messalians addressed themselves to an almost heathen population; the atrocious fanaticism of the Priscillianists, the fury of the Arian women of Alexandria and Constantinople, and the savage cruelty of the Circumcellions can hardly be exaggerated. These various sectaries had their orders of clergy, bishops, priests and deacons; their readers and ministers; their celebrants and altars; their hymns and litanies. They preached to the crowds in public, and their meeting-houses bore the semblance of churches. They had their sacristies and cemeteries; their farms; their professors and doctors; their schools. Miracles were ascribed to the Arian Theophilus, to the Luciferian Gregory of Elvira, to a Macedonian in Cyzicus, and to the Donatists in Africa.

### 4.

How was an individual inquirer to find, or a private Christian to keep the Truth, amid so many rival teachers? The misfortunes or perils of holy men and Saints show us the difficulty; St. Augustine was nine years a Manichee; St. Basil for a time was in admiration of the Semi-Arians; St. Sulpicius gave a momentary countenance to the Pelagians; St. Paula listened, and Melania assented, to the Origenists. Yet the rule was simple, which would direct every one right; and in that age, at least, no one could be wrong for any long time without his own fault. The Church is everywhere, but it is one; sects are everywhere, but they are many, independent and discordant. Catholicity is the attribute of the Church, independency of sectaries. It is true that some sects might seem almost Catholic in their diffusion; Novatians or Marcionites were in all quarters of the empire; yet it is hardly more than the name, or the general doctrine or philosophy, that was universal: the different portions which professed it seem to have been bound together by no strict or definite tie. The Church might be evanescent or lost for a while in particular countries, or it might be levelled and buried among sects, when the eye was confined to one spot, or it might be confronted by the one and same heresy in various places; but, on looking round the *orbis terrarum*, there was no mistaking that body which, and which alone, had possession of it. The Church is a kingdom; a heresy is a family rather than a kingdom; and as a family continually divides and sends out branches, founding new houses, and propagating itself in colonies, each of them as independent as its original head, so was it with heresy. Simon Magus, the first heretic, had been Patriarch of Menandrians, Basilidians, Valentinians, and the whole family of Gnostics; Tatian of Encratites, Severians, Aquarians, Apotactites, and Saccophori. The Montanists had been propagated into Tascodrugites, Pepuzians, Artotyrites, and Quartodecimans. Eutyches, in a later time, gave birth to the Dioscorians, Gaianites, Theodosians, Agnoetæ, Theopaschites, Acephali, Semi-dalitæ, Nagranitæ, Jacobites, and others. This is the uniform history of heresy. The patronage of the civil power might for a time counteract the law of its nature, but it showed it as soon as that obstacle was removed. Scarcely was Arianism deprived of the churches of Constantinople, and left to itself, than it split in that very city into the Dorotheans, the Psathyrians, and the Curtians; and the Eunomians into the Theophronians and Eutychians. One fourth part of the Donatists speedily became Maximinianists; and besides these were the Rogatians, the Primianists, the Urbanists, and the Claudianists. If such was the fecundity of the heretical principle in one place, it is not to be supposed that Novatians or Marcionites in Africa or the East would feel themselves bound to think or to act with their fellow-sectaries of Rome or Constantinople; and the great varieties or inconsistencies of statement, which have come down to us concerning the tenets of heresies, may thus be explained. This had been the case with the pagan rites, whether indigenous or itinerant, to which heresy succeeded. The established priesthoods were local properties, as independent theologically as they were geographically of each other; the fanatical companies which spread over the Empire dissolved and formed again as the circumstances of the moment occasioned. So was it with heresy: it was, by its very nature, its own master, free to change, self-sufficient; and, having thrown off the yoke of the Church, it was little likely to submit to any usurped and spurious authority. Montanism and Manicheeism might perhaps in some sort furnish an exception to this remark.

## 5.

In one point alone the heresies seem universally to have agreed—in hatred to the Church. This might at that time be considered one of her surest and most obvious notes. She was that body of which all sects, however divided among themselves, spoke ill; according to the prophecy, "If they have called the Master of the house Beelzebub, how much more them of His household." They disliked and they feared her; they did their utmost to overcome their mutual differences, in order to unite against her. Their utmost indeed was little, for independency was the law of their being; they could not exert themselves without fresh quarrels, both in the bosom of each, and one with another. *"Bellum hæreticorum pax est ecclesiæ"** had become a proverb; but they felt the great desirableness of union against the only body which was the natural antagonist of all, and various are the instances which occur in ecclesiastical history of attempted coalitions. The Meletians of Africa united with the Arians against St. Athanasius; the Semi-Arians of the Council of Sardica corresponded with the Donatists of Africa; Nestorius received and protected the Pelagians; Aspar, the Arian minister of Leo the Emperor, favoured the Monophysites of Egypt; the Jocobites of Egypt sided with the Moslem, who are charged with holding a Nestorian doctrine. It had been so from the beginning: "They huddle up a peace with all everywhere," says Tertullian, "for it maketh no matter to them, although they hold different doctrines, so long as they conspire together in their siege against the one thing, Truth."[55] And even though active co-operation was impracticable, at least hard words cost nothing, and could express that common hatred at all seasons. Accordingly, by Montanists, Catholics were called "the carnal"; by Novatians, "the apostates"; by Valentinians, "the worldly"; by Manichees, "the simple"; by Aerians, "the ancient";[56] by Apollinarians, "the man-worshippers"; by Origenists, "the flesh-lovers," and "the slimy"; by the Nestorians, "Egyptians"; by Monophysites, the "Chalcedonians"; by Donatists, "the traitors," and "the sinners," and "servants of Antichrist"; and St. Peter's chair, "the seat of pestilence"; and by the Luciferians, the Church was called "a brothel," "the devil's harlot," and "synagogue of Satan": so that it might be called a note of the Church, as I have said, for the use of the most busy and the most ignorant, that she was on one side and all other bodies on the other.

## 6.

Yet, strange as it may appear, there was one title of the Church of a very different nature from those which have been enumerated—a title of honour, which all men agreed to give her—and one which furnished a still more simple direction than such epithets of abuse to

---

* "The heretics' war is the church's peace."
[55] De Præscr. Hær. 41, Oxf. tr.
[56] χρονῖται.

aid the busy and the ignorant in finding her, and which was used by the Fathers for that purpose. It was one which the sects could neither claim for themselves, nor hinder being enjoyed by its rightful owner, though, since it was the characteristic designation of the Church in the Creed, it seemed to surrender the whole controversy between the two parties engaged in it. Balaam could not keep from blessing the ancient people of God; and the whole world, heresies inclusive, were irresistibly constrained to call God's second election by its prophetical title of the "Catholic" Church. St. Paul tells us that the heretic is "condemned by himself"; and no clearer witness against the sects of the earlier centuries was needed by the Church than their own testimony to this contrast between her actual position and their own. Sects, say the Fathers, are called after the name of their founders, or from their locality, or from their doctrine. So was it from the beginning: "I am of Paul, and I of Apollos, and I of Cephas"; but it was promised to the Church that she should have no master upon earth, and that she should "gather together in one the children of God that were scattered abroad." Her everyday name, which was understood in the market place and used in the palace, which every chance comer knew, and which state edicts recognized, was the "Catholic" Church. This was that very description of Christianity in those times which we are all along engaged in determining. And it had been recognized as such from the first; the name or the fact is put forth by St. Ignatius, St. Justin, St. Clement; by the Church of Smyrna, St. Irenæus, Rhodon or another, Tertullian, Origen, St. Cyprian, St. Cornelius; by the Martyrs Pionius, Sabina, and Asclepiades; by Lactantius, Eusebius, Adimantius, St. Athanasius, St. Pacian, St. Optatus, St. Epiphanius, St. Cyril, St. Basil, St. Ambrose, St. Chrysostom, St. Jerome, St. Augustine, and Facundus. St. Clement uses it as an argument against the Gnostics, St. Augustine against the Donatists and Manichees, St. Jerome against the Luciferians, and St. Pacian against the Novatians.

### 7.

It was an argument for educated and simple. When St. Ambrose would convert the cultivated reason of Augustine, he bade him study the book of Isaiah, who is the prophet, as of the Messiah, so of the calling of the Gentiles and of the Imperial power of the Church. And when St. Cyril would give a rule to his crowd of catechumens, "If ever thou art sojourning in any city," he says, "inquire not simply where the Lord's house is (for the sects of the profane also make an attempt to call their own dens houses of the Lord) nor merely where the Church is, but where is the Catholic Church. For this is the peculiar name of this Holy Body, the Mother of us all, which is the Spouse of our Lord Jesus Christ."[57] "In the Catholic Church," says St. Augustine to the Manichees, "not to speak of that most pure wisdom, to the knowledge of which few spiritual men attain in this life so as to know it even in its least measure—as men, indeed, yet, without any doubt—(for the multitude of Christians are safest not in understanding with quickness, but in believing with simplicity) not to speak of this wisdom, which ye do not believe to be in the Catholic Church, there are many other considerations which most sufficiently hold me in her bosom. I am held by the consent of people and nations; by that authority which began in miracles, was nourished in hope, was increased by charity, and made steadfast by age; by that succession of priests from the chair of the Apostle Peter, to whose feeding the Lord after His resurrection commended His sheep, even to the present episcopate; lastly, by the very title of Catholic, which, not without cause, hath this Church alone, amid so many heresies, obtained in such sort, that, whereas all heretics wish to be called Catholics, nevertheless to any stranger, who asked where to find the 'Catholic' Church, none of them would dare to point to his own basilica or home. These dearest bonds, then, of the Christian Name, so many and such, rightly hold a man in belief in the Catholic Church, even though, by reason of the slowness of our understanding or our deserts, truth doth not yet show herself in her clearest tokens. But among you, who have none of these reasons to invite and detain me, I hear but the loud sound of a promise of the truth; which truth, verily, if it be so manifestly displayed among you that there can be no mistake about it, is to be preferred to all those things by which I am held in the Catholic Church; but if it is promised alone, and not exhibited, no one shall move me from that faith which by so many and great ties binds my mind to the Christian religion."[58] When Adimantius asked his Marcionite opponent how he was a Christian who did not even bear that name, but was called from Marcion, he retorts, "And you are called from the Catholic Church, therefore ye are not Christians either"; Adimantius answers, "Did we profess man's name, you would have spoken to the point; but if we are called from being all over the world, what is there bad in this?"[59]

[57] Cat. xviii. 26.
[58] Contr. Ep. Manich. 5.
[59] Origen, Opp. t. i. p. 809.

## 8.

"Whereas there is one God and one Lord," says St. Clement, "therefore also that which is the highest in esteem is praised on the score of being sole, as after the pattern of the One Principle. In the nature then of the One, the Church, which is one, hath its portion, which they would forcibly cut up into many heresies. In substance then, and in idea, and in first principle, and in pre-eminence, we call the ancient Catholic Church sole; in order to the unity of one faith, the faith according to her own covenants, or rather that one covenant in different times, which, by the will of one God and through one Lord, is gathering together those who are already ordained, whom God hath predestined, having known that they would be just from the foundation of the world. . . . But of heresies, some are called from a man's name, as Valentine's heresy, Marcion's, and that of Basilides (though they profess to bring the opinion of Matthias, for all the Apostles had, as one teaching, so one tradition); and others from place, as the Peratici; and others from nation, as that of the Phrygians; and others from their actions, as that of the Encratites; and others from their peculiar doctrines, as the Docetæ and Hematites; and others from their hypotheses, and what they have honoured, as Cainites and the Ophites; and others from their wicked conduct and enormities, as those Simonians who are called Eutychites."[60] "There are, and there have been," says St. Justin, "many who have taught atheistic and blasphemous words and deeds, coming in the name of Jesus; and they are called by us from the appellation of the men whence each doctrine and opinion began . . . Some are called Marcians, others Valentinians, others Basilidians, others Saturnilians."[61] "When men are called Phrygians, or Novatians, or Valentinians, or Marcionites, or Anthropians," says Lactantius, "or by any other name, they cease to be Christians; for they have lost Christ's Name, and clothe themselves in human and foreign titles. It is the Catholic Church alone which retains the true worship."[62] "We never heard of Petrines, or Paulines, or Bartholomeans, or Thaddeans," says St. Epiphanius; "but from the first there was one preaching of all the Apostles, not preaching themselves, but Christ Jesus the Lord. Wherefore also all gave one name to the Church, not their own, but that of their Lord Jesus Christ, since they began to be called

[60] Strom. vii. 17.
[61] c. Tryph. 35.
[62] Instit. 4, 30.

Christians first at Antioch; which is the Sole Catholic Church, having nought else but Christ's, being a Church of Christians; not of Christs, but of Christians, He being One, they from that One being called Christians. None, but this Church and her preachers, are of this character, as is shown by their own epithets, Manicheans, and Simonians, and Valentinians, and Ebionites."[63] "If you ever hear those who are said to belong to Christ," says St. Jerome, "named, not from the Lord Jesus Christ, but from some other, say Marcionites, Valentinians, Mountaineers, Campestrians, know that it is not Christ's Church, but the synagogue of Antichrist."[64]

## 9.

St. Pacian's letters to the Novatian Bishop Sympronian require a more extended notice. The latter had required the Catholic faith to be proved to him, without distinctly stating from what portion of it he dissented; and he boasted that he had never found any one to convince him of its truth. St. Pacian observes that there is one point which Sympronian cannot dispute, and which settles the question, the very name Catholic. He then supposes Sympronian to object that "under the Apostles no one was called Catholic." He answers, "Be it thus;[65] it shall have been so; allow even that. When, after the Apostles, heresies had burst forth, and were striving under various names to tear piecemeal and divide 'the Dove' and 'the Queen' of God, did not the Apostolic people require a name of their own, whereby to mark the unity of the people that was uncorrupted, lest the error of some should rend limb by limb 'the undefiled virgin' of God? Was it not seemly that the chief head should be distinguished by its own peculiar appellation? Suppose this very day I entered a populous city. When I had found Marcionites, Apollinarians, Cataphrygians, Novatians, and others of the kind, who call themselves Christians, by what name should I recognize the congregation of my own people, unless it were named Catholic? . . . Whence was it delivered to me? Certainly that which has stood through so many ages was not borrowed from man. This name 'Catholic' sounds not of Marcion, nor of Apelles, nor of Montanus, nor does it take heretics for its authors."

In his second letter, he continues, "Certainly that was no accessory

[63] Hær. 42, p. 366.
[64] In Lucif. fin.
[65] The Oxford translation is used.

name which endured through so many ages. And, indeed, I am glad for thee, that, although thou mayest have preferred others, yet thou agreest that the name attaches to us, which should you deny nature would cry out. But and if you still have doubts, let us hold our peace. We will both be that which we shall be named." After alluding to Sympronian's remark that, though Cyprian was holy, "his people bear the name of Apostaticum, Capitolinum, or Synedrium," which were some of the Novatian titles of the Church, St. Pacian replies, "Ask a century, brother, and all its years in succession, whether this name has adhered to us; whether the people of Cyprian have been called other than Catholic? No one of these names have I ever heard." It followed that such appellations were "taunts, not names," and therefore unmannerly. On the other hand it seems that Sympronian did not like to be called a Novatian, though he could not call himself a Catholic. "Tell me yourselves," says St. Pacian, "what ye are called. Do ye deny that the Novatians are called from Novatian? Impose on them whatever name you like; that will ever adhere to them. Search, if you please, whole annals, and trust so many ages. You will answer, 'Christian.' But if I inquire the genus of the sect, you will not deny that it is Novatian. . . . Confess it without deceit; there is no wickedness in the name. Why, when so often inquired for, do you hide yourself? Why ashamed of the origin of your name? When you first wrote, I thought you a Cataphrygian. . . . Dost thou grudge me my name, and yet shun thine own? Think what there is of shame in a cause which shrinks from its own name."

In a third letter: " 'The Church is the Body of Christ.' Truly, the body, not a member; the body composed of many parts and members knit in one, as saith the Apostle, 'For the Body is not one member, but many.' Therefore, the Church is the full body, compacted and diffused now throughout the whole world; like a city, I mean, all whose parts are united, not as ye are, O Novatians, some small and insolent portion, and a mere swelling that has gathered and separated from the rest of the body. . . . Great is the progeny of the Virgin, and without number her offspring, wherewith the whole world is filled, wherewith the populous swarms ever throng the circumfluous hive." And he founds this characteristic of the Church upon the prophecies: "At length, brother Sympronian, be not ashamed to be with the many; at length consent to despise these festering spots of the Novatians, and these parings of yours; and at length to look upon the flocks of the Catholics, and the people of the Church extending so far and wide. . . . Hear what David saith, 'I will sing unto Thy name in the great congregation'; and again, 'I will praise Thee among much people'; and 'the Lord, even the most mighty God, hath spoken, and called the world from the rising up of the sun unto the going down thereof.' What! shall the seed of Abraham, which is as the stars and the sand on the seashore for number, be contented with your poverty? . . . Recognize now, brother, the Church of God extending her tabernacles and fixing the stakes of her curtains on the right and on the left; understand that 'the Lord's name is praised from the rising up of the sun unto the going down thereof.' "

### 10.

In citing these passages, I am not proving what was the doctrine of the Fathers concerning the Church in those early times, or what were the promises made to it in Scripture; but simply ascertaining what, in matter of fact, was its then condition relatively to the various Christian bodies among which it was found. That the Fathers were able to put forward a certain doctrine, that they were able to appeal to the prophecies, proves that matter of fact; for unless the Church, and the Church alone, had been one body everywhere, they could not have argued on the supposition that it was so. And so as to the word "Catholic"; it is enough that the Church was so called; that title was a confirmatory proof and symbol of what is even otherwise so plain, that she, as St. Pacian explains the word, was everywhere one, while the sects of the day were nowhere one, but everywhere divided. Sects might, indeed, be everywhere, but they were in no two places the same; every spot had its own independent communion, or at least to this result they were inevitably and continually tending.

### 11.

St. Pacian writes in Spain: the same contrast between the Church and sectarianism is presented to us in Africa in the instance of the Donatists; and St. Optatus is a witness both to the fact, and to its notoriety, and to the deep impressions which it made on all parties. Whether or not the Donatists identified themselves with the true Church, and cut off the rest of Christendom from it, is not the question here, nor alters the fact which I wish distinctly brought out and recognized that in those ancient times the Church was that body which was spread over the *orbis terrarum*, and sects were those bodies which were local or transitory.

"What is that one Church," says St. Optatus, "which Christ calls 'Dove' and 'Spouse'? . . . It cannot be in the multitude of heretics and schismatics. If so, it follows that it is but in one place. Thou, brother Parmenian, hast said that it is with you alone; unless, perhaps, you aim at claiming for yourselves a special sanctity from your pride, so that where you will, there the Church may be, and may not be, where you will not. Must it then be in a small portion of Africa, in the corner of a small realm, among you, but not among us in another part of Africa? And not in Spain, in Gaul, in Italy, where you are not? And if you will have it only among you, not in the three Pannonian provinces, in Dacia, Mœsia, Thrace, Achaia, Macedonia, and in all Greece, where you are not? And that you may keep it among yourselves, not in Pontus, Galatia, Cappadocia, Pamphylia, Phrygia, Cilicia, in the three Syrias, in the two Armenias, in all Egypt, and in Mesopotamia, where you are not? Not among such innumerable islands and the other provinces, scarcely numerable, where you are not? What will become then of the meaning of the word Catholic, which is given to the Church, as being according to reason[66] and diffused every where? For if thus at your pleasure you narrow the Church, if you withdraw from her all the nations, where will be the earnings of the Son of God? where will be that which the Father hath so amply accorded to Him, saying in the second Psalm 'I will give thee the heathen for Thine inheritance and the uttermost parts of the earth for Thy possession,' etc.? . . . The whole earth is given Him with the nations; its whole circuit (orbis) is Christ's one possession."[67]

## 12.

An African writer contemporary with St. Augustine, if not St. Augustine himself, enumerates the small portions of the Donatists Sect, in and out of Africa, and asks if they can be imagined to be the fulfilment of the Scripture promise to the Church. "If the holy Scriptures have assigned the Church to Africa alone, or to the scanty Cutzupitans or Mountaineers of Rome, or to the house or patrimony of one Spanish woman, however the argument may stand from other writings, then none but the Donatists have possession of the Church. If holy Scripture determines it to the few Moors of the Cæsarean

[66] Rationabilis; apparently an allusion to the civil officer called Catholicus or Rationalis, receiver-general.
[67] Ad. Parm. ii. init.

province, we must go over to the Rogatists: if to the few Tripolitans or Byzacenes and Provincials, the Maximianists have attained to it; if in the Orientals only, it is to be sought for among Arians, Eunomians, Macedonians, and others that may be there; for who can enumerate every heresy of every nation? But if Christ's Church, by the divine and most certain testimonies of Canonical Scriptures, is assigned to all nations, whatever may be adduced, and from whatever quarter cited, by those who say, 'Lo, here is Christ and lo there,' let us rather hear, if we be His sheep, the voice of our Shepherd saying unto us, 'Do not believe.' For they are not each found in the many nations where she is; but she, who is everywhere, is found where they are."[68]

Lastly, let us hear St. Augustine himself again in the same controversy: "They do not communicate with us, as you say," he observes to Cresconius, "Novatians, Arians, Patripassians, Valentinians, Patricians, Apellites, Marcionites, Ophites, and the rest of those sacrilegious names, as you call them, of nefarious pests rather than sects. Yet, wheresoever they are, there is the Catholic Church; as in Africa it is where you are. On the other hand, neither you, nor any one of those heresies whatever, is to be found wherever is the Catholic Church. Whence it appears, which is that tree whose boughs extend over all the earth by the richness of its fruitfulness, and which be those broken branches which have not the life of the root, but lie and wither, each in its own place."[69]

## 13.

It may be possibly suggested that this universality which the Fathers ascribe to the Catholic Church lay in its Apostolical descent, or again in its Episcopacy; and that it was one, not as being one kingdom or *civitas* "at unity with itself," with one and the same intelligence in every part, one sympathy, one ruling principle, one organization, one communion, but because, though consisting of a number of independent communities, at variance (if so be) with each other even to a breach of communion, nevertheless all these were possessed of a legitimate succession of clergy, or all governed by bishops, priests, and deacons. But who will in seriousness maintain that relationship, or that sameness of structure, makes two bodies one? England and Prussia are both of them monarchies; are they therefore one kingdom? England

[68] De Unit. Eccles. 6.
[69] Contr. Cresc. iv. 75; also iii. 77.

and the United States are from one stock; can they therefore be called one state? England and Ireland are peopled by different races; yet are they not one kingdom still? If unity lies in the Apostolical succession, an act of schism is from the nature of the case impossible; for as no one can reverse his parentage, so no Church can undo the fact that its clergy have come by lineal descent from the Apostles. Either there is no such sin as schism, or unity does not lie in the Episcopal form or in the Episcopal ordination. And this is felt by the controversialists of this day; who in consequence are obliged to invent a sin, and to consider, not division of Church from Church, but the interference of Church with Church to be the sin of schism, as if local dioceses and bishops with restraint were more than ecclesiastical arrangements and by-laws of the Church, however sacred, while schism is a sin against her essence. Thus they strain out a gnat, and swallow a camel. Division is the schism, if schism there be, not interference. If interference is a sin, division which is the cause of it is a greater; but where division is a duty, there can be no sin in interference.

## 14.

Far different from such a theory is the picture which the ancient Church presents to us; true, it was governed by bishops, and those bishops came from the Apostles, but it was a kingdom besides; and as a kingdom admits of the possibility of rebels, so does such a Church involve sectaries and schismatics, but not independent portions. It was a vast organized association, coextensive with the Roman Empire, or rather overflowing it. Its bishops were not mere local officers, but possessed a quasi-ecumenical power, extending wherever a Christian was to be found. "No Christian," says Bingham, "would pretend to travel without taking letters of credence with him from his own bishop, if he meant to communicate with the Christian Church in a foreign country. Such was the admirable unity of the Church Catholic in those days, and the blessed harmony and consent of her bishops among one another."[70] St. Gregory Nazianzen calls St. Cyprian an universal bishop, "presiding," as the same author presently quotes Gregory, "not only over the Church of Carthage and Africa, but over all the regions of the West, and over the East, and South, and Northern parts of the world also." This is evidence of a unity throughout Christendom, not of mere origin or of Apostolical succession, but of government.

[70] Antiq. ii. 4, § 5.

Bingham continues: "[Gregory] says the same of Athanasius; that, in being made Bishop of Alexandria, he was made Bishop of the whole world. Chrysostom, in like manner, styles Timothy, Bishop of the universe. . . . The great Athanasius, as he returned from his exile, made no scruple to ordain in several cities as he went along, though they were not in his own diocese. And the famous Eusebius of Samosata did the like, in the times of the Arian persecution under Valens . . . Epiphanius made use of the same power and privilege in a like case, ordaining Paulinianus, St. Jerome's brother, first deacon and then presbyter, in a monastery out of his own diocese in Palestine."[71] And so in respect of teaching, before Councils met on any large scale, St. Ignatius of Antioch had addressed letters to the Churches along the coast of Asia Minor, when on his way to martyrdom at Rome. St. Irenæus, when a subject of the Church of Smyrna, betakes himself to Gaul, and answers in Lyons the heresies of Syria. The see of St. Hippolytus, as if he belonged to all parts of the *orbis terrarum*, cannot be located, and is variously placed in the neighbourhood of Rome and in Arabia. Hosius, a Spanish bishop, arbitrates in an Alexandrian controversy. St. Athanasius, driven from his Church, makes all Christendom his home, from Treves to Ethiopia, and introduces into the West the discipline of the Egyptian Antony. St. Jerome is born in Dalmatia, studies at Constantinople and Alexandria, is secretary to St. Damasus at Rome, and settles and dies in Palestine. Above all the See of Rome itself is the centre of teaching as well as of action, is visited by Fathers and heretics as a tribunal in controversy, and by ancient custom sends her alms to the poor Christians of all Churches, to Achaia and Syria, Palestine, Arabia, Egypt, and Cappadocia.

## 15.

Moreover, this universal Church was not only one; it was exclusive also. As to the vehemence with which Christians of the Antenicene period denounced the idolatries and sins of paganism, and proclaimed the judgments which would be their consequence, this is well known, and led to their being reputed in the heathen world as "enemies of mankind." "Worthily doth God exert the lash of His stripes and

---

[71] Antiq. 5, § 3. [Bingham apparently in this passage is indirectly replying to the Catholic argument for the Pope's supremacy drawn from the titles and acts ascribed to him in antiquity; but that argument is cumulative in character, being part of a whole body of proof; and there is moreover a great difference between a rhetorical discourse and a synodal enunciation as at Chalcedon.]

scourges," says St. Cyprian to a heathen magistrate; "and since they avail so little, and convert not men to God by all this dreadfulness of havoc, there abides beyond the prison eternal and the ceaseless flame and the everlasting penalty. . . . Why humble yourself and bend to false gods? Why bow your captive body before helpless images and moulded earth? Why grovel in the prostration of death, like the serpent whom ye worship? Why rush into the downfall of the devil, his fall the cause of yours, and he your companion? . . . Believe and live; you have been our persecutors in time; in eternity, be companions of our joy."[72] "These rigid sentiments," says Gibbon, "which had been unknown to the ancient world, appear to have infused a spirit of bitterness into a system of love and harmony."[73] Such, however, was the judgment passed by the first Christians upon all who did not join their own society; and such still more was the judgment of their successors on those who lived and died in the sects and heresies which had issued from it. That very Father, whose denunciation of the heathen has just been quoted, had already declared it even in the third century. "He who leaves the Church of Christ," he says, "attains not to Christ's rewards. He is an alien, an outcast, an enemy. He can no longer have God for a Father, who has not the Church for a Mother. If any man was able to escape who remained without the Ark of Noah, then will that man escape who is out of doors beyond the Church . . . What sacrifice do they believe they celebrate, who are rivals of the Priests? If such men were even killed for confession of the Christian name, not even by their blood is this stain washed out. Inexplicable and heavy is the sin of discord, and is purged by no suffering . . . They cannot dwell with God who have refused to be of one mind in God's Church; a man of such sort may indeed be killed, crowned he cannot be."[74] And so again St. Chrysostom, in the following century, in harmony with St. Cyprian's sentiment: "Though we have achieved ten thousand glorious acts, yet shall we, if we cut to pieces the fulness of the Church, suffer punishment no less sore than they who mangled His body."[75] In like manner St. Augustine seems to consider that a conversion from idolatry to a schismatical communion is no gain. "Those whom Donatists baptize, they heal of the wound of idolatry or infidelity, but inflict a more grievous stroke in the wound of schism; for idolaters among God's people the sword destroyed, but schismatics the gaping

[72] Ad Demetr. 4, etc. Oxf. Tr.
[73] Hist. ch. xv.
[74] De Unit. 5, 12.
[75] Chrys. in Eph. iv.

earth devoured."[76] Elsewhere, he speaks of the "sacrilege of schism, which surpasses all wickednesses."[77] St. Optatus, too, marvels at the Donatist Parmenian's inconsistency in maintaining the true doctrine, that "Schismatics are cut off as branches from the vine, are destined for punishments, and reserved, as dry wood, for hell-fire."[78] "Let us hate them who are worthy of hatred," says St. Cyril, "withdraw we from those whom God withdraws from; let us also say unto God with all boldness concerning all heretics, 'Do not I hate them, O Lord, that hate thee?' "[79] "Most firmly hold, and doubt in no wise," says St. Fulgentius, "that every heretic and schismatic soever, baptized in the name of Father, Son, and Holy Ghost, unless aggregated to the Catholic Church, how great soever have been his alms, though for Christ's Name he has even shed his blood, can in no wise be saved."[80] The Fathers ground this doctrine on St. Paul's words that, though we have knowledge, and give our goods to the poor, and our body to be burned, we are nothing without love.[81]

## 16.

One more remark shall be made: that the Catholic teachers, far from recognizing any ecclesiastical relation as existing between the

[76] De Baptism. i. 10.
[77] c. Ep. Parm. i. 7.
[78] De Schism. Donat. i. 10.
[79] Cat. xvi. 10.
[80] De Fid. ad Petr. 39. [82.]
[81] Of course this solemn truth must not be taken apart from the words of the present Pope, Pius IX., concerning invincible ignorance: "Notum nobis vobisque est, eos, qui invincibili circa sanctissimam nostram religionem ignorantiâ laborant, quique naturalem legem ejusque præcepta in omnium cordibus a Deo insculpta sedulo servantes, ac Deo obedire parati, honestam rectamque vitam agunt, posse, divinæ lucis et gratiæ operante virtute, æternam consequi vitam, cùm Deus, qui omnium mentes, animos, cogitationes, habitusque planè intuetur, scrutatur et noscit, pro summâ suâ bonitate et clementia, minimè patiatur quempiam æternis puniri suppliciis, qui voluntariæ culpæ reatum non habeat" ["You know as well as we do that those who are invincibly ignorant of our most holy religion can, aided by divine light and grace, attain eternal life, if only they conscientiously observe the natural law and its precepts God has inscribed on every person's heart, if they are ready to obey God and lead an honorable, righteous life. For God, who clearly beholds every person's mind, heart, thoughts, and attitudes, would not in his great goodness and mercy let anyone be punished with eternal suffering who was guiltless of voluntary fault."]

sectarian bishops and priests and their people, address the latter immediately, as if those bishops did not exist, and call on them to come over to the Church individually without respect to any one besides; and that because it is a matter of life and death. To take the instance of the Donatists: it was nothing to the purpose that their churches in Africa were nearly as numerous as those of the Catholics, or that they had a case to produce in their controversy with the Catholic Church; the very fact that they were separated from the *orbis terrarum* was a public, a manifest, a simple, a sufficient argument against them. "The question is not about your gold and silver," says St. Augustine to Glorius and others, "not your lands, or farms, nor even your bodily health is in peril, but we address your souls about obtaining eternal life and fleeing eternal death. Rouse yourself therefore. . . . You see it all, and know it, and groan over it; yet God sees that there is nothing to detain you in so pestiferous and sacrilegious a separation, if you will but overcome your carnal affection, for the obtaining the spiritual kingdom, and rid yourselves of the fear of wounding friendships, which will avail nothing in God's judgment for escaping eternal punishment. Go, think over the matter, consider what can be said in answer. . . .

### 17.

On the whole, then, we have reason to say, that if there be a form of Christianity at this day distinguished for its careful organization, and its consequent power; if it is spread over the world; if it is conspicuous for zealous maintenance of its own creed; if it is intolerant towards what it considers error; if it is engaged in ceaseless war with all other bodies called Christian; if it, and it alone, is called "Catholic" by the world, nay, by those very bodies, and if it makes much of the title; if it names them heretics, and warns them of coming woe, and calls on them one by one, to come over to itself, overlooking every other tie; and if they, on the other hand, call it seducer, harlot, apostate, Antichrist, devil; if, however much they differ one with another, they consider it their common enemy; if they strive to unite together against it, and cannot; if they are but local; if they continually subdivide, and it remains one; if they fall one after another, and make way for new sects, and it remains the same; such a religious communion is not unlike historical Christianity, as it comes before us at the Nicene Era.

## SECTION III

### THE CHURCH OF THE FIFTH AND SIXTH CENTURIES

The patronage extended by the first Christian Emperors to Arianism, its adoption by the barbarians who succeeded to their power, the subsequent expulsion of all heresy beyond the limits of the Empire, and then again the Monophysite tendencies of Egypt and part of Syria, changed in some measure the aspect of the Church, and claim our further attention. It was still a body in possession, or approximating to the possession, of the *orbis terrarum*; but it was not simply inter-mixed with sectaries, as we have been surveying it in the earlier periods, rather it lay between or over against large schisms. That same vast association, which, and which only, had existed from the first, which had been identified by all parties with Christianity, which had been ever called Catholic by people and by laws, took a different shape; collected itself in far greater strength on some points of her extended territory than on others; possessed whole kingdoms with scarcely a rival; lost others partially or wholly, temporarily or for good; was stemmed in its course here or there by external obstacles; and was defied by heresy, in a substantive shape and in mass, from foreign lands, and with the support of the temporal power. Thus not to mention the Arianism of the Eastern Empire in the fourth century, the whole of the West was possessed by the same heresy in the fifth; and nearly the whole of Asia, east of the Euphrates, as far as it was Christian, by the Nestorians, in the centuries which followed; while the Monophysites had almost the possession of Egypt, and at times of the whole Eastern Church. I think it no assumption to call Arianism, Nestorianism, and Eutychianism heresies, or to identify the contemporary Catholic Church with Christianity. Now, then, let us consider the mutual relation of Christianity and heresy under these circumstances.

### 1. The Arians of the Gothic Race

No heresy has started with greater violence or more sudden success than the Arian; and it presents a still more remarkable exhibition of these characteristics among the barbarians than in the civilized world. Even among the Greeks it had shown a missionary spirit. Theophilus in the reign of Constantius had introduced the dominant heresy, not without some promising results, to the Sabeans of the Arabian peninsula; but under Valens, Ulphilas became the apostle of a whole race. He taught the Arian doctrine, which he had unhappily learned in the Imperial Court, first to the pastoral Mœsogoths; who, unlike the other branches of their family, had multiplied under the Mœsian mountains with neither military nor religious triumphs. The Visigoths were next corrupted; by whom does not appear. It is one of the singular traits in the history of this vast family of heathens that they so instinctively caught, and so impetuously communicated, and so fiercely maintained, a heresy which had excited in the Empire, except at Constantinople, little interest in the body of the people. The Visigoths are said to have been converted by the influence of Valens; but Valens reigned for only fourteen years, and the barbarian population which had been admitted to the Empire amounted to nearly a million of persons. It is as difficult to trace how the heresy was conveyed from them to the other barbarian tribes. Gibbon seems to suppose that the Visigoths acted the part of missionaries in their career of predatory warfare from Thrace to the Pyrenees. But such is the fact, however it was brought about, that the success in arms and the conversion to Arianism, of Ostrogoths, Alani, Suevi, Vandals, and Burgundians stand as concurrent events in the history of the times; and by the end of the fifth century the heresy had been established by the Visigoths in France and Spain, in Portugal by the Suevi, in Africa by the Vandals, and by the Ostrogoths in Italy. For a while the title of Catholic as applied to the Church seemed a misnomer; for not only was she buried beneath these populations of heresy, but that heresy was one, and maintained the same distinctive tenet, whether at Carthage, Seville, Toulouse, or Ravenna. No one blots out from heaven the Ordinance of God, no one blots out from earth the Church of God: "He hath promised her, she hath filled, the whole world." "Some carnal intimacies," he says to his kinsman Severinus, "hold you where you are. . . . What avails temporal health or relationship, if with it we neglect Christ's eternal heritage and our perpetual health?" "I ask," he says to Celer, a person of influence, "that you would more earnestly urge upon your men Catholic Unity in the region of Hippo." "Why," he says, in the person of the Church, to the whole Donatist population, "Why open your ears to the words of men, who say what they never have been able to prove, and close them to the word of God, saying, 'Ask of Me, and I will give Thee the heathen for Thine inheritance'?" At another time he says to them, "Some of the presbyters of your party have sent to us to say, 'Retire from our flocks, unless you would have us kill you.' How much more justly do we say to them, 'Nay, do you, not retire from, but come in peace, not to our flocks, but to the flocks of Him whose we are all; or if you will not, and are far from peace, then do you rather retire from flocks, for which Christ shed His Blood.' " "I call on you for Christ's sake," he says to a late proconsul, "to write me an answer, and to urge gently and kindly all your people in the district of Sinis or Hippo into the communion of the Catholic Church." He publishes an address to the Donatists at another time to inform them of the defeat of their bishops in a conference: "Whoso," he says, "is separated from the Catholic Church, however laudably he thinks he is living, by this crime alone, that he is separated from Christ's Unity, he shall not have life, but the wrath of God abideth on him." "Let them believe of the Catholic Church," he writes to some converts about their friends who were still in schism, "that is, to the Church diffused over the whole world, rather what the Scriptures say of it than what human tongues utter in calumny." The idea of acting upon the Donatists only as a body and through their bishops, does not appear to have occurred to St. Augustine at all.[82]

## 2.

It cannot be supposed that these northern warriors had attained to any high degree of mental cultivation; but they understood their own religion enough to hate the Catholics, and their bishops were learned enough to hold disputations for its propagation. They professed to stand upon the faith of Ariminum, administering baptism under an altered form of words, and re-baptizing Catholics whom they gained over to their sect. It must be added that, whatever was their cruelty or tyranny, both Goths and Vandals were a moral people, and put to shame the Catholics whom they dispossessed. "What can the prerogative of a religious name profit us," says Salvian, "that we call ourselves Catholic, boast of being the faithful, taunt Goths and Vandals with the reproach of an heretical appellation, while we live in heretical wickedness?"[83] The barbarians were chaste, temperate, just, and de-

---

[82] Epp. 43, 52, 57, 76, 105, 112, 141, 144.

[83] De Gubern. Dei, vii. p. 142. Elsewhere, "Apud Aquitanicos quæ civitas in locupletissimâ ac nobilissimâ sui parte non quasi lupanar fuit? Quis potentum ac divitum non in luto libidinis vixit? Haud multum matrona abest à vilitate servarum, ubi paterfamilias ancillarum maritus est? Quis autem Aquitanorum divitum non hoc fuit?" ["Among the Aquitanians what city did

vout; the Visigoth Theodoric repaired every morning with his domestic officers to his chapel, where service was performed by the Arian priests; and one singular instance is on record of the defeat of a Visigoth force by the Imperial troops on a Sunday, when instead of preparing for battle they were engaged in the religious services of the day.[84] Many of their princes were men of great ability, as the two Theodorics, Euric and Leovigild.

### 3.

Successful warriors, animated by a fanatical spirit of religion, were not likely to be content with a mere profession of their own creed; they proceeded to place their own priests in the religious establishments which they found, and to direct a bitter persecution against the vanquished Catholics. The savage cruelties of the Vandal Hunneric in Africa have often been enlarged upon; Spain was the scene of repeated persecutions; Sicily, too, had its Martyrs. Compared with these enormities, it was but a little thing to rob the Catholics of their churches, and the shrines of their treasures. Lands, immunities, and jurisdictions which had been given by the Emperors to the African Church were made over to the clergy of its conquerors; and by the time of Belisarius, the Catholic bishops had been reduced to less than a third of their original number. In Spain, as in Africa, bishops were driven from their sees, churches were destroyed, cemeteries profaned, martyries rifled.

---

not, in its richest and most fashionable quarter, resemble a brothel? Among their rich and powerful citizens who did not live in a mire of lust? The lady of a house is not far removed from the base condition of slave girls, where the master of the house plays suitor to his serving-maids. And among the wealthy Aquitanians, who does not do that?"] (pp. 134, 135.) "Offenduntur barbari ipsi impuritatibus nostris. Esse inter Gothos non licet scortatorem Gothum; soli inter eos praejudicio nationis ac nominis permittuntur impuri esse Romani" ["The barbarians themselves take offense at our obscenities. Gothic fornicators are not allowed among Goths; they let only Romans be impure, exemplifying their nation and reputation."] (p. 137). "Quid Hispanias nonne vel eadem vel majora forsitan vitia perdiderunt? . . . Accessit hoc ad manifestandam illic impudicitiae damnationem, ut Wandalis potissimum, id est, pudicis barbaris traderentur" ["What? Did not similar or worse vices corrupt the regions of Spain? It was to express condemnation of the immodesty there that they were given up, especially to the Vandals, that is, to modest barbarians."] (p. 137). Of Africa and Carthage, "In urbe Christiana, in urbe ecclesiastica, . . . viri in semetipsis feminas profitebantur," ["In a Christian city, an ecclesiastical city, men offer themselves as women."] etc. (p. 152).

[84]Dunham, His. Spain, vol. i. p. 112.

When it was possible, the Catholics concealed the relics in caves, keeping up a perpetual memory of these provisional hiding-places.[85] Repeated spoliations were exercised upon the property of the Church. Leovigild applied[86] its treasures partly to increasing the splendour of his throne, partly to national works. At other times, the Arian clergy themselves must have been the recipients of the plunder: for when Childebert the Frank had been brought into Spain by the cruelties exercised against the Catholic Queen of the Goths, who was his sister, he carried away with him from the Arian churches, as St. Gregory of Tours informs us, sixty chalices, fifteen patens, twenty cases in which the gospels were kept, all of pure gold and ornamented with jewels.[87]

## 4.

In France, and especially in Italy, the rule of the heretical power was much less oppressive; Theodoric the Ostrogoth reigned from the Alps to Sicily, and till the close of a long reign he gave an ample toleration to his Catholic subjects. He respected their property, suffered their churches and sacred places to remain in their hands, and had about his court some of their eminent bishops, since known as Saints, St. Cæsarius of Arles, and St. Epiphanius of Pavia. Still he brought into the country a new population, devoted to Arianism, or, as we now speak, a new Church. "His march," says Gibbon,[88] "must be considered as the emigration of an entire people; the wives and children of the Goths, their aged parents, and most precious effects, were carefully transported; and some idea may be formed of the heavy luggage that now followed the camp by the loss of two thousand waggons, which had been sustained in a single action in the war of Epirus." To his soldiers he assigned a third of the soil of Italy, and the barbarian families settled down with their slaves and cattle. The original number of the Vandal conquerors of Africa had only been fifty thousand men, but the military colonists of Italy soon amounted to the number of two hundred thousand; which, according to the calculation adopted by the same author elsewhere, involves a population of a million. The least that could be expected was, that an Arian ascendency established through the extent of Italy would provide for the sufficient celebration of the Arian worship, and we hear of the Arians having a church even

[85] Aguirr. Concil. t. 2, p. 191.
[86] Dunham, p. 125.
[87] Hist. Franc. iii. 10.
[88] ch. 39.

in Rome.[89] The rule of the Lombards in the north of Italy succeeded to that of the Goths—Arians, like their predecessors, without their toleration. The clergy whom they brought with them seem to have claimed their share in the possession of the Catholic churches;[90] and though the Court was converted at the end of thirty years, many cities in Italy were for some time afterwards troubled by the presence of heretical bishops.[91] The rule of Arianism in France lasted for eighty years; in Spain for a hundred and eighty; in Africa for a hundred; for about a hundred in Italy. These periods were not contemporaneous; but extend altogether from the beginning of the fifth to the end of the sixth century.

### 5.

It will be anticipated that the duration of this ascendency of error had not the faintest tendency to deprive the ancient Church of the West of the title of Catholic; and it is needless to produce evidence of a fact which is on the very face of the history. The Arians seem never to have claimed the Catholic name. It is more remarkable that the Catholics during this period were denoted by the additional title of "Romans." Of this there are many proofs in the histories of St. Gregory of Tours, Victor of Vite, and the Spanish Councils. Thus, St. Gregory speaks of Theodegisilus, a king of Portugal, expressing his incredulity at a miracle, by saying, "It is the temper of the Romans (for," interposes the author, "they call men of our religion Romans) and not the power of God."[92] "Heresy is everywhere an enemy to Catholics," says the same St. Gregory in a subsequent place, and he proceeds to illustrate it by the story of a "Catholic woman," who had a heretic husband to whom, he says, came "a presbyter of our religion very Catholic"; and whom the husband matched at table with his own Arian presbyter, "that there might be the priests of each religion" in their house at once. When they were eating, the husband said to the Arian, "Let us have some sport with this presbyter of the Romans."[93] The Arian Count Gomachar, seized on the lands of the Church of Agde in France, and was attacked with a fever; on his recovery, at the prayers of the bishop, he repented of having asked for them, observing, "What will

[89] Greg. Dial. iii. 30.
[90] Ibid. 20.
[91] Gibbon, Hist. ch. 37.
[92] De Glor. Mart. i. 25.
[93] Ibid. 80.

these Romans say now? that my fever came of taking their land."[94]
When the Vandal Theodoric would have killed the Catholic Armo-
gastes, after failing to torture him into heresy, his presbyter dissuaded
him, "lest the Romans should begin to call him a Martyr."[95]

### 6.

This appellation had two meanings; one, which will readily suggest
itself, is its use in contrast to the word "barbarian," as denoting the
faith of the Empire, as "Greek" occurs in St. Paul's Epistles. In this
sense it would more naturally be used by the Romans themselves than
by others. Thus Salvian says that "nearly all the Romans are greater
sinners than the barbarians";[96] and he speaks of "Roman heretics, of
which there is an innumerable multitude,"[97] meaning heretics within
the Empire. And so St. Gregory the Great complains, that he "had
become Bishop of the Lombards rather than of the Romans."[98] And
Evagrius, speaking even of the East, contrasts "Romans and barbarians"[99] in his account of St. Simeon; and at a later date, and even to
this day, Thrace and portions of Dacia and of Asia Minor derive their
name from Rome. In like manner, we find Syrian writers sometimes
speaking of the religion of the Romans, sometimes of the Greeks,[100]
as synonyms.

### 7.

But the word certainly contains also an allusion to the faith and
communion of the Roman See. In this sense the Emperor Theodosius,
in his letter to Acacius of Berœa, contrasts it with Nestorianism, which
was within the Empire as well as Catholicism; during the controversy
raised by that heresy, he exhorts him and others to show themselves
"approved priests of the Roman religion."[101] Again when the Ligurian
nobles were persuading the Arian Ricimer to come to terms with

[94] Ibid. 79.
[95] Vict. Vit. i. 14.
[96] De Gub D. iv. p. 73.
[97] Ibid. v. p. 88.
[98] Epp. i. 31.
[99] Hist. vi. 23.
[100] Cf. Assem. t. i. p. 351, note 4, t. 3, p. 393.
[101] Baron. Ann. 432, 47.

Anthemius, the orthodox representative of the Greek Emperor,[102] they propose to him to send St. Epiphanius as ambassador, a man "whose life is venerable to every Catholic and Roman, and at least amiable in the eyes of a Greek (*Græculus*) if he deserves the sight of him."[103] It must be recollected, too, that the Spanish and African Churches actually were in the closest union with the See of Rome at that time, and that that intercommunion was the visible ecclesiastical distinction between them and their Arian rivals. The chief ground of the Vandal Hunneric's persecution of the African Catholics seems to have been their connexion with their brethren beyond the sea,[104] which he looked at with jealousy, as introducing a foreign power into his territory. Prior to this he had published an edict calling on the "Homoousion" bishops (for on this occasion he did not call them Catholic), to meet his own bishops at Carthage and treat concerning the faith, that "their meetings to the seduction of Christian souls might not be held in the provinces of the Vandals."[105] Upon this invitation, Eugenius of Carthage replied, that all the transmarine bishops of the orthodox communion ought to be summoned, "in particular because it is a matter for the whole world, not special to the African provinces," that "they could not undertake a point of faith *sine universitatis assensu*." Hunneric answered that if Eugenius would make him sovereign of the *orbis terrarum*, he would comply with his request. This led Eugenius to say that the orthodox faith was "the only true faith"; that the king ought to write to his allies abroad, if he wished to know it, and that he himself would write to his brethren for foreign bishops, "who," he says, "may assist us in setting before you the true faith, common to them and to us, and especially the Roman Church, which is the head of all Churches." Moreover, the African bishops in their banishment in Sardinia, to the number of sixty, with St. Fulgentius at their head, quote with approbation the words of Pope Hormisdas, to the effect that they hold, "on the point of free will and divine grace, what the Roman, that is, the Catholic, Church follows and preserves."[106] Again, the Spanish Church was under the superintendence of the Pope's Vicar[107] during the persecutions, whose duty it was to hinder all en-

[102] Gibbon, Hist. ch. 36.
[103] Baron. Ann. 471, 18.
[104] Vict. Vit. iv. 4.
[105] Vict. Vit. ii. 3–15.
[106] Aguirr. Conc. t. 2, p. 262.
[107] Aguirr. ibid. p. 232.

croachments upon "the Apostolical decrees, or the limits of the Holy Fathers," through the whole of the country.

### 8.

Nor was the association of Catholicism with the See of Rome an introduction of that age. The Emperor Gratian, in the fourth century, had ordered that the Churches which the Arians had usurped should be restored, not to those who held "the Catholic faith," or "the Nicene Creed," or were "in communion with the *orbis terrarum*," but "who chose the communion of Damasus,"[108] the then Pope. It was St. Jerome's rule, also, in some well-known passages: Writing against Ruffinus, who had spoken of "our faith," he says, "What does he mean by 'his faith'? that which is the strength of the Roman Church? or that which is contained in the volumes of Origen? If he answer, 'The Roman,' then we are Catholics who have borrowed nothing of Origen's error; but if Origen's blasphemy be his faith, then, while he is charging me with inconsistency, he proves himself to be an heretic."[109] The other passage, already quoted, is still more exactly to the point, because it was written on occasion of a schism. The divisions at Antioch had thrown the Catholic Church into a remarkable position; there were two bishops in the See, one in connexion with the East, the other with Egypt and the West—with which then was "Catholic Communion"? St. Jerome has no doubt on the subject: Writing to St. Damasus, he says, "Since the East tears into pieces the Lord's coat . . . therefore by me is the chair of Peter to be consulted, and that faith which is praised by the Apostle's mouth. . . . Though your greatness terrifies me, yet your kindness invites me. From the Priest I ask the salvation of the victim, from the Shepherd the protection of the sheep. Let us speak without offence; I court not the Roman height: I speak with the successor of the Fisherman and the disciple of the Cross. I, who follow none as my chief but Christ, am associated in communion with thy blessedness, that is, with the See of Peter. On that rock the Church is built, I know. Whoso shall eat the Lamb outside that House is profane. . . . I know not Vitalis" [the Apollinarian], "Meletius I reject, I am ignorant of Paulinus. Whoso gathereth not with thee, scattereth; that is, he who is not of Christ is of Antichrist."[110] Again, "The ancient

---

[108] Theod. Hist. v. 2.
[109] c. Ruff. i. 4.
[110] Ep. 15.

authority of the monks, dwelling round about, rises against me; I meanwhile cry out, If any be joined to Peter's chair he is mine."[111]

### 9.

Here was what may be considered a *dignus vindice nodus*, the Church being divided, and an arbiter wanted. Such a case had also occurred in Africa in the controversy with the Donatists. Four hundred bishops, though but in one region, were a fifth part of the whole Episcopate of Christendom, and might seem too many for a schism, and in themselves too large a body to be cut off from God's inheritance by a mere majority, even had it been overwhelming. St. Augustine, then, who so often appeals to the *orbis terrarum*, sometimes adopts a more prompt criterion. He tells certain Donatists to whom he writes, that the Catholic Bishop of Carthage "was able to make light of the thronging multitude of his enemies, when he found himself by letters of credence joined both to the Roman Church, in which ever had flourished the principality of the Apostolical See, and to the other lands whence the gospel came to Africa itself."[112]

There are good reasons then for explaining the Gothic and Arian use of the word "Roman," when applied to the Catholic Church and faith, of something beyond its mere connexion with the Empire, which the barbarians were assaulting; nor would "Roman" surely be the most obvious word to denote the orthodox faith in the mouths of a people who had learned their heresy from a Roman Emperor and Court, and who professed to direct their belief by the great Latin Council of Ariminum.

### 10.

As then the fourth century presented to us in its external aspect the Catholic Church lying in the midst of a multitude of sects, all enemies to it, so in the fifth and sixth we see the same Church lying in the West under the oppression of a huge, farspreading, and schismatical communion. Heresy is no longer a domestic enemy intermingled with the Church, but it occupies its own ground and is extended over against her, even though on the same territory, and is more or less organized, and cannot be so promptly refuted by the simple test of Catholicity.

[111]Ep. 16.
[112]Aug. Epp. 43, 7.

## 2. The Nestorians

The Churches of Syria and Asia Minor were the most intellectual portion of early Christendom. Alexandria was but one metropolis in a large region, and contained the philosophy of the whole Patriarchate; but Syria abounded in wealthy and luxurious cities, the creation of the Seleucidæ, where the arts and the schools of Greece had full opportunities of cultivation. For a time too, for the first two hundred years, as some think, Alexandria was the only See as well as the only school of Egypt; while Syria was divided into smaller dioceses, each of which had at first an authority of its own, and which, even after the growth of the Patriarchal power, received their respective bishops, not from the See of Antioch, but from their own metropolitan. In Syria too the schools were private, a circumstance which would tend both to diversity in religious opinion, and incaution in the expression of it; but the sole catechetical school of Egypt was the organ of the Church, and its bishop could banish Origen for speculations which developed and ripened with impunity in Syria.

### 2.

But the immediate source of that fertility in heresy, which is the unhappiness of the ancient Syrian Church, was its celebrated Exegetical School. The history of that school is summed up in the broad characteristic fact, on the one hand that it devoted itself to the literal and critical interpretation of Scripture, and on the other that it gave rise first to the Arian and then to the Nestorian heresy. If additional evidence be wanted of the connexion of heterodoxy and biblical criticism in that age, it is found in the fact that, not long after this coincidence in Syria, they are found combined in the person of Theodore of Heraclea, so called from the place both of his birth and his bishopric, an able commentator and an active enemy of St. Athanasius, though a Thracian unconnected except by sympathy with the Patriarchate of Antioch.

The Antiochene School appears to have risen in the middle of the third century; but there is no evidence to determine whether it was a local institution, or, as is more probable, a discipline or method characteristic generally of Syrian teaching. Dorotheus is one of its earliest luminaries; he is known as a Hebrew scholar, as well as a commentator on the sacred text, and he was the master of Eusebius of Cæsarea. Lucian, the friend of the notorious Paul of Samosata, and for three successive Episcopates after him separated from the Church

though afterwards a martyr in it, was the author of a new edition of
the Septuagint, and master of the chief original teachers of Arianism.
Eusebius of Cæsarea, Asterius called the Sophist, and Eusebius of
Emesa, Arians of the Nicene period, and Diodorus, a zealous opponent
of Arianism, but the master of Theodore of Mopsuestia, have all a
place in the Exegetical School. St. Chrysostom and Theodoret, both
Syrians, and the former the pupil of Diodorus, adopted the literal
interpretation, though preserved from its abuse. But the principal doctor of the school was that Theodore, the master of Nestorius, who has
just above been mentioned, and who, with his writings, and with the
writings of Theodoret against St. Cyril, and the letter written by Ibas
of Edessa to Maris, was condemned by the fifth Ecumenical Council.
Ibas was the translator into Syriac, and Maris into Persian, of the
books of Theodore and Diodorus;[113] and thus they became immediate
instruments in the formation of the great Nestorian school and Church
in farther Asia.

As many as ten thousand tracts of Theodore are said in this way to
have been introduced to the knowledge of the Christians of Mesopotamia, Adiabene, Babylonia, and the neighbouring countries. He was
called by those Churches absolutely "the Interpreter," and it eventually
became the very profession of the Nestorian communion to follow him
as such. "The doctrine of all our Eastern Churches," says their Council
under the Patriarch Marabas, "is founded on the Creed of Nicæa; but
in the exposition of the Scriptures we follow St. Theodore." "We must
by all means remain firm to the commentaries of the great Commentator," says the Council under Sabarjesus; "whoso shall in any manner
oppose them, or think otherwise, be he anathema."[114] No one since the
beginning of Christianity, except Origen and St. Augustine, has had so
great literary influence on his brethren as Theodore.[115]

### 3.

The original Syrian School had possessed very marked characteristics, which it did not lose when it passed into a new country and into
strange tongues. Its comments on Scripture seem to have been clear,
natural, methodical, apposite, and logically exact. "In all Western
Aramæa," says Lengerke, that is, in Syria, "there was but one mode

[113] Assem. iii. p. 68.
[114] Ibid. t. 3, p. 84, note 3.
[115] Wegnern, Proleg. in Theod. Opp. p. ix.

of treating whether exegetics or doctrine, the practical."[116] Thus Eusebius of Cæsarea, whether as a disputant or a commentator, is commonly a writer of sense and judgment; and he is to be referred to the Syrian School, though he does not enter so far into its temper as to exclude the mystical interpretation or to deny the verbal inspiration of Scripture. Again, we see in St. Chrysostom a direct, straightforward treatment of the sacred text, and a pointed application of it to things and persons; and Theodoret abounds in modes of thinking and reasoning which without any great impropriety may be called English. Again, St. Cyril of Jerusalem, though he does not abstain from allegory, shows the character of his school by the great stress he lays upon the study of Scripture, and, I may add, by the peculiar characteristics of his style, which will be appreciated by a modern reader.

## 4.

It would have been well had the genius of the Syrian theology been ever in the safe keeping of men such as St. Cyril, St. Chrysostom, and Theodoret; but in Theodore of Mopsuestia, nay in Diodorus before him, it developed into those errors of which Paul of Samosata had been the omen on its rise. As its attention was chiefly directed to the examination of the Scriptures, in its interpretation of the Scriptures was its heretical temper discovered; and though allegory can be made an instrument for evading Scripture doctrine, criticism may more readily be turned to the destruction of doctrine and Scripture together. Theodore was bent on ascertaining the literal sense, an object with which no fault could be found; but, leading him of course to the Hebrew text instead of the Septuagint, it also led him to Jewish commentators. Jewish commentators naturally suggested events and objects short of evangelical as the fulfilment of the prophetical announcements, and, when it was possible, an ethical sense instead of a prophetical. The eighth chapter of Proverbs ceased to bear a Christian meaning, because, as Theodore maintained, the writer of the book had received the gift, not of prophecy, but of wisdom. The Canticles must be interpreted literally; and then it was but an easy, or rather a necessary step, to exclude the book from the Canon. The book of Job too professed to be historical; yet what was it really but a Gentile drama? He also gave up the books of Chronicles and Ezra, and, strange to say, the Epistle of St. James, though it was contained in the Peschito Version

[116]De Ephrem. Syr. p. 61.

of his Church. He denied that Psalms 22 and 69 [21 and 68] applied to our Lord; rather he limited the Messianic passages of the whole book to four; of which the eighth Psalm was one, and the forty-fifth [44] another. The rest he explained of Hezekiah and Zerubbabel, without denying that they might be accommodated to an evangelical sense.[117] He explained St. Thomas's words, "My Lord and my God," as an exclamation of joy, and our Lord's "Receive ye the Holy Ghost" as an anticipation of the day of Pentecost. As may be expected he denied the verbal inspiration of Scripture. Also, he held that the deluge did not cover the earth; and, as others before him, he was heterodox on the doctrine of original sin, and denied the eternity of punishment.

### 5.

Maintaining that the real sense of Scripture was not the scope of a Divine Intelligence, but the intention of the mere human organ of inspiration, Theodore was led to hold not only that that sense was one in each text, but that it was continuous and single in a context; that what was the subject of the composition in one verse must be the subject in the next, and that if a Psalm was historical or prophetical in its commencement, it was the one or the other to its termination. Even that fulness, of meaning, refinement of thought, subtle versatility of feeling, and delicate reserve or reverent suggestiveness which poets exemplify seems to have been excluded from his idea of a sacred composition. Accordingly, if a Psalm contained passages which could not be applied to our Lord, it followed that that Psalm did not properly apply to Him at all, except by accommodation. Such at least is the doctrine of Cosmas, a writer of Theodore's school, who on this ground passes over the twenty-second, sixty-ninth, and other Psalms, and limits the Messianic to the second, the eighth, the forty-fifth, and the hundred and tenth. "David," he says, "did not make common to the servants what belongs to the Lord[118] Christ, but what was proper to the Lord he spoke of the Lord, and what was proper to the servants, of servants."[119] Accordingly the twenty-second could not properly belong to Christ, because in the beginning it spoke of the "*verba delictorum meorum.*" A remarkable consequence would follow from this doctrine, that as Christ was to be separated from His Saints, so

---

[117]Lengerke, de Ephrem. Syr. pp. 73–75.
[118]δεσπότου, vid. La Croze, Thesaur. Ep. t. 3, § 145.
[119]Montf. Coll. Nov. t. 2, p. 227.

the Saints were to be separated from Christ; and an opening was made
for a denial of the doctrine of their *cultus*, though this denial in the
event has not been developed among the Nestorians. But a more serious consequence is latently contained in it, and nothing else than the
Nestorian heresy, viz., that our Lord's manhood is not so intimately
included in His Divine Personality that His brethren according to the
flesh may be associated with the Image of the One Christ. Here St.
Chrysostom pointedly contradicts the doctrine of Theodore, though
his fellow-pupil and friend;[120] as does St. Ephrem, though a Syrian
also;[121] and St. Basil.[122]

### 6.

One other peculiarity of the Syrian School, viewed as independent of
Nestorius, should be added: As it tended to the separation of the Divine
Person of Christ from His manhood, so did it tend to explain away His
Divine Presence in the Sacramental elements. Ernesti seems to consider
the school, in modern language, Sacramentarian: and certainly some of
the most cogent testimonies brought by moderns against the Catholic
doctrine of the Eucharist are taken from writers who are connected
with that school; as the author, said to be St. Chrysostom, of the Epistle
to Cæsarius, Theodoret in his Eranistes, and Facundus. Some countenance too is given to the same view of the Eucharist, at least in some
parts of his works, by Origen, whose language concerning the Incarnation also leans to what was afterwards Nestorianism. To these may be
added Eusebius[123] who, far removed, as he was, from that heresy, was
a disciple of the Syrian School. The language of the later Nestorian
writers seems to have been of the same character.[124] Such then on the
whole is the character of that theology of Theodore which passed from
Cilicia and Antioch to Edessa first, and then to Nisibis.

### 7.

Edessa, the metropolis of Mesopotamia, had remained an oriental
city till the third century, when it was made a Roman colony by Cara-

---

[120] Rosenmuller, Hist. Interpr. t. 3, p. 278.
[121] Lengerke, de Ephr. Syr. pp. 165–67.
[122] Ernest. de Proph. Mess. p. 462.
[123] Eccl. Theol. iii. 12.
[124] Professor Lee's Serm. Oct. 1838, pp. 144–52.

calla.[125] Its position on the confines of two empires gave it great ecclesiastical importance, as the channel by which the theology of Rome and Greece was conveyed to a family of Christians, dwelling in contempt and persecution amid a still heathen world. It was the seat of various schools; apparently of a Greek school, where the classics were studied as well as theology, where Eusebius of Emesa[126] had originally been trained, and where perhaps Protogenes taught.[127] There were also Syrian schools attended by heathen and Christian youths in common. The cultivation of the native language had been an especial object of its masters since the time of Vespasian, so that the pure and refined dialect went by the name of the Edessene.[128] At Edessa too St. Ephrem formed his own Syrian School, which lasted long after him; and there too was the celebrated Persian Christian School, over which Maris presided, who has been already mentioned as the translator of Theodore into Persian.[129] Even in the time of the predecessor of Ibas in the See (before A.D. 435) the Nestorianism of this Persian School was so notorious that Rabbula the Bishop had expelled its masters and scholars;[130] and they, taking refuge in a country which might be called their own, had introduced the heresy to the Churches subject to the Persian King.

### 8.

Something ought to be said of these Churches; though little is known except what is revealed by the fact, in itself of no slight value, that they had sustained two persecutions at the hands of the heathen government in the fourth and fifth centuries. One testimony is extant as early as the end of the second century, to the effect that in Parthia, Media, Persia, and Bactria there were Christians who "were not overcome by evil laws and customs."[131] In the early part of the fourth century, a bishop of Persia attended the Nicene Council, and about the same time Christianity is said to have pervaded nearly the whole of Assyria.[132] Monachism had been introduced there before the middle

[125] Noris. Opp. t. 2, p. 112.
[126] Augusti. Euseb. Em. Opp.
[127] Asseman. Bibl. Or. p. cmxxv.
[128] Hoffman, Gram. Syr. Proleg. § 4.
[129] The educated Persians were also acquainted with Syriac. Assem. t. i. p. 351, note.
[130] Asseman. p. lxx.
[131] Euseb. Præp. vi. 10.
[132] Tillemont, Mem. t. 7, p. 77.

of the fourth century, and shortly after commenced that fearful persecution in which sixteen thousand Christians are said to have suffered.
It lasted thirty years, and is said to have recommenced at the end of
the century. The second persecution lasted for at least another thirty
years of the next, at the very time when the Nestorian troubles were
in progress in the Empire. Trials such as these show the populousness
as well as the faith of the Churches in those parts—and the number
of the Sees, for the names of twenty-seven bishops are preserved who
suffered in the former persecution. One of them was apprehended
together with sixteen priests, nine deacons, besides monks and nuns
of his diocese; another with twenty-eight companions, ecclesiastics or
regulars; another with one hundred ecclesiastics of different orders;
another with one hundred and twenty-eight; another with his chorepis-
copus and two hundred and fifty of his clergy. Such was the Church,
consecrated by the blood of so many martyrs, which immediately after
its glorious confession fell a prey to the theology of Theodore; and
which through a succession of ages manifested the energy, when it had
lost the pure orthodoxy of Saints.

## 9.

The members of the Persian School, who had been driven out of
Edessa by Rabbula, found a wide field open for their exertions under
the pagan government with which they had taken refuge. The Persian
monarchs, who had often prohibited by edict[133] the intercommunion
of the Church under their sway with the countries towards the west,
readily extended their protection to exiles, whose very profession was
the means of destroying its Catholicity. Barsumas, the most energetic
of them, was placed in the metropolitan See of Nisibis, where also the
fugitive school was settled under the presidency of another of their
party; while Maris was promoted to the See of Ardaschir. The primacy
of the Church had from an early period belonged to the See of Seleucia
in Babylonia. Catholicus was the title appropriated to its occupant, as
well as to the Persian Primate, as being deputies of the Patriarch of
Antioch, and was derived apparently from the Imperial dignity so
called, denoting their function as procurators-general, or officers in
chief for the regions in which they were placed. Acacius, another of
the Edessene party, was put into this principal see, and suffered, if he
did not further, the innovations of Barsumas. The mode by which the

---

[133] Gibbon, ch. 47.

latter effected those measures has been left on record by an enemy. "Barsumas accused Babuæus, the Catholicus, before King Pherozes, whispering, 'These men hold the faith of the Romans, and are their spies. Give me power against them to arrest them.' "[134] It is said that in this way he obtained the death of Babuæus, whom Acacius succeeded. When a minority resisted[135] the process of schism, a persecution followed. The death of seven thousand seven hundred Catholics is said by Monophysite authorities to have been the price of the severance of the Chaldaic Churches from Christendom.[136] Their loss was compensated in the eyes of the government by the multitude of Nestorian fugitives who flocked into Persia from the Empire, numbers of them industrious artisans, who sought a country where their own religion was in the ascendant.

## 10.

That religion was founded, as we have already seen, in the literal interpretation of Holy Scripture, of which Theodore was the principal teacher. The doctrine, in which it formally consisted, is known by the name of Nestorianism: it lay in the ascription of a human as well as a Divine Personality to our Lord; and it showed itself in denying the title of "Mother of God," or θεοτόκος, to the Blessed Mary. As to our Lord's Personality, the question of language came into the controversy, which always serves to perplex a subject and make a dispute seem a matter of words. The native Syrians made a distinction between the word "Person" and "Prosopon," which stands for it in Greek; they allowed that there was one Prosopon or Parsopa, as they called it, and they held that there were two Persons. If it is asked what they meant by *parsopa*, the answer seems to be, that they took the word merely in the sense of *character* or *aspect*, a sense familiar to the Greek *prosopon*, and quite irrelevant as a guarantee of their orthodoxy. It follows moreover that, since the *aspect* of a thing is its impression upon the beholder, the personality to which they ascribed unity must have laid in our Lord's manhood, and not in His Divine Nature. But it is hardly worth while pursuing the heresy to its limits. Next, as to the phrase "Mother of God," they rejected it as unscriptural; they maintained that St. Mary was Mother of the humanity of Christ, not

---

[134] Asseman. p. lxxviii.
[135] Gibbon, ibid.
[136] Asseman. t. 2, p. 403, t. 3, p. 393.

of the Word, and they fortified themselves by the Nicene Creed, in which no such title is ascribed to her.

## 11.

Whatever might be the obscurity or the plausibility of their original dogma, there is nothing obscure or attractive in the developments, whether of doctrine or of practice, in which it issued. The first act of the exiles of Edessa, on their obtaining power in the Chaldean communion, was to abolish the celibacy of the clergy, or, in Gibbon's forcible words, to allow "the public and reiterated nuptials of the priests, the bishops, and even the patriarch himself." Barsumas, the great instrument of the change of religion, was the first to set an example of the new usage, and is even said by a Nestorian writer to have married a nun.[137] He passed a canon at councils held at Seleucia and elsewhere that bishops and priests might marry, and might renew their wives as often as they lost them. The Catholicus who followed Acacius went so far as to extend the benefit of the canon to monks, that is, to destroy the Monastic order; and his two successors availed themselves of this liberty, and are recorded to have been fathers. A restriction, however, was afterwards placed upon the Catholicus, and upon the Episcopal order.

## 12.

Such were the circumstances, and such the principles, under which the See of Seleucia became the Rome of the East. In the course of time the Catholicus took on himself the loftier and independent title of Patriarch of Babylon; and though Seleucia was changed for Ctesiphon and for Bagdad,[138] still the name of Babylon was preserved from first to last as a formal or ideal Metropolis. In the time of the Caliphs, it was at the head of as many as twenty-five archbishops; its communion extended from China to Jerusalem; and its numbers, with those of the Monophysites, are said to have surpassed those of the Greek and Latin Churches together. The Nestorians seem to have been unwilling, like the Novatians, to be called by the name of their founder,[139] though they confessed it had adhered to them; one instance may be specified

[137] Asseman. t. 3, p. 67.
[138] Gibbon, ibid.
[139] Assem. p. lxxvi.

of their assuming the name of Catholic,[140] but there is nothing to show it was given them by others.

"From the conquest of Persia," says Gibbon, "they carried their spiritual arms to the North, the East, and the South; and the simplicity of the Gospel was fashioned and painted with the colours of the Syriac theology. In the sixth century, according to the report of a Nestorian traveller, Christianity was successfully preached to the Bactrians, the Huns, the Persians, the Indians, the Persarmenians, the Medes, and the Elamites: the Barbaric Churches from the gulf of Persia to the Caspian Sea were almost infinite; and their recent faith was conspicuous in the number and sanctity of their monks and martyrs. The pepper coast of Malabar and the isles of the ocean, Socotra and Ceylon, were peopled with an increasing multitude of Christians, and the bishops and clergy of those sequestered regions derived their ordination from the Catholicus of Babylon. In a subsequent age, the zeal of the Nestorians overleaped the limits which had confined the ambition and curiosity both of the Greeks and Persians. The missionaries of Balch and Samarcand pursued without fear the footsteps of the roving Tartar, and insinuated themselves into the camps of the valleys of Imaus and the banks of the Selinga."[141]

### 3. The Monophysites

Eutyches was Archimandrite, or abbot, of a monastery in the suburbs of Constantinople; he was a man of unexceptionable character, and was of the age of seventy years, and had been abbot for thirty, at the date of his unhappy introduction into ecclesiastical history. He had been the friend and assistant of St. Cyril of Alexandria, and had lately taken part against Ibas, Bishop of Edessa, whose name has occurred in the above account of the Nestorians. For some time he had been engaged in teaching a doctrine concerning the Incarnation, which he maintained indeed to be none other than that of St. Cyril's in his controversy with Nestorius, but which others denounced as a heresy in the opposite extreme, and substantially a reassertion of Apollinarianism. The subject was brought before a Council of Constantinople, under the presidency of Flavian, the Patriarch, in the year 448; and Eutyches was condemned by the assembled bishops of holding the doctrine of One, instead of Two Natures in Christ.

[140] Ibid. t. 3, p. 441.
[141] ch. 47.

## 2.

It is scarcely necessary for our present purpose to ascertain accurately what he held, and there has been a great deal of controversy on the subject; partly from confusion between him and his successors, partly from the indecision or the ambiguity which commonly attaches to the professions of heretics. If a statement must here be made of the doctrine of Eutyches himself, in whom the controversy began, let it be said to consist in these two tenets: in maintaining first, that "before the Incarnation there were two natures, after their union one," or that our Lord was of or from two natures, but not in two; and, secondly, that His flesh was not of one substance with ours, that is, not of the substance of the Blessed Virgin. Of these two points, he seemed willing to abandon the second, but was firm in his maintenance of the first. But let us return to the Council of Constantinople.

In his examination Eutyches allowed that the Holy Virgin was consubstantial with us, and that "our God was incarnate of her"; but he would not allow that He was therefore, as man, consubstantial with us, his notion apparently being that union with the Divinity had changed what otherwise would have been human nature. However, when pressed, he said, that, though up to that day he had not permitted himself to discuss the nature of Christ, or to affirm that "God's body is man's body though it was human," yet he would allow, if commanded, our Lord's consubstantiality with us. Upon this Flavian observed that "the Council was introducing no innovation, but declaring the faith of the Fathers." To his other position, however, that our Lord had but one nature after the Incarnation, he adhered: when the Catholic doctrine was put before him, he answered, "Let St. Athanasius be read; you will find nothing of the kind in him."

His condemnation followed: it was signed by twenty-two bishops and twenty-three abbots;[142] among the former were Flavian of Constantinople, Basil, Metropolitan of Seleucia in Isauria, the Metropolitans of Amasea in Pontus, and Marcianopolis in Mœsia, and the Bishop of Cos, the Pope's minister at Constantinople.

## 3.

Eutyches appealed to the Pope of the day, St. Leo, who at first hearing took his part. He wrote to Flavian that, "judging by the statement

[142] Fleur. Hist. xxvii. 29.

of Eutyches, he did not see with what justice he had been separated from the communion of the Church." "Send therefore," he continued, "some suitable person to give us a full account of what has occurred, and let us know what the new error is." St. Flavian, who had behaved with great forbearance throughout the proceedings, had not much difficulty in setting the controversy before the Pope in its true light.

Eutyches was supported by the Imperial Court, and by Dioscorus, the Patriarch of Alexandria; the proceedings therefore at Constantinople were not allowed to settle the question. A general Council was summoned for the ensuing summer at Ephesus, where the third Ecumenical Council had been held twenty years before against Nestorius. It was attended by sixty metropolitans, ten from each of the great divisions of the East; the whole number of bishops assembled amounted to one hundred and thirty-five.[143] Dioscorus was appointed President by the Emperor, and the object of the assembly was said to be the settlement of a question of faith which had arisen between Flavian and Eutyches. St. Leo, dissatisfied with the measure altogether, nevertheless sent his legates, but with the object, as their commission stated, and a letter he addressed to the Council, of "condemning the heresy, and reinstating Eutyches if he retracted." His legates took precedence after Dioscorus and before the other patriarchs. He also published at this time his celebrated Tome on the Incarnation, in a letter addressed to Flavian.

The proceedings which followed were of so violent a character that the Council has gone down to posterity under the name of the Latrocinium or "Gang of Robbers." Eutyches was honourably acquitted, and his doctrine received; but the assembled Fathers showed some backwardness to depose St. Flavian. Dioscorus had been attended by a multitude of monks, furious zealots for the Monophysite doctrine from Syria and Egypt, and by an armed force. These broke into the church at his call; Flavian was thrown down and trampled on, and received injuries of which he died the third day after. The Pope's legates escaped as they could; and the bishops were compelled to sign a blank paper, which was afterwards filled up with the condemnation of Flavian. These outrages, however, were subsequent to the Synodical acceptance of the Creed of Eutyches, which seems to have been the spontaneous act of the assembled Fathers. The proceedings ended by Dioscorus excommunicating the Pope, and the Emperor issuing an edict in approval of the decision of the Council.

[143] Gibbon, ch. 47.

## 4.

Before continuing the narrative, let us pause awhile to consider what it has already brought before us. An aged and blameless man, the friend of a Saint, and him the great champion of the faith against the heresy of his day, is found in the belief and maintenance of a doctrine which he declares to be the very doctrine which that Saint taught in opposition to that heresy. To prove it, he and his friends refer to the very words of St. Cyril; Eustathius of Berytus quoting from him at Ephesus as follows: "We must not then conceive two natures, but one nature of the Word incarnate."[144] Moreover, it seems that St. Cyril had been called to account for this very phrase, and had appealed more than once to a passage, which is extant as he quoted it, in a work by St. Athanasius.[145] Whether the passage in question is genuine is very doubtful, but that is not to the purpose; for the phrase which it contains is also attributed by St. Cyril to other Fathers, and was admitted by Catholics generally, as by St. Flavian, who deposed Eutyches, nay was indirectly adopted by the Council of Chalcedon itself.

## 5.

But Eutyches did not merely insist upon a phrase; he appealed for his doctrine to the Fathers generally; "I have read the blessed Cyril, and the holy Fathers, and the holy Athanasius," he says at Constantinople, "that they said, 'Of two natures before the union,' but that 'after the union' they said 'but one.' "[146] In his letter to St. Leo, he appeals in particular to Pope Julius, Pope Felix, St. Gregory Thaumaturgus, St. Gregory Nazianzen, St. Basil, Atticus, and St. Proclus. He did not appeal to them unreservedly certainly, as shall be presently noticed; he allowed that they might err, and perhaps had erred, in their expressions: but it is plain, even from what has been said, that there could be no consensus against him, as the word is now commonly understood. It is also undeniable that, though the word "nature" is applied to our Lord's manhood by St. Ambrose, St. Gregory Nazianzen and others, yet on the whole it is for whatever reason avoided by the previous Fathers; certainly by St. Athanasius, who uses the words "manhood," "flesh," "the man," "economy," where a later writer

---

[144] Concil. Hard. t. 2, p. 127.
[145] Petav. de Incarn. iv. 6, § 4.
[146] Concil. Hard. t. 2, p. 168.

would have used "nature"; and the same is true of St. Hilary.[147] In
like manner, the Athanasian Creed, written, as it is supposed, some
twenty years before the date of Eutyches, does not contain the word
"nature." Much might be said on the plausibility of the defence which
Eutyches might have made for his doctrine from the history and documents of the Church before his time.

## 6.

Further, Eutyches professed to subscribe heartily the decrees of the
Council of Nicæa and Ephesus, and his friends appealed to the latter
of these Councils and to previous Fathers, in proof that nothing could
be added to the Creed of the Church. "I," he says to St. Leo, "even
from my elders have so understood, and from my childhood have so
been instructed, as the holy and Ecumenical Council at Nicæa of the
three hundred and eighteen most blessed bishops settled the faith, and
which the holy Council held at Ephesus maintained and defined anew
as the only faith; and I have never understood otherwise than as the
right or only true orthodox faith hath enjoined." He says at the Latrocinium, "When I declared that my faith was conformable to the decision of Nicæa, confirmed at Ephesus, they demanded that I should add
some words to it; and I, fearing to act contrary to the decrees of the
First Council of Ephesus and of the Council of Nicæa, desired that your
holy Council might be made acquainted with it, since I was ready to
submit to whatever you should approve."[148] Dioscorus states the matter more strongly: "We have heard," he says, "what this Council" of
Ephesus "decreed, that if any one affirm or opine anything, or raise any
question, beyond the Creed aforesaid" of Nicæa, "he is to be condemned."[149] It is remarkable that the Council of Ephesus, which laid

[147]Vid. the Author's Athan. trans. [ed. 1881, vol. ii. pp. 331–33, 426–29,
and on the general subject his Theol. Tracts, art. v].

[148]Fleury, Oxf. tr. xxvii. 39.

[149]Ibid. 41. In like manner, St. Athanasius in the foregoing age had said,
"The faith confessed at Nicæa by the Fathers, according to the Scriptures, is
sufficient for the overthrow of all misbelief." ad Epict. init. Elsewhere, however, he explains his statement, "The decrees of Nicæa are right and sufficient
for the overthrow of all heresy, *especially* the Arian." ad. Max. fin. St. Gregory
Nazianzen, in like manner, appeals to Nicæa; but he "adds an explanation on
the doctrine of the Holy Spirit which was left deficient by the Fathers, because
the question had not then been raised." Ep. 102, init. This exclusive maintenance, and yet extension of the Creed, according to the exigencies of the times,
is instanced in other Fathers. Vid. Athan. tr. [ed. 1881, vol. ii. p. 82].

down this rule, had itself sanctioned the Theotocos, an addition, greater perhaps than any before or since, to the letter of the primitive faith.

7.

Further, Eutyches appealed to Scripture, and denied that a human nature was there given to our Lord; and this appeal obliged him in consequence to refuse an unconditional assent to the Councils and Fathers, though he so confidently spoke about them at other times. It was urged against him that the Nicene Council itself had introduced into the Creed extra-scriptural terms. " 'I have never found in Scripture,' he said," according to one of the Priests who were sent to him, " 'that there are two natures.' I replied, 'Neither is the Consubstantiality [the Homoousion of Nicæa] to be found in the Scriptures, but in the Holy Fathers who well understood them and faithfully expounded them.' "[150] Accordingly, on another occasion, a report was made of him, that "he professed himself ready to assent to the Exposition of Faith made by the Holy Fathers of the Nicene and Ephesine Councils and he engaged to subscribe their interpretations. However, if there were any accidental fault or error in any expressions which they made, this he would neither blame nor accept; but only search the Scriptures, as being surer than the expositions of the Fathers; that since the time of the Incarnation of God the Word . . . he worshipped one Nature . . . that the doctrine that our Lord Jesus Christ came of Two Natures personally united, this it was that he had learned from the expositions of the Holy Fathers; nor did he accept, if ought was read to him from any author to [another] effect, because the Holy Scriptures, as he said, were better than the teaching of the Fathers."[151] This appeal to the Scriptures will remind us of what has lately been said of the school of Theodore in the history of Nestorianism, and of the challenge of the Arians to St. Avitus before the Gothic King.[152] It had also been the characteristic of heresy in the antecedent period. St. Hilary brings together a number of instances in point, from the history of Marcellus, Photinus, Sabellius, Montanus, and Manes; then he adds, "They all speak Scripture without the sense of Scripture, and profess a faith without faith."[153]

[150] Fleury, ibid. 27.
[151] Concil. Hard. t. 2, p. 141. [A negative is omitted in the Greek, but inserted in the Latin.]
[152] Supr. p. 241.
[153] Ad Const. ii. 9. Vid. Athan. tr. [ed. 1881, vol. ii. p. 261].

## 8.

Once more; the Council of the Latrocinium, however, tyrannized over by Dioscorus in the matter of St. Flavian, certainly did acquit Eutyches and accept his doctrine canonically, and, as it would appear, cordially; though their change at Chalcedon, and the subsequent variations of the East, make it a matter of little moment how they decided. The Acts of Constantinople were read to the Fathers of the Latrocinium; when they came to the part where Eusebius of Dorylaeum, the accuser of Eutyches, asked him whether he confessed Two Natures after the Incarnation, and the Consubstantiality according to the flesh, the Fathers broke in upon the reading: "Away with Eusebius; burn him; burn him alive; cut him in two; as he divided, so let him be divided."[154] The Council seems to have been unanimous, with the exception of the Pope's legates, in the restoration of Eutyches; a more complete decision can hardly be imagined.

It is true the whole number of signatures now extant, one hundred and eight, may seem small out of a thousand, the number of sees in the East; but the attendance of Councils always bore a representative character. The whole number of East and West was about eighteen hundred, yet the second Ecumenical Council was attended by only one hundred and fifty, which is but a twelfth part of the whole number; the Third Council by about two hundred, or a ninth; the Council of Nicæa itself numbered only three hundred and eighteen bishops. Moreover, when we look through the names subscribed to the Synodal decision, we find that the misbelief, or misapprehension, or weakness to which this great offence must be attributed was no local phenomenon, but the unanimous sin of bishops in every patriarchate and of every school of the East. Three out of the four patriarchs were in favor of the heresiarch, the fourth being on his trial. Of these Domnus of Antioch and Juvenal of Jerusalem acquitted him, on the ground of his confessing the faith of Nicæa and Ephesus: and Domnus was a man of the fairest and purest character, and originally a disciple of St. Euthemius, however inconsistent on this occasion, and ill-advised in former steps of his career. Dioscorus, violent and bad man as he showed himself, had been Archdeacon to St. Cyril, whom he attended at the Council of Ephesus; and was on this occasion supported by those Churches which had so nobly stood by their patriarch Athanasius in the great Arian conflict. These three Patriarchs were supported by the Exarchs of Ephesus and

---

[154]Concil. Hard. t. 2, p. 162.

Cæsarea in Cappadocia; and both of these, as well as Domnus and Juvenal, were supported in turn by their subordinate Metropolitans. Even the sees under the influence of Constantinople, which was the remaining sixth division of the East, took part with Eutyches. We find among the signatures to his acquittal the Bishops of Dyrrachium, of Heraclea in Macedonia, of Messene in the Peloponese, of Sebaste in Armenia, of Tarsus, of Damascus, of Berytus, of Bostra in Arabia, of Amida in Mesopotamia, of Himeria in Orshoëne, of Babylon, of Arsinoe in Egypt, and of Cyrene. The Bishops of Palestine, of Macedonia, and of Achaia, where the keen eye of St. Athanasius had detected the doctrine in its germ, while Apollinarianism was but growing into form, were his actual partisans. Another Barsumas, a Syrian abbot, ignorant of Greek, attended the Latrocinium as the representative of the monks of his nation, whom he formed into a force, material or moral, of a thousand strong, and whom at that infamous assembly he cheered on to the murder of St. Flavian.

### 9.

Such was the state of Eastern Christendom in the year 449; a heresy, appealing to the Fathers, to the Creed, and, above all, to Scripture, was by a general Council, professing to be Ecumenical, received as true in the person of its promulgator. If the East could determine a matter of faith independently of the West, certainly the Monophysite heresy was established as Apostolic truth in all its provinces from Macedonia to Egypt.

There has been a time in the history of Christianity, when it had been Athanasius against the world, and the world against Athanasius. The need and straitness of the Church had been great, and one man was raised up for her deliverance. In this second necessity, who was the destined champion of her who cannot fail? Whence did he come, and what was his name? He came with an augury of victory upon him, which even Athanasius could not show; it was Leo, Bishop of Rome.

### 10.

Leo's augury of success, which even Athanasius had not, was this, that he was seated in the chair of St. Peter and the heir of his prerogatives. In the very beginning of the controversy, St. Peter Chrysologus had urged this grave consideration upon Eutyches himself, in words which have already been cited: "I exhort you, my venerable brother," he had said, "to submit yourself in everything to what has been written by the blessed Pope of Rome; for St. Peter, who lives and presides in his own See, gives the true faith to those who seek it."[155] This voice had come from Ravenna, and now after the Latrocinium it was echoed back from the depths of Syria by the learned Theodoret. "That all-holy See," he says in a letter to one of the Pope's legates, "has the office of heading (ἡγεμονίαν) the whole world's Churches for many reasons; and above all others, because it has remained free of the communion of heretical taint, and no one of heterodox sentiments hath sat in it, but it hath preserved the Apostolic grace unsullied."[156] And a third testimony in encouragement of the faithful at the same dark moment issued from the Imperial Court of the West. "We are bound," says Valentinian to the Emperor of the East, "to preserve inviolate in our times the prerogative of particular reverence to the blessed Apostle Peter; that the most blessed Bishop of Rome, to whom Antiquity assigned the priesthood over all (κατὰ πάντων) may have place and opportunity of judging concerning the faith and the priests."[157] Nor had Leo himself been wanting at the same time in "the confidence" he had "obtained from the most blessed Peter and head of the Apostles, that he had authority to defend the truth for the peace of the Church."[158] Thus Leo introduces us to the Council of Chalcedon, by which he rescued the East from a grave heresy.

## 11.

The Council met on the eighth of October, 451, and was attended by the largest number of bishops of any Council before or since; some say by as many as six hundred and thirty. Of these, only four came from the West, two Roman legates and two Africans.[159]

Its proceedings were opened by the Pope's legates, who said that they had it in charge from the Bishop of Rome, "which is the head of all the Churches," to demand that Dioscorus should not sit, on the ground that "he had presumed to hold a Council without the authority of the Apostolic See, which had never been done nor was lawful to do."[160] This was immediately allowed them.

[155] Fleury, Hist. Oxf. tr. xxvii. 37.
[156] Ep. 116.
[157] Conc. Hard. t. 2, p. 36.
[158] Ep. 43.
[159] Fleury, Hist. Oxf. tr. xxviii. 17, note *l*.
[160] Concil. Hard. t. 2, p. 68.

The next act of the Council was to give admission to Theodoret, who had been deposed at the Latrocinium. The Imperial officers present urged his admission, on the ground that "the most holy Archbishop Leo hath restored him to the Episcopal office, and the most pious Emperor hath ordered that he should assist at the holy Council."[161]

Presently, a charge was brought forward against Dioscorus, that, though the legates had presented a letter from the Pope to the Council, it had not been read. Dioscorus admitted not only the fact, but its relevancy; but alleged in excuse that he had twice ordered it to be read in vain.

In the course of the reading of the Acts of the Latrocinium and Constantinople, a number of bishops moved from the side of Dioscorus and placed themselves with the opposite party. When Peter, Bishop of Corinth, crossed over, the Orientals whom he joined shouted, "Peter thinks as does Peter; orthodox Bishop, welcome."

## 12.

In the second session it was the duty of the Fathers to draw up a confession of faith condemnatory of the heresy. A committee was formed for the purpose, and the Creed of Nicæa and Constantinople was read; then some of the Epistles of St. Cyril; lastly, St. Leo's Tome, which had been passed over in silence at the Latrocinium. Some discussion followed upon the last of these documents, but at length the bishops cried out, "This is the faith of the Fathers; this is the faith of the Apostles: we all believe thus; the orthodox believe thus; anathema to him who does not believe thus. Peter has thus spoken through Leo; the Apostles taught thus." Readings from the other Fathers followed; and then some days were allowed for private discussion, before drawing up the confession of faith which was to set right the heterodoxy of the Latrocinium.

During the interval, Dioscorus was tried and condemned; sentence was pronounced against him by the Pope's legates, and ran thus: "The most holy Archbishop of Rome, Leo, through us and this present Council, with the Apostle St. Peter, who is the rock and foundation of the Catholic Church and of the orthodox faith, deprives him of the Episcopal dignity and every sacerdotal ministry."

In the fourth session the question of the definition of faith came on again, but the Council got no further than this, that it received the

---

[161] Fleury, Oxf. tr. xxviii. 2, 3.

definitions of the three previous Ecumenical Councils; it would not add to them what Leo required. One hundred and sixty bishops however subscribed his Tome.

## 13.

In the fifth session the question came on once more; some sort of definition of faith was the result of the labours of the committee, and was accepted by the great majority of the Council. The bishops cried out, "We are all satisfied with the definition; it is the faith of the Fathers: anathema to him who thinks otherwise: drive out the Nestorians." When objectors appeared, Anatolius, the new Patriarch of Constantinople, asked "Did not every one yesterday consent to the definition of faith?" on which the bishops answered, "Every one consented; we do not believe otherwise; it is the Faith of the Fathers; let it be set down that Holy Mary is the Mother of God: let this be added to the Creed; put out the Nestorians."[162] The objectors were the Pope's legates, supported by a certain number of Orientals: those clear-sighted, firm-minded Latins understood full well what and what alone was the true expression of orthodox doctrine under the emergency of the existing heresy. They had been instructed to induce the Council to pass a declaration to the effect, that Christ was not only "of" but "in" two natures. However, they did not enter upon disputation on the point, but they used a more intelligible argument: If the Fathers did not consent to the letter of the blessed Bishop Leo, they would leave the Council and go home. The Imperial officers took the part of the legates. The Council however persisted: "Every one approved the definition; let it be subscribed: he who refuses to subscribe it is a heretic." They even proceeded to refer it to Divine inspiration. The officers asked if they received St. Leo's Tome; they answered that they had subscribed it, but that they would not introduce its contents into their definition of faith. "We are for no other definition," they said; "nothing is wanting in this."

## 14.

Notwithstanding, the Pope's legates gained their point through the support of the Emperor Marcian, who had succeeded Theodosius. A fresh committee was obtained under the threat that, if they resisted,

[162] Ibid. 20.

the Council should be transferred to the West. Some voices were raised against this measure; the cries were repeated against the Roman party, "They are Nestorians; let them go to Rome." The Imperial officers remonstrated, "Dioscorus said, 'Of two natures'; Leo says, 'Two natures': which will you follow, Leo or Dioscorus?" On their answering "Leo," they continued, "Well then, add to the definition, according to the judgment of our most holy Leo." Nothing more was to be said. The committee immediately proceeded to their work, and in a short time returned to the assembly with such a definition as the Pope required. After reciting the Creed of Nicæa and Constantinople, it observes, "This Creed were sufficient for the perfect knowledge of religion, but the enemies of the truth have invented novel expressions"; and therefore it proceeds to state the faith more explicitly. When this was read through, the bishops all exclaimed, "This is the faith of the Fathers; we all follow it." And thus ended the controversy once for all.

The Council, after its termination, addressed a letter to St. Leo; in it the Fathers acknowledge him as "constituted interpreter of the voice of Blessed Peter"[163] (with an allusion to St. Peter's Confession in Matthew xvi.) and speak of him as "the very one commissioned with the guardianship of the Vine by the Saviour."

### 15.

Such is the external aspect of those proceedings by which the Catholic faith has been established in Christendom against the Monophysites. That the definition passed at Chalcedon is the Apostolic Truth once delivered to the Saints is most firmly to be received, from faith in that overruling Providence which is by special promise extended over the acts of the Church; moreover, that it is in simple accordance with the faith of St. Athanasius, St. Gregory Nazianzen, and all the other Fathers will be evident to the theological student in proportion as he becomes familiar with their works; but the historical account of the Council is this, that a formula which the Creed did not contain, which the Fathers did not unanimously witness, and which some eminent Saints had almost in set terms opposed, which the whole East refused as a symbol, not once, but twice, patriarch by patriarch, metropolitan by metropolitan, first by the mouth of above a hundred, then by the mouth of above six hundred of its bishops, and refused upon

---

[163] Conc. Hard. t. 2, p. 656.

the grounds of its being an addition to the Creed was forced upon the Council, not indeed as being such an addition, yet, on the other hand, not for subscription merely, but for acceptance as a definition of faith under the sanction of an anathema—forced on the Council by the resolution of the Pope of the day, acting through his legates and supported by the civil power.[164]

## 16.

It cannot be supposed that such a transaction would approve itself to the Churches of Egypt, and the event showed it: they disowned the authority of the Council, and called its adherents Chalcedonians[165] and Synodites.[166] For here was the West tyrannizing over the East, forcing it into agreement with itself, resolved to have one and one only form of words, rejecting the definition of faith which the East had drawn up in council, bidding it and making it frame another, dealing peremptorily and sternly with the assembled bishops, and casting contempt on the most sacred traditions of Egypt! What was Eutyches to them? He might be guilty or innocent; they gave him up: Dioscorus had given him up at Chalcedon;[167] they did not agree with him;[168] he was an extreme man; they would not call themselves by human titles; they were not Eutychians; Eutyches was not their master, but Athanasius and Cyril were their doctors.[169] The two great lights of their Church, the two greatest and most successful polemical Fathers that Christianity had seen, had both pronounced "One Nature Incarnate," though allowing Two before the Incarnation; and though Leo and his Council had not gone so far as to deny this phrase, they had proceeded to say what was the contrary to it, to explain away, to overlay the truth, by defining that the Incarnate Saviour was "in Two Natures." At Ephesus it had been declared that the Creed should not be touched; the Chalcedonian Fathers had, not literally, but virtually added to it: by subscribing Leo's Tome, and promulgating their definition of faith, they had added what might be called "The Creed of Pope Leo."

[164] Can any so grave an *ex parte* charge as this be urged against the recent Vatican Council?

[165] I cannot find my reference for this fact; the sketch is formed from notes made some years since, though I have now verified them.

[166] Leont. de Sect. v. p. 512.

[167] Concil. Hard. t. 2, p. 99, vid. also p. 418.

[168] Renaud. Patr. Alex. p. 115.

[169] Assem. t. 2, pp. 133–37.

## 17.

It is remarkable, as has been just stated, that Dioscorus, wicked man as he was in act, was of the moderate or middle school in doctrine, as the violent and able Severus after him; and from the first the great body of the protesting party disowned Eutyches, whose form of the heresy took refuge in Armenia, where it remains to this day. The Armenians alone were pure Eutychians, and so zealously such that they innovated on the ancient and recognized custom of mixing water with the wine in the Holy Eucharist, and consecrated the wine by itself in token of the one nature, as they considered, of the Christ. Elsewhere both name and doctrine of Eutyches were abjured; the heretical bodies in Egypt and Syria took a title from their special tenet, and formed the Monophysite communion. Their theology was at once simple and specious. They based it upon the illustration which is familiar to us in the Athanasian Creed, and which had been used by St. Gregory Nazianzen, St. Cyril, St. Augustine, Vincent of Lerins, not to say St. Leo himself. They argued that as body and soul made up one man, so God and man made up but one, though one compound Nature, in Christ. It might have been charitably hoped that their difference from the Catholics had been a simple matter of words, as it is allowed by Vigilius of Thapsus really to have been in many cases; but their refusal to obey the voice of the Church was a token of real error in their faith, and their implicit heterodoxy is proved by their connexion, in spite of themselves, with the extreme or ultra party whom they so vehemently disowned.

It is very observable that, ingenious as is their theory and sometimes perplexing to a disputant, the Monophysites never could shake themselves free of the Eutychians; and though they could draw intelligible lines on paper between the two doctrines, yet in fact by a hidden fatality their partisans were ever running into or forming alliance with the anathematized extreme. Thus Peter the Fuller the Theopaschite (Eutychian) is at one time in alliance with Peter the Stammerer, who advocated the Henoticon (which was Monophysite). The Acephali, though separating from the latter Peter for that advocacy, and accused by Leontius of being Gaianites[170] (Eutychians), are considered by Facundus as Monophysites.[171] Timothy the Cat, who is said to have agreed with Dioscorus and Peter the Stammerer, who signed the Henoticon, that is, with two Monophysite patriarchs, is said nevertheless,

[170] Leont. de Sect. vii. pp. 521–22.
[171] Fac. i. 5, circ. init.

according to Anastasius, to have maintained the extreme tenet, that "the Divinity is the sole nature of Christ."[172] Severus, according to Anastasius, symbolized with the Phantasiasts (Eutychians), yet he is more truly, according to Leontius, the chief doctor and leader of the Monophysites. And at one time there was an union, though temporary, between the Theodosians (Monophysites) and the Gaianites.

### 18.

Such a division of an heretical party into the maintainers of an extreme and a moderate view, perspicuous and plausible on paper, yet in fact unreal, impracticable, and hopeless, was no new phenomenon in the history of the Church. As Eutyches put forward an extravagant tenet, which was first corrected into the Monophysite, and then relapsed hopelessly into the doctrine of the Phantasiasts and the Theopaschites, so had Arius been superseded by the Eusebians and had revived in Eunomius; and as the moderate Eusebians had formed the great body of the dissentients from the Nicene Council, so did the Monophysites include the mass of those who protested against Chalcedon; and as the Eusebians had been moderate in creed, yet unscrupulous in act, so were the Monophysites. And as the Eusebians were ever running individually into pure Arianism, so did the Monophysites run into pure Eutychianism. And as the Monophysites set themselves against Pope Leo, so had the Eusebians, with even less provocation, withstood and complained of Pope Julius. In like manner, the Apollinarians had divided into two sects; one, with Timotheus, going the whole length of the inferences which the tenet of their master involved, and the more cautious or timid party making an unintelligible stand with Valentinus. Again, in the history of Nestorianism, though it admitted less opportunity for division of opinion, the See of Rome was with St. Cyril in one extreme, Nestorius in the other, and between them the great Eastern party, headed by John of Antioch and Theodoret, not heretical, but for a time dissatisfied with the Council of Ephesus.

### 19.

The Nestorian heresy, I have said, gave less opportunity for doctrinal varieties than the heresy of Eutyches. Its spirit was rationalizing, and

[172]Hodeg. 20, p. 319.

had the qualities which go with rationalism. When cast out of the Roman Empire, it addressed itself, as we have seen, to a new and rich field of exertion, got possession of an Established Church, co-operated with the civil government, adopted secular fashions, and, by whatever means, pushed itself out into an Empire. Apparently, though it requires a very intimate knowledge of its history to speak except conjecturally, it was a political power rather than a dogma, and despised the science of theology. Eutychianism, on the other hand, was mystical, severe, enthusiastic; with the exception of Severus, and one or two more, it was supported by little polemical skill; it had little hold upon the intellectual Greeks of Syria and Asia Minor, but flourished in Egypt, which was far behind the East in civilization, and among the native Syrians. Nestorianism, like Arianism[173] before it, was a cold religion, and more fitted for the schools than for the many; but the Monophysites carried the people with them. Like modern Jansenism, and unlike Nestorianism, the Monophysites were famous for their austerities. They have, or had, five Lents in the year, during which laity as well as clergy abstain not only from flesh and eggs, but from wine, oil, and fish.[174] Monachism was a characteristic part of their ecclesiastical system: their bishops, and Maphrian or Patriarch, were always taken from the monks, who are even said to have worn an iron shirt or breastplate as a part of their monastic habit.[175]

## 20.

Severus, Patriarch of Antioch at the end of the fifth century, has already been mentioned as an exception to the general character of the Monophysites, and, by his learning and ability, may be accounted the founder of its theology. Their cause, however, had been undertaken by the Emperors themselves before him. For the first thirty years after the Council of Chalcedon, the protesting Church of Egypt had been the scene of continued tumult and bloodshed. Dioscorus had been popular with the people for his munificence, in spite of the extreme laxity of his morals, and for a while the Imperial government failed in obtaining the election of a Catholic successor. At length Proterius, a

[173] *I.e.* Arianism in the East: "Sanctiores aures plebis quam corda sunt sacerdotum." ["There is more holiness in the ears of the people than in the hearts of the priests."] S. Hil. contr. Auxent. 6. It requires some research to account for its hold on the barbarians. Vid. supr. pp. 266–67.

[174] Gibbon, ch. 47.

[175] Assem. t. 2, de Monoph. circ. fin.

man of fair character, and the Vicar-general of Dioscorus on his absence at Chalcedon, was chosen, consecrated, and enthroned; but the
people rose against the civil authorities, and the military, coming to
their defence, were attacked with stones, and pursued into a church,
where they were burned alive by the mob. Next, the popular leaders
prepared to intercept the supplies of grain which were destined for
Constantinople; and, a defensive retaliation taking place, Alexandria
was starved. Then a force of two thousand men was sent for the
restoration of order, who permitted themselves in scandalous excesses
towards the women of Alexandria. Proterius's life was attempted, and
he was obliged to be attended by a guard. The bishops of Egypt would
not submit to him; two of his own clergy, who afterward succeeded
him, Timothy and Peter, seceded, and were joined by four or five of
the bishops and by the mass of the population;[176] and the Catholic
Patriarch was left without a communion in Alexandria. He held a
council, and condemned the schismatics; and the Emperor, seconding
his efforts, sent them out of the country, and enforced the laws against
the Eutychians. An external quiet succeeded; then Marcian died; and
then forthwith Timothy (the Cat) made his appearance again, first in
Egypt, then in Alexandria. The people rose in his favour, and carried
in triumph their persecuted champion to the great Cæsarean Church,
where he was consecrated Patriarch by two deprived bishops, who
had been put out of their sees, whether by a Council of Egypt or of
Palestine.[177] Timothy, now raised to the episcopal rank, began to create
a new succession; he ordained bishops for the Churches of Egypt, and
drove into exile those who were in possession. The Imperial troops,
who had been stationed in Upper Egypt, returned to Alexandria; the
mob rose again, broke into the church where St. Proterius was in
prayer and murdered him. A general ejectment of the Catholic clergy
throughout Egypt followed. On their betaking themselves to Constantinople to the new Emperor, Timothy and his party addressed him
also. They quoted the Fathers, and demanded the abrogation of the
Council of Chalcedon. Next they demanded a conference; the Catholics said that what was once done could not be undone; their opponents
agreed to this and urged it, as their very argument against Chalcedon,
that it added to the faith, and reversed former decisions.[178] After a rule
of three years, Timothy was driven out and Catholicism restored; but

[176] Leont. Sect. v. init.
[177] Tillemont, t. 15, p. 784.
[178] Tillemont, Mem. t. 15, pp. 790–811.

then in turn the Monophysites rallied, and this state of warfare and alternate success continued for thirty years.

### 21.

At length the Imperial government, wearied out with a dispute which was interminable, came to the conclusion that the only way of restoring peace to the Church was to abandon the Council of Chalcedon. In the year 482 was published the famous *Henoticon* or Pacification of Zeno, in which the Emperor took upon himself to determine a matter of faith. The Henoticon declared that no symbol of faith but that of the Nicene Creed, commonly so called, should be received in the Churches; it anathematized the opposite heresies of Nestorius and Eutyches, and it was silent on the question of the "One" or "Two Natures" after the Incarnation. This middle measure had the various effects which might be anticipated. It united the great body of the Eastern bishops, who readily relaxed into the vague profession of doctrine from which they had been roused by the authority of St. Leo. All the Eastern bishops signed this Imperial formulary. But this unanimity of the East was purchased by a breach with the West; for the Popes cut off the communication between Greeks and Latins for thirty-five years. On the other hand, the more zealous Monophysites, disgusted at their leaders for accepting what they considered an unjustifiable compromise, split off from the Eastern Churches, and formed a sect by themselves, which remained without bishops (*acephali*) for three hundred years, when at length they were received back into the communion of the Catholic Church.

### 22.

Dreary and waste was the condition of the Church, and forlorn her prospects, at the period which we have been reviewing. After the brief triumph which attended the conversion of Constantine, trouble and trial had returned upon her. Her imperial protectors were failing in power or in faith. Strange forms of evil were rising in the distance and were thronging for the conflict. There was but one spot in the whole of Christendom, one voice in the whole Episcopate, to which the faithful turned in hope in that miserable day. In the year 493, in the Pontificate of Gelasius, the whole of the East was in the hands of traitors to Chalcedon, and the whole of the West under the tyranny of the open enemies of Nicæa. Italy was the prey of robbers; mercenary bands had overrun its territory, and barbarians were seizing on its farms and settling in its villas. The peasants were thinned by famine and pestilence; Tuscany might be even said, as Gelasius words it, to contain scarely a single inhabitant.[179] Odoacer was sinking before Theodoric, and the Pope was changing one Arian master for another. And as if one heresy were not enough, Pelagianism was spreading with the connivance of the bishops in the territory of Picenum. In the North of the dismembered Empire, the Britons had first been infected by Pelagianism, and now were dispossessed by the heathen Saxons. The Armoricans still preserved a witness of Catholicism in the West of Gaul; but Picardy, Champagne, and the neighbouring provinces, where some remnant of its supremacy had been found, had lately submitted to the yet heathen Clovis. The Arian kingdoms of Burgundy in France, and of the Visigoths in Aquitaine and Spain, oppressed a zealous and Catholic clergy, Africa was in still more deplorable condition under the cruel sway of the Vandal Gundamond; the people indeed uncorrupted by the heresy,[180] but their clergy in exile and their worship suspended. While such was the state of the Latins, what had happened in the East? Acacius, the Patriarch of Constantinople, had secretly taken part against the Council of Chalcedon and was under Papal excommunication. Nearly the whole East had sided with Acacius, and a schism had begun between East and West, which lasted, as I have above stated, for thirty-five years. The Henoticon was in force, and at the Imperial command had been signed by all the patriarchs and bishops throughout the Eastern Empire.[181] In Armenia the Churches were ripening for the pure Eutychianism which they adopted in the following century; and in Egypt the Acephali, already separated from the Monophysite Patriarch, were extending in the east and west of the country, and preferred the loss of the Episcopal Succession to the reception of the Council of Chalcedon. And while Monophysites or their favourers occupied the Churches of the Eastern Empire, Nestorianism was making progress in the territories beyond it. Barsumas had held the See of Nisibis, Theodore was read in the schools of Persia, and the successive Catholici of Seleucia had abolished Monachism and were secularizing the clergy.

[179] Gibbon, Hist. ch. 36, fin.
[180] Gibbon, Hist. ch. 36, fin.
[181] Gibbon, Hist. ch. 47.

## 23.

If then there is now a form of Christianity such that it extends throughout the world, though with varying measures of prominence or prosperity in separate places; that it lies under the power of sovereigns and magistrates, in various ways alien to its faith; that flourishing nations and great empires, professing or tolerating the Christian name, lie over against it as antagonists; that schools of philosophy and learning are supporting theories, and following out conclusions, hostile to it, and establishing an exegetical system subversive of its Scriptures; that it has lost whole Churches by schism, and is now opposed by powerful communions once part of itself; that it has been altogether or almost driven from some countries; that in others its line of teachers is overlaid, its flocks oppressed, its Churches occupied, its property held by what may be called a duplicate succession; that in others its members are degenerate and corrupt, and are surpassed in conscientiousness and in virtue, as in gifts of intellect, by the very heretics whom it condemns; that heresies are rife and bishops negligent within its own pale; and that amid its disorders and its fears there is but one Voice for whose decisions the peoples wait with trust, one Name and one See to which they look with hope, and that name Peter, and that see Rome; such a religion is not unlike the Christianity of the fifth and sixth centuries.[182]

---

[182]The above sketch has run to great length, yet it is only part of what might be set down in evidence of the wonderful identity of type which characterizes the Catholic Church from first to last. I have confined myself for the most part to her political aspect; but a parallel illustration might be drawn simply from her doctrinal, or from her devotional. As to her devotional aspect, Cardinal Wiseman has shown its identity in the fifth compared with the nineteenth century, in an article of the *Dublin Review*, quoted in part in *Via Media*, vol. ii. p. 378. Indeed it is confessed on all hands, as by Middleton, Gibbon, etc., that from the time of Constantine to their own, the system and the phenomena of worship in Christendom, from Moscow to Spain, and from Ireland to Chili, is one and the same. I have myself paralleled medieval Europe with modern Belgium or Italy, in point of ethical character in "Difficulties of Anglicans," vol. i. Lecture ix., referring the identity to the operation of a principle, insisted on presently, the Supremacy of Faith. And so again, as to the system of Catholic doctrine, the type of the religion remains the same, because it has developed according to the "analogy of faith," as is observed in *Apol.*, p. 196. "The idea of the Blessed Virgin was, as it were, *magnified* in the Church of Rome, as time went on, but so were *all* the Christian ideas, as that of the Blessed Eucharist," etc.

# CHAPTER VII

# APPLICATION OF THE SECOND NOTE OF A TRUE DEVELOPMENT: CONTINUITY OF PRINCIPLES

It appears then that there has been a certain general type of Christianity in every age, by which it is known at first sight, differing from itself only as what is young differs from what is mature, or as found in Europe or in America, so that it is named at once and without hesitation, as forms of nature are recognized by experts in physical science; or as some work of literature or art is assigned to its right author by the critic, difficult as may be the analysis of that specific impression by which he is enabled to do so. And it appears that this type has remained entire from first to last, in spite of that process of development which seems to be attributed by all parties, for good or bad, to the doctrines, rites, and usages in which Christianity consists; or, in other words, that the changes which have taken place in Christianity have not been such as to destroy that type—that is, that they are not corruptions, because they are consistent with that type. Here then, in the *preservation of type*, we have a first Note of the fidelity of the existing developments of Christianity. Let us now proceed to a second.

## 1. The Principles of Christianity

When developments in Christianity are spoken of, it is sometimes supposed that they are deductions and diversions made at random, according to accident or the caprice of individuals; whereas it is because they have been conducted all along on definite and continuous principles that the type of the religion has remained from first to last unalterable. What then are the principles under which the developments have been made? I will enumerate some obvious ones.

## 2.

They must be many and positive, as well as obvious, if they are to be effective; thus the Society of Friends seems in the course of years to have changed its type in consequence of its scarcity of principles, a fanatical spiritualism and an intense secularity, types simply contrary to each other, being alike consistent with its main principle, "Forms of worship are Antichristian." Christianity, on the other hand, has principles so distinctive, numerous, various, and operative, as to be unlike any other religious, ethical, or political system that the world has ever seen, unlike, not only in character, but in persistence in that character. I cannot attempt here to enumerate more than a few by way of illustration.

## 3.

For the convenience of arrangement, I will consider the Incarnation the central truth of the gospel, and the source whence we are to draw out its principles. This great doctrine is unequivocally announced in numberless passages of the New Testament, especially by St. John and St. Paul; as is familiar to us all: "The Word was made flesh and dwelt among us, full of grace and truth." "That which was from the beginning, which we have heard, which we have seen with our eyes, which we have looked upon, and our hands have handled, of the Word of life, that declare we to you." "For ye know the grace of our Lord Jesus Christ, that, though he was rich, yet for your sakes He became poor, that ye through His poverty might be rich." "Not I, but Christ liveth in me, and the life which I now live in the flesh, I live by the faith of the Son of God, who loved me and gave Himself for me."

## 4.

In such passages as these we have

1. The principle of *dogma*, that is, supernatural truths irrevocably committed to human language, imperfect because it is human, but definitive and necessary because given from above.

2. The principle of *faith*, which is the correlative of dogma, being the absolute acceptance of the divine Word with an internal assent, in opposition to the informations, if such, of sight and reason.

3. Faith, being an act of the intellect, opens a way for inquiry,

comparison and inference, that is, for science in religion, in subservience to itself; this is the principle of *theology*.

4. The doctrine of the Incarnation is the announcement of a divine gift conveyed in a material and visible medium, it being thus that heaven and earth are in the Incarnation united. That is, it establishes in the very idea of Christianity the *sacramental* principle as its characteristic.

5. Another principle involved in the doctrine of the Incarnation, viewed as taught or as dogmatic, is the necessary use of language, e.g., of the text of Scripture, in a second or *mystical sense*. Words must be made to express new ideas, and are invested with a sacramental office.

6. It is our Lord's intention in His Incarnation to make us what He is Himself; this is the principle of *grace*, which is not only holy but sanctifying.

7. It cannot elevate and change us without mortifying our lower nature; here is the principle of *asceticism*.

8. And involved in this death of the natural man is necessarily a revelation of the *malignity of sin*, in corroboration of the forebodings of conscience.

9. Also by the fact of an Incarnation we are taught that matter is an essential part of us, and, as well as mind, is *capable of sanctification*.

### 5.

Here are nine specimens of Christian principles out of the many[1] which might be enumerated, and will any one say that they have not been retained in vigorous action in the Church at all times amid whatever development of doctrine Christianity has experienced, so as even to be the very instruments of that development, and as patent, and as operative, in the Latin and Greek Christianity of this day as they were in the beginning?

[1] E.g., development itself is such a principle also. "And thus I was led on to a further consideration. I saw that the principle of development not only accounted for certain facts, but was in itself a remarkable philosophical phenomenon, giving a character to the whole course of Christian thought. It was discernible from the first years of Catholic teaching up to the present day, and gave to that teaching a unity and individuality. It served as a sort of test, which the Anglican could not stand, that modern Rome was in truth ancient Antioch, Alexandria, and Constantinople, just as a mathematical curve has its own law and expression." *Apol.* p. 198, vid. also Angl. Diff. vol. i. Lect. xii. 7.

This continuous identity of principles in ecclesiastical action has been seen in part in treating of the Note of unity of type, and will be seen also in the Notes which follow; however, as some direct account of them, in illustration, may be desirable, I will single out four as specimens—Faith, Theology, Scripture, and Dogma.

## 2. Supremacy of Faith

This principle which, as we have already seen, was so great a jest to Celsus and Julian, is of the following kind: That belief in Christianity is in itself better than unbelief; that faith, though an intellectual action, is ethical in its origin; that it is safer to believe; that we must begin with believing; that as for the reasons of believing, they are for the most part implicit, and need be but slightly recognized by the mind that is under their influence; that they consist moreover rather of presumptions and ventures after the truth than of accurate and complete proofs; and that probable arguments, under the scrutiny and sanction of a prudent judgment, are sufficient for conclusions which we even embrace as most certain, and turn to the most important uses.

### 2.

Antagonistic to this is the principle that doctrines are only so far to be considered true as they are logically demonstrated. This is the assertion of Locke, who says in defence of it, "Whatever God hath revealed is certainly true; no doubt can be made of it. This is the proper object of Faith; but, whether it be a divine revelation or no, reason must judge." Now, if he merely means that proofs can be given for Revelation, and that Reason comes in logical order before Faith, such a doctrine is in no sense uncatholic; but he certainly holds that for an individual to act on Faith without proof, or to make Faith a personal principle of conduct for themselves, without waiting till they have got their reasons accurately drawn out and serviceable for controversy, is enthusiastic and absurd. "How a man may know whether he be [a lover of truth for truth's sake] is worth inquiry; and I think there is this one unerring mark of it, viz., the not entertaining any proposition with greater assurance than the proofs it is built upon, will warrant. Whoever goes beyond this measure of assent, it is plain, receives not truth in the love of it; loves not truth for truth's sake, but for some other by-end."

## 3.

It does not seem to have struck him that our "by-end" may be the desire to please our Maker, and that the defect of scientific proof may be made up to our reason by our love of Him. It does not seem to have struck him that such a philosophy as his cut off from the possibility and the privilege of faith all but the educated few, all but the learned, the clear-headed, the men of practised intellects and balanced minds, men who had leisure, who had opportunities of consulting others, and kind and wise friends to whom they deferred. How could a religion ever be Catholic, if it was to be called credulity or enthusiasm in the multitude to use those ready instruments of belief, which alone Providence had put into their power? On such philosophy as this, were it generally received, no great work ever would have been done for God's glory and the welfare of man. The "enthusiasm" against which Locke writes may do much harm, and act at times absurdly; but calculation never made a hero. However, it is not to our present purpose to examine this theory, and I have done so elsewhere.[2] Here I have but to show the unanimity of Catholics, ancient as well as modern, in their absolute rejection of it.

## 4.

For instance, it is the very objection urged by Celsus, that Christians were but parallel to the credulous victims of jugglers or of devotees, who itinerated through the pagan population. He says "that some do not even wish to give or to receive a reason for their faith, but say, 'Do not inquire but believe,' and 'Thy faith will save thee'; and 'A bad thing is the world's wisdom, and foolishness is a good.' " How does Origen answer the charge? by denying the fact, and speaking of the reason of each individual as demonstrating the divinity of the Scriptures, and Faith as coming after that argumentative process, as it is now popular to maintain? Far from it; he grants the fact alleged against the Church and defends it. He observes that, considering the engagements and the necessary ignorance of the multitude of men, it is a very happy circumstance that a substitute is provided for those philosophical exercises, which Christianity allows and encourages, but does not impose on the individual. "Which," he asks, "is the better,

[2]University Sermons [but, more carefully in the "Essay on Assent"].

for them to believe without reason, and thus to reform any how and gain a benefit, from their belief in the punishment of sinners and the reward of well-doers, or to refuse to be converted on mere belief, or except they devote themselves to an intellectual inquiry?"[3] Such a provision then is a mark of divine wisdom and mercy. In like manner, St. Irenæus, after observing that the Jews had the evidence of prophecy, which the Gentiles had not, and that to the latter it was a foreign teaching and a new doctrine to be told that the gods of the Gentiles were not only not gods, but were idols of devils, and that in consequence St. Paul laboured more upon them, as needing it more, adds, "On the other hand, the faith of the Gentiles is thereby shown to be more generous, who followed the word of God without the assistance of Scriptures." To believe on less evidence was generous faith, not enthusiasm. And so again, Eusebius, while he contends of course that Christians are influenced by "no irrational faith," that is, by a faith which is capable of a logical basis, fully allows that in the individual believing, it is not necessarily or ordinarily based upon argument, and maintains that it is connected with that very "hope," and inclusively with that desire of the things beloved, which Locke in the above extract considers incompatible with the love of truth. "What do we find," he says, "but that the whole life of man is suspended on these two, hope and faith?"[4]

I do not mean of course that the Fathers were opposed to inquiries into the intellectual basis of Christianity, but that they held that men were not obliged to wait for logical proof before believing; on the contrary, that the majority were to believe first on presumptions and let the intellectual proof come as their reward.[5]

## 5.

St. Augustine, who had tried both ways, strikingly contrasts them in his *De Utilitate credendi*, though his direct object in that work is to decide, not between Reason and Faith, but between Reason and Authority. He addresses in it a very dear friend, who, like himself, had become a Manichee, but who, with less happiness than his own, was still retained in the heresy. "The Manichees," he observes, "inveigh against those who, following the authority of the Catholic faith, fortify

[3] c. Cels. i. 9.
[4] Hær. iv. 24. Euseb. Præp. Ev. i. 5.
[5] This is too large a subject to admit of justice being done to it here: I have treated of it at length in the "Essay on Assent."

themselves in the first instance with believing, and before they are able to set eyes upon that truth, which is discerned by the pure soul, prepare themselves for a God who shall illuminate. You, Honoratus, know that nothing else was the cause of my falling into their hands, than their professing to put away Authority which was so terrible, and by absolute and simple Reason to lead their hearers to God's presence, and to rid them of all error. For what was there else that forced me, for nearly nine years, to slight the religion which was sown in me when a child by my parents, and to follow them and diligently attend their lectures, but their assertion that I was terrified by superstition, and was bidden to have Faith before I had Reason, whereas they pressed no one to believe before the truth had been discussed and unravelled? Who would not be seduced by these promises, and especially a youth, such as they found me then, desirous of truth, nay conceited and forward, by reason of the disputations of certain men of school learning, with a contempt of old-wives' tales, and a desire of possessing and drinking that clear and unmixed truth which they promised me?"[6]

Presently he goes on to describe how he was reclaimed. He found the Manichees more successful in pulling down than in building up; he was disappointed in Faustus, whom he found eloquent and nothing besides. Upon this, he did not know what to hold, and was tempted to a general scepticism. At length he found he must be guided by authority; then came the question, Which authority among so many teachers? He cried earnestly to God for help, and at last was led to the Catholic Church. He then returns to the question urged against that Church, that "she bids those who come to her believe," whereas heretics "boast that they do not impose a yoke of believing, but open a fountain of teaching." On which he observes, "True religion cannot in any manner be rightly embraced, without a belief in those things which each individual afterwards attains and perceives, if he behave himself well and shall deserve it, nor altogether without some weighty and imperative Authority."[7]

## 6.

These are specimens of the teaching of the ancient Church on the subject of Faith and Reason; if, on the other hand, we would know what has been taught on the subject in those modern schools, in and

[6] Init.
[7] Vid. also supr. p. 251.

through which the subsequent developments of Catholic doctrines have proceeded, we may turn to the extracts made from their writings by Huet, in his "Essay on the Human Understanding"; and, in so doing, we need not perplex ourselves with the particular theory, true or not, for the sake of which he has collected them. Speaking of the weakness of the Understanding, Huet says:

"God, by His goodness, repairs this defect of human nature, by granting us the inestimable gift of Faith, which confirms our staggering Reason, and corrects that perplexity of doubts which we must bring to the knowledge of things. For example: my reason not being able to inform me with absolute evidence, and perfect certainty, whether there are bodies, what was the origin of the world, and many other like things, after I had received the Faith, all those doubts vanish, as darkness at the rising of the sun. This made St. Thomas Aquinas say: 'It is necessary for man to receive as articles of Faith, not only the things which are above Reason, but even those that for their certainty may be known by Reason. For human Reason is very deficient in things divine; a sign of which we have from philosophers, who, in the search of human things by natural methods, have been deceived, and opposed each other on many heads. To the end then that men may have a certain and undoubted cognizance of God, it was necessary things divine should be taught them by way of Faith, as being revealed of God Himself, who cannot lie.'[8] . . . .

"Then St. Thomas adds afterwards: 'No search by natural Reason is sufficient to make man know things divine, nor even those which we can prove by Reason.' And in another place he speaks thus: 'Things which may be proved demonstratively, as the Being of God, the Unity of the Godhead, and other points, are placed among articles we are to believe, because previous to other things that are of Faith; and these must be presupposed, at least by such as have no demonstration of them.'

### 7.

"What St. Thomas says of the cognizance of divine things extends also to the knowledge of human, according to the doctrine of Suarez. 'We often correct,' he says, 'the light of Nature by the light of Faith, even in things which seem to be first principles, as appears in this: those things that are the same to a third, are the same between them-

_____
[8] Pp. 142–43, Combe's tr.

selves; which, if we have respect to the Trinity, ought to be restrained to finite things. And in other mysteries, especially in those of the Incarnation and the Eucharist, we use many other limitations, that nothing may be repugnant to the Faith. This is then an indication that the light of Faith is most certain, because founded on the first truth, which is God, to whom it's more impossible to deceive or be deceived than for the natural science of man to be mistaken and erroneous.'[9]. . . .

"If we hearken not to Reason, say you, you overthrow that great foundation of Religion which Reason has established in our understanding, viz. God is. To answer this objection, you must be told that men know God in two manners. By Reason, with entire human certainty; and by Faith, with absolute and divine certainty. Although by Reason we cannot acquire any knowledge more certain than that of the Being of God; insomuch that all the arguments, which the impious oppose to this knowledge are of no validity and easily refuted; nevertheless this certainty is not absolutely perfect.[10]. . . .

## 8.

"Now although, to prove the existence of the Deity, we can bring arguments which, accumulated and connected together, are not of less power to convince men that geometrical principles, and theorems deduced from them, and which are of entire human certainty, notwithstanding, because learned philosophers have openly opposed even these principles, 'tis clear we cannot, neither in the natural knowledge we have of God, which is acquired by Reason, nor in science founded on geometrical principles and theorems, find absolute and consummate certainty, but only that human certainty I have spoken of, to which nevertheless every wise man ought to submit his understanding. This being not repugnant to the testimony of the Book of Wisdom and the Epistle to the Romans, which declares that men who do not from the make of the world acknowledge the power and divinity of the Maker are senseless and inexcusable.

"For to use the terms of Vasquez: 'By these words the Holy Scripture means only that there has ever been a sufficient testimony of the Being of a God in the fabric of the world, and in His other works, to make Him known unto men: but the Scripture is not under any concern

[9]Pp. 144–45.
[10]P. 219.

whether this knowledge be evident or of greatest probability; for these terms are seen and understood, in their common and usual acceptation, to signify all the knowledge of the mind with a determined assent.' He adds after: 'For if any one should at this time deny Christ, that which would render him inexcusable would not be because he might have had an evident knowledge and reason for believing Him, but because he might have believed it by Faith and a prudential knowledge.'

" 'Tis with reason then that Suarez teaches that 'the natural evidence of this principle, God is the first truth, who cannot be deceived, is not necessary, nor sufficient enough to make us believe by infused Faith, what God reveals.' He proves, by the testimony of experience, that it is not necessary; for ignorant and illiterate Christians, though they know nothing clearly and certainly of God, do believe nevertheless that God is. Even Christians of parts and learning, as St. Thomas has observed, believe that God is, before they know it by Reason. Suarez shows afterwards that the natural evidence of this principle is not sufficient, because divine Faith, which is infused into our understanding, cannot be bottomed upon human faith alone, how clear and firm soever it is, as upon a formal object, because an assent most firm, and of an order most noble and exalted, cannot derive its certainty from a more infirm assent.[11]. . . .

### 9.

"As touching the motives of credibility, which, preparing the mind to receive Faith, ought according to you to be not only certain by supreme and human certainty, but by supreme and absolute certainty, I will oppose Gabriel Biel to you, who pronounces that to receive Faith 'tis sufficient that the motives of credibility be proposed as probable. Do you believe that children, illiterate, gross, ignorant people, who have scarcely the use of Reason, and notwithstanding have received the gift of Faith, do most clearly and most steadfastly conceive those forementioned motives of credibility? No, without doubt; but the grace of God comes in to their assistance, and sustains the imbecility of Nature and Reason.

"This is the common opinion of divines. Reason has need of divine grace, not only in gross, illiterate persons, but even in those of parts and learning; for how clear-sighted soever that may be, yet it cannot make us have Faith, if celestial light does not illuminate us within,

[11] Pp. 221–23.

because, as I have said already, divine Faith being of a superior order cannot derive its efficacy from human faith.[12]. . . . This is likewise the doctrine of St. Thomas Aquinas: 'The light of Faith makes things seen that are believed.' He says moreover, 'Believers have knowledge of the things of Faith, not in a demonstrative way, but so as by the light of Faith it appears to them that they ought to be believed.' "[13]

### 10.

It is evident what a special influence such doctrine as this must exert upon the theological method of those who hold it. Arguments will come to be considered as suggestions and guides rather than logical proofs; and developments as the slow, spontaneous, ethical growth, not the scientific and compulsory results, of existing opinions.

### 3. Theology

I have spoken and have still to speak of the action of logic, implicit and explicit, as a safeguard, and thereby a note, of legitimate developments of doctrine; but I am regarding it here as that continuous tradition and habit in the Church of a scientific analysis of all revealed truth, which is an ecclesiastical principle rather than a note of any kind, as not merely bearing upon the process of development, but applying to all religious teaching equally, and which is almost unknown beyond the pale of Christendom. Reason, thus considered, is subservient to faith, as handling, examining, explaining, recording, cataloguing, defending the truths which faith, not reason, has gained for us, as providing an intellectual expression of supernatural facts, eliciting what is implicit, comparing, measuring, connecting each with each, and forming one and all into a theological system.

### 2.

The first step in theology is investigation, an investigation arising out of the lively interest and devout welcome which the matters investigated claim of us; and, if Scripture teaches us the duty of faith, it teaches quite as distinctly that loving inquisitiveness which is the life of the *Schola*. It attributes that temper both to the Blessed Virgin and

[12] Pp. 229–30.
[13] Pp. 230–31.

to the Angels. The Angels are said to have "desired to look into the mysteries of Revelation," and it is twice recorded of Mary that she "kept these things and pondered them in her heart." Moreover, her words to the Archangel, "How shall this be?" show that there is a questioning in matters revealed to us compatible with the fullest and most absolute faith. It has sometimes been said in defence and commendation of heretics that "their misbelief at least showed that they had thought upon the subject of religion"; this is an unseemly paradox—at the same time there certainly is the opposite extreme of a readiness to receive any number of dogmas at a minute's warning, which, when it is witnessed, fairly creates a suspicion that they are merely professed with the tongue, not intelligently held. Our Lord gives no countenance to such lightness of mind; He calls on His disciples to use their reason, and to submit it. Nathanael's question "Can there any good thing come out of Nazareth?" did not prevent our Lord's praise of him as "an Israelite without guile." Nor did He blame Nicodemus, except for want of theological knowledge, on his asking, "How can these things be?" Even towards St. Thomas He was gentle, as if towards one of those who had "eyes too tremblingly awake to bear with dimness for His sake." In like manner He praised the centurion when he argued himself into a confidence of divine help and relief from the analogy of his own profession; and left his captious enemies to prove for themselves from the mission of the Baptist His own mission; and asked them "if David called Him Lord, how was He his Son?" and, when His disciples wished to have a particular matter taught them, chid them for their want of "understanding." And these are but some out of the various instances which He gives us of the same lesson.

### 3.

Reason has ever been awake and in exercise in the Church after Him from the first. Scarcely were the Apostles withdrawn from the world, when the Martyr Ignatius, in his way to the Roman Amphitheatre, wrote his strikingly theological Epistles; he was followed by Irenæus, Hippolytus, and Tertullian; thus we are brought to the age of Athanasius and his contemporaries, and to Augustine. Then we pass on by Maximus and John Damascene to the Middle Age, when theology was made still more scientific by the Schoolmen; nor has it become less so, by passing on from St. Thomas to the great Jesuit writers Suarez and Vasquez, and then to Lambertini.

## 4. Scripture and Its Mystical Interpretation

Several passages have occurred in the foregoing chapters, which serve to suggest another principle on which some words are now to be said. Theodore's exclusive adoption of the literal, and repudiation of the mystical interpretation of Holy Scripture, leads to the consideration of the latter, as one of the characteristic conditions or principles on which the teaching of the Church has ever proceeded. Thus Christianity developed, as we have incidentally seen, into the form, first, of a Catholic, then of a Papal Church. Now it was Scripture that was made the rule on which this development proceeded in each case, and Scripture moreover interpreted in a mystical sense; and, whereas at first certain texts were inconsistently confined to the letter, and a Millennium was in consequence expected, the very course of events, as time went on, interpreted the prophecies about the Church more truly, and that first in respect of her prerogative as occupying the *orbis terrarum*, next in support of the claims of the See of St. Peter. This is but one specimen of a certain law of Christian teaching, which is this—a reference to Scripture throughout, and especially in its mystical sense.[14]

## 2.

1. This is a characteristic which will become more and more evident to us, the more we look for it. The divines of the Church are in every age engaged in regulating themselves by Scripture, appealing to Scripture in proof of their conclusions, and exhorting and teaching in the thoughts and language of Scripture. Scripture may be said to be the medium in which the mind of the Church has energized and developed.[15] When St. Methodius would enforce the doctrine of vows of

[14] Vid. Proph. Offic. Lect. xiii. [Via Med. vol. i. p. 309, etc.]

[15] A late writer goes farther, and maintains that it is not determined by the Council of Trent, whether the whole of the Revelation is in Scripture or not. "The Synod declares that the Christian 'truth and discipline are contained in written books and unwritten traditions.' They were well aware that the controversy then was, whether the Christian doctrine was only *in part* contained in Scripture. But they did not dare to frame their decree openly in accordance with the modern Romish view; they did not venture to affirm, as they might easily have done, that the Christian verity 'was contained *partly* in written books, and *partly* in unwritten traditions.' "—*Palmer on the Church*, vol. 2, p. 15. Vid. Difficulties of Angl. vol. ii. pp. 11, 12.

celibacy, he refers to the book of Numbers; and if St. Irenæus proclaims
the dignity of St. Mary, it is from a comparison of St. Luke's Gospel
with Genesis. And thus St. Cyprian, in his Testimonies, rests the prerogatives of martyrdom, as indeed the whole circle of Christian doctrine, on the declaration of certain texts; and, when in his letter to
Antonian he seems to allude to Purgatory, he refers to our Lord's
words about "the prison" and "paying the last farthing." And if St.
Ignatius exhorts to unity, it is from St. Paul; and he quotes St. Luke
against the Phantasiasts of his day. We have a first instance of this law
in the Epistle of St. Polycarp, and a last in the practical works of St.
Alphonso Liguori. St. Cyprian, or St. Ambrose, or St. Bede, or St.
Bernard, or St. Carlo, or such popular books as Horstius's *Paradisus
Animæ*, are specimens of a rule which is too obvious to need formal
proof. It is exemplified in the theological decisions of St. Athanasius
in the fourth century, and of St. Thomas in the thirteenth; in the
structure of the Canon Law, and in the Bulls and Letters of Popes. It
is instanced in the notion so long prevalent in the Church, which
philosophers of this day do not allow us to forget, that all truth, all
science, must be derived from the inspired volume. And it is recognized
as well as exemplified; recognized as distinctly by writers of the Society
of Jesus, as it is copiously exemplified by the Antenicene Fathers.

### 3.

"Scriptures are called canonical," says Salmeron, "as having been
received and set apart by the Church into the Canon of sacred books,
and because they are to us a rule of right belief and good living; also
because they ought to rule and moderate all other doctrines, laws,
writings, whether ecclesiastical, apocryphal, or human. For as these
agree with them, or at least do not disagree, so far are they admitted;
but they are repudiated and reprobated so far as they differ from them
even in the least matter."[16] Again: "The main subject of Scripture is
nothing else than to treat of the God-Man, or the Man-God, Christ
Jesus, not only in the New Testament, which is open, but in the
Old. . . . . . . For whereas Scripture contains nothing but the precepts
of belief and conduct, or faith and works, the end and the means
towards it, the Creator and the creature, love of God and our
neighbour, creation and redemption, and whereas all these are found
in Christ, it follows that Christ is the proper subject of Canonical

[16]Opp. t. 1, p. 4.

Scripture. For all matters of faith, whether concerning Creator or creatures, are recapitulated in Jesus, whom every heresy denies, according to that text, 'Every spirit that divides (*solvit*) Jesus is not of God'; for He as man is united to the Godhead, and as God to the manhood, to the Father from whom He is born, to the Holy Ghost who proceeds at once from Christ and the Father, to Mary his most Holy Mother, to the Church, to Scriptures, Sacraments, Saints, Angels, the Blessed, to Divine Grace, to the authority and ministers of the Church, so that it is rightly said that every heresy divides Jesus."[17] And again: "Holy Scripture is so fashioned and composed by the Holy Ghost as to be accommodated to all plans, times, persons, difficulties, dangers, diseases, the expulsion of evil, the obtaining of good, the stifling of errors, the establishment of doctrines, the ingrafting of virtues, the averting of vices. Hence it is deservedly compared by St. Basil to a dispensary which supplies various medicines against every complaint. From it did the Church in the age of Martyrs draw her firmness and fortitude; in the age of Doctors, her wisdom and light of knowledge; in the time of heretics, the overthrow of error; in time of prosperity, humility and moderation; fervour and diligence, in a lukewarm time; and in times of depravity and growing abuse, reformation from corrupt living and return to the first estate."[18]

## 4.

"Holy Scripture," says Cornelius à Lapide, "contains the beginnings of all theology: for theology is nothing but the science of conclusions which are drawn from principles certain to faith, and therefore is of all sciences most august as well as certain; but the principles of faith and faith itself both Scripture contain; whence it evidently follows that Holy Scripture lays down those principles of theology by which the theologian begets of the mind's reasoning his demonstrations. He, then, who thinks he can tear away Scholastic Science from the work of commenting on Holy Scripture is hoping for offspring without a mother."[19] Again: "What is the subject matter of Scripture? Must I say it in a word? Its aim is *de omni scibili*; it embraces in its bosom all studies, all that can be known: and thus it is a certain university of sciences containing all sciences either 'formally' or 'eminently.' "[20]

[17] Opp. t. i. pp. 4, 5.
[18] Ibid. p. 9.
[19] Proem. 5.
[20] P. 4.

Nor am I aware that later Posttridentine writers deny that the whole Catholic faith may be proved from Scripture, though they would certainly maintain that it is not to be found on the surface of it, nor in such sense that it may be gained from Scripture without the aid of tradition.

### 5.

2. And this has been the doctrine of all ages of the Church, as is shown by the disinclination of her teachers to confine themselves to the mere literal interpretation of Scripture. Her most subtle and powerful method of proof, whether in ancient or modern times, is the mystical sense, which is so frequently used in doctrinal controversy as on many occasions to supersede any other. Thus the Council of Trent appeals to the peace-offering spoken of in Malachi in proof of the Eucharistic Sacrifice; to the water and blood issuing from our Lord's side, and to the mention of "waters" in the Apocalypse, in admonishing on the subject of the mixture of water with the wine in the Oblation. Thus Bellarmine defends Monastic celibacy by our Lord's words in Matthew xix, and refers to "We went through fire and water," etc., in the Psalm, as an argument for Purgatory; and these, as is plain, are but specimens of a rule. Now, on turning to primitive controversy, we find this method of interpretation to be the very basis of the proof of the Catholic doctrine of the Holy Trinity. Whether we betake ourselves to the Antenicene writers or the Nicene, certain texts will meet us, which do not obviously refer to that doctrine, yet are put forward as palmary proofs of it. Such are, in respect of our Lord's divinity, "My heart is inditing of a good matter," or "has burst forth with a good Word"; "The Lord made" or "possessed Me in the beginning of His ways"; "I was with Him, in whom He delighted"; "In Thy Light shall we see Light"; "Who shall declare His generation?" "She is the Breath of the Power of God"; and "His Eternal Power and Godhead."

On the other hand, the School of Antioch, which adopted the literal interpretation, was, as I have noticed above, the very metropolis of heresy. Not to speak of Lucian, whose history is but imperfectly known (one of the first masters of this school, and also teacher of Arius and his principal supporters), Diodorus and Theodore of Mopsuestia, who were the most eminent masters of literalism in the succeeding generation, were, as we have seen, the forerunners of Nestorianism. The case had been the same in a still earlier age; the Jews clung to the literal sense of the Scriptures and hence rejected the Gospel; the Christian

Apologists proved its divinity by means of the allegorical. The formal connexion of this mode of interpretation with Christian theology is noticed by Porphyry, who speaks of Origen and others as borrowing it from heathen philosophy, both in explanation of the Old Testament and in defence of their own doctrine. It may be almost laid down as an historical fact, that the mystical interpretation and orthodoxy will stand or fall together.

### 6.

This is clearly seen, as regards the primitive theology, by a recent writer, in the course of a dissertation upon St. Ephrem. After observing that Theodore of Heraclea, Eusebius, and Diodorus gave a systematic opposition to the mystical interpretation, which had a sort of sanction from antiquity and the orthodox Church, he proceeds: "Ephrem is not as sober in his interpretations, *nor could it be, since* he was a zealous disciple of the orthodox faith. For all those who are most eminent in such sobriety were as far as possible removed from the faith of the Councils. . . . . On the other hand, all who retained the faith of the Church never entirely dispensed with the spiritual sense of the Scriptures. For the Councils watched over the orthodox faith; nor was it safe in those ages, as we learn especially from the instance of Theodore of Mopsuestia, to desert the spiritual for an exclusive cultivation of the literal method. Moreover, the allegorical interpretation, even when the literal sense was not injured, was also preserved; because in those times, when both heretics and Jews in controversy were stubborn in their objections to Christian doctrine, maintaining that the Messiah was yet to come, or denying the abrogation of the Sabbath and ceremonial law, or ridiculing the Christian doctrine of the Trinity, and especially that of Christ's Divine Nature, under such circumstances ecclesiastical writers found it to their purpose, in answer to such exceptions, violently to refer every part of Scripture by allegory to Christ and His Church."[21]

### 7.

With this passage from a learned German, illustrating the bearing of the allegorical method upon the Judaic and Athanasian controversies, it will be well to compare the following passage from the latitudi-

[21]Lengerke, de Ephr. S. pp. 78–80.

narian Hale's "Golden Remains," as directed against the theology of Rome. "The literal, plain, and uncontroversible meaning of Scripture," he says, "without any addition or supply by way of interpretation, is that alone which for ground of faith we are necessarily bound to accept; except it be there, where the Holy Ghost Himself treads us out another way. I take not this to be any particular conceit of mine, but that unto which our Church stands necessarily bound. When we receded from the Church of Rome, one motive was, because she added unto Scripture her glosses as Canonical, to supply what the plain text of Scripture could not yield. If, in place of hers, we set up our own glosses, thus to do were nothing else but to pull down Baal, and set up an Ephod, to run round and meet the Church of Rome again in the same point in which at first we left her. . . . This doctrine of the literal sense was never grievous or prejudicial to any, but only to those who were inwardly conscious that their positions were not sufficiently grounded. When Cardinal Cajetan, in the days of our grandfathers, had forsaken that vein of postilling and allegorizing on Scripture, which for a long time had prevailed in the Church, and betaken himself unto the literal sense, it was a thing so distasteful unto the Church of Rome that he was forced to find out many shifts and make many apologies for himself. The truth is (as it will appear to him that reads his writings), this sticking close to the literal sense was that alone which made him to shake off many of those tenets upon which the Church of Rome and the reformed Churches differ. But when the importunity of the Reformers, and the great credit of Calvin's writings in that kind, had forced the divines of Rome to level their interpretations by the same line; when they saw that no pains, no subtlety of wit was strong enough to defeat the literal evidence of Scripture, it drove them on those desperate shoals, on which at this day they stick, to call in question, as far as they durst, the credit of the Hebrew text, and countenance against it a corrupt translation; to add traditions unto Scripture, and to make the Church's interpretation, so pretended, to be above exception."[22]

### 8.

He presently adds concerning the allegorical sense: "If we absolutely condemn these interpretations, then must we condemn a great part of

[22] Pp. 24–26.

Antiquity, who are very much conversant in this kind of interpreting. For the most partial for Antiquity cannot choose but see and confess thus much, that for the literal sense, the interpreters of our own times, because of their skill in the original languages, their care of pressing the circumstances and coherence of the text, of comparing like places of Scripture with like, have generally surpassed the best of the ancients."[23]

The use of Scripture then, especially its spiritual or second sense, as a medium of thought and deduction, is a characteristic principle of doctrinal teaching in the Church.

## 5. Dogma

1. That opinions in religion are not matters of indifference, but have a definite bearing on the position of their holders in the Divine Sight, is a principle on which the Evangelical Faith has from the first developed, and on which that Faith has been the first to develop. I suppose, it hardly had any exercise under the Law; the zeal and obedience of the ancient people being mainly employed in the maintenance of divine worship and the overthrow of idolatry, not in the action of the intellect. Faith is in this, as in other respects, a characteristic of the Gospel, except so far as it was anticipated, as its time drew near. Elijah and the prophets down to Ezra resisted Baal or restored the Temple Service; the Three Children refused to bow down before the golden image; Daniel would turn his face towards Jerusalem; the Maccabees spurned the Grecian paganism. On the other hand, the Greek Philosophers were authoritative indeed in their teaching, enforced the "*Ipse dixit*," and demanded the faith of their disciples; but they did not commonly attach sanctity or reality to opinions, or view them in a religious light. Our Saviour was the first to "bear witness to the Truth," and to die for it, when "before Pontius Pilate he witnessed a good confession." St. John and St. Paul, following his example, both pronounce anathema on those who denied "the Truth" or "brought in another Gospel." Tradition tells us that the Apostle of love seconded his word with his deed, and on one occasion hastily quitted a bath because an heresiarch of the day had entered it. St. Ignatius, his contemporary, compares false teachers to raging dogs; and St. Polycarp, his disciple, exercised the same severity upon Marcion which St. John had shown towards Cerinthus.

[23] P. 27.

## 2.

St. Irenæus after St. Polycarp exemplifies the same doctrine: "I saw thee," he says to the heretic Florinus, "when I was yet a boy, in lower Asia, with Polycarp, when thou wast living splendidly in the Imperial Court, and trying to recommend thyself to him. I remember indeed what then happened better than more recent occurrences, for the lessons of boyhood grow with the mind and become one with it. Thus I can name the place where blessed Polycarp sat and conversed, and his goings out and comings in, and the fashion of his life, and the appearance of his person, and his discourses to the people, and his familiarity with John, which he used to tell of, and with the rest who had seen the Lord, and how he used to repeat their words, and what it was that he had learned about the Lord from them. . . . And in the sight of God, I can protest, that, if that blessed and apostolical Elder had heard aught of this doctrine, he had cried out and stopped his ears, saying after his wont, 'O Good God, for what times hast thou reserved me that I should endure this?' and he had fled the place where he was sitting or standing when he heard it." It seems to have been the duty of every individual Christian from the first to witness in his place against all opinions which were contrary to what he had received in his baptismal catechizing, and to shun the society of those who maintained them. "So religious," says Irenæus after giving his account of St. Polycarp, "were the Apostles and their disciples, in not even conversing with those who counterfeited the truth."[24]

## 3.

Such a principle, however, would but have broken up the Church the sooner, resolving it into the individuals of which it was composed, unless the Truth, to which they were to bear witness, had been a something definite, and formal, and independent of themselves. Christians were bound to defend and to transmit the faith which they had received, and they received it from the rulers of the Church; and, on the other hand, it was the duty of those rulers to watch over and define this traditionary faith. It is unnecessary to go over ground which has been traversed so often of late years. St. Irenæus brings the subject before us in his description of St. Polycarp, part of which has already

[24] Euseb. Hist. iv. 14, v. 20.

been quoted; and to it we may limit ourselves. "Polycarp," he says when writing against the Gnostics, "whom we have seen in our first youth, ever taught those lessons which he learned from the Apostles, which the Church also transmits, which alone are true. All the Churches of Asia bear witness to them; and the successors of Polycarp down to this day, who is a much more trustworthy and sure witness of truth than Valentinus, Marcion, or their perverse companions. The same was in Rome in the time of Anicetus, and converted many of the aforenamed heretics to the Church of God, preaching that he had received from the Apostles this one and only truth, which had been transmitted by the Church."[25]

## 4.

Nor was this the doctrine and practice of one school only, which might be ignorant of philosophy; the cultivated minds of the Alexandrian Fathers, who are said to owe so much to pagan science, certainly showed no gratitude or reverence towards their alleged instructors, but maintained the supremacy of Catholic tradition. Clement[26] speaks of heretical teachers as perverting Scripture, and essaying the gate of heaven with a false key, not raising the veil, as he and his, by means of tradition from Christ, but digging through the Church's wall, and becoming mystagogues of misbelief; "for," he continues, "few words are enough to prove that they have formed their human assemblies later than the Catholic Church," and "from that previously existing and most true Church it is very clear that these later heresies, and others which have been since, are counterfeit and novel inventions."[27] "When the Marcionites, Valentinians, and the like," says Origen, "appeal to apocryphal works, they are saying, 'Christ is in the desert'; when to canonical Scripture, 'Lo, He is in the chambers'; but we must not depart from that first and ecclesiastical tradition, nor believe otherwise than as the Churches of God by succession have transmitted to us." And it is recorded of him in his youth, that he never could be brought to attend the prayers of a heretic who was in the house of his patroness, from abomination of his doctrine, "observing," adds Eusebius, "the rule of the Church." Eusebius too himself, unsatisfac-

[25] Contr. Hær. iii. 3, § 4.
[26] Ed. Potter, p. 897.
[27] Ed. Potter, p. 899.

tory as is his own theology, cannot break from this fundamental rule; he ever speaks of the Gnostic teachers, the chief heretics of his period (at least before the rise of Arianism), in terms most expressive of abhorrence and disgust.

### 5.

The African, Syrian, and Asian Schools are additional witnesses; Tertullian at Carthage was strenuous for the dogmatic principle even after he had given up the traditional. The Fathers of Asia Minor, who excommunicated Noëtus, rehearse the Creed, and add, "We declare as we have learned"; the Fathers of Antioch, who depose Paul of Samosata, set down in writing the Creed from Scripture, "which," they say, "we received from the beginning, and have, by tradition and in custody, in the Catholic and Holy Church, until this day, by succession, as preached by the blessed Apostles, who were eyewitnesses and ministers of the Word."[28]

### 6.

Moreover, it is as plain, or even plainer, that what the Christians of the first ages anathematized, included deductions from the Articles of Faith, that is, false developments, as well as contradictions of those Articles. And, since the reason they commonly gave for using the anathema was that the doctrine in question was strange and startling, it follows that the truth, which was its contradictory, was also in some respect unknown to them hitherto; which is also shown by their temporary perplexity, and their difficulty of meeting heresy, in particular cases. "Who ever heard the like hitherto?" says St. Athanasius, of Apollinarianism; "who was the teacher of it, who the hearer? 'From Sion shall go forth the Law of God, and the Word of the Lord from Jerusalem'; but from whence hath this gone forth? What hell hath burst out with it?" The Fathers at Nicæa stopped their ears; and St. Irenæus, as above quoted, says that St. Polycarp, had he heard the Gnostic blasphemies, would have stopped his ears, and deplored the times for which he was reserved. They anathematized the doctrine, not because it was old, but because it was new; the anathema would have

[28] Clem. Strom. vii. 17. Origen in Matth. Comm. Ser. 46. Euseb. Hist. vi. 2, fin. Epiph. Hær. 57, p. 480. Routh, t. 2, p. 465.

altogether slept, if it could not have been extended to propositions not anathematized in the beginning; for the very characteristic of heresy is this novelty and originality of manifestation.

Such was the exclusiveness of Christianity of old: I need not insist on the steadiness with which that principle has been maintained ever since, for bigotry and intolerance is one of the ordinary charges brought at this day against both the medieval Church and the modern.

### 7.

The Church's consistency and thoroughness in teaching is another aspect of the same principle, as is illustrated in the following passage from M. Guizot's history of civilization. "The adversaries," he says, "of the Reformation, knew very well what they were about, and what they required; they could point to their first principles, and boldly admit all the consequences that might result from them. No government was ever more consistent and systematic than that of the Romish Church. In fact, the Court of Rome was much more accommodating, yielded much more than the Reformers; but in principle it much more completely adopted its own system, and maintained a much more consistent conduct. There is an immense power in this full confidence of what is done; this perfect knowledge of what is required; this complete and rational adaptation of a system and a creed." Then he goes on to the history of the Society of Jesus in illustration. "Everything," he says, "was unfavourable to the Jesuits, both fortune and appearances; neither practical sense which requires success, nor the imagination which looks for splendour, were gratified by their destiny. Still it is certain that they possessed the elements of greatness; a grand idea is attached to their name, to their influence, and to their history. Why? because they worked from fixed principles, which they fully and clearly understood, and the tendency of which they entirely comprehended. In the Reformation, on the contrary, when the event surpassed its conception, something incomplete, inconsequent, and narrow has remained, which has placed the conquerors themselves in a state of rational and philosophical inferiority, the influence of which has occasionally been felt in events. The conflict of the new spiritual order of things against the old, is, I think, the weak side of the Reformation."[29]

[29] Eur. Civil. pp. 394–98.

### 6. Additional Remarks

Such are some of the intellectual principles which are characteristic of Christianity. I observe—

That their continuity down to this day, and the vigour of their operation, are two distinct guarantees that the theological conclusions to which they are subservient are, in accordance with the Divine Promise, true developments, and not corruptions of the Revelation.

Moreover, if it be true that the principles of the later Church are the same as those of the earlier, then, whatever are the variations of belief between the two periods, the later in reality agrees more than it differs with the earlier, for principles are responsible for doctrines. Hence they who assert that the modern Roman system is the corruption of primitive theology are forced to discover some difference of principle between the one and the other; for instance, that the right of private judgment was secured to the early Church and has been lost to the later, or, again, that the later Church rationalizes and the earlier went by faith.

### 2.

On this point I will but remark as follows. It cannot be doubted that the horror of heresy, the law of absolute obedience to ecclesiastical authority, and the doctrine of the mystical virtue of unity were as strong and active in the Church of St. Ignatius and St. Cyprian as in that of St. Carlo and St. Pius the Fifth, whatever be thought of the theology respectively taught in the one and in the other. Now we have before our eyes the effect of these principles in the instance of the later Church; they have entirely succeeded in preventing departure from the doctrine of Trent for three hundred years. Have we any reason for doubting, that from the same strictness the same fidelity would follow, in the first three, or any three, centuries of the Antetridentine period? Where then was the opportunity of corruption in the three hundred years between St. Ignatius and St. Augustine? or between St. Augustine and St. Bede? or between St. Bede and St. Peter Damiani? or again, between St. Irenæus and St. Leo, St. Cyprian and St. Gregory the Great, St. Athanasius and St. John Damascene? Thus the tradition of eighteen centuries becomes a collection of indefinitely many *catenæ*, each commencing from its own point, and each crossing the other; and each year, as it comes, is guaranteed with various degrees of cogency by every year which has gone before it.

### 3.

Moreover, while the development of doctrine in the Church has been in accordance with, or in consequence of these immemorial principles, the various heresies, which have from time to time arisen, have in one respect or other, as might be expected, violated those principles with which she rose into existence, and which she still retains. Thus Arian and Nestorian schools denied the allegorical rule of Scripture interpretation; the Gnostics and Eunomians for Faith professed to substitute knowledge; and the Manichees also, as St. Augustine so touchingly declares in the beginning of his work *De Utilitate credendi.* The dogmatic Rule, at least so far as regards its traditional character, was thrown aside by all those sects which, as Tertullian tells us, claimed to judge for themselves from Scripture; and the Sacramental principle was violated, *ipso facto*, by all who separated from the Church—was denied also by Faustus the Manichee when he argued against the Catholic ceremonial, by Vigilantius in his opposition to relics, and by the Iconoclasts. In like manner the contempt of mystery, of reverence, of devoutness, of sanctity, are other notes of the heretical spirit. As to Protestantism it is plain in how many ways it has reversed the principles of Catholic theology.

# CHAPTER VIII

# APPLICATION OF THE THIRD NOTE OF A TRUE DEVELOPMENT: ITS ASSIMILATIVE POWER

Since religious systems, true and false, have one and the same great and comprehensive subject matter, they necessarily interfere with one another as rivals, both in those points in which they agree together, and in those in which they differ. That Christianity on its rise was in these circumstances of competition and controversy is sufficiently evident even from a foregoing chapter; it was surrounded by rites, sects, and philosophies, which contemplated the same questions, sometimes advocated the same truths, and in no slight degree wore the same external appearance. It could not stand still, it could not take its own way, and let them take theirs: they came across its path, and a conflict was inevitable. The very nature of a true philosophy relatively to other systems is to be polemical, eclectic, unitive: Christianity was polemical; it could not but be eclectic; but was it also unitive? Had it the power, while keeping its own identity, of absorbing its antagonists, as Aaron's rod, according to St. Jerome's illustration, devoured the rods of the sorcerers of Egypt? Did it incorporate them into itself, or was it dissolved into them? Did it assimilate them into its own substance, or, keeping its name, was it simply infected by them? In a word, were its developments faithful or corrupt? Nor is this a question merely of the early centuries. When we consider the deep interest of the controversies which Christianity raises, the various characters of mind it has swayed, the range of subjects which it embraces, the many countries it has entered, the deep philosophies it has encountered, the vicissitudes it has undergone, and the length of time through which it has lasted, it requires some assignable explanation, why we should not consider it substantially modified and changed, that is, corrupted, from the first, by the numberless influences to which it has been exposed.

## 2.

Now there was this cardinal distinction between Christianity and the religions and philosophies by which it was surrounded, nay even the Judaism of the day, that it referred all truth and revelation to one source, and that the Supreme and Only God. Pagan rites which honoured one or other out of ten thousand deities; philosophies which scarcely taught any source of revelation at all; Gnostic heresies which were based on dualism, adored Angels, or ascribed the two Testaments to distinct authors, could not regard truth as one, unalterable, consistent, imperative, and saving. But Christianity started with the principle that there was but "one God and one Mediator," and that He, "who at sundry times and in divers manners spake in time past unto the fathers by the Prophets, had in these last days spoken unto us by His Son." He had never left Himself without witness, and now He had come, not to undo the past, but to fulfil and perfect it. His Apostles, and they alone, possessed, venerated, and protected a Divine Message, as both sacred and sanctifying; and, in the collision and conflict of opinions, in ancient times or modern, it was that Message, and not any vague or antagonist teaching, that was to succeed in purifying, assimilating, transmuting, and taking into itself the many-coloured beliefs, forms of worship, codes of duty, schools of thought, through which it was ever moving. It was Grace, and it was Truth.

### 1. The Assimilating Power of Dogmatic Truth

That there is a truth then; that there is one truth; that religious error is in itself of an immoral nature; that its maintainers, unless involuntarily such, are guilty in maintaining it; that it is to be dreaded; that the search for truth is not the gratification of curiosity; that its attainment has nothing of the excitement of a discovery; that the mind is below truth, not above it, and is bound, not to descant upon it, but to venerate it; that truth and falsehood are set before us for the trial of our hearts; that our choice is an awful giving forth of lots on which salvation or rejection is inscribed; that "before all things it is necessary to hold the Catholic faith"; that "he that would be saved must thus think," and not otherwise; that, "if thou criest after knowledge, and liftest up thy voice for understanding, if thou seekest her as silver, and searchest for her as for hid treasure, then shalt thou understand the fear of the Lord, and find the knowledge of God"—this is the dogmatical principle, which has strength.

That truth and falsehood in religion are but matter of opinion; that one doctrine is as good as another; that the Governor of the world does not intend that we should gain the truth; that there is no truth; that we are not more acceptable to God by believing this than by believing that; that no one is answerable for his opinions; that they are a matter of necessity or accident; that it is enough if we sincerely hold what we profess; that our merit lies in seeking, not in possessing; that it is a duty to follow what seems to us true, without a fear lest it should not be true; that it may be a gain to succeed, and can be no harm to fail; that we may take up and lay down opinions at pleasure; that belief belongs to the mere intellect, not to the heart also; that we may safely trust to ourselves in matters of Faith, and need no other guide—this is the principle of philosophies and heresies, which is very weakness.

## 2.

Two opinions encounter; each may be abstractedly true; or again, each may be a subtle, comprehensive doctrine, vigorous, elastic, expansive, various; one is held as a matter of indifference, the other as a matter of life and death; one is held by the intellect only, the other also by the heart: it is plain which of the two must succumb to the other. Such was the conflict of Christianity with the old established paganism, which was almost dead before Christianity appeared; with the Oriental Mysteries, flitting wildly to and fro like spectres; with the Gnostics, who made Knowledge all in all, despised the many, and called Catholics mere children in the Truth; with the Neoplatonists, men of literature, pedants, visionaries, or courtiers; with the Manichees, who professed to seek Truth by Reason, not by Faith; with the fluctuating teachers of the School of Antioch, the time-serving Eusebians, and the reckless versatile Arians; with the fanatic Montanists and harsh Novatians, who shrank from the Catholic doctrine, without power to propagate their own. These sects had no stay or consistence, yet they contained elements of truth amid their error, and had Christianity been as they, it might have resolved into them; but it had that hold of the truth which gave its teaching a gravity, a directness, a consistency, a sternness, and a force, to which its rivals for the most part were strangers. It could not call evil good, or good evil, because it discerned the difference between them; it could not make light of what was so solemn, or desert what was so solid. Hence, in the collision, it broke in pieces its antagonists, and divided the spoils.

## 3.

This was but another form of the spirit that made martyrs. Dogmatism was in teaching what confession was in act. Each was the same strong principle of life in a different aspect, distinguishing the faith which was displayed in it from the world's philosophies on the one side, and the world's religions on the other. The heathen sects and the heresies of Christian history were dissolved by the breath of opinion which made them; paganism shuddered and died at the very sight of the sword of persecution, which it had itself unsheathed. Intellect and force were applied as tests both upon the divine and upon the human work; they prevailed with the human, they did but become instruments of the Divine. "No one," says St. Justin, "has so believed Socrates as to die for the doctrine which he taught." "No one was ever found undergoing death for faith in the sun."[1] Thus Christianity grew in its proportions, gaining aliment and medicine from all that it came near, yet preserving its original type, from its perception and its love of what had been revealed once for all and was no private imagination.

## 4.

There are writers who refer to the first centuries of the Church as a time when opinion was free, and the conscience exempt from the obligation or temptation to take on trust what it had not proved; and that, apparently on the mere ground that the series of great theological decisions did not commence till the fourth. This seems to be M. Guizot's meaning when he says that Christianity "in the early ages was a belief, a sentiment, an individual conviction";[2] that "the Christian society appears as a pure association of men animated by the same sentiments and professing the same creed. The first Christians," he continues, "assembled to enjoy together the same emotions, the same religious convictions. We do not find any doctrinal system established, any form of discipline or of laws, or any body of magistrates."[3] What can be meant by saying that Christianity had no magistrates in the earliest ages?—but, any how, in statements such as these the distinction is not properly recognized between a principle and its exhibitions and instances, even if the fact were as is represented. The principle

---

[1] Justin, Apol. ii. 10, Tryph. 121.
[2] Europ. Civ. p. 56, tr.
[3] P. 58.

indeed of dogmatism develops into Councils in the course of time; but it was active, nay sovereign from the first, in every part of Christendom. A conviction that truth was one; that it was a gift from without, a sacred trust, an inestimable blessing; that it was to be reverenced, guarded, defended, transmitted; that its absence was a grievous want, and its loss an unutterable calamity; and again, the stern words and acts of St. John, of Polycarp, Ignatius, Irenæus, Clement, Tertullian, and Origen—all this is quite consistent with perplexity or mistake as to what was truth in particular cases, in what way doubtful questions were to be decided, or what were the limits of the Revelation. Councils and Popes are the guardians and instruments of the dogmatic principle: they are not that principle themselves; they presuppose the principle; they are summoned into action at the call of the principle, and the principle might act even before they had their legitimate place, and exercised a recognized power, in the movements of the Christian body.

## 5.

The instance of Conscience, which has already served us in illustration, may assist us here. What Conscience is in the history of an individual mind, such was the dogmatic principle in the history of Christianity. Both in the one case and the other, there is the gradual formation of a directing power out of a principle. The natural voice of Conscience is far more imperative in testifying and enforcing a rule of duty than successful in determining that duty in particular cases. It acts as a messenger from above, and says that there is a right and a wrong, and that the right must be followed; but it is variously, and therefore erroneously, trained in the instance of various persons. It mistakes error for truth; and yet we believe that on the whole, and even in those cases where it is ill-instructed, if its voice be diligently obeyed, it will gradually be cleared, simplified, and perfected, so that minds, starting differently will, if honest, in course of time converge to one and the same truth. I do not hereby imply that there is indistinctness so great as this in the theology of the first centuries; but so far is plain, that the early Church and Fathers exercised far more a ruler's than a doctor's office: it was the age of Martyrs, of acting not of thinking. Doctors succeeded Martyrs, as light and peace of conscience follow upon obedience to it; yet, even before the Church had grown into the full measure of its doctrines, it was rooted in its principles.

## 6.

So far, however, may be granted to M. Guizot, that even principles were not so well understood and so carefully handled at first, as they were afterwards. In the early period, we see traces of a conflict, as well as of a variety, in theological elements, which were in course of combination, but which required adjustment and management before they could be used with precision as one. In a thousand instances of a minor character, the statements of the early Fathers are but tokens of the multiplicity of openings which the mind of the Church was making into the treasure-house of Truth; real openings, but incomplete or irregular. Nay, the doctrines even of the heretical bodies are indices and anticipations of the mind of the Church. As the first step in settling a question of doctrine is to raise and debate it, so heresies in every age may be taken as the measure of the existing state of thought in the Church, and of the movement of her theology; they determine in what way the current is setting, and the rate at which it flows.

## 7.

Thus, St. Clement may be called the representative of the eclectic element, and Tertullian of the dogmatic, neither element as yet being fully understood by Catholics; and Clement perhaps went too far in his accommodation to philosophy, and Tertullian asserted with exaggeration the immutability of the Creed. Nay, the two antagonist principles of dogmatism and assimilation are found in Tertullian alone, though with some deficiency of amalgamation, and with a greater leaning towards the dogmatic. Though the Montanists professed to pass over the subject of doctrine, it is chiefly in Tertullian's Montanistic works that his strong statements occur of the unalterableness of the Creed; and extravagance on the subject is not only in keeping with the stern and vehement temper of that Father, but with the general severity and harshness of his sect. On the other hand the very foundation of Montanism is development, though not of doctrine, yet of discipline and conduct. It is said that its founder professed himself the promised Comforter, through whom the Church was to be perfected; he provided prophets as organs of the new revelation, and called Catholics Psychici or animal. Tertullian distinctly recognizes even the process of development in one of his Montanistic works. After speaking of an innovation upon usage, which his newly revealed truth required, he proceeds, "Therefore hath the Lord sent the Paraclete, that, since human infirmity çould not take all things in at once, discipline might be gradually directed, regulated and brought to perfection by the Lord's Vicar, the Holy Ghost. 'I have yet many things to say to you,' He saith, etc. What is this dispensation of the Paraclete but this, that discipline is directed, Scriptures opened, intellect reformed, improvements effected? Nothing can take place without age, and all things wait their time. In short, the Preacher says, 'There is a time for all things.' Behold the creature itself gradually advancing to fruit. At first there is a seed, and a stalk springs out of the seed, and from the stalk bursts out a shrub, and then its branches and foliage grow vigorous, and all that we mean by a tree is unfolded; then there is a swelling of the bud, and the bud is resolved into a blossom, and the blossom is opened into a fruit, and is for a while rudimental and unformed, till, by degrees following out its life, it is matured into mellowness of flavour. So too righteousness (for there is the same God both of righteousness and of the creation) was at first in its rudiments, a nature fearing God; thence, by means of Law and Prophets, it advanced into infancy; thence, by the gospel, it burst forth into its youth; and now by the Paraclete, it is fashioned into maturity."[4]

## 8.

Not in one principle or doctrine only, but in its whole system, Montanism is a remarkable anticipation or presage of developments which soon began to show themselves in the Church, though they were not perfected for centuries after. Its rigid maintenance of the original Creed, yet its admission of a development, at least in the ritual, has just been instanced in the person of Tertullian. Equally Catholic in their principle, whether in fact or anticipation, were most of the other peculiarities of Montanism: its rigorous fasts, its visions, its commendation of celibacy and martyrdom, its contempt of temporal goods, its penitential discipline, and its maintenance of a centre of unity. The doctrinal determinations and the ecclesiastical usages of the Middle Ages are the true fulfilment of its self-willed and abortive attempts at precipitating the growth of the Church. The favour shown to it for a while by Pope Victor is an evidence of its external resemblance to orthodoxy; and the celebrated Martyrs and Saints in Africa, in the beginning of the third century, Perpetua and Felicitas, or at least their

[4]De Virg. Vel. 1.

Acts, betoken that same peculiar temper of religion, which, when cut off from the Church a few years afterwards, quickly degenerated into a heresy. A parallel instance occurs in the case of the Donatists. They held a doctrine on the subject of Baptism similar to that of St. Cyprian: "Vincentius Lirinensis," says Gibbon, referring to Tillemont's remarks on that resemblance, "has explained why the Donatists are eternally burning with the devil, while St. Cyprian reigns in heaven with Jesus Christ."[5] And his reason is intelligible: it is, says Tillemont, "as St. Augustine often says, because the Donatists had broken the bond of peace and charity with the other Churches, which St. Cyprian had preserved so carefully."[6]

## 9.

These are specimens of the raw material, as it may be called, which, whether as found in individual Fathers within the pale of the Church, or in heretics external to it, she had the power, by means of the continuity and firmness of her principles, to convert to her own uses. She alone has succeeded in thus rejecting evil without sacrificing the good, and in holding together in one things which in all other schools are incompatible. Gnostic or Platonic words are found in the inspired theology of St. John; to the Platonists Unitarian writers trace the doctrine of our Lord's divinity; Gibbon the idea of the Incarnation to the Gnostics. The Gnostics too seem first to have systematically thrown the intellect upon matters of faith; and the very term "Gnostic" has been taken by Clement to express his perfect Christian. And, though ascetics existed from the beginning, the notion of a religion higher than the Christianity of the many, was first prominently brought forward by the Gnostics, Montanists, Novatians, and Manichees. And while the prophets of the Montanists prefigure the Church's Doctors, and their professed inspiration her infallibility, and their revelations her developments, and the heresiarch himself is the unsightly anticipation of St. Francis, in Novatian again we discern the aspiration of nature after such creations of grace as St. Benedict or St. Bruno. And so the effort of Sabellius to complete the enunciation of the mystery of the Everblessed Trinity failed: it became a heresy; grace would not be constrained; the course of thought could not be forced—at length it was realized in the true Unitarianism of St. Augustine.

[5] Hist. t. 3, p. 312.
[6] Mem. Eccl. t. 6, p. 83.

## 10.

Doctrine too is percolated, as it were, through different minds, beginning with writers of inferior authority in the Church, and issuing at length in the enunciation of her Doctors. Origen, Tertullian, nay Eusebius and the Antiochenes, supply the materials, from which the Fathers have wrought out comments or treatises. St. Gregory Nazianzen and St. Basil digested into form the theological principles of Origen; St. Hilary and St. Ambrose are both indebted to the same great writer in their interpretations of Scripture; St. Ambrose again has taken his comment on St. Luke from Eusebius, and certain of his Tracts from Philo; St. Cyprian called Tertullian his Master; and traces of Tertullian, in his almost heretical treatises, may be detected in the most finished sentences of St. Leo. The School of Antioch, in spite of the heretical taint of various of its Masters, formed the genius of St. Chrysostom. And the Apocryphal gospels have contributed many things for the devotion and edification of Catholic believers.[7]

The deep meditation which seems to have been exercised by the Fathers on points of doctrine, the disputes and turbulence yet lucid determination which characterize the Councils, the indecision of Popes, are all in different ways, at least when viewed together, portions and indications of the same process. The theology of the Church is no random combination of various opinions, but a diligent, patient working out of one doctrine from many materials. The conduct of Popes, Councils, Fathers, betokens the slow, painful, anxious taking up of new truths into an existing body of belief. St. Athanasius, St. Augustine, St. Leo are conspicuous for the repetition *in terminis* of their own theological statements; on the contrary, it has been observed of the heterodox Tertullian, that his works "indicate no ordinary fertility of mind in that he so little repeats himself or recurs to favourite thoughts, as is frequently the case even with the great St. Augustine."[8]

## 11.

Here we see the difference between originality of mind and the gift and calling of a Doctor in the Church; the holy Fathers just mentioned were intently fixing their minds on what they taught, grasping it more

---

[7] Galland. t. 3, p. 673, note 3.

[8] Vid. Preface to Oxford Transl. of Tertullian, where the character of his mind is admirably drawn out.

and more closely, viewing it on various sides, trying its consistency, weighing their own separate expressions. And thus if in some cases they were even left in ignorance, the next generation of teachers completed their work, for the same unwearied anxious process of thought went on. St. Gregory Nyssen finishes the investigations of St. Athanasius; St. Leo guards the polemical statements of St. Cyril. Clement may hold a purgatory, yet tend to consider all punishment purgatorial; St. Cyprian may hold the unsanctified state of heretics, but include in his doctrine a denial of their baptism; St. Hippolytus may believe in the personal existence of the Word from eternity, yet speak confusedly on the eternity of His Sonship; the Council of Antioch might put aside the Homoousion, and the Council of Nicæa impose it; St. Hilary may believe in a purgatory, yet confine it to the day of judgment; St. Athanasius and other Fathers may treat with almost supernatural exactness the doctrine of our Lord's incarnation, yet imply, as far as words go, that He was ignorant viewed in His human nature; the Athanasian Creed may admit the illustration of soul and body, and later Fathers may discountenance it; St. Augustine might first be opposed to the employment of force in religion, and then acquiesce in it. Prayers for the faithful departed may be found in the early liturgies, yet with an indistinctness which included the Blessed Virgin and the Martyrs in the same rank with the imperfect Christian whose sins were as yet unexpiated; and succeeding times might keep what was exact, and supply what was deficient. Aristotle might be reprobated by certain early Fathers, yet furnish the phraseology for theological definitions afterwards. And in a different subject matter, St. Isidore and others might be suspicious of the decoration of Churches; St. Paulinus and St. Helena advance it. And thus we are brought on to dwell upon the office of grace, as well as of truth, in enabling the Church's creed to develop and to absorb without the risk of corruption.

## 2. The Assimilating Power of Sacramental Grace

There is in truth a certain virtue or grace in the Gospel which changes the quality of doctrines, opinions, usages, actions, and personal characters when incorporated with it, and makes them right and acceptable to its Divine Author, whereas before they were either infected with evil, or at best but shadows of the truth. This is the principle, above spoken of, which I have called the Sacramental. "We know that we are of God, and the whole world lieth in wickedness," is an enunciation of the principle; or, the declaration of the Apostle of the Gentiles, "If any man be

324 DOCTRINAL DEVELOPMENTS VIEWED TO CORRUPTIONS

in Christ, he is a new creature; old things are passed away, behold all things are become new." Thus it is that outward rites, which are but worthless in themselves, lose their earthly character and become Sacraments under the Gospel; circumcision, as St. Paul says, is carnal and has come to an end, yet Baptism is a perpetual ordinance, as being grafted upon a system which is grace and truth. Elsewhere, he parallels, while he contrasts, "the cup of the Lord" and "the cup of devils," in this respect, that to partake of either is to hold communion with the source from which it comes; and he adds presently that "we have been all made to drink into one spirit." So again he says, no one is justified by the works of the old Law; while both he implies, and St. James declares, that Christians are justified by works of the New Law. Again he contrasts the exercises of the intellect as exhibited by heathen and Christian. "Howbeit," he says, after condemning heathen wisdom, "we speak wisdom among them that are perfect, yet not the wisdom of this world"; and it is plain that nowhere need we look for more glowing eloquence, more distinct profession of reasoning, more careful assertion of doctrine, than is to be found in the Apostle's writings.

### 2.

In like manner when the Jewish exorcists attempted to "call over them which had evil spirits the Name of the Lord Jesus," the evil spirit professed not to know them, and inflicted on them a bodily injury; on the other hand, the occasion of this attempt of theirs was a stupendous instance or type, in the person of St. Paul, of the very principle I am illustrating. "God wrought special miracles by the hands of Paul, so that from his body were brought unto the sick handkerchiefs and aprons, and the diseases departed from them, and the evil spirits went out of them." The grace given him was communicable, diffusive; an influence passing from him to others, and making what it touched spiritual, as enthusiasm may be or tastes or panics.

Parallel instances occur of the operation of this principle in the history of the Church, from the time that the Apostles were taken from it. St. Paul denounces distinctions in meat and drink, the observance of Sabbaths and holy days, and of ordinances, and the worship of Angels; yet Christians, from the first, were rigid in their stated fastings, venerated, as St. Justin tells us, the Angelic intelligences,[9] and established the observance of the Lord's day as soon as persecution ceased.

[9] Infra. pp. 386–90, etc.

### 3.

In like manner Celsus objects that Christians did not "endure the sight of temples, altars, and statues"; Porphyry, that "they blame the rites of worship, victims, and frankincense"; the heathen disputant in Minucius asks, "Why have Christians no altars, no temples, no conspicuous images?" and "no sacrifices"; and yet it is plain from Tertullian that Christians had altars of their own, and sacrifices and priests. And that they had churches is again and again proved by Eusebius who had seen "the houses of prayer levelled" in the Diocletian persecution; from the history too of St. Gregory Thaumaturgus, nay from Clement.[10] Again, St. Justin and Minucius speak of the form of the Cross in terms of reverence, quite inconsistent with the doctrine that external emblems of religion may not be venerated. Tertullian speaks of Christians signing themselves with it whatever they set about, whether they walk, eat, or lie down to sleep. In Eusebius's life of Constantine, the figure of the Cross holds a most conspicuous place; the Emperor sees it in the sky and is converted; he places it upon his standards; he inserts it into his own hand when he puts up his statue; wherever the Cross is displayed in his battles, he conquers; he appoints fifty men to carry it; he engraves it on his soldiers' arms; and Licinius dreads its power. Shortly after, Julian plainly accuses Christians of worshipping the wood of the Cross, though they refused to worship the ancile. In a later age the worship of images was introduced.[11]

### 4.

The principle of the distinction, by which these observances were pious in Christianity and superstitious in paganism, is implied in such passages of Tertullian, Lactantius, and others, as speak of evil spirits lurking under the pagan statues. It is intimated also by Origen, who, after saying that Scripture so strongly "forbids temples, altars, and images," that Christians are "ready to go to death, if necessary, rather than pollute their notion of the God of all by any such transgression," assigns as a reason "that, as far as possible, they might not fall into the notion that images were gods." St. Augustine, in replying to Por-

[10] Orig. c. Cels. vii. 63, viii. 17 (vid. note Bened. in loc.), August. Ep. 102, 16; Minuc. F. 10, and 32; Tertull. de Orat. fin. ad Uxor. i. fin. Euseb. Hist. viii. 2; Clem. Strom. vii. 6, p. 846.
[11] Tertull. de Cor. 3; Just. Apol. i. 55; Minuc. F. 29; Julian ap. Cyr. vi. p. 194, Spanh.

phyry, is more express: "Those," he says, "who are acquainted with Old and New Testament do not blame in the pagan religion the erection of temples or institution of priesthoods, but that these are done to idols and devils . . . True religion blames in their superstitions, not so much their sacrificing, for the ancient saints sacrificed to the True God, as their sacrificing to false gods."[12] To Faustus the Manichee he answers, "We have some things in common with the gentiles, but our purpose is different."[13] And St. Jerome asks Vigilantius, who made objections to lights and oil, "Because we once worshipped idols, is that a reason why we should not worship God, for fear of seeming to address him with an honour like that which was paid to idols and then was detestable, whereas this is paid to Martyrs and therefore to be received?"[14]

## 5.

Confiding then in the power of Christianity to resist the infection of evil, and to transmute the very instruments and appendages of demon-worship to an evangelical use, and feeling also that these usages had originally come from primitive revelations and from the instinct of nature, though they had been corrupted; and that they must invent what they needed, if they did not use what they found; and that they were moreover possessed of the very archetypes, of which paganism attempted the shadows; the rulers of the Church from early times were prepared, should the occasion arise, to adopt, or imitate, or sanction the existing rites and customs of the populace, as well as the philosophy of the educated class.

St. Gregory Thaumaturgus supplies the first instance on record of this economy. He was the Apostle of Pontus, and one of his methods for governing an untoward population is thus related by St. Gregory of Nyssa. "On returning," he says, "to the city, after revisiting the country round about, he increased the devotion of the people everywhere by instituting festive meetings in honour of those who had fought for the faith. The bodies of the Martyrs were distributed in different places, and the people assembled and made merry, as the year came round, holding festival in their honour. This indeed was a proof of his great wisdom . . . for, perceiving that the childish and untrained

[12] Epp. 102, 18.
[13] Contr. Faust, 20, 23.
[14] Lact. ii. 15, 16; Tertull. Spect. 12; Origen, c. Cels. vii. 64–66, August. Epp. 102, 18; Contr. Faust. xx. 23; Hieron. c. Vigil. 8.

populace were retained in their idolatrous error by creature comforts, in order that what was of first importance should at any rate be secured to them, viz. that they should look to God in place of their vain rites, he allowed them to be merry, jovial, and gay at the monuments of the holy Martyrs, as if their behaviour would in time undergo a spontaneous change into greater seriousness and strictness, since faith would lead them to it; which has actually been the happy issue in that population, all carnal gratification having turned into a spiritual form of rejoicing."[15] There is no reason to suppose that the licence here spoken of passed the limits of harmless though rude festivity; for it is observable that the same reason, the need of holidays for the multitude, is assigned by Origen, St. Gregory's master, to explain the establishment of the Lord's Day also, and the Paschal and the Pentecostal festivals, which have never been viewed as unlawful compliances; and, moreover, the people were in fact eventually reclaimed from their gross habits by his indulgent policy, a successful issue which could not have followed an accommodation to what was sinful.

## 6.

The example set by St. Gregory in an age of persecution was impetuously followed when a time of peace succeeded. In the course of the fourth century two movements or developments spread over the face of Christendom, with a rapidity characteristic of the Church; the one ascetic, the other ritual or ceremonial. We are told in various ways by Eusebius[16] that Constantine, in order to recommend the new religion to the heathen, transferred into it the outward ornaments to which they had been accustomed in their own. It is not necessary to go into a subject which the diligence of Protestant writers has made familiar to most of us. The use of temples, and these dedicated to particular saints, and ornamented on occasions with branches of trees; incense, lamps, and candles; votive offerings on recovery from illness; holy water; asylums; holidays and seasons, use of calendars, processions, blessings on the fields; sacerdotal vestments, the tonsure, the ring in marriage, turning to the East, images at a later date, perhaps the ecclesiastical chant, and the Kyrie Eleison,[17] are all of pagan origin, and sanctified by their adoption into the Church.

[15] Vit. Thaum. p. 1006.
[16] V. Const. iii. 1, iv. 23, etc.
[17] According to Dr. E.D. Clarke, Travels, vol. i. p. 352.

### 7.

The eighth book of Theodoret's work *Adversus Gentiles*, which is "On the Martyrs," treats so largely on the subject that we must content ourselves with only a specimen of the illustrations which it affords, of the principle acted on by St. Gregory Thaumaturgus. "Time, which makes all things decay," he says, speaking of the Martyrs, "has preserved their glory incorruptible. For as the noble souls of those conquerors traverse the heavens, and take part in the spiritual choirs, so their bodies are not consigned to separate tombs, but cities and towns divide them among them; and call them saviours of souls and bodies, and physicians, and honour them as the protectors and guardians of cities, and, using their intervention with the Lord of all, obtain through them divine gifts. And though each body be divided, the grace remains indivisible; and that small, that tiny particle is equal in power with the Martyr that hath never been dispersed about. For the grace which is ever blossoming distributes the gifts, measuring the bounty according to the faith of those who come for it.

"Yet not even this persuades you to celebrate their God, but ye laugh and mock at the honour which is paid them by all, and consider it a pollution to approach their tombs. But though all men made a jest of them, yet at least the Greeks could not decently complain, to whom belonged libations and expiations, and heroes and demigods and deified men. To Hercules, though a man ... and compelled to serve Eurystheus, they built temples, and constructed altars, and offered sacrifices in honour, and allotted feasts; and that, not Spartans only and Athenians, but the whole of Greece and the greater part of Europe."

### 8.

Then, after going through the history of many heathen deities, and referring to the doctrine of the philosophers about great men, and to the monuments of kings and emperors, all of which at once are witnesses and are inferior, to the greatness of the Martyrs, he continues: "To their shrines we come, not once or twice a year or five times, but often do we hold celebrations; often, nay daily, do we present hymns to their Lord. And the sound in health ask for its preservation, and those who struggle with any disease for a release from their sufferings; the childless for children, the barren to become mothers, and those who enjoy the blessing for its safe keeping. Those too who are setting out for a foreign land beg that the Martyrs may be their fellow-travellers and guides of the journey; those who have come safe back acknowledge the grace, not coming to them as to gods, but beseeching them as divine men, and asking their intercession. And that they obtain what they ask in faith, their dedications openly witness, in token of their cure. For some bring likenesses of eyes, others of feet, others of hands; some of gold, others of silver; and their Lord accepts even the small and cheap, measuring the gift by the offerer's ability. . . . . Philosophers and Orators are consigned to oblivion, and kings and captains are not known even by name to the many; but the names of the Martyrs are better known to all than the names of those dearest to them. And they make a point of giving them to their children, with a view of gaining for them thereby safety and protection. . . . Nay, of the so-called gods, so utterly have the sacred places been destroyed, that not even their outline remains, nor the shape of their altars is known to men of this generation, while their materials have been dedicated to the shrines of the Martyrs. For the Lord has introduced His own dead in place of your gods; of the one He hath made a riddance, on the other He hath conferred their honours. For the Pandian festival, the Diasia, and the Dionysia, and your other such, we have the feasts of Peter, of Paul, of Thomas, of Sergius, of Marcellus, of Leontius, of Panteleëmon, of Antony, of Maurice, and of the other Martyrs; and for that old-world procession, and indecency of work and word, are held modest festivities, without intemperance, or revel, or laughter, but with divine hymns, and attendance on holy discourses and prayers, adorned with laudable tears." This was the view of the "Evidences of Christianity" which a bishop of the fifth century offered for the conversion of unbelievers.

### 9.

The introduction of images was still later, and met with more opposition in the West than in the East. It is grounded on the same great principle which I am illustrating; and as I have given extracts from Theodoret for the developments of the fourth and fifth centuries, so will I now cite St. John Damascene in defence of the further developments of the eighth.

"As to the passages you adduce," he says to his opponents, "they abominate not the worship paid to our Images, but that of the Greeks, who made them gods. It needs not therefore, because of the absurd use of the Greeks, to abolish our use which is so pious. Enchanters and wizards use adjurations, so does the Church over its Catechumens; but they invoke devils, and she invokes God against devils. Greeks dedicate images to devils, and call them gods; but we to True God Incarnate, and to God's servants and friends, who drive away the troops of devils."[18] Again, "As the holy Fathers overthrew the temples and shrines of the devils, and raised in their places shrines in the names of Saints and we worship them, so also they overthrew the images of the devils, and in their stead raised images of Christ, and God's Mother, and the Saints. And under the Old Covenant, Israel neither raised temples in the name of men, nor was memory of man made a festival; for, as yet, man's nature was under a curse, and death was condemnation, and therefore was lamented, and a corpse was reckoned unclean and he who touched it; but now that the Godhead has been combined with our nature, as some life-giving and saving medicine, our nature has been glorified and is trans-elemented into incorruption. Wherefore the death of Saints is made a feast, and temples are raised to them, and Images are painted . . . For the Image is a triumph, and a manifestation, and a monument in memory of the victory of those who have done nobly and excelled, and of the shame of the devils defeated and overthrown." Once more, "If because of the Law thou dost forbid Images, you will soon have to sabbatize and be circumcised, for these ordinances the Law commands as indispensable; nay, to observe the whole law, and not to keep the festival of the Lord's Pascha out of Jerusalem: but know that if you keep the Law, Christ hath profited you nothing. . . . But away with this, for whoever of you are justified in the Law have fallen from grace."[19]

## 10.

It is quite consistent with the tenor of these remarks to observe, or to allow, that real superstitions have sometimes obtained in parts of Christendom from its intercourse with the heathen; or have even been admitted, or all but admitted, though commonly resisted strenuously, by authorities in the Church, in consequence of the resemblance which exists between the heathen rites and certain portions of her ritual. As philosophy has at times corrupted her divines, so has paganism corrupted her worshippers; and as the more intellectual have been involved in heresy, so have the ignorant been corrupted by superstition.

[18] De Imag. i. 24.
[19] Ibid. ii. 11. 14.

Thus St. Chrysostom is vehement against the superstitious usages which Jews and Gentiles were introducing among Christians at Antioch and Constantinople. "What shall we say," he asks in one place, "about the amulets and bells which are hung upon the hands, and the scarlet woof, and other things full of such extreme folly; when they ought to invest the child with nothing else save the protection of the Cross? But now that is despised which hath converted the whole world, and given the sore wound to the devil, and overthrown all his power; while the thread, and the woof, and the other amulets of that kind, are entrusted with the child's safety." After mentioning further superstitions, he proceeds, "Now that among Greeks such things should be done, is no wonder; but among the worshippers of the Cross, and partakers in unspeakable mysteries, and professors of such morality, that such unseemliness should prevail, this is especially to be deplored again and again."[20]

And in like manner St. Augustine suppressed the feasts called Agapæ, which had been allowed the African Christians on their first conversion. "It is time," he says, "for men who dare not deny that they are Christians, to begin to live according to the will of Christ, and, now being Christians, to reject what was only allowed that they might become Christians." The people objected the example of the Vatican Church at Rome, where such feasts were observed every day; St. Augustine answered, "I have heard that it has been often prohibited, but the place is far off from the Bishop's abode (the Lateran), and in so large a city there is a multitude of carnal persons, especially of strangers who resort daily thither."[21] And in like manner it certainly is possible that the consciousness of the sanctifying power in Christianity may have acted as a temptation to sins, whether of deceit or of violence; as if the habit or state of grace destroyed the sinfulness of certain acts, or as if the end justified the means.

## 11.

It is but enunciating in other words the principle we are tracing, to say that the Church has been entrusted with the dispensation of grace. For if she can convert heathen appointments into spiritual rites and usages, what is this but to be in possession of a treasure, and to exercise a discretionary power in its application? Hence there has been from the

---

[20] Hom. xii. in Cor. 1, Oxf. Tr.
[21] Fleury, Hist. xx. 11, Oxf. Tr.

first much variety and change, in the Sacramental acts and instruments which she has used. While the Eastern and African Churches baptized heretics on their reconciliation, the Church of Rome, as the Catholic Church since, maintained that imposition of hands was sufficient, if their prior baptism had been formally correct. The ceremony of imposition of hands was used on various occasions with a distinct meaning; at the rite of Catechumens, on admitting heretics, in Confirmation, in Ordination, in Benediction. Baptism was sometimes administered by immersion, sometimes by infusion. Infant baptism was not at first enforced as afterwards. Children or even infants were admitted to the Eucharist in the African Church and the rest of the West, as now in the Greek. Oil had various uses, as for healing the sick, or as in the rite of extreme unction. Indulgences in works or in periods of penance, had a different meaning, according to circumstances. In like manner the Sign of the Cross was one of the earliest means of grace; then holy seasons, and holy places, and pilgrimage to them; holy water; prescribed prayers, or other observances; garments, as the scapular, and sacred vestments; the rosary; the crucifix. And for some wise purpose doubtless, such as that of showing the power of the Church in the dispensation of divine grace, as well as the perfection and spirituality of the Eucharistic Presence, the Chalice is in the West withheld from all but the celebrant in the Holy Eucharist.


### 12.

Since it has been represented as if the power of assimilation, spoken of in this chapter, is in my meaning nothing more than a mere accretion of doctrines or rites from without, I am led to quote the following passage in further illustration of it from my *Essays*, vol. ii. p. 231:

"The phenomenon, admitted on all hands, is this: That great portion of what is generally received as Christian truth is, in its rudiments or in its separate parts, to be found in heathen philosophies and religions. For instance, the doctrine of a Trinity is found both in the East and in the West; so is the ceremony of washing; so is the rite of sacrifice. The doctrine of the Divine Word is Platonic; the doctrine of the Incarnation is Indian; of a divine kingdom is Judaic; of Angels and demons is Magian; the connexion of sin with the body is Gnostic; celibacy is known to Bonze and Talapoin; a sacerdotal order is Egyptian; the idea of a new birth is Chinese and Eleusinian; belief in sacramental virtue is Pythagorean; and honours to the dead are a polytheism. Such is the general nature of the fact before us; Mr. Milman argues from it—

'These things are in heathenism, therefore they are not Christian': we, on the contrary, prefer to say, 'these things are in Christianity, therefore they are not heathen.' That is, we prefer to say, and we think that Scripture bears us out in saying, that from the beginning the Moral Governor of the world has scattered the seeds of truth far and wide over its extent; that these have variously taken root, and grown up as in the wilderness, wild plants indeed but living; and hence that, as the inferior animals have tokens of an immaterial principle in them, yet have not souls, so the philosophies and religions of men have their life in certain true ideas, though they are not directly divine. What man is amid the brute creation, such is the Church among the schools of the world; and as Adam gave names to the animals about him, so has the Church from the first looked round upon the earth, noting and visiting the doctrines she found there. She began in Chaldea, and then sojourned among the Canaanites, and went down into Egypt, and thence passed into Arabia, till she rested in her own land. Next she encountered the merchants of Tyre, and the wisdom of the East country, and the luxury of Sheba. Then she was carried away to Babylon, and wandered to the schools of Greece. And wherever she went, in trouble or in triumph, still she was a living spirit, the mind and voice of the Most High; 'sitting in the midst of the doctors, both hearing them and asking them questions'; claiming to herself what they said rightly, correcting their errors, supplying their defects, completing their beginnings, expanding their surmises, and thus gradually by means of them enlarging the range and refining the sense of her own teaching. So far then from her creed being of doubtful credit because it resembles foreign theologies, we even hold that one special way in which Providence has imparted divine knowledge to us has been by enabling her to draw and collect it together out of the world, and, in this sense, as in others, to 'suck the milk of the Gentiles and to suck the breast of kings.'

"How far in fact this process has gone, is a question of history; and we believe it has before now been grossly exaggerated and misrepresented by those who, like Mr. Milman, have thought that its existence told against Catholic doctrine; but so little antecedent difficulty have we in the matter, that we could readily grant, unless it were a question of fact not of theory, that Balaam was an Eastern sage, or a Sibyl was inspired, or Solomon learnt of the sons of Mahol, or Moses was a scholar of the Egyptian hierophants. We are not distressed to be told that the doctrine of the angelic host came from Babylon, while we know that they did sing at the Nativity; nor that the vision of a

Mediator is in Philo, if in very deed He died for us on Calvary. Nor are we afraid to allow, that, even after His coming, the Church has been a treasure-house, giving forth things old and new, casting the gold of fresh tributaries into her refiner's fire, or stamping upon her own, as time required it, a deeper impress of her Master's image.

"The distinction between these two theories is broad and obvious. The advocates of the one imply that Revelation was a single, entire, solitary act, or nearly so, introducing a certain message; whereas we, who maintain the other, consider that Divine teaching has been in fact, what the analogy of nature would lead us to expect, 'at sundry times and in divers manners,' various, complex, progressive, and supplemental of itself. We consider the Christian doctrine, when analyzed, to appear, like the human frame, 'fearfully and wonderfully made'; but they think it some one tenet or certain principles given out at one time in their fulness, without gradual enlargement before Christ's coming or elucidation afterwards. They cast off all that they also find in Pharisee or heathen; we conceive that the Church, like Aaron's rod, devours the serpents of the magicians. They are ever hunting for a fabulous primitive simplicity; we repose in Catholic fulness. They seek what never has been found; we accept and use what even they acknowledge to be a substance. They are driven to maintain, on their part, that the Church's doctrine was never pure; we say that it can never be corrupt. We consider that a divine promise keeps the Church Catholic from doctrinal corruption; but on what promise, or on what encouragement, they are seeking for their visionary purity does not appear."

# CHAPTER IX

# APPLICATION OF THE FOURTH NOTE OF A TRUE DEVELOPMENT: ITS LOGICAL SEQUENCE

Logical Sequence has been set down above as a fourth test of fidelity in development, and shall now be briefly illustrated in the history of Christian doctrine. That is, I mean to give instances of one doctrine leading to another; so that, if the former be admitted, the latter can hardly be denied, and the latter can hardly be called a corruption without taking exception to the former. And I use "logical sequence" in contrast both to that process of incorporation and assimilation which was last under review, and also to that principle of science, which has put into order and defended the developments after they have been made. Accordingly it will include any progress of the mind from one judgment to another, as, for instance, by way of moral fitness, which may not admit of analysis into premise and conclusion. Thus St. Peter argued in the case of Cornelius and his friends, "Can any man forbid water that these should not be baptized, which have received the Holy Ghost as well as we?"

Such is the series of doctrinal truths, which start from the dogma of our Lord's Divinity, and again from such texts of Scripture as "Thou art Peter," and which I should have introduced here, had I not already used them for a previous purpose in the fourth chapter. I shall confine myself then for an example to the instance of the developments which follow on the consideration of sin after Baptism, a subject which was touched upon in the same chapter.

## 1. Pardons

It is not necessary here to enlarge on the benefits which the primitive Church held to be conveyed to the soul by means of the Sacrament of Baptism. Its distinguishing gift, which is in point to mention, was the plenary forgiveness of sins past. It was also held that the Sacrament could not be repeated. The question immediately followed, how, since there was but "one Baptism for the remission of sins," the guilt of such sin was to be removed as was incurred after its administration. There must be some provision in the revealed system for so obvious a need. What could be done for those who had received the one remission of sins, and had sinned since? Some who thought upon the subject appear to have conceived that the Church was empowered to grant one, and one only, reconciliation after grievous offences. Three sins seemed to many, at least in the West, to be irremissible, idolatry, murder, and adultery. But such a system of Church discipline, however suited to a small community, and even expedient in a time of persecution, could not exist in Christianity, as it spread into the *orbis terrarum*, and gathered like a net of every kind. A more indulgent rule gradually gained ground; yet the Spanish Church adhered to the ancient even in the fourth century, and a portion of the African in the third, and in the remaining portion there was a relaxation only as regards the crime of incontinence.

## 2.

Meanwhile a protest was made against the growing innovation: at the beginning of the third century Montanus, who was a zealot for the more primitive rule, shrank from the laxity, as he considered it, of the Asian Churches;[1] as, in a different subject matter, Jovinian and Vigilantius were offended at the developments in divine worship in the century which followed. The Montanists had recourse to the See of Rome, and at first with some appearance of success. Again, in Africa, where there had been in the first instance a schism headed by Felicissimus in favour of a milder discipline than St. Cyprian approved, a far more formidable stand was soon made in favour of antiquity, headed by Novatus, who originally had been of the party of Felicissimus. This was taken up at Rome by Novatian, who professed to adhere to the original, or at least the primitive rule of the Church, viz., that those who had once fallen from the faith could in no case be received again.[2] The controversy seems to have found the following issue—whether the Church had the *means* of pardoning sins committed after baptism, which the Novatians, at least practically, denied. "It is fitting," says the Novatian Acesius, "to exhort those who have sinned after Baptism to repentance, but to expect hope of remission, not from the priests,

---

[1] Gieseler, Text-book, vol. i. p. 108.
[2] Gieseler, ibid. p. 164.

but from God, who hath power to forgive sins."[3] The schism spread
into the East, and led to the appointment of a penitentiary priest in
the Catholic Churches. By the end of the third century as many as four
degrees of penance were appointed, through which offenders had to
pass in order to a reconciliation.

## 2. Penances

The length and severity of the penance varied with times and places.
Sometimes, as we have seen, it lasted, in the case of grave offences,
through life and on to death, without any reconciliation; at other times
it ended only in the *viaticum*; and if, after reconciliation they did not
die, their ordinary penance was still binding on them either for life or
for a certain time. In other cases it lasted ten, fifteen, or twenty years.
But in all cases, from the first, the bishop had the power of shortening
it, and of altering the nature and quality of the punishment. Thus in
the instance of the Emperor Theodosius, whom St. Ambrose shut out
from communion for the massacre at Thessalonica, "according to the
mildest rules of ecclesiastical discipline, which were established in the
fourth century," says Gibbon, "the crime of homicide was expiated
by the penitence of twenty years; and as it was impossible, in the
period of human life, to purge the accumulated guilt of the massacre
. . . the murderer should have been excluded from the holy communion
till the hour of his death." He goes on to say that the public edification
which resulted from the humiliation of so illustrious a penitent was a
reason for abridging the punishment. "It was sufficient that the Emperor of the Romans, stripped of the ensigns of royalty, should appear
in a mournful and suppliant posture, and that, in the midst of the
Church of Milan, he should humbly solicit with sighs and tears the
pardon of his sins." His penance was shortened to an interval of about
eight months. Hence arose the phrase of a "*pœnitentia legitima, plena,
et justa*"; which signifies a penance sufficient, perhaps in length of
time, perhaps in intensity of punishment.

## 3. Satisfactions

Here a serious question presented itself to the minds of Christians,
which was now to be wrought out: Were these punishments merely
signs of contrition, or in any sense satisfactions for sin? If the former,

[3] Socr. Hist. i. 10.

they might be absolutely remitted at the discretion of the Church, as soon as true repentance was discovered; the end had then been attained, and nothing more was necessary. Thus St. Chrysostom says in one of his Homilies,[4] "I require not continuance of time, but the correction of the soul. Show your contrition, show your reformation, and all is done." Yet, though there might be a reason of the moment for shortening the penance imposed by the Church, this does not at all decide the question whether that ecclesiastical penance be not part of an expiation made to the Almighty Judge for the sin; and supposing this really to be the case, the question follows, How is the complement of that satisfaction to be wrought out, which on just grounds of present expedience has been suspended by the Church now?

As to this question, it cannot be doubted that the Fathers considered penance as not a mere expression of contrition, but as an act done directly towards God and a means of averting His anger. "If the sinner spare not himself, he will be spared by God," says the writer who goes under the name of St. Ambrose. "Let him lie in sackcloth, and by the austerity of his life make amends for the offence of his past pleasures," says St. Jerome. "As we have sinned greatly," says St. Cyprian, "let us weep greatly; for a deep wound diligent and long tending must not be wanting, the repentance must not fall short of the offence." "Take heed to thyself," says St. Basil, "that, in proportion to the fault, thou admit also the restoration from the remedy."[5] If so, the question follows which was above contemplated—if in consequence of death, or in the exercise of the Church's discretion, the "*plena pœnitentia*" is not accomplished in its ecclesiastical shape, how and when will the residue be exacted?

### 4. Purgatory

Clement of Alexandria answers this particular question very distinctly, according to Bishop Kaye, though not in some other points expressing himself conformably to the doctrine afterwards received. "Clement," says that author, "distinguishes between sins committed before and after baptism: the former are remitted at baptism; the latter are purged by discipline. . . . The necessity of this purifying discipline is such, that if it does not take place in this life, it must after death,

---

[4]Hom. 14, in 2 Cor. fin.
[5]Vid. Tertull. Oxf. tr. pp. 374–75.

and is then to be effected by fire, not by a destructive, but a discriminating fire, pervading the soul which passes through it."[6]

There is a celebrated passage in St. Cyprian, on the subject of the punishment of lapsed Christians, which certainly seems to express the same doctrine. "St. Cyprian is arguing in favour of readmitting the lapsed, when penitent; and his argument seems to be that it does not follow that we absolve them simply because we simply restore them to the Church. He writes thus to Antonian: 'It is one thing to stand for pardon, another to arrive at glory; one to be sent to prison (*missum in carcerem*) and not to go out till the last farthing be paid, another to receive at once the reward of faith and virtue; one thing to be tormented for sin in long pain, and so to be cleansed and purged a long while by fire (*purgari diu igne*), another to be washed from all sin in martyrdom; one thing, in short, to wait for the Lord's sentence in the Day of Judgment, another at once to be crowned by Him.' Some understand this passage to refer to the penitential discipline of the Church which was imposed on the penitent; and, as far as the context goes, certainly no sense could be more apposite. Yet . . . the words in themselves seem to go beyond any mere ecclesiastical, though virtually divine censure; especially '*missum in carcerem*' and '*purgari diu igne*.' "[7]

## 2.

The Acts of the Martyrs St. Perpetua and St. Felicitas, which are prior to St. Cyprian, confirm this interpretation. In the course of the narrative, St. Perpetua prays for her brother Dinocrates, who had died at the age of seven; and has a vision of a dark place, and next of a pool of water, which he was not tall enough to reach. She goes on praying; and in a second vision the water descended to him, and he was able to drink, and went to play as children use. "Then I knew," she says, "that he was translated from his place of punishment."[8]

The prayers in the Eucharistic Service for the faithful departed inculcate, at least according to the belief of the fourth century, the same doctrine, that the sins of accepted and elect souls, which were not expiated here, would receive punishment hereafter. Certainly such was

[6] Clem. ch. 12. Vid. also Tertull. de Anim. fin.
[7] Tracts for the Times, No. 79, p. 38.
[8] Ruinart, Mart. p. 96.

St. Cyril's belief: "I know that many say," he observes, "what is a soul profited, which departs from this world either with sins or without sins, if it be commemorated in the [Eucharistic] Prayer? Now, surely, if when a king had banished certain who had given him offence, their connexions should weave a crown and offer it to him on behalf of those under his vengeance, would he not grant a respite to their punishments? In the same way we, when we offer to Him our supplications for those who have fallen asleep, though they be sinners, weave no crown, but offer up Christ, sacrificed for our sins, propitiating our merciful God, both for them and for ourselves."[9]

### 3.

Thus we see how, as time went on, the doctrine of Purgatory was brought home to the minds of the faithful as a portion or form of penance due for post-baptismal sin. And thus the apprehension of this doctrine and the practice of infant baptism would grow into general reception together. Cardinal Fisher gives another reason for Purgatory being then developed out of earlier points of faith. He says, "Faith, whether in Purgatory or in Indulgences, was not so necessary in the Primitive Church as now. For then love so burned, that every one was ready to meet death for Christ. Crimes were rare, and such as occurred were avenged by the great severity of the Canons."[10]

### 4.

An author, who quotes this passage, analyzes the circumstances and the reflections which prepared the Christian mind for the doctrine, when it was first insisted on, and his remarks with a few corrections may be accepted here. "Most men," he says, "to our apprehensions, are too little formed in religious habits either for heaven or for hell, yet there is no middle state when Christ comes in judgment. In consequence it is obvious to have recourse to the interval before His coming, as a time during which this incompleteness may be remedied; as a season, not of changing the spiritual bent and character of the soul departed, whatever that be, for probation ends with mortal life, but of developing it in a more determinate form, whether of good or of evil. Again, when the mind once allows itself to speculate, it will

[9] Mystagog. 5.
[10] Vid. Via Med. vol. i. p. 72.

discern in such a provision a means, whereby those, who, not without true faith at bottom, yet have committed great crimes, or those who have been carried off in youth while still undecided, or who die after a barren though not an immoral or scandalous life, may receive such chastisement as may prepare them for heaven, and render it consistent with God's justice to admit them thither. Again, the inequality of the sufferings of Christians in this life, compared one with another, leads the mind to the same speculations; the intense suffering, for instance, which some men undergo on their death-bed, seeming as if but an anticipation in their case of what comes after death upon others, who, without greater claim on God's forbearance, live without chastisement, and die easily. The mind will inevitably dwell upon such thoughts, unless it has been taught to subdue them by education or by the fear or the experience of their dangerousness.

5.

"Various suppositions have, accordingly, been made, as pure suppositions, as mere specimens of the capabilities (if one may so speak) of the Divine Dispensation, as efforts of the mind reaching forward and venturing beyond its depth into the abyss of the Divine Counsels. If one supposition could be hazarded, sufficient to solve the problem, the existence of ten thousand others is conceivable, unless indeed the resources of God's Providence are exactly commensurate with man's discernment of them. Religious men, amid these searchings of heart, have naturally gone to Scripture for relief; to see if the inspired word anywhere gave them any clue for their inquiries. And from what was there found, and from the speculations of reason upon it, various notions have been hazarded at different times; for instance, that there is a certain momentary ordeal to be undergone by all men after this life, more or less severe according to their spiritual state; or that certain gross sins in good men will be thus visited, or their lighter failings and habitual imperfections; or that the very sight of Divine Perfection in the invisible world will be in itself a pain, while it constitutes the purification of the imperfect but believing soul; or that, happiness admitting of various degrees of intensity, penitents late in life may sink for ever into a state, blissful as far as it goes, but more or less approaching to unconsciousness; and infants dying after baptism may be as gems paving the courts of heaven, or as the living wheels of the Prophet's vision; while matured Saints may excel in capacity of bliss, as well as in dignity, the highest Archangels.

## 6.

"Now, as to the punishments and satisfactions for sin, the texts to which the minds of the early Christians seem to have been principally drawn, and from which they ventured to argue in behalf of these vague notions, were these two: 'The fire shall try every man's work,' etc., and 'He shall baptize you with the Holy Ghost and with fire.' These passages, with which many more were found to accord, directed their thoughts one way, as making mention of 'fire,' whatever was meant by the word, as the instrument of trial and purification; and that, at some time between the present time and the Judgment, or at the Judgment.

"As the doctrine, thus suggested by certain striking texts, grew in popularity and definiteness, and verged towards its present Roman form, it seemed a key to many others. Great portions of the books of Psalms, Job, and the Lamentations, which express the feelings of religious men under suffering, would powerfully recommend it by the forcible and most affecting and awful meaning which they received from it. When this was once suggested, all other meanings would seem tame and inadequate.

"To these may be added various passages from the Prophets, as that in the beginning of the third chapter of Malachi, which speaks of fire as the instrument of judgment and purification, when Christ comes to visit His Church.

"Moreover, there were other texts of obscure and indeterminate bearing, which seemed on this hypothesis to receive a profitable meaning; such as our Lord's words in the Sermon on the Mount, 'Verily, I say unto thee, thou shalt by no means come out thence till thou hast paid the uttermost farthing'; and St. John's expression in the Apocalypse, that 'no man in heaven, nor in earth, neither under the earth, was able to open the book.' "[11]

## 7.

When then an answer had to be made to the question, how is post-baptismal sin to be remitted, there was an abundance of passages in Scripture to make easy to the faith of the inquirer the definitive decision of the Church.

[11] Via Med. vol. i. pp. 174–77.

## 5. Meritorious Works

The doctrine of post-baptismal sin, especially when realized in the doctrine of Purgatory, leads the inquirer to fresh developments beyond itself. Its effect is to convert a Scripture statement, which might seem only of temporary application, into a universal and perpetual truth. When St. Paul and St. Barnabas would "confirm the souls of the disciples," they taught them "that we must through much tribulation enter into the kingdom of God." It is obvious what very practical results would follow on such an announcement, in the instance of those who simply accepted the Apostolic decision; and in like manner a conviction that sin must have its punishment, here or hereafter, and that we all must suffer, how overpowering will be its effect, what a new light does it cast on the history of the soul, what a change does it make in our judgment of the external world, what a reversal of our natural wishes and aims for the future! Is a doctrine conceivable which would so elevate the mind above this present state, and teach it so successfully to dare difficult things, and to be reckless of danger and pain? He who believes that suffer he must, and that delayed punishment may be the greater, will be above the world, will admire nothing, fear nothing, desire nothing. He has within his breast a source of greatness, self-denial, heroism. This is the secret spring of strenuous efforts and persevering toil, of the sacrifice of fortune, friends, ease, reputation, happiness. There is, it is true, a higher class of motives which will be felt by the Saint; who will do from love what all Christians who act acceptably do from faith. And, moreover, the ordinary measures of charity which Christians possess suffice for securing such respectable attention to religious duties as the routine necessities of the Church require. But if we would raise an army of devoted men to resist the world, to oppose sin and error, to relieve misery, or to propagate the truth, we must be provided with motives which keenly affect the many. Christian love is too rare a gift, philanthropy is too weak a material, for the occasion. Nor is there an influence to be found to suit our purpose, besides this solemn conviction, which arises out of the very rudiments of Christian theology, and is taught by its most ancient masters—this sense of the awfulness of post-baptismal sin. It is in vain to look out for missionaries for China or Africa, or evangelists for our great towns, or Christian attendants on the sick, or teachers of the ignorant, on such a scale of numbers as the need requires, without the doctrine of Purgatory. For thus the sins of youth are turned

344 DOCTRINAL DEVELOPMENTS VIEWED TO CORRUPTIONS

to account by the profitable penance of manhood; and terrors, which the philosopher scorns in the individual, become the benefactors and earn the gratitude of nations.

### 6. *The Monastic Rule*

But there is one form of penance which has been more prevalent and uniform than any other, out of which the forms just noticed have grown, or on which they have been engrafted—the Monastic Rule. In the first ages, the doctrine of the punishments of sin, whether in this world or in the next, was little called for. The rigid discipline of the infant Church was the preventive of greater offences, and its persecutions the penance of their commission; but when the canons were relaxed and confessorship ceased, then some substitute was needed, and such was Monachism, being at once a sort of continuation of primeval innocence, and a school of self-chastisement. And, as it is a great principle in economical and political science that everything should be turned to account, and there should be no waste, so, in the instance of Christianity, the penitential observances of individuals, which were necessarily on a large scale as its professors increased, took the form of works, whether for the defence of the Church, or the spiritual and temporal good of mankind.

### 2.

In no aspect of the Divine system do we see more striking developments than in the successive fortunes of Monachism. Little did the youth Antony foresee, when he set off to fight the evil one in the wilderness, what a sublime and various history he was opening, a history which had its first developments even in his own lifetime. He was himself a hermit in the desert; but when others followed his example, he was obliged to give them guidance, and thus he found himself, by degrees, at the head of a large family of solitaries, five thousand of whom were scattered in the district of Nitria alone. He lived to see a second stage in the development; the huts in which they lived were brought together, sometimes round a church, and a sort of subordinate community, or college, formed among certain individuals of their number. St. Pachomius was the first who imposed a general rule of discipline upon the brethren, gave them a common dress, and set before them the objects to which the religious life was dedicated. Manual labour, study, devotion, bodily mortification, were now their peculiarities; and the institution, thus defined, spread and established itself through Eastern and Western Christendom.

The penitential character of Monachism is not prominent in St. Antony, though it is distinctly noticed by Pliny in his description of the Essenes of the Dead Sea, who anticipated the monastic life at the rise of Christianity. In St. Basil, however, it becomes a distinguishing feature; so much so that the monastic profession was made a disqualification for the pastoral office,[12] and in theory involved an absolute separation from mankind; though in St. Basil's, as well as St. Antony's disciples, it performed the office of resisting heresy.

Next, the monasteries, which in their ecclesiastical capacity had been at first separate churches under a presbyter or abbot, became schools for the education of the clergy.[13]

### 3.

Centuries passed, and after many extravagant shapes of the institution, and much wildness and insubordination in its members, a new development took place under St. Benedict. Revising and digesting the provisions of St. Antony, St. Pachomius, and St. Basil, he bound together his monks by a perpetual vow, brought them into the cloister, united the separate convents into one Order,[14] and added objects of an ecclesiastical and civil nature to that of personal edification. Of these objects, agriculture seemed to St. Benedict himself of first importance; but in a very short time it was superseded by study and education, and the monasteries of the following centuries became the schools and libraries, and the monks the chroniclers and copyists, of a dark period. Centuries later, the Benedictine Order was divided into separate Congregations, and propagated in separate monastic bodies. The Congregation of Cluni was the most celebrated of the former; and of the latter, the hermit order of the Camaldoli and the agricultural Cistercians.

[12] Gieseler, vol. ii. p. 288.
[13] Ibid. p. 279.
[14] Or rather his successors, as St. Benedict of Anian, were the founders of the Order; but minute accuracy on these points is unnecessary in a mere sketch of the history.

## 4.

Both a unity and an originality are observable in the successive phases under which Monachism has shown itself; and while its developments bring it more and more into the ecclesiastical system, and subordinate it to the governing power, they are true to their first idea, and spring fresh from the parent stock, which from time immemorial had thriven in Syria and Egypt. The sheepskin and desert of St. Antony did but revive "the mantle"[15] and the mountain of the first Carmelite, and St. Basil's penitential exercises had already been practised by the Therapeutæ. In like manner the congregational principle, which is ascribed to St. Benedict, had been anticipated by St. Antony and St. Pachomius; and after centuries of disorder, another function of early Monachism, for which there had been little call for centuries, the defence of Catholic truth, was exercised with singular success by the rival orders of Dominicans and Franciscans.

St. Benedict had come as if to reserve a principle of civilization, and a refuge for learning, at a time when the old framework of society was falling, and new political creations were taking their place. And when the young intellect within them began to stir, and a change of another kind discovered itself, then appeared St. Francis and St. Dominic to teach and chastise it; and in proportion as Monachism assumed this public office, so did the principle of penance, which had been the chief characteristic of its earlier forms, hold a less prominent place. The Tertiaries indeed, or members of the third order of St. Francis and St. Dominic, were penitents; but the friar himself, instead of a penitent, was made a priest, and was allowed to quit cloister. Nay, they assumed the character of what may be called an Ecumenical Order, as being supported by begging, not by endowments, and being under the jurisdiction, not of the local bishop, but of the Holy See. The Dominicans too came forward especially as a learned body, and as entrusted with the office of preaching, at a time when the mind of Europe seemed to be developing into infidelity. They filled the chairs at the Universities, while the strength of the Franciscans lay among the lower orders.

[15] μηλωτής, 2 Kings ii. Sept. Vid. also, "They wandered about in sheepskins and goatskins" (Heb. xi. 37).

## 5.

At length, in the last era of ecclesiastical revolution, another principle of early Monachism, which had been but partially developed, was brought out into singular prominence in the history of the Jesuits. "Obedience," said an ancient abbot, "is a monk's service, with which he shall be heard in prayer, and shall stand with confidence by the Crucified, for so the Lord came to the cross, being made obedient even unto death";[16] but it was reserved for modern times to furnish the perfect illustration of this virtue, and to receive the full blessing which follows it. The great Society, which bears no earthly name, still more secular in its organization, and still more simply dependent on the See of St. Peter, has been still more distinguished than any order before it for the rule of obedience, while it has compensated the danger of its free intercourse with the world by its scientific adherence to devotional exercises. The hermitage, the cloister, the inquisitor, and the friar were suited to other states of society; with the Jesuits, as well as with the religious communities, which are their juniors, usefulness, secular and religious, literature, education, the confessional, preaching, the oversight of the poor, missions, the care of the sick, have been chief objects of attention; great cities have been the scene of operation: bodily austerities and the ceremonial of devotion have been made of but secondary importance. Yet it may fairly be questioned, whether, in an intellectual age, when freedom both of thought and of action is so dearly prized, a greater penance can be devised for the soldier of Christ than the absolute surrender of judgment and will to the command of another.

[16] Rosweyde. V. P. p. 618.

# CHAPTER X

# APPLICATION OF THE FIFTH NOTE OF A TRUE DEVELOPMENT: ANTICIPATION OF ITS FUTURE

It has been set down above as a fifth argument in favour of the fidelity of developments, ethical or political, if the doctrine from which they have proceeded has, in any early stage of its history, given indications of those opinions and practices in which it has ended. Supposing then the so-called Catholic doctrines and practices are true and legitimate developments, and not corruptions, we may expect from the force of logic to find instances of them in the first centuries. And this I conceive to be the case: the records indeed of those times are scanty, and we have little means of determining what daily Christian life then was: we know little of the thoughts, and the prayers, and the meditations, and the discourses of the early disciples of Christ, at a time when these professed developments were not recognized and duly located in the theological system; yet it appears, even from what remains, that the atmosphere of the Church was, as it were, charged with them from the first, and delivered itself of them from time to time, in this way or that, in various places and persons, as occasion elicited them, testifying the presence of a vast body of thought within it, which one day would take shape and position.

## 1. Resurrection and Relics

As a chief specimen of what I am pointing out, I will direct attention to a characteristic principle of Christianity, whether in the East or in the West, which is at present both a special stumbling-block and a subject of scoffing with Protestants and free-thinkers of every shade and colour: I mean the devotions which both Greeks and Latins show towards bones, blood, the heart, the hair, bits of clothes, scapulars, cords, medals, beads, and the like, and the miraculous powers which they often ascribe to them. Now, the principle from which these beliefs and usages proceed is the doctrine that Matter is susceptible of grace, or capable of a union with a Divine Presence and influence. This principle, as we shall see, was in the first age both energetically manifested and variously developed; and that chiefly in consequence of the diametrically opposite doctrine of the schools and the religions of the day. And thus its exhibition in that primitive age becomes also an instance of a statement often made in controversy, that the profession and the developments of a doctrine are according to the emergency of the time, and that silence at a certain period implies, not that it was not then held, but that it was not questioned.

## 2.

Christianity began by considering Matter as a creature of God, and in itself "very good." It taught that Matter, as well as Spirit, had become corrupt, in the instance of Adam; and it contemplated its recovery. It taught that the Highest had taken a portion of that corrupt mass upon Himself, in order to the sanctification of the whole; that, as a first fruits of His purpose, He had purified from all sin that very portion of it which He took into His Eternal Person, and thereunto had taken it from a Virgin Womb, which He had filled with the abundance of His Spirit. Moreover, it taught that during His earthly sojourn He had been subject to the natural infirmities of man, and had suffered from those ills to which flesh is heir. It taught that the Highest had in that flesh died on the Cross, and that His blood had an expiatory power; moreover, that He had risen again in that flesh, and had carried that flesh with Him into heaven, and that from that flesh, glorified and deified in Him, He never would be divided. As a first consequence of these awful doctrines comes that of the resurrection of the bodies of His Saints, and of their future glorification with Him; next, that of the sanctity of their relics; further, that of the merit of Virginity; and, lastly, that of the prerogatives of Mary, Mother of God. All these doctrines are more or less developed in the Antenicene period, though in very various degrees, from the nature of the case.

## 3.

And they were all objects of offence or of scorn to philosophers, priests, or populace of the day. With varieties of opinions which need not be mentioned, it was a fundamental doctrine in the schools, whether Greek or Oriental, that Matter was essentially evil. It had not been created by the Supreme God; it was in eternal enmity with Him;

it was the source of all pollution; and it was irreclaimable. Such was the doctrine of Platonist, Gnostic, and Manichee—whereas then St. John had laid it down that "every spirit that confesseth not that Jesus Christ is come in the flesh is the spirit of Antichrist"; the Gnostics obstinately denied the Incarnation, and held that Christ was but a phantom, or had come on the man Jesus at his baptism, and left him at his passion. The one great topic of preaching with Apostles and Evangelists was the Resurrection of Christ and of all mankind after Him; but when the philosophers of Athens heard St. Paul, "some mocked," and others contemptuously put aside the doctrine. The birth from a Virgin implied not only that the body was not intrinsically evil, but that one state of it was holier than another, and St. Paul explained that, while marriage was good, celibacy was better; but the Gnostics, holding the utter malignity of Matter, one and all condemned marriage as sinful, and, whether they observed continence or not, or abstained from eating flesh or not, maintained that all functions of our animal nature were evil and abominable.

### 4.

"Perish the thought," says Manes, "that our Lord Jesus Christ should have descended through the womb of a woman." "He descended," says Marcion, "but without touching her or taking aught from her." "Through her, not of her," said another. "It is absurd to assert," says a disciple of Bardesanes, "that this flesh in which we are imprisoned shall rise again, for it is well called a burden, a tomb, and a chain." "They execrate the funeral-pile," says Cæcilius, speaking of Christians, "as if bodies, though withdrawn from the flames, did not all resolve into dust by years, whether beasts tear, or sea swallows, or earth covers, or flame wastes." According to the old paganism, both the educated and vulgar held corpses and sepulchres in aversion. They quickly rid themselves of the remains even of their friends, thinking their presence a pollution, and felt the same terror even of burying-places which assails the ignorant and superstitious now. It is recorded of Hannibal that, on his return to the African coast from Italy, he changed his landing-place to avoid a ruined sepulchre. "May the god who passes between heaven and hell," says Apuleius in his *Apology*, "present to thy eyes, O Emilian, all that haunts the night, all that alarms in burying-places, all that terrifies in tombs." George of Cappadocia could not direct a more bitter taunt against the Alexandrian pagans than to call the temple of Serapis a sepulchre. The case had been the same even among the Jews; the Rabbins taught that even the corpses of holy men "did but serve to diffuse infection and defilement." "When deaths were Judaical," says the writer who goes under the name of St. Basil, "corpses were an abomination; when death is for Christ, the relics of Saints are precious. It was anciently said to the priests and the Nazarites, 'If any one shall touch a corpse, he shall be unclean till evening, and he shall wash his garment'; now, on the contrary, if any one shall touch a Martyr's bones, by reason of the grace dwelling in the body, he receives some participation of his sanctity."[1] Nay, Christianity taught a reverence for the bodies even of heathen. The care of the dead is one of the praises which, as we have seen above, is extorted in their favour from the Emperor Julian; and it was exemplified during the mortality which spread through the Roman world in the time of St. Cyprian. "They did good," says Pontius of the Christians of Carthage, "in the profusion of exuberant works to all, and not only to the household of faith. They did somewhat more than is recorded of the incomparable benevolence of Tobias. The slain of the king and the outcasts, whom Tobias gathered together, were of his own kin only."[2]

## 5.

Far more of course than such general reverence was the honour that they showed to the bodies of the Saints. They ascribed virtue to their martyred tabernacles, and treasured, as something supernatural, their blood, their ashes, and their bones. When St. Cyprian was beheaded, his brethren brought napkins to soak up his blood. "Only the harder portion of the holy relics remained," say the Acts of St. Ignatius, who was exposed to the beasts in the amphitheatre, "which were conveyed to Antioch, and deposited in linen, bequeathed, by the grace that was in the Martyr, to that holy Church as a priceless treasure." The Jews attempted to deprive the brethren of St. Polycarp's body, "lest, leaving the Crucified, they begin to worship him," says his Acts; "ignorant," they continue, "that we can never leave Christ"; and they add, "We, having taken up his bones which were more costly than precious stones, and refined more than gold, deposited them where was fitting; and there when we meet together, as we can, the Lord will grant us to

[1] Act. Arch. p. 85. Athan. c. Apoll. ii. 3.—Adam. Dial. iii. init. Minuc. Dial. 11. Apul. Apol. p. 535. Kortholt. Cal. p. 63. Calmet, Dict. t. 2, p. 736. Basil in Ps. 115, 4.
[2] Vit. S. Cypr. 10.

celebrate with joy and gladness the birthday of his martyrdom." On one occasion in Palestine, the Imperial authorities disinterred the bodies and cast them into the sea, "lest as their opinion went," says Eusebius, "there should be those who in their sepulchres and monuments might think them gods, and treat them with divine worship."

Julian, who had been a Christian, and knew the Christian history more intimately than a mere infidel would know it, traces the superstition, as he considers it, to the very lifetime of St. John, that is, as early as there were Martyrs to honour; makes the honour paid them contemporaneous with the worship paid to our Lord, and equally distinct and formal; and, moreover, declares that first it was secret, which for various reasons it was likely to have been. "Neither Paul," he says, "nor Matthew, nor Luke, nor Mark dared to call Jesus God; but honest John, having perceived that a great multitude had been caught by this disease in many of the Greek and Italian cities, and hearing, I suppose, that the monuments of Peter and Paul were, secretly indeed, but still hearing that they were honoured, first dared to say it." "Who can feel fitting abomination?" he says elsewhere; "you have filled all places with tombs and monuments, though it has been nowhere told you to tumble down at tombs or to honour them. . . . . If Jesus said that they were full of uncleanness, why do ye invoke God at them?" The tone of Faustus the Manichæan is the same. "Ye have turned," he says to St. Augustine, "the idols" of the heathen "into your Martyrs, whom ye honour (*colitis*) with similar prayers (*votis*)."[3]

<h2 style="text-align:center">6.</h2>

It is remarkable that the attention of both Christians and their opponents turned from the relics of the Martyrs to their persons. Basilides at least, who was founder of one of the most impious Gnostic sects, spoke of them with disrespect; he considered that their sufferings were the penalty of secret sins or evil desires, or transgressions committed in another body, and a sign of divine favour only because they were allowed to connect them with the cause of Christ.[4] On the other hand, it was the doctrine of the Church that Martyrdom was meritori-

[3] Act. Procons. 5. Ruinart, Act. Mart. pp. 22, 44. Euseb. Hist. viii. 6. Julian. ap. Cyr. pp. 327, 335. August. c. Faust. xx. 4.
[4] Clem. Strom. iv. 12.

ous, that it had a certain supernatural efficacy in it, and that the blood of the Saints received from the grace of the One Redeemer a certain expiatory power. Martyrdom stood in the place of Baptism, where the Sacrament had not been administered. It exempted the soul from all preparatory waiting, and gained its immediate admittance into glory. "All crimes are pardoned for the sake of this work," says Tertullian.

And in proportion to the near approach of the martyrs to their Almighty Judge, was their high dignity and power. St. Dionysius speaks of their reigning with Christ; Origen even conjectures that "as we are redeemed by the precious blood of Jesus, so some are redeemed by the precious blood of the Martyrs." St. Cyprian seems to explain his meaning when he says, "We believe that the merits of Martyrs and the works of the just avail much with the Judge," that is, for those who were lapsed, "when, after the end of this age and the world, Christ's people shall stand before His judgment-seat." Accordingly they were considered to intercede for the Church militant in their state of glory, and for individuals whom they had known. St. Potamiæna of Alexandria, in the first years of the third century, when taken out for execution, promised to obtain after her departure the salvation of the officer who led her out; and did appear to him, according to Eusebius, on the third day, and prophesied his own speedy martyrdom. And St. Theodosia in Palestine came to certain confessors who were in bonds, "to request them," as Eusebius tells us, "to remember her when they came to the Lord's Presence." Tertullian, when a Montanist, betrays the existence of the doctrine in the Catholic body by protesting against it.[5]

## 2. The Virgin Life

Next to the prerogatives of bodily suffering or Martyrdom came, in the estimation of the early Church, the prerogatives of bodily, as well as moral, purity or Virginity; another form of the general principle which I am here illustrating. "The first reward," says St. Cyprian to the Virgins, "is for the Martyrs an hundredfold; the second, sixtyfold, is for yourselves."[6] Their state and its merit is recognized by a consensus of the Antenicene writers; of whom Athenagoras distinctly connects Virginity with the privilege of divine communion: "You will find many of our people," he says to the Emperor Marcus, "both men and

[5] Tertull. Apol. fin. Euseb. Hist. vi. 42. Orig. ad Martyr. 50. Ruinart, Act. Mart. pp. 122, 323.
[6] De Hab. Virg. 12.

women, grown old in their single state, in hope thereby of a closer union with God."[7]

## 2.

Among the numerous authorities which might be cited, I will confine myself to a work, elaborate in itself, and important from its author. St. Methodius was a bishop and Martyr of the latter years of the Antenicene period, and is celebrated as the most variously endowed divine of his day. His learning, elegance in composition, and eloquence, are all commemorated.[8] The work in question, the *Convivium Virginum*, is a conference in which ten Virgins successively take part, in praise of the state of life to which they have themselves been specially called. I do not wish to deny that there are portions of it which strangely grate upon the feelings of an age which is formed on principles of which marriage is the centre. But here we are concerned with its doctrine. Of the speakers in this colloquy, three at least are real persons prior to St. Methodius's time; of these Thecla, whom tradition associates with St. Paul, is one, and Marcella, who in the Roman Breviary is considered to be St. Martha's servant, and who is said to have been the woman who exclaimed, "Blessed is the womb that bare Thee," etc., is described as a still older servant of Christ. The latter opens the discourse, and her subject is the gradual development of the doctrine of Virginity in the Divine Dispensations; Theophila, who follows, enlarges on the sanctity of Matrimony, with which the special glory of the higher state does not interfere; Thalia discourses on the mystical union which exists between Christ and His Church, and on the seventh chapter of the first Epistle to the Corinthians; Theopatra on the merit of Virginity; Thallusa exhorts to a watchful guardianship of the gift; Agatha shows the necessity of other virtues and good works, in order to the real praise of their peculiar profession; Procilla extols Virginity as the special instrument of becoming a spouse of Christ; Thecla treats of it as the great combatant in the warfare between heaven and hell, good and evil; Tysiana with reference to the Resurrection; and Domnina allegorizes Jotham's parable in Judges ix. Virtue, who has been introduced as the principal personage in the representation from the first, closes the discussion with an exhortation

[7] Athenag. Leg. 33.
[8] Lumper, Hist. t. 13, p. 439.

to inward purity, and they answer her by an hymn to our Lord as the Spouse of His Saints.

## 3.

It is observable that St. Methodius plainly speaks of the profession of Virginity as a vow. "I will explain," says one of his speakers, "how we are dedicated to the Lord. What is enacted in the Book of Numbers, 'to vow a vow mightily,' shows what I am insisting on at great length, that Chastity is a mighty vow beyond all vows."[9] This language is not peculiar to St. Methodius among the Antenicene Fathers. "Let such as promise Virginity and break their profession be ranked among digamists," says the Council of Ancyra in the beginning of the fourth century. Tertullian speaks of being "married to Christ," and marriage implies a vow; he proceeds, "to Him thou hast pledged (*sponsasti*) thy ripeness of age"; and before he had expressly spoken of the *continentiæ votum*. Origen speaks of "devoting one's body to God" in chastity; and St. Cyprian "of Christ's Virgin, dedicated to Him and destined for His sanctity," and elsewhere of "members dedicated to Christ, and for ever devoted by virtuous chastity to the praise of continence"; and Eusebius of those "who had consecrated themselves body and soul to a pure and all-holy life."[10]

### 3. Cultus of Saints and Angels

The Spanish Church supplies us with an anticipation of the later devotions to Saints and Angels. The canons are extant of a Council of Illiberis, held shortly before the Council of Nicæa, and representative of course of the doctrine of the third century. Among these occurs the following: "It is decreed, that pictures ought not to be in church, lest what is worshipped or adorned be painted on the walls."[11] Now these words are commonly taken to be decisive against the use of pictures in the Spanish Church at that era. Let us grant it; let us grant that the use of all pictures is forbidden, pictures not only of our Lord, and

[9] Galland. t. 3, p. 670.
[10] Routh, Reliqu. t. 3, p. 414. Tertull. de Virg. Vel. 16 and 11. Orig. in Num. Hom. 24, 2. Cyprian. Ep. 4, p. 8, ed. Fell. Ep. 62, p. 147. Euseb. V. Const. iv. 26.
[11] Placuit picturas in ecclesiâ esse non debere, ne quod colitur aut adoratur, in parietibus depingatur. Can. 36.

sacred emblems, as of the Lamb and the Dove, but pictures of Angels
and Saints also. It is not fair to restrict the words, nor are controversialists found desirous of doing so; they take them to include the images
of the Saints. "For keeping of pictures out of the Church, the Canon
of the Eliberine or Illiberitine Council, held in Spain, about the time
of Constantine the Great, is most plain,"[12] says Ussher: he is speaking
of "the representations of God and of Christ, and of Angels and of
Saints."[13] "The Council of Eliberis is very ancient, and of great fame,"
says Taylor, "in which it is expressly forbidden that what is worshipped should be depicted on the walls, and that therefore pictures
ought not to be in churches."[14] He too is speaking of the Saints. I
repeat, let us grant this freely. This inference then seems to be undeniable, that the Spanish Church considered the Saints to be in the number
of objects either of "worship or adoration"; for it is of such objects
that the representations are forbidden. The very drift of the prohibition
is this—*lest* what is in itself an object of worship (*quod colitur*) should
be worshipped *in painting*; unless then Saints and Angels were objects
of worship, their pictures would have been allowed.

## 2.

This mention of Angels leads me to a memorable passage about the
honour due to them in Justin Martyr.

St. Justin, after "answering the charge of Atheism," as Dr. Burton
says, "which was brought against Christians of his day, and observing
that they were punished for not worshipping evil demons which were
not really gods," continues, "But Him [God] and the Son who came
from Him, and taught us these things, and the host of the other good
Angels who follow and resemble Him, and the prophetic Spirit, we
worship and adore, paying them a reasonable and true honour, and
not grudging to deliver to any one, who wishes to learn, as we ourselves
have been taught."[15]

[12] Answ. to a Jes. 10, p. 437.
[13] P. 430. The "colitur *aut* adoratur" marks a difference of worship.
[14] Dissuasive, i. 1, 8.
[15] Ἐκεῖνον τε, καὶ τὸν παρ' αὐτοῦ υἱὸν ἐλθόντα καὶ διδάξαντα ἡμᾶς ταῦτα,
[καὶ τὸν τῶν ἄλλων ἑπομένων καὶ ἐξομοιουμένων ἀγαθῶν ἀγγέλων στρατὸν,] πνεῦμα τε τὸ προφητικὸν σεβόμεθα καὶ προσκυνοῦμεν, λόγῳ καὶ
ἀληθείᾳ τιμῶντες καὶ παντὶ βουλομένῳ μαθεῖν, ὡς ἐδιδάχθημεν, ἀφθόνως
παραδιδόντες.—*Apol.* i. 6. The passage is parallel to the Prayer in the Breviary: "Sacrosanctæ et individuæ Trinitati, Crucifixi Domini nostri Jesu Christi
humanitati, beatissimæ et gloriosissimæ semperque Virginis Mariæ fœundæ

A more express testimony to the *cultus Angelorum* cannot be required; nor is it unnatural in the connexion in which it occurs, considering St. Justin has been speaking of the heathen worship of demons, and therefore would be led without effort to mention, not only the incommunicable adoration paid to the One God, who "will not give His glory to another," but such inferior honour as may be paid to creatures, without sin on the side whether of giver or receiver. Nor is the construction of the original Greek harsher than is found in other authors; nor need it surprise us in one whose style is not accurate, that two words should be used in combination to express worship, and that one should include Angels, and that the other should not.

## 3.

The following is Dr. Burton's account of the passage:

"Scultetus, a Protestant divine of Heidelberg, in his *Medulla Theologiæ Patrum*, which appeared in 1605, gave a totally different meaning to the passage; and instead of connecting '*the host*' with '*we worship*,' connected it with '*taught us*.' The words would then be rendered thus: 'But Him, and the Son who came from Him, who also gave us instructions concerning these things, and concerning the host of the other good angels we worship,' etc. This interpretation is adopted and defended at some length by Bishop Bull, and by Stephen Le Moyne; and even the Benedictine Le Nourry supposed Justin to mean that Christ had taught us not to worship the bad angels, as well as the existence of good angels. Grabe, in his edition of 'Justin's Apology,' which was printed in 1703, adopted another interpretation, which had been before proposed by Le Moyne and by Cave. This also connects '*the host*' with '*taught*,' and would require us to render the passage thus: '. . . and the Son who came from Him, who also taught these things to us, and to the host of the other Angels,' etc. It might be thought that Langus, who published a Latin translation of Justin in 1565, meant to adopt one of these interpretations, or at least to connect '*host*' with '*taught these things*.' Both of them certainly are ingenious, and are not perhaps opposed to the literal construction of the Greek words; but I cannot say that they are satisfactory, or that I am surprised at Roman

---

integritati, et omnium Sanctorum universitati, sit sempiterna laus, honor, virtus, et gloria ab omni creaturâ," etc. ["To the holy and undivided Trinity, to the humanity of our crucified Lord Jesus Christ, to the life-giving integrity of the most blessed and glorious ever virgin Mary, and to all the saints, may every creature give endless praise, honour, power, and glory."]

Catholic writers describing them as forced and violent attempts to evade a difficulty. If the words enclosed in brackets were removed, the whole passage would certainly contain a strong argument in favour of the Trinity; but as they now stand, Roman Catholic writers will naturally quote them as supporting the worship of Angels.

"There is, however, this difficulty in such a construction of the passage: it proves too much. By coupling the Angels with the three persons of the Trinity, as objects of religious adoration, it seems to go beyond even what Roman Catholics themselves would maintain concerning the worship of Angels. Their well-known distinction between *latria* and *dulia* would be entirely confounded; and the difficulty felt by the Benedictine editor appears to have been as great, as his attempt to explain it is unsuccessful, when he wrote as follows: 'Our adversaries in vain object the twofold expression, *we worship* and *adore*. For the former is applied to Angels themselves, regard being had to the distinction between the creature and the Creator; the latter by no means necessarily includes the Angels.' This sentence requires concessions, which no opponent could be expected to make; and if one of the two terms, *we worship* and *adore*, may be applied to Angels, it is unreasonable to contend that the other must not also. Perhaps, however, the passage may be explained so as to admit a distinction of this kind. The interpretations of Scultetus and Grabe have not found many advocates; and upon the whole I should be inclined to conclude, that the clause, which relates to the Angels, is connected particularly with the words, *'paying them a reasonable and true honour.'* "[16]

Two violent alterations of the text have also been proposed: one to transfer the clause which creates the difficulty, after the words *paying them honour*; the other to substitute στρατηγὸν (*commander*) for στρατὸν (*host*).

### 4.

Presently Dr. Burton continues: "Justin, as I observed, is defending the Christians from the charge of Atheism; and after saying that the gods, whom they refused to worship, were no gods, but evil demons, he points out what were the Beings who were worshipped by the Christians. He names the true God, who is the source of all virtue; the Son, who proceeded from Him; the good and ministering spirits; and the Holy Ghost. To these Beings, he says, we pay all the worship, adora-

[16]Test. Trin. pp. 16, 17, 18.

tion, and honour, which is due to each of them; *i.e.* worship where worship is due, honour where honour is due. The Christians were accused of worshipping no gods, that is, of acknowledging no superior beings at all. Justin shows that so far was this from being true, that they acknowledged more than one order of spiritual Beings; they offered divine worship to the true God, and they also believed in the existence of good spirits, which were entitled to honour and respect. If the reader will view the passage as a whole, he will perhaps see that there is nothing violent in thus restricting the words *worship* and *adore*, and *honouring*, to certain parts of it respectively. It may seem strange that Justin should mention the ministering spirits before the Holy Ghost: but this is a difficulty which presses upon the Roman Catholics as much as upon ourselves; and we may perhaps adopt the explanation of the Bishop of Lincoln,[17] who says, 'I have sometimes thought that in this passage, "*and the host*," is equivalent to "*with the host*," and that Justin had in his mind the glorified state of Christ, when He should come to judge the world, surrounded by the host of heaven.' The bishop then brings several passages from Justin, where the Son of God is spoken of as attended by a company of Angels; and if this idea was then in Justin's mind, it might account for his naming the ministering spirits immediately after the Son of God, rather than after the Holy Ghost, which would have been the natural and proper order."[18]

This passage of St. Justin is the more remarkable, because it cannot be denied that there was a worship of the Angels at that day, of which St. Paul speaks, which was Jewish and Gnostic, and utterly reprobated by the Church.

## 4. Office of the Blessed Virgin

The special prerogatives of St. Mary, the *Virgo Virginum*, are intimately involved in the doctrine of the Incarnation itself, with which these remarks began, and have already been dwelt upon above. As is well known, they were not fully recognized in the Catholic ritual till a late date, but they were not a new thing in the Church, or strange to her earlier teachers. St. Justin, St. Irenæus, and others, had distinctly laid it down, that she not only had an office, but bore a part, and was a voluntary agent, in the actual process of redemption, as Eve had been instrumental and responsible in Adam's fall. They taught that, as the

[17]Dr. Kaye.
[18]Pp. 19–21.

first woman might have foiled the Tempter and did not, so, if Mary had been disobedient or unbelieving on Gabriel's message, the Divine Economy would have been frustrated. And certainly the parallel between "the Mother of all living" and the Mother of the Redeemer may be gathered from a comparison of the first chapters of Scripture with the last. It was noticed in a former place, that the only passage where the serpent is directly identified with the evil spirit occurs in the twelfth chapter of the Revelation; now it is observable that the recognition, when made, is found in the course of a vision of a "woman clothed with the sun and the moon under her feet": thus two women are brought into contrast with each other. Moreover, as it is said in the Apocalypse," "The dragon was wroth with the woman, and went about to make war with the remnant of her seed," so is it prophesied in Genesis, "I will put enmity between thee and the woman, and between thy seed and her Seed. He shall bruise thy head, and thou shalt bruise His heel." Also the enmity was to exist not only between the serpent and the Seed of the woman, but between the serpent and the woman herself; and here too there is a correspondence in the Apocalyptic vision. If then there is reason for thinking that this mystery at the close of the Scripture record answers to the mystery in the beginning of it, and that "the Woman" mentioned in both passages is one and the same, then she can be none other than St. Mary, thus introduced prophetically to our notice immediately on the transgression of Eve.

## 2.

Here, however, we are not so much concerned to interpret Scripture as to examine the Fathers. Thus St. Justin says, "Eve, being a virgin and incorrupt, having conceived the word from the Serpent, bore disobedience and death; but Mary the Virgin, receiving faith and joy, when Gabriel the Angel evangelized her, answered, 'Be it unto me according to thy word.' "[19] And Tertullian says that, whereas Eve believed the Serpent, and Mary believed Gabriel, "the fault of Eve in believing, Mary by believing hath blotted out."[20] St. Irenæus speaks more explicitly: "As Eve," he says . . . "becoming disobedient, became the cause of death to herself and to all mankind, so Mary too, having the predestined Man, and yet a Virgin, being obedient, became cause

---

[19] Tryph. 100.
[20] Carn. Christ. 17.

of salvation both to herself and to all mankind."[21] This becomes the received doctrine in the Postnicene Church.

One well-known instance occurs in the history of the third century of St. Mary's interposition, and it is remarkable from the names of the two persons, who were, one the subject, the other the historian of it. St. Gregory Nyssen, a native of Cappadocia in the fourth century, relates that his namesake bishop of Neo-cæsarea, surnamed Thaumaturgus, in the preceding century, shortly before he was called to the priesthood, received in a vision a Creed, which is still extant, from the Blessed Virgin at the hands of St. John. The account runs thus: He was deeply pondering theological doctrine, which the heretics of the day depraved. "In such thoughts," says his namesake of Nyssa, "he was passing the night, when one appeared, as if in human form, aged in appearance, saintly in the fashion of his garments, and very venerable both in grace of countenance and general mien. . . . Following with his eyes his extended hand, he saw another appearance opposite to the former, in shape of a woman, but more than human. . . . When his eyes could not bear the apparition, he heard them conversing together on the subject of his doubts; and thereby not only gained a true knowledge of the faith, but learned their names, as they addressed each other by their respective appellations. And thus he is said to have heard the person in woman's shape bid 'John the Evangelist' disclose to the young man the mystery of godliness; and he answered that he was ready to comply in this matter with the wish of 'the Mother of the Lord,' and enunciated a formulary, well-turned and complete, and so vanished." Gregory proceeds to rehearse the Creed thus given, "There is One God, Father of a Living Word," etc.[22] Bull, after quoting it in his work upon the Nicene Faith, refers to this history of its origin, and adds, "No one should think it incredible that such a providence should befall a man whose whole life was conspicuous for revelations and miracles, as all ecclesiastical writers who have mentioned him (and who has not?) witness with one voice."[23]

## 3.

It is remarkable that St. Gregory Nazianzen relates an instance, even more pointed, of St. Mary's intercession, contemporaneous with this

[21] Hær. iii. 22, § 4.
[22] Nyss. Opp. t. ii. p. 977.
[23] Def. F. N. ii. 12.

appearance to Thaumaturgus; but it is attended with mistake in the narrative, which weakens its cogency as an evidence of the belief, not indeed of the fourth century, in which St. Gregory lived, but of the third. He speaks of a Christian woman having recourse to the protection of St. Mary, and obtaining the conversion of a heathen who had attempted to practise on her by magical arts. They were both martyred.

In both these instances the Blessed Virgin appears especially in that character of Patroness or Paraclete, which St. Irenæus and other Fathers describe and which the Medieval Church exhibits—a loving Mother with clients.

# CHAPTER XI

# APPLICATION OF THE SIXTH NOTE OF A TRUE DEVELOPMENT: CONSERVATIVE ACTION ON ITS PAST

It is the general pretext of heretics that they are but serving and protecting Christianity by their innovations; and it is their charge against what by this time we may surely call the Catholic Church that her successive definitions of doctrine have but overlaid and obscured it. That is, they assume, what we have no wish to deny, that a true development is that which is conservative of its original, and a corruption is that which tends to its destruction. This has already been set down as a Sixth Test, discriminative of a development from a corruption, and must now be applied to the Catholic doctrines; though this essay has so far exceeded its proposed limits that both reader and writer may well be weary, and may content themselves with a brief consideration of the portions of the subject which remain.

It has been observed already that a strict correspondence between the various members of a development, and those of the doctrine from which it is derived, is more than we have any right to expect. The bodily structure of a grown man is not merely that of a magnified boy; he differs from what he was in his make and proportions; still manhood is the perfection of boyhood, adding something of its own, yet keeping what it finds. "*Ut nihil novum,*" says Vincentius, "*proferatur in senibus, quod non in pueris jam antea latitaverit.*"* This character of addition—that is, of a change which is in one sense real and perceptible, yet without loss or reversal of what was before, but, on the contrary, protective and confirmative of it—in many respects and in a special way belongs to Christianity.

* "So that nothing should present itself in old age that had not already been latent in youth."

## SECTION I

### VARIOUS INSTANCES

If we take the simplest and most general view of its history, as existing in an individual mind, or in the Church at large, we shall see in it an instance of this peculiarity. It is the birth of something virtually new, because latent in what was before. Thus we know that no temper of mind is acceptable in the Divine Presence without love; it is love which makes Christian fear differ from servile dread, and true faith differ from the faith of devils; yet in the beginning of the religious life, fear is the prominent evangelical grace, and love is but latent in fear, and has in course of time to be developed out of what seems its contradictory. Then, when it is developed, it takes that prominent place which fear held before, yet protecting not superseding it. Love is added, not fear removed, and the mind is but perfected in grace by what seems a revolution. "They that sow in tears, reap in joy"; yet afterwards still they are "sorrowful," though "always rejoicing."

And so was it with the Church at large. She started with suffering, which turned to victory; but when she was set free from the house of her prison, she did not quit it so much as turn it into a cell. Meekness inherited the earth; strength came forth from weakness; the poor made many rich; yet meekness and poverty remained. The rulers of the world were monks, when they could not be Martyrs.

### 2.

Immediately on the overthrow of the heathen power, two movements simultaneously ran through the world from East to West, as quickly as the lightning in the prophecy, a development of worship and of asceticism. Hence, while the world's first reproach in heathen times had been that Christianity was a dark malevolent magic, its second has been that it is a joyous carnal paganism—according to that saying, "We have piped unto you, and ye have not danced; we have mourned unto you, and ye have not lamented. For John came neither eating nor drinking, and they say, He hath a devil. The Son of man came eating and drinking, and they say, Behold a man gluttonous and a winebibber, a friend of publicans and sinners." Yet our Lord too was "a man of sorrows" all the while, but softened His austerity by His gracious gentleness.

## 3.

The like characteristic attends also on the mystery of His Incarnation. He was first God and He became man; but Eutyches and heretics of his school refused to admit that He was man, lest they should deny that He was God. In consequence the Catholic Fathers are frequent and unanimous in their asseverations, that "the Word" had become flesh, not to His loss, but by an addition. Each Nature is distinct, but the created Nature lives in and by the Eternal. *Non amittendo quod erat, sed sumendo quod non erat** is the Church's principle. And hence, though the course of development, as was observed in a former chapter, has been to bring into prominence the divine aspect of our Lord's mediation, this has been attended by even a more open manifestation of the doctrine of His atoning sufferings. The passion of our Lord is one of the most imperative and engrossing subjects of Catholic teaching. It is the great topic of meditations and prayers; it is brought into continual remembrance by the sign of the Cross; it is preached to the world in the Crucifix; it is variously honoured by the many houses of prayer, and associations of religious men, and pious institutions and undertakings, which in some way or other are placed under the name and the shadow of Jesus, or the Saviour, or the Redeemer, or His Cross, or His Passion, or His sacred Heart.

## 4.

Here a singular development may be mentioned of the doctrine of the Cross, which some have thought so contrary to its original meaning[1] as to be a manifest corruption; I mean the introduction of the Sign of the meek Jesus into the armies of men, and the use of an emblem of peace as a protection in battle. If light has no communion with darkness, or Christ with Belial, what has He to do with Moloch, who would not call down fire on His enemies, and came not to destroy but to save? Yet this seeming anomaly is but one instance of a great law which is seen in developments generally, that changes which appear at first sight to contradict that out of which they grew, are really its

---

* "Not giving up what was present, but taking up what was not."
[1] Supr. p. 178.

protection or illustration. Our Lord Himself is represented in the Prophets as a combatant inflicting wounds while He received them, as coming from Bozrah with dyed garments, sprinkled and red in His apparel with the blood of His enemies; and, whereas no war is lawful but what is just, it surely beseems that they who are engaged in so dreadful a commission as that of taking away life at the price of their own, should at least have the support of His Presence, and fight under the mystical influence of His Name, who redeemed His elect as a combatant by the Blood of Atonement, with the slaughter of His foes, the sudden overthrow of the Jews, and the slow and awful fall of the pagan Empire. And if the wars of Christian nations have often been unjust, this is a reason against much more than the use of religious symbols by the parties who engage in them, though the pretence of religion may increase the sin.

### 5.

The same rule of development has been observed in respect of the doctrine of the Blessed Trinity. It is the objection of the School of Socinus, that belief in the Trinity is destructive of any true maintenance of the Divine Unity, however strongly the latter may be professed; but Petavius, as we have seen,[2] sets it down as one especial recommendation of the Catholic doctrine, that it subserves that original truth which at first sight it does but obscure and compromise.

### 6.

This representation of the consistency of the Catholic system will be found to be true, even in respect of those peculiarities of it, which have been considered by Protestants most open to the charge of corruption and innovation. It is maintained, for instance, that the veneration paid to images in the Catholic Church directly contradicts the command of Scripture, and the usage of the primitive ages. As to primitive usage, that part of the subject has been incidentally observed upon already; here I will make one remark on the argument from Scripture.

It may be reasonably questioned, then, whether the Commandment which stands second in the Protestant Decalogue, on which the prohibition of images is grounded, was intended in its letter for more than

[2]Supr. p. 179.

temporary observance. So far is certain, that, though none could surpass the later Jews in its literal observance, nevertheless this did not save them from the punishments attached to the violation of it. If this be so, the literal observance is not its true and evangelical import.

### 7.

"When the generation to come of your children shall rise up after you," says their inspired lawgiver, "and the stranger that shall come from a far land shall say, when they see the plagues of that land, and its sickness which the Lord hath laid upon it; and that the whole land thereof is brimstone, and salt, and burning, that it is not sown, nor beareth, nor any grass groweth therein, . . . even all nations shall say, Wherefore hath the Lord done thus unto this land? What meaneth the heat of this great anger? Then men shall say, Because they have forsaken the covenants of the Lord God of their fathers, which He made with them when He brought them forth out of the land of Egypt; for they went and served other gods, and worshipped them, gods whom they knew not, and whom He had not given them." Now the Jews of our Lord's day did not keep this covenant, for they incurred the penalty; yet they kept the letter of the Commandment rigidly, and were known among the heathen far and wide for their devotion to the "Lord God of their fathers who brought them out of the land of Egypt," and for their abhorrence of the "gods whom He had not given them." If then adherence to the letter was no protection to the Jews, departure from the letter may be no guilt in Christians.

It should be observed, moreover, that there certainly is a difference between the two covenants in their respective view of symbols of the Almighty. In the Old, it was blasphemy to represent Him under "the similitude of a calf that eateth hay"; in the New, the Third Person of the Holy Trinity has signified His Presence by the appearance of a Dove, and the Second Person has presented His sacred Humanity for worship under the name of the Lamb.

### 8.

It follows that, if the letter of the Decalogue is but partially binding on Christians, it is as justifiable, in setting it before persons under instruction, to omit such parts as do not apply to them, as, when we quote passages from the Pentateuch in sermons or lectures generally, to pass over verses which refer simply to the temporal promises or the ceremonial law, a practice which we allow without any intention or appearance of dealing irreverently with the sacred text.

## SECTION II

### DEVOTION TO THE BLESSED VIRGIN

It has been anxiously asked, whether the honours paid to St. Mary, which have grown out of devotion to her Almighty Lord and Son, do not, in fact, tend to weaken that devotion; and whether, from the nature of the case, it is possible so to exalt a creature without withdrawing the heart from the Creator.

In addition to what has been said on this subject in foregoing chapters, I would here observe that the question is one of fact, not of presumption or conjecture. The abstract lawfulness of the honours paid to St. Mary, and their distinction in theory from the incommunicable worship paid to God, are points which have already been dwelt upon; but here the question turns upon their practicability or expedience, which must be determined by the fact whether they are practicable, and whether they have been found to be expedient.

### 1.

Here I observe, first, that, to those who admit the authority of the Fathers of Ephesus, the question is in no slight degree answered by their sanction of the θεοτόκος, or "Mother of God," as a title of St. Mary, and as given in order to protect the doctrine of the Incarnation, and to preserve the faith of Catholics from a specious Humanitarianism. And if we take a survey at least of Europe, we shall find that it is not those religious communions which are characterized by devotion towards the Blessed Virgin that have ceased to adore her Eternal Son, but those very bodies (when allowed by the law) which have renounced devotion to her. The regard for His glory, which was professed in that keen jealousy of her exaltation, has not been supported by the event. They who were accused of worshipping a creature in His stead, still worship Him; their accusers, who hoped to worship Him so purely, they, wherever obstacles to the development of their principles have been removed, have ceased to worship Him altogether.

## 2.

Next, it must be observed, that the tone of the devotion paid to the Blessed Mary is altogether distinct from that which is paid to her Eternal Son, and to the Holy Trinity, as we must certainly allow on inspection of the Catholic services. The supreme and true worship paid to the Almighty is severe, profound, awful, as well as tender, confiding, and dutiful. Christ is addressed as true God, while He is true Man; as our Creator and Judge, while He is most loving, gentle, and gracious. On the other hand, towards St. Mary the language employed is affectionate and ardent, as towards a mere child of Adam; though subdued, as coming from her sinful kindred. How different, for instance, is the tone of the *Dies Iræ* from that of the *Stabat Mater*. In the "Tristis et afflicta Mater Unigeniti" ["Sorrowful and afflicted mother of the only-begotten son"], in the "Virgo virginum praeclara Mihi jam non sis amara, Poenas mecum divide" ["Most excellent virgin of virgins, do not be harsh to me, but let me share your sufferings"], in the "Fac me vere tecum flere" ["Let me truly weep with you"], we have an expression of the feelings with which we regard one who is a creature and a mere human being; but in the "Rex tremendae majestatis qui salvandos salvas gratis, salva me Fons pietatis" ["King of awesome majesty, freely saving those destined for salvation, save me, fountain of love"], the "Ne me perdas illa die" ["Let not that day destroy me"], the "Juste judex ultionis, donum fac remissionis" ["Righteous judge of vengeance, grant me the gift of forgiveness"], the "Oro supplex et acclinis, cor contritum quasi cinis" ["I implore you, prostrate and suppliant, for a heart contrite as ashes"], the "Pie Jesu Domine, dona eis requiem" ["Loving Lord Jesus, grant them rest"], we hear the voice of the creature raised in hope and love, yet in deep awe to his Creator, Infinite Benefactor, and Judge.

Or again, how distinct is the language of the Breviary services on the Festival of Pentecost, or of the Holy Trinity, from the language of the services for the Assumption! How indescribably majestic, solemn, and soothing is the "Veni Creator Spiritus" ["Come Creator Spirit"], the "Altissimi donum Dei, Fons vivus, ignis, charitas" ["Gift of God most high, living spring, fire love"], or the "Vera et una Trinitas, una et summa Deitas, sancta et una Unitas" ["True and single Trinity, single supreme Deity, holy single Unity"], the "Spes nostra, salus nostra, honor noster, O beata Trinitas" ["Our hope, salvation, honor, O blessed Trinity"], the "Charitas Pater, gratia Filius, communicatio Spiritus Sanctus, O beata Trinitas" ["Love, the Father; grace, the Son;

communication, the Holy Spirit, O blessed Trinity"]; "Libera nos, salva nos, vivifica nos, O beata Trinitas!" ["Free us, save us, give us life, O blessed Trinity!"]. How fond, on the contrary, how full of sympathy and affection, how stirring and animating, in the Office for the Assumption, is the "Virgo prudentissima, quo progrederis, quasi aurora valde rutilans? filia Sion, tota formosa et suavis es, pulcra ut luna, electa ut sol" ["Virgin most wise, where do you advance to, all golden as the dawn? daughter of Sion, fair, delightful, beautiful as the moon, choice as the sun"]; the "Sicut dies verni circumdabant eam flores rosarum, et lilia convallium" ["Surrounded with rose blossoms and lilies of the valley like a day in spring"]; the "Maria Virgo assumpta est ad aethereum thalamum in quo Rex regum stellato sedet solio" ["Virgin Mary, raised to the heavenly nuptial chamber where the King is seated in a starry throne"]; and the "Gaudent Angeli, laudantes benedicunt Dominum" ["The angels rejoice and bless the Lord with praise."]. And so again, the Antiphon, the "Ad te clamamus exules filii Hevae, ad te suspiramus gementes et flentes in hac lacrymarum valle" ["We banished children of Eve cry out to you, we sigh to you, lamenting and weeping in this valley of tears."], and "Eia ergo, advocata nostra, illos tuos misericordes oculos ad nos converte" ["So turn, advocate, your merciful eyes toward us."], and "O clemens, O pia, O dulcis Virgo Maria" ["O merciful, loving, sweet virgin Mary"]. Or the hymn, "Ave Maris stella, Dei Mater alma" ["Hail star of the sea, sweet Mother of God"], and "Virgo singularis, inter omnes mitis, nos culpis solutos, mites fac et castos" ["Singular virgin, meek among all, make us meek and pure, set free from guilt."].

### 3.

Nor does it avail to object that, in this contrast of devotional exercises, the human will supplant the Divine, from the infirmity of our nature; for, I repeat, the question is one of fact, whether it has done so. And next it must be asked, whether the character of much of the Protestant devotion towards our Lord has been that of adoration at all; and not rather such as we pay to an excellent human being, that is, no higher devotion than that which Catholics pay to St. Mary, differing from it, however, in often being familiar, rude, and earthly. Carnal minds will ever create a carnal worship for themselves; and to forbid them the service of the Saints will have no tendency to teach them the worship of God.

Moreover, it must be observed, what is very important, that great and constant as is the devotion which the Catholic pays to the Blessed Mary, it has a special province, and has far more connexion with the public services and the festive aspect of Christianity, and with certain extraordinary offices which she holds, than with what is strictly personal and primary in religion.

Two instances will serve in illustration of this, and they are but samples of many others.[3]

## 4.

(1.) For example, St. Ignatius's Spiritual Exercises are among the most approved methods of devotion in the modern Catholic Church; they proceed from one of the most celebrated of her Saints, and have the praise of Popes, and of the most eminent masters of the spiritual life. A Bull of Paul the Third's "approves, praises, and sanctions all and everything contained in them"; indulgences are granted to the performance of them by the same Pope, by Alexander the Seventh, and by Benedict the Fourteenth. St. Carlo Borromeo declared that he learned more from them than from all other books together; St. Francis de Sales calls them "a holy method of reformation," and they are the model on which all the extraordinary devotions of religious men or bodies, and the course of missions, are conducted. If there is a document which is the authoritative exponent of the inward communion of the members of the modern Catholic Church with their God and Saviour, it is this work.

The Exercises are directed to the removal of obstacles in the way of the soul's receiving and profiting by the gifts of God. They undertake to effect this in three ways: by removing all objects of this world, and, as it were, bringing the soul "into the solitude where God may speak to its heart"; next, by setting before it the ultimate end of man, and its own deviations from it, the beauty of holiness, and the pattern of Christ; and, lastly, by giving rules for its correction. They consist of a course of prayers, meditations, self-examinations, and the like, which in its complete extent lasts thirty days; and these are divided into

---

[3] E.g. the "De Imitatione," the "Introduction à la Vie Dévote," the "Spiritual Combat," the "Anima Divota," the "Paradisus Animæ," the "Regula Cleri," the "Garden of the Soul," etc. etc. [Also, the Roman Catechism, drawn up expressly for Parish instruction, a book in which, out of nearly 600 pages, scarcely half-a-dozen make mention of the Blessed Virgin, though without any disparagement thereby, or thought of disparagement, of her special prerogatives.]

three stages—the *Via Purgativa*, in which sin is the main subject of consideration; the *Via Illuminativa*, which is devoted to the contemplation of our Lord's passion, involving the process of the determination of our calling; and the *Via Unitiva*, in which we proceed to the contemplation of our Lord's Resurrection and Ascension.

## 5.

No more need be added in order to introduce the remark for which I have referred to these Exercises; viz., that in a work so highly sanctioned, so widely received, so intimately bearing upon the most sacred points of personal religion, very slight mention occurs of devotion to the Blessed Virgin, Mother of God. There is one mention of her in the rule given for the first prelude or preparation, in which the person meditating is directed to consider as before him a church, or other place with Christ in it, St. Mary, and whatever else is suitable to the subject of meditation. Another is in the third Exercise, in which one of the three addresses is made to our Lady, Christ's Mother, requesting earnestly "her intercession with her Son"; to which is to be added the Ave Mary. In the beginning of the Second Week there is a form of offering ourselves to God in the presence of "His infinite goodness," and with the witness of His "glorious Virgin Mother Mary, and the whole host of heaven." At the end of the Meditation upon the Angel Gabriel's mission to St. Mary, there is an address to each Divine Person, to "the Word Incarnate and to His Mother." In the Meditation upon the Two Standards, there is an address prescribed to St. Mary to implore grace from her Son through her, with an Ave Mary after it.

In the beginning of the Third Week one address is prescribed to Christ; or three, if devotion incites, to Mother, Son, and Father. In the description given of three different modes of prayer we are told, if we would imitate the Blessed Mary, we must recommend ourselves to her, as having power with her Son, and presently the Ave Mary, *Salve Regina*, and other forms are prescribed, as is usual after all prayers. And this is pretty much the whole of the devotion, if it may so be called, which is recommended towards St. Mary in the course of so many apparently as a hundred and fifty meditations, and those chiefly on the events in our Lord's earthly history as recorded in Scripture. It would seem then that whatever be the influence of the doctrines connected with the Blessed Virgin and the Saints in the Catholic Church, at least they do not impede or obscure the freest exercise and the fullest manifestation of the devotional feelings towards God and Christ.

### 6.

(2.) The other instance which I give in illustration is of a different kind, but is suitable to mention. About forty little books have come into my possession which are in circulation among the laity at Rome, and answer to the smaller publications of the Christian Knowledge Society among ourselves. They have been taken almost at hazard from a number of such works, and are of various lengths; some running to as many as two or three hundred pages, others consisting of scarce a dozen. They may be divided into three classes: a third part consists of books on practical subjects; another third is upon the Incarnation and Passion; and of the rest, a portion is upon the Sacraments, especially the Holy Eucharist, with two or three for the use of Missions, but the greater part is about the Blessed Virgin.

As to the class on practical subjects, they are on such as the following: *La Consolazione degl' Infermi* ["Comfort of the Sick"], *Pensieri di una donna sul vestire moderno* ["A Woman's Thoughts on Modern Dress"], *L'Inferno Aperto* ["Hell Exposed"], *Il Purgatorio Aperto* ["Purgatory Exposed"], St. Alphonso Liguori's *Massime eterne* ["Eternal Maxims"], other maxims by St. Francis de Sales for every day in the year, *Practica per ben confessarsi e communicarsi* ["Practice of Confessing and Communicating Well"], and the like.

The titles of the second class on the Incarnation and Passion are such as *Gesu dalla Croce al cuore del peccatore* ["Jesus From the Cross to the Sinner's Heart"], *Novena del Ss. Natale di G. C.* ["Novena of St. Natale of Jesus Christ"], *Associazione pel culto perpetuo del divin cuore* ["Association for Perpetual Worship of the Divine Heart"], *Compendio della Passione* ["Compendium of the Passion"].

In the third are *Il Mese Eucaristico* ["Eucharist Month"], *Il divoto di Maria* ["Mary's Devout"], *Feasts of the Blessed Virgin*, etc.

### 7.

These books in all three divisions are, as even the titles of some of them show, in great measure made up of meditations; such are the *Breve e pie Meditazioni* ["Short Pious Meditations"] of P. Crasset, the *Meditazioni per ciascun giorno del mese sulla Passione* ["Meditations on the Passion for Each Day of the Month"], the *Meditazioni per l'ora Eucaristica* ["Meditations for the Eucharistic Hour"]. Now of these it may be said generally, that in the body of the Meditation, St. Mary is hardly mentioned at all. For instance, in the *Meditations on the Passion*, a book used for distribution, through two hundred and seventy-seven pages St. Mary is not once named. In the Prayers for Mass which are added, she is introduced, at the Confiteor, thus, "I pray the Virgin, the Angels, the Apostles, and all the Saints of heaven to intercede," etc.; and in the Preparation for Penance, she is once addressed, after our Lord, as the Refuge of sinners, with the Saints and Guardian Angel; and at the end of the exercise there is a similar prayer of four lines for the intercession of St. Mary, Angels and Saints of heaven. In the Exercise for Communion, in a prayer to our Lord, "my only and infinite good, my treasure, my life, my paradise, my all," the merits of the Saints are mentioned, "especially of St. Mary." She is also mentioned with Angels and Saints at the termination.

In a collection of *Spiritual Lauds* for Missions, of thirty-six hymns, we find as many as eleven addressed to St. Mary, or relating to her, among which are translations of the *Ave Maris Stella*, and the *Stabat Mater*, and the *Salve Regina*; and one is on "the sinner's reliance on Mary." Five, however, which are upon Repentance, are entirely engaged upon the subjects of our Lord and sin, with the exception of an address to St. Mary at the end of two of them. Seven others, upon sin, the Crucifixion, and the Four Last Things, do not mention the Blessed Virgin's name.

To the *Manual for the Perpetual Adoration of the Divine Heart of Jesus* there is appended one chapter on the Immaculate Conception.

### 8.

One of the most important of these books is the French *Pensez-y bien*, which seems a favourite, since there are two translations of it, one of them being the fifteenth edition; and it is used for distribution in Missions. In these reflections there is scarcely a word said of St. Mary. At the end there is a Method of reciting the Crown of the Seven Dolours of the Virgin Mary, which contains seven prayers to her, and the *Stabat Mater*.

One of the longest in the whole collection is a tract consisting principally of Meditations on the Holy Communion; under the title of the "Eucharistic Month," as already mentioned. In these "Preparations," "Aspirations," etc., St. Mary is but once mentioned, and that in a prayer addressed to our Lord. "O my sweetest Brother," it says with an allusion to the Canticles, "who, being made Man for my salvation, hast sucked the milk from the virginal breast of her, who is my Mother by grace," etc. In a small "Instruction" given to children on their first Communion, there are the following questions and answers: "Is our Lady in the Host? No. Are the Angels and the Saints? No. Why not? Because they have no place there."

## 9.

Now coming to those in the third class, which directly relate to the Blessed Mary, such as *Esercizio ad Onore dell' addolorato cuore di Maria* ["Exercise in Honor of Mary's Most Sorrowful Heart"], *Novena di Preparazione alla festa dell' Assunzione* ["Novena in Preparation for the Feast of the Assumption"], *Li Quindici Misteri del Santo Rosario* ["The Fifteen Mysteries of the Rosary"], the principal is Father Segneri's *Il divoto di Maria* ["Mary's Devout"], which requires a distinct notice. It is far from the intention of these remarks to deny the high place which the Holy Virgin holds in the devotion of Catholics; I am but bringing evidence of its not interfering with that incommunicable and awful relation which exists between the creature and the Creator; and, if the foregoing instances show, as far as they go, that that relation is preserved inviolate in such honours as are paid to St. Mary, so will this treatise throw light upon the rationale by which the distinction is preserved between the worship of God and the honour of an exalted creature, and that in singular accordance with the remarks made in the foregoing section.

## 10.

This work of Segneri is written against persons who continue in sins under pretence of their devotion to St. Mary, and in consequence he is led to draw out the idea which good Catholics have of her. The idea is this, that she is absolutely the first of created beings. Thus the treatise says, that "God might have easily made a more beautiful firmament, and a greener earth, but it was not possible to make a higher Mother than the Virgin Mary; and in her formation there has been conferred on mere creatures all the glory of which they are capable, remaining mere creatures," page 34. And as containing all created perfection, she has all those attributes, which, as was noticed above, the Arians and other heretics applied to our Lord, and which the Church denied of

Him as infinitely below His Supreme Majesty. Thus she is "the created Idea in the making of the world," page 20; "which, as being a more exact copy of the Incarnate Idea than was elsewhere to be found, was used as the original of the rest of the creation," page 21. To her are applied the words, "Ego primo-genita prodivi ex ore Altissimi,"* because she was predestinated in the Eternal Mind coevally with the Incarnation of her Divine Son. But to Him alone the title of Wisdom Incarnate is reserved, page 25. Again, Christ is the First-born by nature; the Virgin in a less sublime order, viz., that of adoption. Again, if omnipotence is ascribed to her, it is a participated omnipotence (as she and all Saints have a participated sonship, divinity, glory, holiness, and worship), and is explained by the words, "Quod Deus imperio, tu prece, Virgo, potes."**

## 11.

Again, a special office is assigned to the Blessed Virgin, that is, special as compared with all other Saints; but it is marked off with the utmost precision from that assigned to our Lord. Thus she is said to have been made "the arbitress of every *effect* coming from God's mercy." Because she is the Mother of God, the salvation of mankind is said to be given to her prayers "*de congruo*, but *de condigno* it is due only to the blood of the Redeemer," page 113. Merit is ascribed to Christ, and prayer to St. Mary, page 162. The whole may be expressed in the words, "*Unica* spes mea Jesus, et post Jesum Virgo Maria. Amen."***

Again, a distinct *cultus* is assigned to Mary, but the reason of it is said to be the transcendent dignity of her Son. "A particular *cultus* is due to the Virgin beyond comparison greater than that given to any other Saint, because her dignity belongs to another order, namely to one which in some sense belongs to the order of the Hypostatic Union itself, and is necessarily connected with it," page 41. And "Her being the Mother of God is the source of all the extraordinary honours due to Mary," page 35.

It is remarkable that the "Monstra te esse Matrem" is explained, page 158, as "Show thyself to be *our* Mother"; an interpretation which I think I have found elsewhere in these tracts, and also in a book

---

* "I came forth first-born from the mouth of the Most High."
** "What God can achieve by command you can achieve by prayer."
*** "Jesus my only hope, and after Jesus the virgin Mary. Amen."

commonly used in religious houses, called the "Journal of Meditations," and elsewhere.[4]

It must be kept in mind that my object here is not to prove the dogmatic accuracy of what these popular publications teach concerning the prerogatives of the Blessed Virgin, but to show that that teaching is not such as to obscure the divine glory of her Son. We must ask for clearer evidence before we are able to admit so grave a charge; and so much may suffice on the sixth test of fidelity in the development of an idea, as applied to the Catholic system.

[4]Vid. Via Med. vol. ii. pp. 121–22.

# CHAPTER XII

# APPLICATION OF THE SEVENTH NOTE OF A TRUE DEVELOPMENT: ITS CHRONIC VIGOUR

We have arrived at length at the seventh and last test, which was laid down when we started, for distinguishing the true development of an idea from its corruptions and perversions; it is this: A corruption, if vigorous, is of brief duration, runs itself out quickly, and ends in death; on the other hand, if it lasts, it fails in vigour and passes into a decay. This general law gives us additional assistance in determining the character of the developments of Christianity commonly called Catholic.

## 2.

When we consider the succession of ages during which the Catholic system has endured, the severity of the trials it has undergone, the sudden and wonderful changes without and within which have befallen it, the incessant mental activity and the intellectual gifts of its maintainers, the enthusiasm which it has kindled, the fury of the controversies which have been carried on among its professors, the impetuosity of the assaults made upon it, the ever-increasing responsibilities to which it has been committed by the continuous development of its dogmas, it is quite inconceivable that it should not have been broken up and lost, were it a corruption of Christianity. Yet it is still living, if there be a living religion or philosophy in the world; vigorous, energetic, persuasive, progressive; *vires acquirit eundo*; it grows and is not overgrown; it spreads out, yet is not enfeebled; it is ever germinating, yet ever consistent with itself. Corruptions indeed are to be found which sleep and are suspended; and these, as I have said, are usually called "decays"; such is not the case with Catholicity; it does not sleep, it is not stationary even now; and that its long series of developments should be corruptions would be an instance of sustained error, so novel, so unaccountable, so preternatural, as to be little short of a

miracle, and to rival those manifestations of Divine Power which
constitute the evidence of Christianity. We sometimes view with surprise and awe the degree of pain and disarrangement which the human
frame can undergo without succumbing; yet at length there comes an
end. Fevers have their crisis, fatal or favourable; but this corruption
of a thousand years, if corruption it be, has ever been growing nearer
death, yet never reaching it, and has been strengthened, not debilitated,
by its excesses.

### 3.

For instance: when the Empire was converted, multitudes, as is very
plain, came into the Church on but partially religious motives, and
with habits and opinions infected with the false worships which they
had professedly abandoned. History shows us what anxiety and effort
it cost her rulers to keep paganism out of her pale. To this tendency
must be added the hazard which attended on the development of the
Catholic ritual, such as the honours publicly assigned to Saints and
Martyrs, the formal veneration of their relics, and the usages and
observances which followed. What was to hinder the rise of a sort of
refined pantheism, and the overthrow of dogmatism *pari passu* with
the multiplication of heavenly intercessors and patrons? If what is
called in reproach "Saint-worship" resembled the polytheism which it
supplanted, or was a corruption, how did dogmatism survive? Dogmatism is a religion's profession of its own reality as contrasted with
other systems; but polytheists are liberals, and hold that one religion
is as good as another. Yet the theological system was developing and
strengthening, as well as the monastic rule, which is intensely anti-
pantheistic, all the while the ritual was assimilating itself, as Protestants
say, to the paganism of former ages.

### 4.

Nor was the development of dogmatic theology, which was then
taking place, a silent and spontaneous process. It was wrought out
and carried through under the fiercest controversies, and amid the
most fearful risks. The Catholic faith was placed in a succession of
perils, and rocked to and fro like a vessel at sea. Large portions of
Christendom were, one after another, in heresy or in schism; the leading Churches and the most authoritative schools fell from time to time
into serious error; three Popes, Liberius, Vigilius, Honorius, have left

to posterity the burden of their defence: but these disorders were no interruption to the sustained and steady march of the sacred science from implicit belief to formal statement. The series of ecclesiastical decisions, in which its progress was ever and anon signified, alternate between the one and the other side of the theological dogma especially in question, as if fashioning it into shape by opposite strokes. The controversy began in Apollinaris, who confused or denied the Two Natures in Christ, and was condemned by Pope Damasus. A reaction followed, and Theodore of Mopsuestia suggested by his teaching the doctrine of Two Persons. After Nestorius had brought that heresy into public view, and had incurred in consequence the anathema of the Third Ecumenical Council, the current of controversy again shifted its direction; for Eutyches appeared, maintained the One Nature, and was condemned at Chalcedon. Something however was still wanting to the overthrow of the Nestorian doctrine of Two Persons, and the Fifth Council was formally directed against the writings of Theodore and his party. Then followed the Monothelite heresy, which was a revival of the Eutychian or Monophysite, and was condemned in the Sixth. Lastly, Nestorianism once more showed itself in the Adoptionists of Spain, and gave occasion to the great Council of Frankfort. Any one false step would have thrown the whole theory of the doctrine into irretrievable confusion; but it was as if some one individual and perspicacious intellect, to speak humanly, ruled the theological discussion from first to last. That in the long course of centuries, and in spite of the failure, in points of detail, of the most gifted Fathers and Saints, the Church thus wrought out the one and only consistent theory which can be taken on the great doctrine in dispute, proves how clear, simple, and exact her vision of that doctrine was. But it proves more than this. Is it not utterly incredible, that with this thorough comprehension of so great a mystery, as far as the human mind can know it, she should be at that very time in the commission of the grossest errors in religious worship, and should be hiding the God and Mediator, whose Incarnation she contemplated with so clear an intellect, behind a crowd of idols?

### 5.

The integrity of the Catholic developments is still more evident when they are viewed in contrast with the history of other doctrinal systems. Philosophies and religions of the world have each its day, and are parts of a succession. They supplant and are in turn supplanted. But the Catholic religion alone has had no limits; it alone has ever been greater than the emergence, and can do what others cannot do. If it were a falsehood, or a corruption, like the systems of men, it would be weak as they are; whereas it is able even to impart to them a strength which they have not, and it uses them for its own purposes, and locates them in its own territory. The Church can extract good from evil, or at least gets no harm from it. She inherits the promise made to the disciples, that they should take up serpents, and, if they drank any deadly thing, it should not hurt them. When evil has clung to her, and the barbarian people have looked on with curiosity or in malice, till she should have swollen or fallen down suddenly, she has shaken the venomous beast into the fire, and felt no harm.

## 6.

Eusebius has set before us this attribute of Catholicism in a passage in his history. "These attempts," he says, speaking of the acts of the enemy, "did not long avail him, Truth ever consolidating itself, and, as time goes on, shining into broader day. For, while the devices of adversaries were extinguished at once, undone by their very impetuosity—one heresy after another presenting its own novelty, the former specimens ever dissolving and wasting variously in manifold and multiform shapes—the brightness of the Catholic and only true Church went forward increasing and enlarging, yet ever in the same things, and in the same way, beaming on the whole race of Greeks and barbarians with the awfulness, and simplicity, and nobleness, and sobriety, and purity of its divine polity and philosophy. Thus the calumny against our whole creed died with its day, and there continued alone our Discipline, sovereign among all, and acknowledged to be preeminent in awfulness, sobriety, and divine and philosophical doctrines; so that no one of this day dares to cast any base reproach upon our faith, nor any calumny, such as it was once usual for our enemies to use."[1]

[1] Euseb. Hist. iv. 7, *ap.* Church of the Fathers [Historical Sketches, vol. i. p. 408].

## 7.

The Psalmist says, "We went through fire and water"; nor is it possible to imagine trials fiercer or more various than those from which Catholicism has come forth uninjured, as out of the Egyptian sea or the Babylonian furnace. First of all were the bitter persecutions of the pagan Empire in the early centuries; then its sudden conversion, the liberty of Christian worship, the development of the *cultus sanctorum*,* and the reception of Monachism into the ecclesiastical system. Then came the irruption of the barbarians, and the occupation by them of the *orbis terrarum* from the North, and by the Saracens from the South. Meanwhile the anxious and protracted controversy concerning the Incarnation hung like some terrible disease upon the faith of the Church. Then came the time of thick darkness; and afterwards two great struggles, one with the material power, the other with the intellect, of the world, terminating in the ecclesiastical monarchy, and in the theology of the schools. And lastly came the great changes consequent upon the controversies of the sixteenth century. Is it conceivable that any one of those heresies, with which ecclesiastical history abounds, should have gone through a hundredth part of these trials, yet have come out of them so nearly what it was before, as Catholicism has done? Could such a theology as Arianism have lasted through the scholastic contest? or Montanism have endured to possess the world, without coming to a crisis, and failing? or could the imbecility of the Manichean system, as a religion, have escaped exposure, had it been brought into conflict with the barbarians of the Empire, or the feudal system?

## 8.

A similar contrast discovers itself in the respective effects and fortunes of certain influential principles or usages, which have both been introduced into the Catholic system, and are seen in operation elsewhere. When a system really is corrupt, powerful agents, when applied to it, do but develop that corruption, and bring it the more speedily to an end. They stimulate it preternaturally; it puts forth its strength, and dies in some memorable act. Very different has been the history of Catholicism, when it has committed itself to such formidable influences. It has borne, and can bear, principles or doctrines, which in

* "veneration of the saints"

other systems of religion quickly degenerate into fanaticism or infidelity. This might be shown at great length in the history of the Aristotelic philosophy within and without the Church; or in the history of Monachism, or of Mysticism—not that there has not been at first a conflict between these powerful and unruly elements and the Divine System into which they were entering, but that it ended in the victory of Catholicism. The theology of St. Thomas, nay of the Church of his period, is built on that very Aristotelism, which the early Fathers denounce as the source of all misbelief, and in particular of the Arian and Monophysite heresies. The exercises of asceticism, which are so graceful in St. Antony, so touching in St. Basil, and so awful in St. Germanus, do but become a melancholy and gloomy superstition even in the most pious persons who are cut off from Catholic communion. And while the highest devotion in the Church is the mystical, and contemplation has been the token of the most singularly favoured Saints, we need not look deeply into the history of modern sects, for evidence of the excesses in conduct, or the errors in doctrine, to which mystics have been commonly led, who have boasted of their possession of reformed truth, and have rejected what they called the corruptions of Catholicism.

## 9.

It is true, there have been seasons when, from the operation of external or internal causes, the Church has been thrown into what was almost a state of *deliquium*,* but her wonderful revivals, while the world was triumphing over her, is a further evidence of the absence of corruption in the system of doctrine and worship into which she has developed. If corruption be an incipient disorganization, surely an abrupt and absolute recurrence to the former state of vigour, after an interval, is even less conceivable than a corruption that is permanent. Now this is the case with the revivals I speak of. After violent exertion men are exhausted and fall asleep; they awake the same as before, refreshed by the temporary cessation of their activity; and such has been the slumber and such the restoration of the Church. She pauses in her course, and almost suspends her functions; she rises again, and she is herself once more; all things are in their place and ready for action. Doctrine is where it was, and usage, and precedence, and principle, and policy; there may be changes, but they are consolidations

* "collapse"

or adaptations; all is unequivocal and determinate, with an identity which there is no disputing. Indeed it is one of the most popular charges against the Catholic Church at this very time, that she is "incorrigible"—change she cannot, if we listen to St. Athanasius or St. Leo; change she never will, if we believe the controversialist or alarmist of the present day.

# CONCLUSION

Such were the thoughts concerning the "Blessed Vision of Peace," of one whose long-continued petition had been that the Most Merciful would not despise the work of His own Hands, nor leave him to himself—while yet his eyes were dim, and his breast laden, and he could but employ Reason in the things of Faith. And now, dear Reader, time is short, eternity is long. Put not from you what you have here found; regard it not as mere matter of present controversy; set not out resolved to refute it, and looking about for the best way of doing so; seduce not yourself with the imagination that it comes of disappointment, or disgust, or restlessness, or wounded feeling, or undue sensibility, or other weakness. Wrap not yourself round in the associations of years past, nor determine that to be truth which you wish to be so, nor make an idol of cherished anticipations. Time is short, eternity is long.

NUNC DIMITTIS SERVUM TUUM DOMINE,
SECUNDUM VERBUM TUUM IN PACE
QUIA VIDERUNT OCULI MEI SALUTARE TUUM.*

---

*The prayer of Simeon on receiving the infant Jesus into his arms (Luke 2.29–30): "Lord, now lettest thou thy servant depart in peace according to thy word; for mine eyes have seen thy salvation . . ." Compare this closing biblical citation with the opening one, heading the "Advertisement to the First Edition."

# III

# ON CONSULTING THE FAITHFUL
# IN MATTERS OF DOCTRINE
*(July, 1859)*

# THE DOCTRINAL ROLE OF THE LAITY

The background of Newman's "On Consulting the Faithful in Matters of Doctrine" is complicated, and may strike modern readers as a tempest in a teapot. Ecclesiastical teapots can, however, generate formidable storms, and in this one Newman came near to drowning.

In 1848 a new Catholic periodical, *The Rambler*, was started. In an effort to vindicate the intellectual seriousness of Roman Catholics, it adopted high standards of scholarship and unaccustomed frankness in criticizing Church authority. After a decade it was in imminent danger of being officially censured by the bishops and thereby losing much of its influence among loyal Catholics. To avert this crisis, Newman agreed to become its editor, and tried to modify its controversial tone. Its enemies, however, remained unmollified and alert to any new grounds for offense. Their opportunity was provided in an article by a highly respected government school inspector, Stokes, a Catholic layman, who argued that Catholic schools, receiving public funds, should not resist government inspection but welcome it as an opportunity to demonstrate their academic soundness. Unfortunately, the bishops had already taken the very opposite position, but without as yet issuing any public statement. Informed that *The Rambler* was once again out of tune with hierarchical views, Newman wrote what he supposed to be a conciliatory editorial. While apologizing for having published a piece that unwittingly contradicted the bishops, he went on to express confidence that the bishops must surely want to know lay opinions about matters that chiefly concerned the laity—like the schooling of their children. He reinforced that opinion with the following *a fortiori* statement which proved to be almost unquenchably incendiary: "If even in the preparation of a dogmatic definition the faithful are consulted, as lately in the instance of the Immaculate Conception, it is at least as natural to anticipate such an act of kind feeling and sympathy in great practical questions . . ."

The hierarchy were so far from being satisfied that Newman's own bishop, Ullathorne, who in March had urged him to accept editorship of *The Rambler*, in May urged him to resign it. He agreed to do so after the very next issue. In that July issue, however, he published an anonymous explanation and defense of his own views "On Consulting the Faithful in Matters of Doctrine."

The article's anonymity was transparent to critics of Newman and *The Rambler*, and several leaders of the hierarchy came in person to rebuke the author. One bishop denounced him to the Vatican as a disseminator of heretical opinions, and it became clear that the charge was not taken lightly by papal officialdom. During the five years following this debacle, aware that his reputation was in jeopardy and his orthodoxy under hostile scrutiny, Newman entirely ceased to write and, under continuing insensitive criticism, sank into deep dejection. This dreariest period of his life ended when a personal attack by the Anglican writer Kingsley stung him to reply in a work that became an overnight classic, the *Apologia Pro Vita Sua*, which earned him the admiration of his countrymen and reestablished him as a heroic champion of his co-religionists.

Apart from its poignancy as a factor in his personal life, Newman's article "On Consulting the Faithful . . ." was a distinctive contribution to his account of doctrinal development, in that it maintained that there are times when an instinctive consensus of devout lay believers sustains the vitality of important doctrines even when these are generally neglected by the hierarchy.

Newman's critics were especially distressed by his use of the word "consult." His article accordingly begins by arguing that consulting the laity did not imply deferring or submitting to them but simply attending to or considering their views. Newman complains of his critics' seeming inability to distinguish ordinary vernacular usage from technical theological vocabulary. He then goes on to the theological heart of his argument in explaining why the laity must not be ignored in matters of doctrine, because they are witnesses to tradition whose consensus is expressed as the "voice of the infallible Church." Finally, in historical confirmation of this interpretation of the laity's role, he reviews the Arian controversy, contending that over a lengthy period of the fourth century it was in fact the laity who clung firmly to belief in the divinity of Christ while their bishops, with few exceptions, "failed in their confession of the faith."

Not until the era of the Second Vatican Council did this conception of the laity's role gain wide support among Catholic theologians. In 1871, Newman reprinted only a part of the historical section of the article as an appendix to his book on the Arians, with some additional notes in its defense. The work as a whole was not included in the standard edition of Newman's works, and remained largely inaccessible until 1961, when John Coulson republished it in England with a lengthy introduction. The text that occupies the following pages is that of the original article published in *The Rambler*. Words in [   ] were omitted from the 1871 reprinting; words in <   > were added at that time.

# On Consulting the Faithful
# in Matters of Doctrine

A question has arisen among persons of theological knowledge and fair and candid minds, about the wording and the sense of a passage in the *Rambler* for May. It admits to my own mind of so clear and satisfactory an explanation, that I should think it unnecessary to intrude myself, an anonymous person, between the conductors and readers of this Magazine, except that, as in dogmatic works the replies made to objections often contain the richest matter, so here too, plain remarks on a plain subject may open to the minds of others profitable thoughts, which are more due to their own superior intelligence than to the very words of the writer.

The *Rambler*, then, has these words at p. 122: "In the preparation of a dogmatic definition, the faithful are consulted, as lately in the instance of the Immaculate Conception." Now two questions bearing upon doctrine have been raised on this sentence, putting aside the question of fact as regards the particular instance cited, which must follow the decision on the doctrinal questions: viz. first, whether it can, with doctrinal correctness, be said that an *appeal* to the faithful is one of the preliminaries of a definition of doctrine; and secondly, granting that the faithful are taken into account, still, whether they can correctly be said to be *consulted*. I shall remark on both these points, and I shall begin with the second.

## 1.

Now doubtless, if a divine were expressing himself formally, and in Latin, he would not commonly speak of the laity being "consulted" among the preliminaries of a dogmatic definition, because the technical, or even scientific, meaning of the word "consult" is to "consult *with*," or to "take *counsel*." But the English word "consult," in its popular and ordinary use, is not so precise and narrow in its meaning; it is doubtless a word expressive of trust and deference, but not of submission. It includes the idea of inquiring into a matter of *fact*, as well as asking a judgment. Thus we talk of "consulting our barometer" about the weather:—the barometer only attests the *fact* of the state of the atmosphere. In like manner, we may consult a watch or a sun-dial about the time of day. A physician consults the pulse of his patient; but not in the same sense in which his patient consults *him*. It is but an index of the state of his health. Ecclesiastes says, "Qui *observat* ventum, non seminat" we might translate it, "he who consults," without meaning that we ask the wind's opinion. This being considered, it was, I conceive, quite allowable for a writer, who was not teaching or treating theology, but, as it were, conversing, to say, as in the passage in question, "In the preparation of a dogmatic definition, the faithful are consulted." Doubtless their advice, their opinion, their judgment on the question of definition is not asked; but the matter of fact, viz. their belief, *is* sought for, as a testimony to that apostolical tradition, on which alone any doctrine whatsoever can be defined. In like manner, we may "consult" the liturgies or the rites of the Church; not that they speak, not that can take any part whatever in the definition, for they are documents or customs; but they are witnesses to the antiquity or universality of the doctrines which they contain, and about which they are "consulted." And, in like manner, I certainly understood the writer in the *Rambler* to mean (and I think any lay reader might so understand him) that the *fidelium sensus* and *consensus* is a branch of evidence which it is natural or necessary for the Church to regard and consult, before she proceeds to any definition, from its intrinsic cogency; and by consequence, that it ever has been so regarded and consulted. And the writer's use of the word "opinion" in the foregoing sentence, and his omission of it in the sentence in question, seemed to show that, though the two cases put therein were analogous, they were not identical.

Having said as much as this, I go further, and maintain that the word "consulted," used as it was used, was in no respect unadvisable, except so far as it distressed any learned and good men, who identified it with the Latin. I might, indeed, even have defended the word as it was used, in the Latin sense of it. Regnier both uses it of the laity and explains it. "Cùm receptam apud populos traditionem *consulunt* et *sequuntur* Episcopi, non illos habent pro magistris et ducibus, &c."* (*De Eccles. Christ.* p. i. §l, c. i., ed. Migne, col. 234) But in my bountifulness I will give up this use of the word as untheological; still I will maintain that the true theological sense is unknown to all *but* theologians. Accord-

---

* "When the bishops consult and follow a tradition received by the people they do not thereby make the people into their teachers and leaders, &c."

ingly, the use of it in the *Rambler* was in no sense dangerous to any lay reader, who, if he knows Latin, still is not called upon, in the structure of his religious ideas, to draw those careful lines and those fine distinctions, which in theology itself are the very means of anticipating and repelling heresy. The laity would not have a truer, or a clearer, or a different view of the doctrine itself, though the sentence had run, "in the preparation of a dogmatic decree, *regard* is had to the sense of the faithful;" or, "there is an *appeal* to the general voice of the faithful;" or, "*inquiry* is made into the belief of the Christian people;" or, "the definition is not made without a previous *reference* to what the faithful will think of it and say to it;" or though any other form of words had been used, stronger or weaker, expressive of the same general idea, viz. that *the sense of the faithful is not left out of the question* by the Holy See among the preliminary acts of defining a doctrine.

Now I shall go on presently to remark on the proposition itself which is conveyed in the words on which I have been commenting; here, however, I will first observe, that such misconceptions as I have been setting right will and must occur, from the nature of the case, whenever we speak on theological subjects in the vernacular; and if we do not use the vernacular, I do not see how the bulk of the Catholic people are to be catechised or taught at all. English has innovated on the Latin sense of its own Latin words; and if we are to speak according to the conditions of the language, and are to make ourselves intelligible to the multitude, we shall necessarily run the risk of startling those who are resolved to act as mere critics and scholastics in the process of popular instruction.

This divergence from a classical or ecclesiastical standard is a great inconvenience, I grant; but we cannot remodel our mother-tongue. *Crimen* does not properly mean *crime; amiable* does not yet convey the idea of *amabilis; compassio* is not *compassion; princeps* is not a *prince; disputatio* is not *a dispute; praevenire* is not *to prevent. Cicero imperator* is not *the Emperor Cicero; scriptor egregius* is not *an egregious writer; virgo singularis* is not *a singular virgin; retractare dicta* is not *to retract what he has said;* and, as we know from the sacred passage, *traducere* is not necessarily *to traduce.*

Now this is not merely sharp writing, for mistakes do in matter of fact occur not unfrequently from this imperfect correspondence between theological Latin and English; showing that readers of English are bound ever to bear in mind that they are not reading Latin, and that learned divines must ever exercise charity in their interpretations of vernacular religious teaching.

For instance, I know of certain English sermons which were translated into French by some French priests. They, good and friendly
men, were surprised to find in these compositions such language as
"weak evidence and strong evidence," and "insufficient, probably,
demonstrative evidence;" they read that "some writers had depreciated
the evidences of religion," and that "the last century, when love was
cold, was an age of evidences." *Evidentia*, they said, meant that luminousness which attends on demonstration, conviction, certainty; how
can it be more or less? how can it be unsatisfactory? how can a sane
man disparage it? how can it be connected with religious coldness? The
simple explanation of the difficulty was, that the writer was writing for
his own people, and that in English "an evidence" is not *evidentia*.

Another instance. An excellent Italian religious, now gone to his
reward, was reading a work of the same author; and he came upon a
sentence to the effect, I think, that the doctrine of the Holy Trinity
was to be held with "implicit" faith. He was perplexed and concerned.
He thought the writer held that the Church did not explicitly teach,
had not explicitly defined, the dogma; that is, he confused the English
meaning of the word, according to which it is a sort of correlative to
*imperative*, meaning simple, unconditional, absolute, with its sense in
theology.

It is not so exactly apposite to refer,—yet I will refer,—to another
instance, as supplying a general illustration of the point I am urging.
It was in a third country that a lecturer spoke in terms of disparagement
of "Natural Theology," on the ground of its deciding questions of
revelation by reasonings from physical phenomena. It was objected to
him, that *Naturalis Theologia* embraced *all* truths and arguments from
natural reason bearing upon the Divine Being and Attributes. Certainly
he would have been the last to depreciate what he had ever made
the paramount preliminary science to Christian faith; but he spoke
according to the sense of those to whom his words might come. He
considered that in the Protestant school of Paley and other popular
writers, the idea of Natural Theology had practically merged in a
scientific view of the argument from Design.

Once more. Supposing a person were to ask me whether a friend,
who has told me the fact in confidence, had written a certain book,
and I were to answer, "Well, if he did, he certainly would tell *me*,"
and the inquirer went away satisfied that he did *not* write it,—I do
not see that I have done any thing to incur the reproach of the English
word "equivocation;" I have but adopted a mode of turning off a
difficult question, to which any one may be obliged any day to have

recourse. I am not speaking of spontaneous and gratuitous assertions, statements on solemn occasions, or answers to formal authorities. I am speaking of impertinent or unjustifiable questions; and I should like to know the man who thinks himself bound to say every thing to every one. Physicians evade the questions of sick persons about themselves; friends break bad news gradually, and with temporary concealments, to those whom it may shock. Parents shuffle with their children. Statesmen, ministers in Parliament, baffle adversaries in every possible way short of a direct infringement of veracity. When St. Athanasius saw that he was pursued on the Nile by the imperial officers, he turned round his boat and met them; when they came up to his party and hailed them, and asked whether they had seen any thing of Athanasius, Athanasius cried out, "O yes, he is not far from you:" and off the vessels went in different directions as swiftly as they could go, each boat on its own errand, the pursuer and the pursued. I do not see that there is in any of these instances what is expressed by the English word "equivocation;" but it *is* the *equivocatio* of a Latin treatise; and when Protestants hear that *aequivocamus sine scrupulo*, they are shocked at the notion or our "unscrupulous equivocation."

Now, in saying all this, I must not be supposed to be forgetful of the sacred and imperative duty of preserving with religious exactness all those theological terms which are ecclesiastically recognised as portions of dogmatic statements, such as *Trinity, Person, Consubstantial, Nature, Transubstantiation, Sacrament*, &c. It would be unpardonable for a Catholic to teach "justification by faith only," and say that he meant by "faith" *fides formata*, or "justification without works," and say that he meant by "works" the works of the Jewish ritual; but granting all this fully, still if our whole religious phraseology is, as a matter of duty, to be modelled in strict conformity to theological Latin, neither the poor nor children will understand us. I have always fancied that to preachers great license was allowed, not only in the wording, but even in the matter of their discourses: they exaggerate and are rhetorical, and they are understood *piè* as speaking *more praedicatorio*. I have always fancied that, when Catholics were accused of hyperbolical language towards the Blessed Virgin, it was replied that devotion was not the measure of doctrine; nor surely is the vernacular of a magazine writer. I do not see that I am wrong in considering that a periodical, not treating theology *ex professo*, but accidentally alluding to an ecclesiastical act, commits no real offence if it uses an unscientific word, since it speaks, not *more digladiatorio*, but *colloquialiter*.

I shall conclude this head of my subject with allusion to a passage in the history of St. Dionysius the Great, Bishop of Alexandria, though it is beyond my purpose; but I like to quote a saint whom, *multis nominibus* (not "with many *names*, or "by many *nouns*"), I have always loved most of all the Ante-Nicene Fathers. It relates to an attack which was made on his orthodoxy; a very serious matter. Now I know every one will be particular on his own special science or pursuits. I am the last man to find fault with such particularity. Drill-sergeants think much of deportment; hard logicians come down with a sledge-hammer even on a Plato who does not happen to enumerate in his beautiful sentences all the argumentative considerations which go to make up his conclusion; scholars are horrified, as if with sensible pain, at the perpetration of a false quantity. I am far from ridiculing, despising, or even undervaluing such precision; it is for the good of every art and science that it should have vigilant guardians. Nor am I comparing such precision (far from it) with that true religious zeal which leads theologians to keep the sacred Ark of the Covenant in every letter of its dogma, as a tremendous deposit for which they are responsible. In this curious sceptical world, such sensitiveness is the only human means by which the treasure of faith can be kept inviolate. There is a woe in Scripture against the unfaithful shepherd. We do not blame the watch-dog because he sometimes flies at the wrong person. I conceive the force, the peremptoriness, the sternness, with which the Holy See comes down upon the vagrant or the robber, trespassing upon the enclosure of revealed truth, is the only sufficient antagonist to the power and subtlety of the world, to imperial comprehensiveness, monarchical selfishness, nationalism, the liberalism of philosophy, the encroachments and usurpations of science. I grant, I maintain all this; and after this avowal, lest I be misunderstood, I venture to introduce my notice of St. Dionysius. He was accused on a far worse charge, and before a far more formidable tribunal, than commonly befalls a Catholic writer; for he was brought up before the Holy See on a denial of our Lord's divinity. He had been controverting with the Sabellians; and he was in consequence accused of the doctrine to which Arius afterwards gave his name, that is, of considering our Lord a creature. He says, writing in his defence, that when he urged his opponents with the argument that "a vine and a vine-dresser were not the same," neither, therefore, were the "Father and the Son," these were not the only illustrations that he made use of, nor those on which he dwelt, for he also spoke of "a root and a plant," "a fount and a stream," which are not only *distinct* from each other, but of one and the same *nature*. Then he adds, "But my accusers have no eyes to see this portion of my treatise; but they take up two little words detached from the context, and proceed to discharge them at me as pebbles from a sling."[1] If even a saint's words are not always precise enough to allow of being made a dogmatic text, much less are those of any modern periodical.

The conclusion I would draw from all I have been saying is this: Without deciding whether or not it is advisable to introduce points of theology into popular works, and especially whether it is advisable for laymen to do so, still, if this actually *is* done, we are not to expect in them that perfect accuracy of expression which is demanded in a Latin treatise or a lecture *ex cathedrâ*; and if there be a want of this exactness, we must not at once think it proceeds from self-will and undutifulness in the writers.

## 2.

Now I come to the *matter* of what the writer in the *Rambler* really said, putting aside the question of the *wording*; and I begin by expressing my belief that, whatever he may be willing to admit on the score of theological Latinity in the use of the word "consult" when applied to the faithful, yet one thing he cannot deny, viz. that in using it, he implied, from the very force of the term, that they are treated by the Holy See, on occasions such as that specified, with attention and consideration.

Then follows the question, Why? and the answer is plain, viz. because the body of the faithful is one of the witnesses to the fact of the tradition of revealed doctrine, and because their *consensus* through Christendom is the voice of the Infallible Church.

I think I am right in saying that the tradition of the Apostles, committed to the whole Church in its various constituents and functions *per modum unius*, manifests itself variously at various times: sometimes by the mouth of the episcopacy, sometimes by the doctors, sometimes by the people, sometimes by liturgies, rites, ceremonies, and customs, by events, disputes, movements, and all those other phenomena which are comprised under the name of history. It follows that none of these channels of tradition may be treated with disrespect; granting at the same time fully, that the gift of discerning, discriminating, defining, promulgating, and enforcing any portion of that tradition resides solely in the *Ecclesia docens*.

[1] Athan. de Sent. Dion. 8.

One man will lay more stress on one aspect of doctrine, another on another; for myself, I am accustomed to lay great stress on the *consensus fidelium*, and I will say how it has to come about.

1. It had long been to me a difficulty, that I could not find certain portions of the defined doctrine of the Church in ecclesiastical writers. I was at Rome in the year 1847; and then I had the great advantage and honour of seeing Fathers Perrone and Passaglia, and having various conversations with them on this point. The point of difficulty was this, that up to the date of the definition of certain articles of doctrine respectively, there was so very deficient evidence from existing documents that Bishops, doctors, theologians, held them. I do not mean to say that I expressed my difficulty in this formal shape; but that what passed between us in such interviews as they were kind enough to give me, ran into or impinged upon this question. Nor would I ever dream of making them answerable for the impression which their answers made on me; but, speaking simply on my own responsibility, I should say that, while Father Passaglia seemed to maintain that the Ante-Nicene writers were clear in their testimonies in behalf (*e.g.*) of the doctrines of the Holy Trinity and Justification, expressly praising and making much of the Anglican Bishop Bull; Father Perrone, on the other hand, not speaking, indeed directly upon those particular doctrines, but rather on such as I will presently introduce in his own words, seemed to me to say *"transeat"* to the alleged fact which constituted the difficulty, and to lay a great stress on what he considered to be the *sensus* and *consensus fidelium*, as a compensation for whatever deficiency there might be of patristical testimony in behalf of various points of the Catholic dogma.

2. I should have been led to fancy, perhaps, that he was shaping his remarks in the direction in which he considered he might be especially serviceable to myself, who had been accustomed to account for the (supposed) phenomena in another way, had it not been for his work on the Immaculate Conception, which I read the next year with great interest, and which was passing through the press when I saw him. I am glad to have this opportunity of expressing my gratitude and attachment to a venerable man, who never grudged me his valuable time.

But now for his treatise, to which I have referred, so far as it speaks of the *sensus fidelium*, and of its bearing upon the doctrine, of which his work treats, and upon its definition.

(1.) He states the historical *fact* of such *sensus*. Speaking of the "Ecclesiae sensus" on the subject, he says that, though the liturgies of the Feast of the Conception "satis apertè patefaciant quid Ecclesia antiquitùs de hoc senserit argumento,"* yet it may be worth while to add some direct remarks on the sense itself of the Church. Then he says, "Ex duplici fonte eum colligi posse arbitramur, tum scilicet ex pastorum, *tum ex fidelium* sese gerendi ratione"** (pp. 74, 75). Let it be observed, he not only joins together the *pastores* and *fideles*, but contrasts them; I mean (for it will bear on what is to follow), the "faithful" do not *include* the "pastors."

(2.) Next he goes on to describe the relation of that *sensus fidelium* to the *sensus Ecclesiae.* He says, that to inquire into the sense of the Church on any question, is nothing else but to investigate towards which side of it she has more inclined. And the "indicia et manifestationes hujus propensionis" are her public acts, liturgies, feasts, prayers, "pastorum ac *fidelium* in unum veluti conspiratio" (p. 101). Again, at p. 109, joining together in one this twofold consent of pastors and people, he speaks of the "unanimis pastorum ac *fidelium* consensio . . . per liturgias, per festa, per euchologia, per fidei controversias, per conciones patefacta."***

(3.) These various "indicia" are also the *instrumenta traditionis,* and vary one with another in the evidence which they give in favour of particular doctrines; so that the strength of one makes up in a particular case for the deficiency of another, and the strength of the "sensus communis fidelium" can make up (*e.g.*) for the silence of the Fathers. "Istiusmodi instrumenta interdum simul conjunctè conspirare possunt ad traditionem aliquam apostolicam atque divinam patefaciendam, interdum vero seorsum. . . . Perperam nonnulli solent ad inficiandam traditionis alicujus existentiam urgere silentium Patrum . . . quid enim si silentium istud alio pacto . . . compensetur?" (p. 139). He instances this from St. Irenaeus and Tertullian in the "Successio Episcoporum," who transmit the doctrines "tum activi operâ ministerii, tum usu et praxi, tum institutis ritibus . . . adeò ut catholica atque apostolica doctrina inoculata . . . fuerit . . . communi Ecclesiae coetui"**** (p. 142).

* "It is plain enough what the ancient Church thought about this argument."
** "We think it can be gathered from two sources, the behavior of the pastors and that of the faithful."
*** "Signs and manifestations of this tendency . . . a combining of pastors and faithful . . . unanimous consensus of pastors and faithful, exhibited through liturgies, celebrations, prayers, debates, and discourses."
**** "Such instruments may illustrate some divine and apostolic tradition, sometimes in combination, sometimes separately . . . Some are accustomed wrongly to urge silence on the part of the Fathers as impugning the existence of some tradition . . . But what if that silence is compensated in some other

(4.) He then goes on to speak directly of the force of the "sensus fidelium," as distinct (not separate) from the teaching of their pastors. "*Praestantissimi* theologi maximam *probandi* vim huic communi sensui inesse *uno ore* fatentur. Etenim Canus, 'In quaestione fidei,' inquit, 'communis fidelis populi sensus haud levem facit fidem' "*(p. 143). He gives another passage from him in a note, which he introduces with the words, "Illud *praeclarè* addit;" what Canus adds is, "Quaero ex te, quando de rebus Christianae fidei inter nos contendimus, non de philosophae decretis, utrùm potius *quaerendum* est, quid philosophi atque ethnici, an quid homines Christiani, et *doctrinâ et fide* instituti, *sentiant?*"**

Now certainly "quaerere quid sentiant homines doctrinâ et fide instituti," though not asking advice, is an act implying not a little deference on the part of the persons addressing towards the parties addressed.

Father Perrone continues, "Gregorious verò de Valentiâ fusius vim ejusmodi fidelium consensus evolvit. 'Est enim,' inquit, "in *definitionibus fidei* habenda ratio, quoad fieri potest, consensûs fidelium.' "*** Here, again, "habere rationem," to have regard to, is an act of respect and consideration. However, Gregory continues, "Quoniam *et ii* sanè, quatenus *ex ipsis* constat Ecclesia, sic *Spiritu Sancto assistente*, divinas revelationes *integrè et purè conservant*, ut omnes illi quidem aberrare non possunt. . . . Illud solùm contendo; Si quando de re aliquâ *in materie religionis* controversia (controversâ?) constaret fidelium omnium concordem esse sententiam (solet autem id constare, vel ex ipsâ praxi alicujus cultûs communiter apud christianos populos receptâ, vel ex *scandalo et offensione communi*, quae opinione

----

way? . . . by the exertion of an active ministry, by usage and practice, and established rituals, so as to implant a Catholic and apostolic doctrine in the community of the Church."

* "The most distinguished theologians agree in attributing the greatest probative force to this common sentiment. Cano asserts that 'in a question of faith, common sentiment of the faithful people provides a warrant that is by no means insignificant.' "

** "Cano excellently adds . . . 'I ask you, when we discuss not philosophical conclusions but matters of Christian belief, whether it is preferable to ascertain the views of philosophers and pagans, or the thoughts of Christians formed by doctrine and faith.' "

*** "Gregory of Valencia, who brought out the force of this consensus of the faithful, says that 'as far as possible, account must be taken of the consensus of the faithful in definitions of faith.'"

aliquâ oritur, &c.) meritò *posse et debere* Pontificem illâ *niti*, ut quae esset *Ecclesiae sententia infallibilis*"\* (p. 144). Thus Gregory says that, in controversy about a matter of faith, the consent of all the faithful has such a force in the proof of this side or that, that the Supreme Pontiff *is able and ought* to *rest* upon it, as being the *judgment or sentiment* of the *infallible* Church. These are surely exceedingly strong words; not that I take them to mean strictly that infallibility is *in* the "consensus fidelium," but that that "consensus" is an *indicium* or *instrumentum* to us of the judgement of that Church which *is* infallible.

Father Perrone proceeds to quote from Petavius, who supplies us with the following striking admonition from St. Paulinus, viz. "ut de omnium fidelium *ore pendeamus*, quia in omnem fidelem Spiritus Dei spirat."\*\*

Petavius speaks thus, as he quotes him (p. 156): "*Movet me*, ut in cam (viz. piam) sententiam sim propensior, *communis maximus sensus fidelium omnium*."\*\*\* By "movet me" he means, that he *attends* to what the *coetus fidelium* says: this is certainly not passing over the *fideles*, but making much of them.

In a later part of his work (p. 186), Father Perrone speaks of the "consensus fidelium" under the strong image of a *seal*. After mentioning various arguments in favour of the Immaculate Conception, such as the testimony of so many universities, religious bodies, theologians, &c., he continues, "Haec demum omnia firmissimo veluti *sigillo obsignat* totius christiani populi consensus."\*\*\*\*

(5.) He proceeds to give several instances, in which the definition of doctrine was made in consequence of nothing else but the "sensus fidelium" and the "juge et vivum magisterium" of the Church.

For his meaning of the "juge et vivum magisterium Ecclesiae," he refers us to his *Praelectiones* (part ii. §2, c.ii.). In that passage I do not see that he defines the sense of the word; but I understand him to mean

---

\* "For inasmuch as they comprise the Church, by assistance of the Holy Spirit they so preserve divine revelations in their purity and integrity that they cannot all go astray . . . I contend only this: If a consensus of the faithful is established in some disputed matter of religion, the Pope may and should rely upon it as the judgment of the infallible Church. (Such consensus is usually verified either from some practice of worship adopted universally among Christians, or by general scandal and offense caused by some opinion.)

\*\* "We should hang upon the lips of all the faithful, because the Spirit of God breathes into every believer."

\*\*\* "The main consensus of all the faithful moves me to favor that view."

\*\*\*\* "All these are ratified by consensus of the whole Christian people as by the most authoritative seal."

that high authoritative voice or act which is the Infallible Church's prerogative, inasmuch as she is the teacher of the nations; and which is a sufficient warrant to all men for a doctrine being true and being *de fide*, by the mere fact of its formally occurring. It is distinct from, and independent of, tradition, though never in fact separated from it. He says, "Fit ut traditio dogmatica identificetur cum ipsâ Ecclesiae doctrinâ, a quâ separari nequit; qua propter, *etsi documenta deficerent omnia*, solum hoc vivum et juge magisterium *satis esset* ad cognoscendam doctrinam divinitus traditam, habito praesertim respectu ad solennes Christi promissiones"* (p. 303).

This being understood, he speaks of several points of faith which have been determined and defined by the "magisterium" of the Church and, as to tradition, on the "consensus fidelium," prominently, if not solely.

The most remarkable of these is the "dogma de visione Dei beatificâ" possessed by souls after purgatory and before the day of judgment; a point which Protestants, availing themselves of the comment of the Benedictines of St. Maur upon St. Ambrose, are accustomed to urge in controversy. "Nemo est qui nesciat," says Father Perrone, "quot utriusque Ecclesiae, tum Graecae tum Latinae, Patres contrarium sensisse visi sunt"** (p. 147). He quotes in a note the words of the Benedictine editor, as follows: "Propemodum incredibile videri potest, quàm in eâ quaestione sancti Patres ab ipsis Apostolorum temporibus ad Gregorii XI. (Benedicti XII) pontificatum florentinumque concilium, hoc est toto quatuordecim seculorum spatio, incerti ac parùm constantes exstiterint."*** Father Perrone continues: "Certè quidem in Ecclesiâ non deerat quoad hunc fidei articulum divina traditio; alioquin nunquam is definiri potuisset: verùm non omnibus illa erat comperta; divina eloquia haud satis in re sunt conspicua; *Patres*, ut vidimus, in varias abierunt sententias; *liturgiae ipsae* non modicam prae se ferunt difficultatem. *His omnibus succurrit* juge Ecclesiae magisterium, *com-*

* "Dogmatic tradition is identified with the teachings of the Church, from which it cannot be separated. Hence, even if all documentation were lacking, this living, consistent magisterium would suffice by itself to make known the divinely transmitted doctrine, especially in consideration of Christ's solemn promises."

** "Everyone is aware how many Fathers in both the Eastern and Western Churches seem to have held an opposite opinion."

*** "It may seem almost incredible how diffident and inconsistent the holy Fathers were about this question, all the way from the Apostolic age to the pontificate of Gregory XI (Benedict XII) and the Council of Florence, that is, over a period of fully fourteen hundred years."

*munis praeterea fidelium sensus*; qui altè adeò defixum . . . habebant
mentibus, purgatas animas statim ad Deum videndum eoque fruendum
admitti, ut non minimum eorum animi vel ex ipsâ controversiâ fuerint
*offensi*, quae sub Joanne XXII. agitabatur, et cujus definitio *diu nimis
protrahebatur.*"\* Now does not this imply that the tradition, on which
the definition was made, was manifested in the *consensus fidelium* with
a luminousness which the succession of Bishops, though many of them
were "Sancti Patres ab ipsis Apostolorum temporibus," did not furnish? that the definition was delayed till the *fideles* would bear the delay
no longer? that it was made because of them and for their sake, because
of their strong feelings? If so, surely, in plain English, most considerable
deference was paid to the "sensus fidelium;" their opinion and advice
indeed was not asked, but their testimony was taken, their feelings consulted, their impatience, I had almost said, feared.

In like manner, as regards the doctrine, though not the definition,
of the Immaculate Conception, he says, not denying, of course, the
availableness of the other "instrumenta traditionis" in this particular
case, "Ratissimum est, Christi fideles omnes circa hunc articulum unius
esse animi, idque ita, ut maximo afficerentur *scandalo*, si vel minima
de Immaculatâ Virginis Conceptione quaestio moveretur"\*\* (p. 156).

3. A year had hardly passed from the appearance of Fr. Perrone's
book in England, when the Pope published his Encyclical Letter. In it
he asked the Bishops of the Catholic world, "ut nobis significare velitis,
quâ devotione vester clerus *populusque fidelis* erga Immaculatae Virginis conceptionem sit animatus, et quo desiderio flagret, ut ejusmodi
res ab apostolicâ sede decernatur;"\*\*\* that is, when it came to the
point to take measures for the definition of the doctrine, he did lay a

---

\* "Certainly the Church was not without any divine tradition regarding this
article of faith; otherwise it could not have been defined. Yet it was scarcely
obvious to everyone. Divine eloquence on this subject was not abundant. The
Fathers' thoughts, as noted, strayed in different directions. Even the liturgies
present considerable difficulty. The unfailing magisterium of the Church came
to the aid of all these along with the consensus of the faithful. In their minds
it was so deeply established that souls, once purified, had immediate access to
the vision and enjoyment of God, that they were no little offended by the
controversy that went on under John XXII, and the unwarranted postponement of a definition."

\*\* "It is well established that all the Christian faithful are in such complete
agreement about this article that they would be deeply scandalized if the
Virgin's Immaculate Conception were even mildly questioned."

\*\*\* "Make known to us how devoted your clergy and faithful people are
with respect to the conception of the Immaculate Virgin, and how eager they
are for a decision on the matter to be issued by the Apostolic See."

special stress on this particular preliminary, viz. the ascertainment of the feeling of the faithful both towards the doctrine and its definition; as the *Rambler* stated in the passage out of which this argument has arisen. It seems to me important to keep this in view, whatever becomes of the word "consulted," which, I have already said, is not to be taken in its ordinary Latin sense.

4. At length, in 1854, the definition took place, and the Pope's Bull containing it made its appearance. In it the Holy Father speaks as he had spoken in his Encyclical, viz. that although he *already* knew the sentiments of the Bishops, still he had wished to know the sentiments of the *people* also: "*Quamvis* nobis ex receptis postulationibus de definiendâ tandem aliquando Immaculatâ Virginis Conceptione *perspectus* esset plurimorum sociorum *Antistitum* sensus, tamen Encyclicas literas, &c. ad omnes Ven. FF. totius Catholici orbis sacrorum Antistites misimus, ut, adhibitis ad Deum precibus, nobis scripto *etiam* significarent, quae esset suorum *fidelium* erga Immaculatam Deiparae Conceptionem pietas et devotio,"\* &c. And when, before the formal definition, he enumerates the various witnesses to the apostolicity of the doctrine, he sets down "divina eloquia, veneranda traditio, perpetuus Ecclesiae sensus, singularis catholicorum Antistitum ac *fidelium* conspiratio."\*\* *Conspiratio*; the two, the Church teaching and the Church taught, are put together, as one twofold testimony, illustrating each other, and never to be divided.

5. A year or two passed, and the Bishop of Birmingham published his treatise on the doctrine. I close this portion of my paper with an extract from his careful view of the argument. "Nor should the universal conviction of pious Catholics be passed over, as of small account in the general argument; for that pious belief, and the devotion which springs from it, are the *faithful reflection* of the pastoral teaching" (p. 172). Reflection; that is, the people are a *mirror*, in which the Bishops see themselves. Well, I suppose a person may *consult* his glass, and in that way may know things about himself which he can learn in no other way. This is what Fr. Perrone above seems to say has sometimes

---

\* "Even though the requests we had received left no doubt about the opinion of most of our fellow bishops concerning eventual definition of the Immaculate Conception of the Virgin, we nevertheless sent encyclical letters and the like to all our venerable brother bishops in the whole Catholic world, requesting them, after prayer, to inform us in writing about the piety and devotion of their faithful concerning the Immaculate Conception of the Mother of God."

\*\* "divine eloquence, revered tradition, the perpetual mind of the Church, and the singular joint accord of Catholic bishops and faithful . . ."

actually been the case, as in the instance of the "beatifica visio" of the saints; at least he does not mention the "*pastorum* ac fidelium *conspiratio*" in reviewing the grounds of its definition, but simply the "juge Ecclesiae magisterium" and the "communis fidelium sensus."

His lordship proceeds: "The more devout the faithful grew, the more devoted they showed themselves towards this mystery. And it is the devout who have the surest instinct in discerning the mysteries of which the Holy Spirit breathes the grace through the Church, and who, with as sure a tact, reject what is alien from her teaching. The common accord of the faithful has weight much as an argument even with the most learned divines. St. Augustine says, that amongst many things which most justly held him in the bosom of the Catholic Church, was the 'accord of populations and of nations.' In another work he says, 'It seems that I have believed nothing but the confirmed opinion and the exceedingly wide-spread report of populations and of nations.' Elsewhere he says: 'In matters whereupon the Scripture has not spoken clearly, the custom of the people of God, or the institutions of our predecessors, are to be held as law.' In the same spirit St. Jerome argues, whilst defending the use of relics against Vigilantius: 'So the people of all the Churches who have gone out to meet holy relics, and have received them with so much joy, are to be accounted foolish' " (pp. 172, 173).

And here I might come to an end; but, having got so far, I am induced, before concluding, to suggest an historical instance of the same great principle, which Father Perrone does not draw out.

### 3.

First, I will set down the various ways in which theologians put before us the bearing of the Consent of the faithful upon the manifestation of the tradition of the Church. Its *consensus* is to be regarded: 1. as a testimony to the fact of the apostolical dogma; 2. as a sort of instinct, or φρόνημα, deep in the bosom of the mystical body of Christ; 3. as a direction of the Holy Ghost; 4. as an answer to its prayer; 5. as a jealousy of error, which it at once feels as a scandal.

1. The first of these I need not enlarge upon, as it is illustrated in the foregoing passages from Father Perrone.

2. The second is explained in the well-known passages of Möhler's *Symbolique*; e.g. "L'esprit de Dieu, qui gouverne et vivifie L'Eglise, enfante dans l'homme, en s'unissant à lui, *un instinct*, un tact éminemment chrétien, qui le conduit à toute vraie doctrine. . . . Ce sentiment commun, cette conscience de l'Eglise est la tradition dans le sens sub-

jectif du mot. Qu'est-ce donc que la tradition considérée sous ce point de vue? C'est le sens chrétien existant dans l'Eglise, et transmis par l'Eglise; sens, toutefois, qu'on ne peut séparer des vérités qu'il contient, puisqu'il est formé de ces vérités et par ces vérités."* Ap. Perrone, p. 142.

3. Cardinal Fisher seems to speak of the third, as he is quoted by Petavius, *De Incarn.* xiv. 2; that is, he speaks of a custom imperceptibly gaining a position, "nullâ praeceptorum vi, sed consensu quodam tacito tam populi quàm cleri, quasi tacitis omnium suffragiis recepta fuit, priusquàm ullo conciliorum decreto legimus eam fuisse firmatam." And then he adds, "This custom has its birth *in that people which is ruled by the Holy Ghost*,"** &c.

4. Petavius speaks of a fourth aspect of it. "It is well said by St. Augustine, that to the minds of individuals certain things are revealed by God, not only by extraordinary means, as in visions, &c., but also in those usual ways, according to which what is unknown to them is opened *in answer to their prayer*. After this manner it is to be believed that God has revealed to Christians the sinless Conception of the Immaculate Virgin." *De Incarn.* xiv. 2, 11.

5. The fifth is enlarged upon in Dr. Newman's second *Lecture on Anglican Difficulties,* from which I quote a few lines: "We know that it is the property of life to be impatient of any foreign substance in the body to which it belongs. It will be sovereign in its own domain, and it conflicts with what it cannot assimilate into itself, and *is irritated and disordered* till it has expelled it. Such expulsion, then, is emphatically a test of uncongeniality, for it shows that the substance ejected, not only is not one with the body that rejects it, but cannot be made one with it; that its introduction is not only useless, or superfluous, or adventitious, but that it is intolerable." Presently he continues: "The religious life of a people is of a certain quality and direction, and these are tested by the mode in which it encounters the various opinions,

* "The Spirit of God who directs and animates the Church, in becoming united to a human being, engenders a distinctively Christian sensitivity which shows the way to all true doctrine. This common sensibility, this consciousness of the Church, is tradition in the subjective sense of that word. What, from that point of view, is tradition? It is the Christian mentality, existing in the Church and transmitted by the Church; a mentality, however, inseparable from the truths it contains, because it is formed out of and by those very truths."

** "Not compelled by any precepts, but carried forward by a kind of tacit consensus of clergy and people, as though silent votes had come in from them all, long before we read of its confirmation by conciliar decree."

customs, and institutions which are submitted to it. Drive a stake into a river's bed, and you will at once ascertain which way it is running, and at what speed; throw up even a straw upon the air, and you will see which way the wind blows; submit your heretical and Catholic principle to the action of the multitude, and you will be able to pronounce at once whether it is imbued with Catholic truth or with heretical falsehood." And then he proceeds to exemplify this by a passage in the history of Arianism, the very history which I intend now to take, as illustrative of the truth and importance of the thesis on which I am insisting.

It is not a little remarkable, that, though, historically speaking, the fourth century is the age of doctors, illustrated, as it was, by the saints Athanasius, Hilary, the two Gregories, Basil, Chrysostom, Ambrose, Jerome, and Augustine, and all of these saints bishops also, except one, nevertheless in that very day the divine tradition committed to the infallible Church was proclaimed and maintained far more by the faithful than by the Episcopate.

Here, of course, I must explain:—in saying this, then, undoubtedly I am not denying that the great body of the Bishops were in their internal belief orthodox; nor that there were numbers of clergy who stood by the laity, and acted as their centres and guides; nor that the laity actually received their faith, in the first instance, from the Bishops and clergy; nor that some portions of the laity were ignorant, and other portions at length corrupted by the Arian teachers, who got possession of the sees and ordained an heretical clergy;—but I mean still, that in that time of immense confusion the divine dogma of our Lord's divinity was proclaimed, enforced, maintained, and (humanly speaking) preserved, far more by the "Ecclesia docta" than by the "Ecclesia docens;" that the body of the episcopate was unfaithful to its commission, while the body of the laity was faithful to its baptism; that at one time the Pope, at other times the patriarchal, metropolitan, and other great sees, at other times general councils, said what they should not have said, or did what obscured and compromised revealed truth; while, on the other hand, it was the Christian people who, under Providence, were the ecclesiastical strength of Athanasius, Hilary, Eusebius of Vercellae, and other great solitary confessors, who would have failed without them.

I see, then, in the Arian history a palmary example of a state of the Church, during which, in order to know the tradition of the Apostles, we must have recourse to the faithful; for I fairly own, that if I go to writers, since I must adjust the letter of Justin, Clement, and Hippolytus with the Nicene Doctors, I get confused; and what revives and reinstates me, as far as history goes, is the faith of the people. For I argue that, unless they had been catechised, as St. Hilary says, in the orthodox faith from the time of their baptism, they never could have had that horror, which they show, of the heterodox Arian doctrine. Their voice, then, is the voice of tradition; and the instance comes to us with still greater emphasis, when we consider—1. that it occurs in the very beginning of the history of the "Ecclesia docens," for there can scarcely be said to be any history of her teaching till the age of martyrs was over; 2. that the doctrine in controversy was so momentous, being the very foundation of the Christian system; 3. that the state of controversy and disorder lasted over the long space of sixty years; and 4. that it involved serious persecutions, in life, limb, and property, to the faithful whose loyal perseverance decided it.

It seems, then, as striking an instance as I could take in fulfilment of Father Perrone's statement, that the voice of tradition may in certain cases express itself, not by Councils, nor Fathers, nor Bishops, but the "communis fidelium sensus."

I shall set down some authorities for the two points successively, which I have to enforce, viz. that the Nicene dogma was maintained during the greater part of the 4th century,

1. not by the unswerving firmness of the Holy See, Councils, or Bishops, but

2. by the "consensus fidelium."

I. On the one hand, then, I say, that there was a temporary suspense of the functions of the "Ecclesia docens." The body of Bishops failed in their confession of the faith. They spoke variously, one against another; there was nothing, after Nicaea, of firm, unvarying, consistent testimony, for nearly sixty years. There were untrustworthy Councils, unfaithful Bishops; there was weakness, fear of consequences, misguidance, delusion, hallucination, endless, hopeless, extending itself into nearly every corner of the Catholic Church. The comparatively few who remained faithful were discredited and driven into exile; the rest were either deceivers or were deceived.

1. A.D. 325. The great council of Nicaea, of 318 Bishops, chiefly from the eastern provinces of Christendom, under the presidency of Hosius of Cordova, as the Pope's Legate. It was convoked against Arianism, which it once for all anathematized; and it inserted the formula of the "Consubstantial" into the Creed, with the view of establishing the fundamental dogma which Arianism impugned. It is the first Oecumenical Council, and recognised at the time its own

authority as the voice of the infallible Church. It is so received by the *orbis terrarum* at this day. <A.D. 326. St. Athanasius, the great champion of the Homoüison, was elected Bishop of Alexandria.>

[The history of the Arian controversy, from its date, A.D. 325, to the date of the second Oecumenical Council, A.D. 381, is the history of the struggle through Christendom for the universal acceptance or the repudiation of the formula of the "Consubstantial."]

2. A.D. 334, 335. The synods of Caesarea and Tyre <sixty Bishops> against Athanasius, who was therein accused and formally condemned of rebellion, sedition, and ecclesiastical tyranny; of murder, sacrilege, and magic; deposed from his see, forbidden to set foot in Alexandria for life, and banished to Gaul. [Constantine confirmed the sentence.] <Also, they received Arius into communion.>

3. A.D. 341. Council of Rome of fifty Bishops, attended by the exiles from Thrace, Syria, &c., by Athanasius, &c., in which Athanasius was pronounced innocent.

4. A.D. 341. Great Council of the Dedication at Antioch, attended by ninety or a hundred Bishops. The council ratified the proceedings of the councils of Caesarea and Tyre, and placed an Arian in the see of Athanasius. Then it proceeded to pass a dogmatic decree in reversal of the formula of the "Consubstantial." Four or five creeds, instead of the Nicene, were successively adopted by the assembled fathers. [The first was a creed which they ascribed to Lucian, a martyr and saint of the preceding century, in whom the Arians always gloried as their master. The second was fuller and stronger in its language, and made more pretension to orthodoxy. The third was more feeble again. These three creeds][1] were circulated in the neighbourhood; but, as they wished to send one to Rome, they directed a fourth to be drawn up. This, too, apparently failed. [So little was known at the time of the real history of this synod and its creeds, that St. Hilary calls it "sanctorum synodus."]

5. A.D. 345. Council of the creed called Macrostich. This creed suppresses, as did the third, the word "substance." The eastern Bishops sent this to the Bishops of [the West][2], who rejected it.

6. A.D. 347. The great council of Sardica, attended by [380][3] Bishops. Before it commenced, the division between its members broke out

---

[1] [These three creeds] Three of these
[2] [the West] France
[3] [380] more than 300

on the question whether or not Athanasius should have a seat in it. In consequence, seventy-six retired to Philippopolis, on the Thracian side of Mount Haemus, and there excommunicated the Pope and the Sardican fathers. These seceders published a sixth confession of faith. The synod of Sardica, including Bishops from Italy, Gaul, Africa, Egypt, Cyprus, and Palestine, confirmed the act of the Roman council, and restored Athanasius and the other exiles to their sees. The synod of Philippopolis, on the contrary, sent letters to the civil magistrates of those cities, forbidding them to admit the exiles into them. The imperial power took part with the Sardican fathers, and Athanasius went back to Alexandria.

7. A.D. 351. [Before many years had run out, the great eastern party was up again.] <The Bishops of the East met at Sirmium. The semi-Arian Bishops began to detach themselves from the Arians, and to form a separate party.>

Under pretence of putting down a kind of Sabellianism, they drew up a new creed, into which they introduced [certain inadvisable expressions][1] of some of the ante-Nicene writers, on the subject of our Lord's divinity, and dropped the word "substance." [St. Hilary thought this creed also Catholic; and other Catholic writers style its fathers "holy Bishops."]

[8. There is considerable confusion of dates here. Anyhow, there was a second Sirmian creed, in which the eastern party first came to a division among themselves. St. Hilary at length gives up these creeds as indefensible, and calls this one a "blasphemy." It is the first creed which criticises the words "substance," &c., as unscriptural. Some years afterwards this "blasphemia" seems to have been interpolated, and sent into the East in the name of Hosius. At a later date, there was a third Sirmian creed; and a second edition of it, with alterations, was published at Nice in Thrace.]

9. A.D. 353. The council of Arles.[2] [I cannot find how many Bishops attended it. As the Pope sent several Bishops as legates, it must have been one of great importance. The Bishop of Arles was an Arian, and managed to seduce, or to force, a number of orthodox Bishops, including the Pope's legate, Vincent, to subscribe the condemnation of

---

[1] Certain inadvisable expressions] the language

[2] The Council of Arles <The Pope sent to it several Bishops as legates. The Fathers of the Council, including the Pope's legate, Vincent, subscribed the condemnation of Athanasius. Paulinus, Bishop of Trêves, was nearly the only one who stood up for the Nicene faith and for Athanasius.>

Athanasius. Paulinus, Bishop of Trêves, was nearly the only champion of the Nicene faith and of Athanasius.] He was accordingly banished into Phrygia, where he died.

10. A.D. 355. The council of Milan, of more than 300 Bishops of the West. Nearly all of them, subscribed the condemnation of Athanasius; whether they generally subscribed the heretical creed, which was brought forward, does not appear. The Pope's four legates remained firm, and St. Dionysius of Milan, who died an exile in Asia Minor. An Arian was put into his see. Saturninus, the Bishop of Arles, proceeded to hold a council at Beziers; and its fathers banished St. Hilary to Phrygia.

<A.D. 357-9. The Arians and Semi-Arians successively drew up fresh creeds at Sirmium.>

11. A.D. 357< – 8.> Hosius falls. "Constantius used such violence towards the old man, and confined him so straitly, that at last, broken by suffering, he was brought, though hardly, to hold communion with Valens and Ursacius (the Arian leaders), though he would not subscribe against Athanasius." Athan. *Arian. Hist.* 45.

12. <And> Liberius. A.D. 357 < – 8> "The tragedy was not ended in the lapse of Hosius, but in the evil which befell Liberius, the Roman Pontiff, it became far more dreadful and mournful, considering that he was Bishop of so great a city, and of the whole Catholic Church, and that he had so bravely resisted Constantius two years previously. There is nothing, whether in the historians and holy fathers, or in his own letters, to prevent our coming to the conclusion, that Liberius communicated with the Arians, and confirmed the sentence passed against Athanasius; but he is not at all on that account to be called a heretic." Baron. Ann. 357, 38–45. Athanasius says: "Liberius, after he had been in banishment <for> two years, gave way, and from fear of threatened death was induced to subscribe." *Arian. Hist.* §41. St. Jerome says: "Liberius, taedio victus exilii, in haereticam pravitatem subscribens, Roman quasi victor intraverat."* *Chron.* <ed. Val. p. 797>

13. A.D. 359. The great councils of Seleucia and Ariminum, being one bi-partite council, representing the East and West respectively. At Seleucia there were 150 Bishops, of which only the twelve or thirteen from Egypt were champions of the Nicene "Consubstantial." At Ari-

---

* "Liberius, worn out by the tedium of exile and subscribing to the heretical error, had entered Rome almost as a conqueror."

minum there were as many as 400 Bishops, who, worn out by the artifice of long delay on the part of the Arians, abandoned the "Consubstantial," and subscribed the ambiguous formula which the heretics had substituted for it.

[14. A.D. 361. The death of Constantius; the Catholic Bishops breathe again, and begin at once to remedy the miseries of the Church, though troubles were soon to break out anew.]

15. A.D. 362. State of the Church of Antioch at this time. There were four Bishops or communions of Antioch; first, the old succession and communion, which had possession before the Arian troubles; secondly, the Arian succession, which had lately conformed to orthodoxy in the person of Meletius; thirdly, the new Latin succession, lately created by Lucifer, whom some have thought the Pope's legate there; and, fourthly, the new Arian succession, which was [begun]¹ upon the recantation of Meletius. At length, as Arianism was brought under, the evil reduced itself to two <Episcopal> successions, that of Meletius and the Latin, which went on for many years, the West and Egypt holding communion with the latter, and the East with the former.

[16. A.D. 370–379. St. Basil was Bishop of Caesarea in Cappadocia through these years. The judgments formed about this great doctor in his lifetime show us vividly the extreme confusion which prevailed. He was accused by one party of being a follower of Apollinaris, and lost in consequence some of the sees over which he was metropolitan. He was accused by the monks in his friend Gregory's diocese of favouring the semi-Arians. He was accused by the Neocaesareans of inclining towards Arianism. And he was treated with suspicion and coldness by Pope Damasus].

17. About A.D. 360, St. Hilary says: "I am not speaking of things foreign to my knowledge; I am not writing about what I am ignorant of; I have heard and I have seen the shortcomings of persons who are [present to]² me, not of laymen <merely>, but of Bishops. For, excepting the Bishop Eleusius and a few with him, for the most part the ten Asian provinces, within whose boundaries I am situate, are truly ignorant of God." <De Syn. 63.> It is observable, that even Eleusius, who is here spoken of as somewhat better than the rest, was a semi-Arian, according to Socrates, and even a persecutor of Catholics

¹[begun] started
²[present to] round about

at Constantinople; and, according to Sozomen, one of those who [urged][1] Pope Liberius to give up the Nicene formula of the "Consubstantial." By the ten Asian provinces is meant the east and south provinces of Asia Minor, pretty nearly as cut off by a line passing from Cyzicus to Seleucia through Synnada.

18. A.D. 360. St. Gregory Nazianzen says, about this date: "Surely the pastors have done foolishly; for, excepting a very few, who, either on account of their insignificance were passed over, or who by reason of their virtue resisted, and who were to be left as a seed and root for the springing up again and revival of Israel by the influences of the Spirit, all temporised, only differing from each other in this, that some succumbed earlier, and others later; some were foremost champions and leaders in the impiety, and others joined the second rank of the battle, being overcome by fear, or by interest, or by flattery, or, what was the most excusable, by their own ignorance." *Orat.* xxi. 24.

19. A.D. 363. About this time, St. Jerome says: "Nearly all the churches in the whole world, under the pretence of peace and the emperor, are polluted with the communion of the Arians." *Chron.* Of the same date, that is, upon the council of Ariminum, are his famous words, "Ingemuit totus orbis et se esse Arianum miratus est."* *In Lucif.* <19.> [That is,] the Catholics of Christendom were surprised indeed to find that [their rulers][2] had made Arians of them.

[20. A.D. 364. And St. Hilary: "Up to this date, the only cause why Christ's people is not murdered by the priests of Anti-christ, with this deceit of impiety, is, that they take the words which the heretics use, to denote the faith which they themselves hold. Sanctiores aures plebis quàm corda sunt sacerdotum."** *In Aux.* 6.]

21. St. Hilary speaks of the series of ecclesiastical councils of that time in the following well-known passage: ["It is most dangerous to us, and it is lamentable, that there are at present as many creeds as there are sentiments, and as many doctrines among us as dispositions, while we write creeds and explain them according to our fancy.] Since the Nicene council, we have done nothing but write the creed. While we fight about words, inquire about novelties, take advantage of ambiguities, criticise authors, fight on party questions, have difficulties in agreeing, and prepare to anathematise each other, there is scarce a

---

[1] [urged] were active in causing
* "The whole world groaned, and marveled to see itself Arian."
[2] [their rulers] the Council
** "There is more holiness in the ears of the people than in the hearts of the priests."

man who belongs to Christ. Take, for instance, last year's creed, what alteration is there not in it already? First, we have the creed, which bids us not to use the Nicene 'consubstantial;' then comes another, which decrees and preaches it; next, the third, excuses the word 'substance,' as adopted by the fathers in their simplicity; lastly, the fourth, <which> instead of excusing, condemns. We [impose][1] creeds by the year or by the month, we change our [minds about our own imposition of them, then][2] we prohibit our changes, [then] we anathematise our prohibitions. Thus, we either condemn others in our own persons, or ourselves in the instance of others, and while we bite and devour one another, are like to be consumed one of another." <Ad Const. ii. 4, 5.>

22. A.D. 382. St. Gregory writes: "If I must speak the truth, I feel disposed to shun every conference of Bishops; for never saw I synod brought to a happy issue, and remedying, and not rather aggravating, existing evils. For rivalry and ambition are stronger than reason,—do not think me extravagant for saying so,—and a mediator is more likely to incur some imputation himself than to clear up the imputations which others lie under." *Ep.* 129. [It must ever be kept in mind that a passage like this only relates, and is here quoted as only relating, to that miserable time of which it is spoken. Nothing more can be argued from it than that the "Ecclesia docens" is not at every time the active instrument of the Church's infallibility.]

II. Now we come secondly to the proofs of the fidelity of the laity, and the effectiveness of that fidelity, during that domination of imperial heresy to which the foregoing passages have related. I have abridged the extracts which follow, but not, I hope, to the injury of their sense.

1. ALEXANDRIA. "We suppose," says Athanasius, "you are not ignorant what outrages they (the Arian Bishops) committed at Alexandria, for they are reported everywhere. They attacked the *holy virgins and brethren* with naked swords; they beat with scourges their persons, esteemed honourable in God's sight, so that their feet were lamed by the stripes, whose souls were whole and sound in purity and all good works." Athan. *Op. c. Arian.* 15, [Oxf: tr.]

"Accordingly Constantius writes letters, and commences *a persecution against all.* Gathering together a multitude of herdsmen and shepherds, and dissolute youths belonging to the town, armed with swords and clubs, they attacked in a body *the Church* of Quirinus: and *some*

---

[1] [impose] determine
[2] [minds about . . . of them, then] own determinations,

they slew, *some* they trampled under foot, *others* they beat with stripes and cast into prison or banished. They hauled away many *women* also, and dragged them openly into the court, and insulted them, dragging them by the hair. *Some* they proscribed; from *some* they took away their bread, for no other reason but that they might be induced to join the Arians, and receive Gregory (the Arian Bishop), who had been sent by the Emperor." Athan. *Hist. Arian.* §10.

"On the week that succeeded the holy Pentecost, when the *people*, after their fast, had gone out to the cemetery to pray, because that *all* refused communion with George (the Arian Bishop), the commander, Sebastian, straightway with a multitude of soldiers proceeded to *attack the people*, though it was the Lord's day; and finding a few praying, (for the greater part had already retired on account of the lateness of the hour,) having lighted a pile, he placed certain *virgins* near the fire, and endeavoured to force them to say that they were of the Arian faith. And having seized on *forty men*, he cut some fresh twigs of the palm-tree, with the thorns upon them, and scourged them on the back so severely that some of them were for a long time under medical treatment, on account of the thorns which had entered their flesh, and others, unable to bear up under their sufferings, died. All those whom they had taken, both the men and the virgins, they sent away into banishment to the great oasis. Moreover, they immediately banished out of Egypt and Libya the following Bishops (sixteen), and the presbyters, Hierax and Dioscorus: some of them died on the way, others in the place of their banishment. They caused also more than thirty Bishops to take to flight." *Apol. de Fug.* 7.

2. EGYPT. "The Emperor Valens having issued an edict commanding that the orthodox should be expelled both from Alexandria and the rest of Egypt, *depopulation and ruin to an immense extent immediately followed; some* were dragged before the tribunals, others cast into prison, and many tortured in various ways; all sorts of punishment being inflicted upon persons who aimed only at peace and quiet." Socr. *Hist.* iv. 24, [Bohn.]

3. THE MONKS OF EGYPT. "*Antony left the solitude* of the desert to go about every part of the city (Alexandria), warning the inhabitants that the Arians were opposing the truth, and that the doctrines of the Apostles were preached only by Athanasius." Theod. *Hist.* iv. 27, [Bohn.]

"Lucius, the Arian, with a considerable body of troops, proceeded to the *monasteries* of Egypt, where he in person assailed the assemblage of holy men with greater fury than the ruthless soldiery. When these excellent persons remained unmoved by all the violence, in despair he advised the military chief to send the fathers of the monks, the Egyptian Macarius and his namesake of Alexandria, into exile." Socr. iv. 24.

OF CONSTANTINOPLE. "*Isaac*, on seeing the emperor depart at the head of his army, exclaimed, 'You who have declared war against God cannot gain His aid. Cease from fighting against Him, and He will terminate the war. Restore the pastors to their flocks, and then you will obtain a bloodless victory." [*Ibid*[1] 34.]

OF SYRIA, &c. "That these heretical doctrines (Apollinarian and Eunomian) did not finally become predominant is *mainly to be attributed to the zeal of the monks* of this period; for *all the monks* of Syria, Cappadocia, and the neighbouring provinces *were sincerely attached to the Nicene faith*. The same fate awaited them which had been experienced by the Arians; for they incurred the full weight of the popular odium and aversion, when it was observed that their sentiments were regarded with suspicion, by the monks." Sozom. [*Hist.* vii.][2] 27, [Bohn.]

OF CAPPADOCIA. "Gregory, the father of Gregory Theologus, otherwise a most excellent man and a zealous defender of the true and Catholic religion, not being on his guard against the artifices of the Arians, such was his simplicity, received with kindness certain men who were contaminated with the poison, and subscribed an impious proposition of theirs. This moved the monks to such indignation, that they *withdrew forthwith from his communion*, and took with them, after their example, *a considerable part of his flock*." Ed. Bened. *Monit. in Greg. Naz.* Orat. 6.

[4. SYRIA. "Syria and the neighbouring provinces were plunged into confusion and disorder, for the Arians were very numerous in these parts, and had possession of the churches. The members of the Catholic Church *were not*, however, *few in numbers*. It was through their instrumentality that the Church of Antioch was preserved from the encroachments of the Arians, and enabled to resist the power of Valens. Indeed, it appears that all the Churches which were governed by men who were firmly attached to the faith did not deviate from the form of doctrine which they had originally embraced." Sozom. vi. 21]

5. ANTIOCH. "Whereas he (the Bishop Leontius) took part in the blasphemy of Arius, he made a point of concealing this disease, partly *for fear of the multitude*, partly for the menaces of Constantius; so

---

[1] [ibid. 34] Theod. iv.
[2] [Hist. vii] vi.

those who followed the apostolical dogmas gained from him neither patronage nor ordination, but those who held Arianism were allowed the fullest liberty of speech, and were placed in the ranks of the sacred ministry. But Flavian and Diodorus, who had embraced the ascetical life, and maintained the apostolical dogmas, *openly withstood* Leontius's machinations against religious doctrine. They threatened that they would retire from the communion of his Church, and would go to the West, and reveal his intrigues. Though they were not as yet in the sacred ministry, but were *in the ranks of the laity*, night and day they used to excite all the people to zeal for religion. They were the first to divide the singers into two choirs, and to teach them to sing [alternately][1] the strains of David. They too, assembling the devout at the shrines of the martyrs, passed the whole night there in hymns to God. These things Leontius seeing, did not think it safe to hinder them, for he saw that *the multitude was especially well affected* towards those excellent persons. Nothing, however, could persuade Leontius to correct his wickedness. It follows, that among the clergy were many who were infected with the heresy: but *the mass of the people were champions of orthodoxy*." Theodor. *Hist.* ii. 24.

6. EDESSA. "There is in that city a magnificent church, dedicated to St. Thomas the Apostle, wherein, on account of the sanctity of the place, religious assemblies are continually held. The Emperor Valens wished to inspect this edifice; when, having learned that *all who usually congregated there were opposed to the heresy* which he favoured, he is said to have struck the prefect with his own hand, because he had neglected to expel them thence. The prefect, to prevent the slaughter of *so great a number* of persons, privately warned them against resorting thither. But his admonitions and menaces were alike unheeded; for on the following day *they all crowded to the church*. When the prefect was going towards it with a large military force, a poor woman, leading her own little child by the hand, hurried hastily by on her way to the church, breaking through the ranks of the soldiery. The prefect, irritated at this, ordered her to be brought to him, and thus addressed her: 'Wretched woman, whither are you running in so disorderly a manner?' She replied, 'To the same place that others are hastening.' 'Have you not heard,' said he, 'that the prefect is about to put to death all that shall be found there?' 'Yes,' said the woman, 'and therefore I hasten, that I may be found there.' 'And whither are you dragging that little child?' said the prefect. The woman answered, *'That he also may*

[1] [alternately] in alternate parts

*be vouchsafed the honour of martyrdom.'* The prefect went back and informed the emperor that *all were ready to die in behalf of their own faith*; and added that it would be preposterous to destroy so many persons at one time, and thus succeeded in restraining the emperor's wrath." Socr. iv. 18. "Thus was the Christian faith confessed by the *whole city* of Edessa." Sozom. vi. 18.

7. SAMOSATA. "The Arians, having deprived this exemplary flock of their shepherd, elected in his place an individual with whom *none of the inhabitants of the city*, whether poor or rich, servants or mechanics, husbandmen or gardeners, men or women, young or old, would hold communion. *He was left quite alone*; no one even calling to see him, or exchanging a word with him. It is, however, said that his disposition was extremely gentle; and this is proved by what I am about to relate. One day, when he went to bathe in the public baths, the attendants closed the doors; but he ordered the doors to be thrown open, that the people might be admitted to bathe with himself. Perceiving that they remained in a standing posture before him, imagining that great deference towards himself was the cause of this conduct, he arose and left the bath. *These people believed that the water had been contaminated by his heresy*, and ordered it to be let out and fresh water to be supplied. When he heard of this circumstance, he left the city, thinking that he ought no longer to remain in a place *where he was the object of public aversion and hatred*. Upon this retirement of Eunomius, Lucius was elected as his successor by the Arians. Some young persons were amusing themselves with playing at ball in the marketplace; Lucius was passing by at the time, and the ball happened to fall beneath the feet of the ass on which he was mounted. *The youths uttered loud exclamations, believing that the ball was contaminated.* They lighted a fire, and hurled the ball through it, believing that by this process the ball would be purified. Although this was only a childish deed, and although it exhibits the remains of ancient superstition, yet it is *sufficient to show the odium which the Arian faction had incurred in this city.* Lucius was far from imitating the mildness of Eunomius, and he persuaded the heads of government to exile most of the clergy." Theodor. iv. 15.

8. OSRHOENE. "Arianism met with similar opposition at the same period in Osrhoëne and Cappadocia. Basil, Bishop of Caesarea, and Gregory, Bishop of Nazianzus, were held in high admiration and esteem *throughout these regions.*" Sozom. vi. 21.

9. CAPPADOCIA. "Valens, in passing through Cappadocia, did all in his power to injure the orthodox, and to deliver up the churches to

the Arians. He thought to accomplish his designs more easily on account of a dispute which was then pending between Basil and Eusebius, who governed the Church of Caesarea. This dissension had been the cause of Basil's departing to Pontus. *The people, and some of the most powerful and wisest men of the city*, began to regard Eusebius with suspicion, and to meditate a secession from his communion. The emperor and the Arian Bishops regarded the absence of Basil, and the hatred of the people towards Eusebius, as circumstances that would tend greatly to the success of their designs. *But their expectations were utterly frustrated.* On the first intelligence of the intention of the emperor to pass through Cappadocia, Basil returned to Caesarea, where he effected a reconciliation with Eusebius. The projects of Valens were thus defeated, and he returned with his Bishops." Sozom. vi. 15.

10. PONTUS. "It is said that when Eulalius, Bishop of Amasia in Pontus, returned from exile, he found that his Church had passed into the hands of an Arian, and that *scarcely fifty inhabitants of the city* had submitted to the control of their new Bishop." Sozom. vii. 2.

11. ARMENIA. "That company of Arians, who came with Eustathius to Nicopolis, had promised that they would bring over this city to compliance with the commands of the imperial vicar. This city had great ecclesiastical importance, both because it was the metropolis of Armenia, and because it had been ennobled by the blood of martyrs, and governed hitherto by Bishops of great reputation, and thus, as Basil calls it, was the nurse of religion and the metropolis of sound doctrine. Fronto, one of the city presbyters, who had hitherto shown himself as a champion of the truth, through ambition gave himself up to the enemies of Christ, and purchased the bishopric of the Arians at the price of renouncing the Catholic faith. This wicked proceeding of Eustathius and the Arians brought a new glory instead of evil to the Nicopolitans, since it gave them an opportunity of defending the faith. Fronto, indeed, the Arians consecrated, *but there was a remarkable unanimity of clergy and people in rejecting him.* Scarcely one or two clerks sided with him; on the contrary, he *became the execration of all Armenia.*" *Vita S. Basil.*, Bened. pp. clvii, clviii.

12. NICOMEDIA. "Eighty pious clergy proceeded to Nicomedia, and there presented to the emperor a supplicatory petition complaining of the ill-usage to which they had been subjected. Valens, dissembling his displeasure in their presence, gave Modestus, the prefect, a secret order to apprehend these persons and put them to death. The prefect, *fearing that he should excite the populace to a seditious movement*

against himself, if he attempted the public execution of so many, pretended to send them away into exile," &c. Socr. iv. 16.

13. [ASIA MINOR.][1] St. Basil says, about the year 372: "Religious people keep silence, but every blaspheming tongue is let loose. Sacred things are profaned; *those of the laity* who are sound in faith *avoid the places of worship* as schools of impiety, and raise their hands in solitude, with groans and tears, to the Lord in heaven." *Ep.* 92. Four years after he writes: "Matters have come to this pass; *the people have left their houses of prayer*, and assemble in deserts: a pitiable sight; *women and children, old men, and [others][2] infirm*, wretchedly faring in the open air, amid the most profuse rains and snow-storms, and winds, and frost<s> of winter; and again in summer under a scorching sun. To this they submit, because they *will have no part in the wicked Arian leaven.*" *Ep.* 242. Again: "Only one offence is now vigorously punished, an accurate observance of our fathers' traditions. For this cause the pious are driven from their countries, and transported into deserts. The *people are in lamentation*, in continual tears at home and abroad. There is a cry in the city, a cry in the country, in the roads, in the deserts. Joy and spiritual cheerfulness are no more; our feasts are turned into mourning; our houses of prayer are shut up, our altars deprived of the spiritual worship." *Ep.* 243.

<PAPHLAGONIA, &c. "I thought," says Julian in one of his Epistles, "that the leaders of the Galilaeans would feel more grateful to me than to my predecessor. For in his time they were in great numbers turned out of their homes, and persecuted, and imprisoned; moreover, multitudes of so-called heretics" (the Novatians who were with the Catholics against the Arians) "were slaughtered, so that in Samosata, Paphlagonia, Bithynia, and Galatia, and many other nations, villages were utterly sacked and destroyed." *Ep.* 52.>

14. SCYTHIA. "There are in this country a great number of cities, of towns, and of fortresses. According to an ancient custom which still prevails, all the churches of the whole country are under the sway of one Bishop. Valens (the emperor) repaired to the church, and strove to gain over the Bishop to the heresy of Arius; but this latter manfully opposed his arguments, and, after a courageous defence of the Nicene doctrines, quitted the emperor, and proceeded to another church, *whither he was followed by the people. Valens was extremely offended at being left alone* in a church with his attendants, and, in resentment,

---

[1] [ASIA MINOR] CAPPADOCIA
[2] [others] men otherwise

condemned Vetranio (the Bishop) to banishment. Not long after, however, he recalled him, because, I believe, *he apprehended an insurrection.*" Sozom. vi. 21.

15. CONSTANTINOPLE. "Those who acknowledged the doctrine of consubstantiality were not only expelled from the churches, but also from the cities. But although expulsion at first satisfied them (the Arians), they soon proceeded to the worse extremity of inducing compulsory communion with them, caring little for such a desecration of the churches. They resorted to all kinds of scourgings, a variety of tortures, and confiscation of property. Many were punished with exile, some died under the torture, and others were put to death while being driven from their country. *These atrocities were exercised throughout all the eastern cities,* but especially at Constantinople." Socr. ii. 27.

[The following passage is quoted for the substantial fact which it contains, viz. the testimony of popular tradition to the Catholic doctrine: "At this period a union was nearly effected between the Novatian and Catholic Churches; for, as they both *held the same sentiments concerning the Divinity,* and were subjected to a common persecution, the members of both Churches assembled and prayed together. The Catholics then possessed no houses of prayer, for the Arians had wrested them from them." Sozom. iv 20.]

16. ILLYRIA. "The parents of Theodosius were Christians, and were attached to the Nicene doctrine, hence he took pleasure in the ministration of Ascholius (Bishop of Thessalonica). He also rejoiced at finding that the *Arian heresy had not been received in Illyria.*" Sozom. vii. 4.

17. NEIGHBOURHOOD OF MACEDONIA. "Theodosius inquired concerning the religious sentiments which were prevalent in the other provinces, and ascertained that, as far as Macedonia, *one form of belief was universally predominant,*" &c. Ibid.

18. ROME. "With respect to doctrine no dissension arose either at Rome or in any other of the Western Churches. *The people unanimously adhered to the form of belief established at Nicaea.*" Sozom. vi. 23. ["Not long after, Liberius (the Pope) was recalled and reinstated in his see; for the people of Rome, *having raised a sedition, and expelled* Felix (whom the Arian party had intruded) from their Church, Constantius deemed it *inexpedient to provoke the popular fury.*" Socr. ii. 37.]

"Liberius, returning to Rome, found the *mind of the mass of men alienated from him,* because he had so shamefully yielded to Constantius. And thus it came to pass, that those persons who had hitherto kept aloof from Felix (the rival Pope), and had avoided his communion in favour of Liberius, on hearing what had happened, *left him for Felix*, who raised the Catholic standard. [Among others, Damasus (afterwards Pope) took the side of Felix. Such had been, even from the times of the Apostles, *the love of Catholic discipline in the Roman people*."] Baron. ann. 357. <56> He tells us besides <57>, that the people would not even go to the public baths, lest they should bathe with the party of Liberius.

19. MILAN. "At the council of Milan, Eusebius of Vercellae, when it was proposed to draw up a declaration against Athanasius, said that the council ought first to be sure of the faith of the Bishops attending it, for he had found out that some of them were polluted with heresy. Accordingly he brought before the Fathers the Nicene creed, and said he was willing to comply with all their demands, after they had sub- scribed that confession. Dionysius, Bishop of Milan, at once took up the paper and began to write his assent; but Valens (the Arian) violently pulled pen and paper out of his hands, crying out that such a course of proceeding was impossible. Whereupon, after much tumult, *the question came before the people, and great was the distress of all of them*; the faith of the Church was [impugned][1] by the Bishops. *They then, dreading the judgment of the people*, transfer their meeting from the church to the imperial palace." Hilar. *ad Const.* i. <8>.

"As the feast of Easter approached, the empress sent to St. Ambrose to ask a church of him, where the Arians who attended her might meet together. He replied, that a Bishop could not give up the temple of God. The pretorian prefect came into the church, where St. Ambrose was, *attended by the people*, and endeavoured to persuade him to yield up at least the Portian Basilica. *The people were clamorous against the proposal*;" and the prefect retired to report how matters stood to the emperor. The Sunday following, St. Ambrose was explaining the creed, when he was informed that the officers were hanging up the imperial hangings in the Portian Basilica, and that upon this news the people were repairing thither. While he was offering up the holy sacrifice, a second message came that the *people had seized an Arian priest* as he was passing through the street. He despatched a number of his clergy to the spot to *rescue the Arian from his danger*. The court looked on this resistance of the people as seditious, and immediately laid considerable fines upon *the whole body of the tradesmen* of the city. Several were thrown into prison. In three days' time these tradesmen

---

[1] [impugned] attacked

were fined two hundred pounds weight of gold, and they said *that they were ready to give as much again, on condition that they might retain their faith*. The prisons were filled with tradesmen: *all the officers of the household*, secretaries, agents of the emperor, and dependent officers who served under various counts, were kept within doors, and were forbidden to appear in public under pretence that they should bear no part in [the] sedition. *Men of higher rank* were menaced with severe consequences, unless the Basilica were surrendered. . . .

"Next morning the Basilica was surrounded by soldiers; but it was reported, that *these soldiers had sent to the emperor to tell him* that if he wished to come abroad he might, and that they would attend him, if he was going to the assembly of the Catholics; otherwise, that they *would go to that which would be held by St. Ambrose*. Indeed, the *soldiers were all Catholics*, as well as the citizens of Milan; there were no heretics there, except a few officers of the emperor and some Goths. . . .

"St. Ambrose was continuing his discourse when he was told that the emperor had withdrawn the soldiers from the Basilica, and that he had restored to the tradesmen the fines which he had exacted from them. *This news gave joy to the people*, who expressed their delight with applauses and thanksgivings; *the soldiers themselves were eager to bring the news*, throwing themselves on the altars, and kissing them in token of peace." Fleury's *Hist.* xviii. 41, 42, Oxf. trans.

[20. THE SOLDIERY. Soldiers having been mentioned in the foregoing extract, I add the following passage. "Terentius, a general distinguished by his valour and by his piety, was able, on his return from Armenia, to erect trophies of victory. Valens promised to give him everything that he might desire. But he asked not for gold or silver, for lands, power, of honours; *he requested that a church might be given to those who preached the apostolical doctrines*." Theodor. iv. 32.

"Valens sent Trajan, the general, against the barbarians. Trajan was defeated, and, on his return, the emperor reproached him severely, and accused him of weakness and cowardice. But Trajan replied with great boldness, 'It is not I, O emperor, who have been defeated; for you, *by fighting against God, have thrown the barbarians upon His protection*. Do you not know who those are whom you have driven from the churches, and who are those to whom you have given them up?' Arintheus and Victor, the other commanders, *accorded in what he had said*, and brought the emperor to reflect on the truth of their remonstrances." Ibid. 33.]

## 21. CHRISTENDOM GENERALLY.

St. Hilary to Constantius: "Not only in words, but in tears, we beseech you to save the Catholic Churches from any longer continuance of these most grievous injuries, and of their present intolerable persecutions and insults, which moreover they are enduring, which is monstrous, from our brethren. Surely your clemency should listen to the *voice of those who cry out so loudly*, 'I am a Catholic, I have no wish to be a heretic.' It should seem equitable to your sanctity, most glorious Augustus, that they who fear the Lord God and His judgment should not be polluted and contaminated with execrable blasphemies, but *should have liberty to follow those Bishops and prelates* who observe inviolate the laws of charity, and who desire a perpetual and sincere peace. It is impossible, it is unreasonable, to mix true and false, to confuse light and darkness, and bring into a union, of whatever kind, night and day. *Give permission to the populations to hear the teaching of the pastors whom they have wished*, whom they fixed on, whom they have chosen, to attend their celebration of the divine mysteries, to offer prayers through them for your safety and prosperity." *ad Const.* i. <i.2.>

Now I know quite well what will be said to so elaborate a collection of instances as I have been making. The "lector benevolus" will quote against me the words of Cicero, "Utitur in re non dubiâ testibus non necessariis."* This is sure to befall a man when he directs the attention of a friend to any truth which hitherto he has thought little of. At first, he seems to be hazarding a paradox, and at length to be committing a truism. The hearer is first of all startled, and then disappointed; he ends by asking, "Is this all?" It is a curious phenomenon in the philosophy of the human mind, that we often do not know whether we hold a point or not, though we hold it; but when our attention is once drawn to it, then forthwith we find it so much part of ourselves, that we cannot recollect when we began to hold it, and we conclude (with truth), and we declare, that it has always been our belief. Now it strikes me as worth noticing, that, though Father Perrone is so clear upon the point of doctrine which I have been urging in 1847, yet in 1842, which is the date of my own copy of his *Praelectiones*, he has not given the *consensus fidelium* any distinct place in his *Loci Theologici*, though he has even given "heretici" a place there. Among the *Media Traditionis*, he enumerates the *magisterium* of the Church, the Acts of the Martyrs, the Liturgy, usages and rites of worship, the

---

* "He invokes, in a matter that is not in doubt, witnesses for whom there is no need."

Fathers, heretics, Church history; but not a word, that I can find, directly and separately, about the *sensus fidelium*. This is the more remarkable, because, speaking of the *Acta Martyrum*, he gives a reason for the force of the testimony of the martyrs which belongs quite as fully to the faithful generally; viz. that, as not being theologians, they can only repeat that objective truth, which, on the other hand, Fathers and theologians do but present subjectively, and thereby coloured with their own mental peculiarities. "We learn from them," he says, "what was the traditionary doctrine in both domestic and public assemblies of the Church, without any admixture of private and (so to say) subjective explanation, such as at times creates a difficulty in ascertaining the real meaning of the Fathers; and so much the more, because many of them were either women or ordinary and untaught laymen, who brought out and avowed just what they believed in a straightforward inartificial way." May we not conjecture that the argument from the Consent of the Faithful was but dimly written among the *Loci* on the tablets of his intellect, till the necessities, or rather the requirements, of the contemplated definition of the Immaculate Conception brought the argument before him with great force? Yet who will therefore for an instant suppose that he did not always hold it? Perhaps I have overlooked some passage of his treatises, and am in consequence inter-preting his course of thought wrongly; but, at any rate, what I seem to see in him, is what actually does occur from time to time in myself and others. A man holds an opinion or a truth, yet without holding it with a simple consciousness and a direct recognition; and thus, though he had never denied, he has never gone so far as to profess it.

As to the particular doctrine to which I have here been directing my view, and the passage in history by which I have been illustrating it, I am not supposing that such times as the Arian will ever come again. As to the present, certainly, if there ever was an age which might dispense with the testimony of the faithful, and leave the maintenance of the truth to the pastors of the Church, it is the age in which we live. Never was the Episcopate of Christendom so devoted to the Holy See, so religious, so earnest in the discharge of its special duties, so little disposed to innovate, so superior to the temptation of theological sophistry. And perhaps this is the reason why the "consensus fidelium" has, in the minds of many, fallen into the background. Yet each constit-uent portion of the Church has its proper functions, and no portion can safely be neglected. Though the laity be but the reflection or echo of the clergy in matters of faith, yet there is something in the "pastorum et fidelium *conspiratio*," which is not in the pastors alone. The history of the definition of the Immaculate Conception shows us this; and it will be one among the blessings which the Holy Mother, who is the subject of it, will gain for us, in repayment of the definition, that by that very definition we are all reminded of the part which the laity have had in the preliminaries of its promulgation. Pope Pius has given us a pattern, in his manner of defining, of the duty of considering the sentiments of the laity upon a point of tradition, in spite of whatever fullness of evidence the Bishops had already thrown upon it.

In most cases when a definition is contemplated, the laity will have a testimony to give; but if ever there be an instance when they ought to be consulted, it is in the case of doctrines which bear directly upon devotional sentiments. Such is the Immaculate Conception, of which the *Rambler* was speaking in the sentence which has occasioned these remarks. The faithful people have ever a special function in regard to those doctrinal truths which relate to the Objects of worship. Hence it is, that, while the Councils of the fourth century were traitors to our Lord's divinity, the laity vehemently protested against its impugners. Hence it is, that, in a later age, when the learned Benedictines of Germany and France were perplexed in their enunciation of the doctrine of the Real Presence, Paschasius was supported by the faithful in his maintenance of it. The saints, again, are the object of a religious *cultus*; and therefore it was the faithful, again, who urged on the Holy See, in the time of John XXII., to declare their beatitude in heaven, though so many Fathers spoke variously. And the Blessed Virgin is preëminently an object of devotion; and therefore it is, I repeat, that though Bishops had already spoken in favour of her absolute sinlessness, the Pope was not content without knowing the feelings of the faithful.

Father Dalgairns gives us another case in point; and with his words I conclude: "While devotion in the shape of a dogma issues from the high places of the Church, in the shape of devotion . . . it starts from below. . . . Place yourselves, in imagination, in a vast city of the East in the fifth century. Ephesus, the capital of Asia Minor, is all in commotion; for a council is to be held there, and Bishops are flocking in from all parts of the world. There is anxiety painted on every face; so that you may easily see that the question is one of general interest. . . . Ask the very children in the streets what is the matter; they will tell you that wicked men are coming to make out that their own mother is not the Mother of God. And so, during a livelong day of June, they crowd around the gates of the old cathedral-church of St. Mary, and watch with anxious faces each Bishop as he goes in. Well might they be anxious; for it is well known that Nestorius has won the court over to his side. It was only the other day that he entered the town, with banners displayed and trumpets sounding, surrounded by the glittering files of the emperor's body-guard, with Count Candidianus, their general and his own partisan, at their head. Besides which, it is known for certain, that at least eighty-four Bishops are ready to vote with him; and who knows how many more? He is himself the patriarch of Constantinople, the rival of Rome, the imperial city of the East; and then John of Antioch is hourly expected with his quota of votes; and he, the patriarch of the see next in influence to that of Nestorius, is, if not a heretic, at least of that wretched party which, in ecclesiastical disputes, ever hovers between the two camps of the devil and of God. The day wears on, and still nothing issues from the church; it proves, at least, that there is a difference of opinion; and as the shades of evening close around them, the weary watchers grow more anxious still. At length the great gates of the Basilica are thrown open; and oh, what a cry of joy bursts from the assembled crowd, as it is announced to them that Mary has been proclaimed to be, what every one with a Catholic heart knew that she was before, the Mother of God! . . . Men, women, and children, the noble and the low-born, the stately matron and the modest maiden, all crowd round the Bishops with acclamations. They will not leave them; they accompany them to their homes with a long procession of lighted torches; they burn incense before them, after the eastern fashion, to do them honour. There was but little sleep in Ephesus that night; for very joy they remained awake; the whole town was one blaze of light, for each window was illuminated."[1]

My own drift is somewhat different from that which has dictated this glowing description; but the substance of the argument of each of us is one and the same. I think certainly that the *Ecclesia docens* is more happy when she has such enthusiastic partisans about her as are here represented, than when she cuts off the faithful from the study of her divine doctrines and the sympathy of her divine contemplations, and requires from them a *fides implicita* in her word, which in the educated classes will terminate in indifference, and in the poorer in superstition.

O.

[1] Sacred Heart

# IV

# A LETTER ADDRESSED TO
# HIS GRACE THE DUKE OF NORFOLK
# ON OCCASION OF MR. GLADSTONE'S
# RECENT EXPOSTULATION

*(December 27, 1874)*

# CATHOLIC LOYALTIES:
# TO COUNTRY, TO POPE, TO
# CONSCIENCE

In the summer of 1870 the first Vatican Council defined papal infallibility as a Catholic dogma. Throughout winter and spring of that year Newman had expressed confident hope that the Council would not define that doctrine, as well as exasperation at the pressure being exerted to obtain the definition by the Ultramontanes—Catholics dedicated to intensifying central control of the Church directly by the Vatican. It was not that Newman disbelieved in papal infallibility; indeed he considered it a general and tranquil belief of Roman Catholics. But he was painfully aware that among Anglicans such a dogma would be misunderstood and resented. He was also persuaded that the motives of Catholics who clamored for the definition were of a much more political than devotional or theological nature. And he knew that the historical scholarship Catholics could bring forward to vindicate the definition was in a most unsatisfactory state. Ironically, Newman's *Essay on Development* was being used, by persons who had hitherto shown little enthusiasm for it, as a rationale for accelerating this latest 'development.' Newman argued that the consistent finding of his own research was to the effect that dogmatic definitions were always emergency measures in the life of the Church. They typically emerged from great controversies that threatened to divide believers. They were remedial measures, a kind of surgery to excise malignant errors that would otherwise spread through the ecclesiastical body. Concerning papal infallibility no such controversy raged among Catholics, and no pernicious errors about it were infecting the Church. To define the doctrine would, within the Church, merely signal the ascendancy and encourage the arrogance of the Ultramontanes, while to outsiders it would confirm prevailing diffidence about a community obliged to suspend all critical thinking at the bidding of a supposedly omniscient autocrat. To persons unfamiliar with Catholic theological distinctions, a declaration that Catholics must deem their pope infallible had an ominously fanatical ring. Nor was it reassuring to be told the infallibility covered all matters of "faith and morals," a formula seemingly able to encompass every kind of social issue.

Newman was acutely aware that after a definition of this kind, Catholics would have a lot of explaining to do. And he joylessly anticipated that in England part of that burden of explanation would devolve upon him. He would be conscripted to defend a dogmatic definition that he had declared publicly and in the strongest terms to be unnecessary and inopportune. For four years he was able to avoid that task, but in 1874 circumstances arose that both impelled him to undertake it, and enabled him to do so in terms he found congenial. The occasion was a pamphlet on *The Vatican Decrees in Their Bearing on Civil Allegiance,* by no less an author than the Liberal Prime Minister of England, William Gladstone. Newman, whose controversial writings are so often two-edged swords, saw in this work an opportunity to defend the Catholic position, but in such a way as to excoriate the pretensions of the Ultramontanes. He framed his answer as a letter in response to the leading Catholic peer, an alumnus of Newman's Oratory School, the Duke of Norfolk.

Gladstone's strongest objection reflected the prevailing view of English non-Catholics, namely that a Catholic population committed to papal infallibility could not be trusted to participate loyally and thoughtfully in the nation's civic life. What the pope said, they were compelled to think, and what the pope bade they were compelled to do; the former, no matter how unreasonable; the latter, no matter how treacherous. In responding to such charges, Newman was able to interpret the doctrine of infallibility as the very circumscribed belief he considered it to be, emphasizing that most secular concerns of everyday life were simply untouched by it. The political opinions of popes, however solemnly enunciated, might be foolish, and their political directives might be pernicious; and if they were, they should be examined critically, refuted candididly, and resisted conscientiously. Popes had as little right to require treason of Catholics as monarchs had to require heresy of them; the Vatican could no more override England's just laws than Parliament could amend the Church's creed.

And yet, Gladstone had anxiously noted, the pope's defined sphere of infallibility was explicitly stated to be not faith only, but faith and morals. What kind of moral responsibility could one expect of a people whose leader's moral judgments were above criticism? In dealing with this objection, Newman appealed to a Catholic tradition that reflected one of his own most cherished convictions, namely that all of morality, as well as all of religion, depended for their legitimacy, and indeed for their very life, on the inviolable sovereignty of conscience. For a pope to contravene conscience would be a supreme irony, for conscience was ultimately the only valid reason for paying any attention to popes. It was the bottom line of morality and religion, and there could be no legitimate moral or religious appeal against it. Even a faulty conscience, if sincere, commanded absolute obedience, for there was no surer standard against which to measure it. If one's conscience and one's pope gave contrary directions, rare and unlikely as that might be, there could be no serious question about which to follow. Any pope who thought otherwise, and acted on such thoughts, would embark on a course of self-destruction.

Newman's *Letter to the Duke* of Norfolk shows his controversialist rapier quite unblunted at the age of 73, and displays his virtuoso talent for obliquely disposing of one adversary while directly attacking another, vindicating the most expansive dogmatic claims ever made for papal authority, in terms that firmly subordinate it to the authority of individual conscience.

Although the letter was addressed to a unique occasion, its 4th chapter, "Divided Allegiance," and its 5th, "Conscience," reproduced in the following pages, remain classic responses to questions that continue to trouble Roman Catholics—and to trouble others about Roman Catholics.

# A Letter Addressed to His Grace the Duke of Norfolk on Occasion of Mr. Gladstone's Recent Expostulation

## Divided Allegiance

. . . One attribute the Church has, and the Pope as head of the Church, whether he be in high estate, as this world goes, or not, whether he has temporal possessions or not, whether he is in honour or dishonour, whether he is at home or driven about, whether those special claims of which I have spoken are allowed or not—and that is Sovereignty. As God has sovereignty, though He may be disobeyed or disowned, so has His Vicar upon earth; and farther than this, since Catholic populations are found everywhere, he ever will be in fact lord of a vast empire; as large in numbers, as far spreading as the British; and all his acts are sure to be such as are in keeping with the position of one who is thus supremely exalted.

I beg not to be interrupted here, as many a reader will interrupt me in his thoughts, for I am using these words, not at random, but as the commencement of a long explanation, and, in a certain sense, limitation, of what I have hitherto been saying concerning the Church's and the Pope's power. To this task the remaining pages, which I have to address to your Grace, will be directed; and I trust that it will turn out, when I come to the end of them, that, by first stating fully what the Pope's claims are, I shall be able most clearly to show what he does not claim.

Now the main point of Mr. Gladstone's Pamphlet is this: that, since the Pope claims infallibility in faith and morals, and since there are no "departments and functions of human life which do not and cannot fall within the domain of morals" (p. 36), and since he claims also "the domain of all that concerns the government and discipline of the Church," and moreover, "claims the power of determining the limits of those domains," and "does not sever them, by any acknowledged or intelligible line from the domains of civil duty and allegiance" (p.

45), therefore Catholics are moral and mental slaves, and "every convert and member of the Pope's Church places his loyalty and civil duty at the mercy of another" (p. 45).

I admit Mr. Gladstone's premises, but I reject his conclusion; and now I am going to show why I reject it.

In doing this, I shall, with him, put aside for the present and at first the Pope's prerogative of infallibility in general enunciations, whether of faith or morals, and confine myself to the consideration of his authority (in respect to which he is not infallible) in matters of conduct, and of our duty of obedience to him. "There is something wider still," he says (than the claim of infallibility), "and that is the claim to an Absolute and entire Obedience" (p. 37). "Little does it matter to me, whether my Superior claims infallibility, so long as he is entitled to demand and exact conformity" (p. 39). He speaks of a third province being opened, "not indeed to the abstract assertion of Infallibility, but to the far more practical and decisive demand of Absolute Obedience" (p. 41), "the Absolute Obedience, at the peril of salvation, of every member of his communion" (p. 42).

Now, I proceed to examine this large, direct, religious, sovereignty of the Pope, both in its relation to his subjects, and to the Civil Power; but first, I beg to be allowed to say just one word on the principle of obedience itself, that is, by way of inquiring whether it is or is not now a religious duty.

Is there then such a duty at all as obedience to ecclesiastical authority now? or is it one of those obsolete ideas, which are swept away, as unsightly cobwebs, by the New Civilization? Scripture says, "Remember them which have the *rule* over you, who have spoken unto you the word of God, whose faith follow." And, "*Obey* them that have the *rule* over you, and *submit yourselves*; for they watch *for your souls*, as they that must give account, that they may do it with joy and not with grief; for that is unprofitable for you." The margin in the Protestant Version reads, "those who are your *guides*"; and the word may also be translated "leaders." Well, as rulers, or guides and leaders, whichever word be right, they are to be *obeyed*. Now Mr. Gladstone dislikes our way of fulfilling this precept, whether as regards our choice of ruler and leader, or our "Absolute Obedience" to him; but he does not give us his own. Is there any liberalistic reading of the Scripture passage? Or are the words only for the benefit of the poor and ignorant, not for the *Schola* (as it may be called) of political and periodical writers, not for individual members of Parliament, not for statesmen and Cabinet ministers, and people of Progress? Which party then is the more "Scriptural," those who recognize and carry out in their conduct texts like these, or those who don't? May not we Catholics claim some mercy from Mr. Gladstone, though we be faulty in the object and the manner of our obedience, since in a lawless day an object and a manner of obedience we have? Can we be blamed if, arguing from those texts which say that ecclesiastical authority comes from above, we obey it in that one form in which alone we find it on earth, in that one person who, of all the notabilities of this nineteenth century into which we have been born, alone claims it of us? The Pope has no rival in his claim upon us; nor is it our doing that his claim has been made and allowed for centuries upon centuries, and that it was he who made the Vatican decrees, and not they him. If we give him up, to whom shall we go? Can we dress up any civil functionary in the vestments of divine authority? Can I, for instance, follow the faith, can I put my soul into the hands, of our gracious Sovereign? or of the Archbishop of Canterbury? or of the Bishop of Lincoln, albeit he is not broad and low, but high? Catholics have "done what they could"—all that any one could: and it should be Mr. Gladstone's business, before telling us that we are slaves, because we obey the Pope, first of all to tear away those texts from the Bible.

With this preliminary remark, I proceed to consider whether the Pope's authority is either a slavery to his subjects, or a menace to the Civil Power; and first, as to his power over his flock.

1. Mr. Gladstone says that "the Pontiff declares to belong to him the *supreme direction* of Catholics in respect to all duty" (p. 37). Supreme direction; true, but "supreme" is not "minute," nor does "direction" mean "supervision" or "management." Take the parallel of human law; the Law is *supreme*, and the Law *directs* our conduct under the manifold circumstances in which we have to act, and may and must be absolutely obeyed; but who therefore says that the Law has the "supreme direction" of us? The State, as well as the Church, has the power at its will of imposing laws upon us, laws bearing on our moral duties, our daily conduct, affecting our actions in various ways, and circumscribing our liberties; yet no one would say that the Law, after all, with all its power in the abstract and its executive vigour in fact, interferes either with our comfort or our conscience. There are numberless laws about property, landed and personal, titles, tenures, trusts, wills, covenants, contracts, partnerships, money transactions, life-insurances, taxes, trade, navigation, education, sanitary measures, trespasses, nuisances, all in addition to the criminal law. Law, to apply

Mr. Gladstone's words, "is the shadow that cleaves to us, go where we will." Moreover, it varies year after year, and refuses to give any pledge of fixedness or finality. Nor can any one tell what restraint is to come next, perhaps painful personally to himself. Nor are its enactments easy of interpretation; for actual cases, with the opinions and speeches of counsel, and the decisions of judges, must prepare the raw material, as it proceeds from the Legislature, before it can be rightly understood; so that "the glorious uncertainty of the Law" has become a proverb. And, after all, no one is sure of escaping its penalties without the assistance of lawyers, and that in such private and personal matters that the lawyers are, as by an imperative duty, bound to a secrecy which even courts of justice respect. And then, besides the Statute Law, there is the common and traditional; and, below this, usage. Is not all this enough to try the temper of a free-born Englishman, and to make him cry out with Mr. Gladstone, "Three fourths of my life are handed over to the Law; I care not to ask if there be dregs or tatters of human life, such as can escape from the description and boundary of Parliamentary tyranny"? Yet, though we may dislike it, though we may at times suffer from it ever so much, who does not see that the thraldom and irksomeness is nothing compared with the great blessings which the Constitution and Legislature secure to us?

Such is the jurisdiction which the Law exercises over us. What rule does the Pope claim which can be compared to its strong and its long arm? What interference with our liberty of judging and acting in our daily work, in our course of life, comes to us from him? Really, at first sight, I have not known where to look for instances of his actual interposition in our private affairs, for it is our routine of personal duties about which I am now speaking. Let us see how we stand in this matter.

We are guided in our ordinary duties by the books of moral theology, which are drawn up by theologians of authority and experience, as an instruction for our Confessors. These books are based on the three Christian foundations of Faith, Hope, and Charity, on the Ten Commandments, and on the six Precepts of the Church, which relate to the observance of Sunday, of fast days, of confession and communion, and, in one shape or other, to paying tithes. A great number of possible cases are noted under these heads, and in difficult questions a variety of opinions are given, with plain directions, when it is that private Catholics are at liberty to choose for themselves whatever answer they like best, and when they are bound to follow some one of them in particular. Reducible as these directions in detail are to the few and simple heads which I have mentioned, they are little more than reflexions and memoranda of our moral sense, unlike the positive enactments of the Legislature; and, on the whole, present to us no difficulty—though now and then some critical question may arise, and some answer may be given (just as by the private conscience itself) which it is difficult to us or painful to accept. And again, cases may occur now and then when our private judgment differs from what is set down in theological works, but even then it does not follow at once that our private judgment must give way, for those books are no utterance of Papal authority.

And this is the point to which I am coming. So little does the Pope come into this whole system of moral theology by which (as by our conscience) our lives are regulated, that the weight of his hand upon us, as private men, is absolutely unappreciable. I have had a difficulty where to find a measure or gauge of his interposition. At length I have looked through Busenbaum's *Medulla*, to ascertain what light such a book would throw upon the question. It is a book of casuistry for the use of Confessors, running to 700 pages, and is a large repository of answers made by various theologians on points of conscience, and generally of duty. It was first published in 1645—my own edition is of 1844—and in this latter are marked those propositions, bearing on subjects treated in it, which have been condemned by Popes in the intermediate 200 years. On turning over the pages I find they are in all between fifty and sixty. This list includes matters sacramental, ritual, ecclesiastical, monastic, and disciplinarian, as well as moral—relating to the duties of ecclesiastics and regulars, of parish priests, and of professional men, as well as of private Catholics. And these condemnations relate for the most part to mere occasional details of duty, and are in reprobation of the lax or wild notions of speculative casuists, so that they are rather restraints upon theologians than upon laymen. For instance, the following are some of the propositions condemned:—"The ecclesiastic, who on a certain day is hindered from saying Matins and Lauds, is not bound to say, if he can, the remaining hours"; "Where there is good cause, it is lawful to swear without the purpose of swearing, whether the matter is of light or grave moment"; "Domestics may steal from their masters, in compensation for their service, which they think greater than their wages"; "It is lawful for a public man to kill an opponent, who tries to fasten a calumny upon him, if he cannot otherwise escape the ignominy." I have taken these instances at random. It must be granted, I think, that in the long course of 200 years the amount of the Pope's authoritative enunciations has not been such as to press heavily on the back of the private Catholic. He leaves us surely far more than that "one fourth of the department of conduct," which Mr. Gladstone allows us. Indeed, if my account and specimens of his sway over us in morals be correct, I do not see what he takes away at all from our private consciences.

But here Mr. Gladstone will object that the Pope does really exercise a claim over the whole domain of conduct, inasmuch as he refuses to draw any line across it in limitation of his interference, and *therefore* it is that we are his slaves—let us see if another illustration or parallel will not show this to be a *non sequitur*. Suppose a man, who is in the midst of various and important lines of business, has a medical adviser, in whom he has full confidence, as knowing well his constitution. This adviser keeps a careful and anxious eye upon him; and, as an honest man, says to him, "You must not go off on a journey to-day," or "You must take some days' rest," or "You must attend to your diet." Now, this is not a fair parallel to the Pope's hold upon us; for the Pope does not speak to us personally, but to all, and, in speaking definitively on ethical subjects, what he propounds must relate to things good and bad in themselves, not to things accidental, changeable, and of mere expedience; so that the argument which I am drawing from the case of a medical adviser is *a fortiori* in its character. However, I say that though a medical man exercises a "supreme direction" over those who put themselves under him, yet we do not therefore say, even of him, that he interferes with our daily conduct, and that we are his slaves. He certainly does thwart many of our wishes and purposes; and in a true sense we are at his mercy: he may interfere any day, suddenly; he will not, he cannot, draw any intelligible line between the acts which he has a right to forbid us, and the acts which he has not. The same journey, the same press of business, the same indulgence at table, which he passes over one year, he sternly forbids the next. Therefore if Mr. Gladstone's argument is good, he has a finger in all the commercial transactions of the great trader or financier who has chosen him. But surely there is a simple fallacy here. Mr. Gladstone asks us whether our political and civil life is not at the Pope's mercy; every act, he says, of at least three quarters of the day, is under his control. No, not *every*, but *any*, and this is all the difference—that is, we have no guarantee given us that there will never be a case when the Pope's general utterances may come to have a bearing upon some personal act of ours. In the same way we are all of us in this age under the control of public opinion and the public prints; nay, much more intimately so. Journalism can be and is very personal; and, when it is in the right, more powerful just now than any Pope; yet we do not go into fits, as if we were slaves, because we are under a *surveillance* much more like tyranny than any sway, so indirect, so practically limited, so gentle, as his is.

But it seems the cardinal point of our slavery lies, not simply in the domain of morals, but in the Pope's general authority over us in all things whatsoever. This count in his indictment Mr. Gladstone founds on a passage in the third chapter of the *Pastor æternus*, in which the Pope, speaking of the Pontifical jurisdiction, says: "Towards it (erga quam) pastors and people of whatsoever rite or dignity, each and all, are bound by the duty of hierarchical subordination and true obedience, not only in matters which pertain to faith and morals, but also in those which pertain to the *discipline* and the *regimen* of the Church spread throughout the world; so that, unity with the Roman Pontiff (both of communion and of profession of the same faith) being preserved, the Church of Christ may be one flock under one supreme Shepherd. This is the doctrine of Catholic truth, from which no one can deviate without loss of faith and salvation."

On Mr. Gladstone's use of this passage I observe, first, that he leaves out a portion of it which has much to do with the due understanding of it (ita ut custoditâ, etc.). Next, he speaks of "*absolute* obedience" so often that any reader who had not the passage before him would think that the word "absolute" was the Pope's word, not his. Thirdly, three times (at pp. 38, 41, and 42) does he make the Pope say that no one can *disobey* him without risking his salvation, whereas what the Pope does say is that no one can *disbelieve* the *duty* of obedience and unity without such risk. And fourthly, in order to carry out this false sense, or rather to hinder its being evidently impossible, he mistranslates (p. 38) "doctrina" (Hæc est doctrina) by the word "rule."

But his chief attack is directed to the words "disciplina" and "regimen." "Thus," he says, "are swept into the Papal net whole multitudes of facts, whole systems of government, prevailing, though in different degrees, in every country of the world" (p. 41). That is, "disciplina" and "regimen" are words of such lax, vague, indeterminate meaning that under them any matters can be slipped in which may be required for the Pope's purpose in this or that country, such as, to take Mr. Gladstone's instances, blasphemy, poor-relief, incorporation, and mortmain; as if no definitions were contained in our theological and ecclesiastical works of words in such common use, and as if in consequence the Pope was at liberty to give them any sense of his own. As to discipline, Fr. Perrone says, "Discipline comprises the exterior worship of God, the liturgy, sacred rites, psalmody, the administration of the sacraments, the canonical form of sacred elections and the institution of ministers, vows, feast-days, and the like"; all of them (observe) matters internal to the Church, and without any relation to the Civil Power and civil affairs. Perrone adds, "Ecclesiastical discipline is a practical and external rule, prescribed by the Church, in order to retain the faithful in their *faith*, and the more easily lead them on to *eternal happiness.*"—*Prœl. Theol.*, t. 2, p. 381, 2nd ed., 1841. Thus discipline is in no sense a political instrument, except as the profession of our faith may accidentally become political. In the same sense Zallinger: "The Roman Pontiff has by divine right the power of passing universal laws pertaining to the *discipline* of the Church; for instance, to divine worship, sacred rites, the ordination and manner of life of the clergy, the order of the ecclesiastical regimen, and the right administration of the temporal possessions of the church."—*Jur. Eccles.*, lib. i. t. 2, § 121.

So too the word "regimen" has a definite meaning, relating to a matter strictly internal to the Church: it means government, or the mode or form of government, or the course of government; and as, in the intercourse of nation with nation, the nature of a nation's government, whether monarchical or republican, does not come into question, so the constitution of the Church simply belongs to its nature, not to its external action. Certainly there are aspects of the Church which involve relations towards secular powers and to nations, as, for instance, its missionary office; but regimen has relation to one of its internal characteristics, viz., its form of government, whether we call it a pure monarchy or with others a monarchy tempered by aristocracy. Thus Tournely says, "Three kinds of regimen or government are set down by philosophers, monarchy, aristocracy, and democracy."— *Theol.*, t. 2, p. 100. Bellarmine says the same, *Rom. Pont.* i. 2; and Perrone takes it for granted, *ibid.*, pp. 70, 71.

Now, why does the Pope speak at this time of regimen and discipline? He tells us in that portion of the sentence, which, thinking it of no account, Mr. Gladstone has omitted. The Pope tells us that all Catholics should recollect their duty of obedience to him, not only in faith and morals, but in such matters of regimen and discipline as belong to the universal Church, "so that unity with the Roman Pontiff, both of communion and of profession of the same faith being preserved, the Church of Christ may be one flock under one supreme Shepherd." I consider this passage to be especially aimed at Nationalism: "Recollect," the Pope seems to say, "the Church is one, and that, not only in faith and morals, for schismatics may profess as much as this, but one, wherever it is, all over the world; and not only one, but one and the same, bound together by its one regimen and discipline and by the same regimen and discipline—the same rites, the same sacraments, the same usages, and the same one Pastor; and in these bad times it is necessary for all Catholics to recollect that this doctrine of the Church's individuality and, as it were, personality, is not a mere received opinion or understanding, which may be entertained or not, as we please, but is a fundamental, necessary truth." This being, speaking under correction, the drift of the passage, I observe that the words "spread throughout the world" or "universal" are so far from turning "discipline and regimen" into what Mr. Gladstone calls a "net," that they contract the range of both of them, not including, as he would have it, "marriage" here, "blasphemy" there, and "poor-relief" in a third country, but noting and specifying that one and the same structure of laws, rites, rules of government, independency, everywhere, of which the Pope himself is the centre and life. And surely this is what every one of us will say as well as the Pope, who is not an Erastian, and who believes that the Gospel is no mere philosophy thrown upon the world at large, no mere quality of mind and thought, no mere beautiful and deep sentiment or subjective opinion, but a substantive message from above, guarded and preserved in a visible polity.

2. And now I am naturally led on to speak of the Pope's supreme authority, such as I have described it, in its bearing towards the Civil Power all over the world—a power which as truly comes from God, as his own does, though diverse, as the Church is invariable.

That collisions can take place between the Holy See and national governments, the history of fifteen hundred years sufficiently teaches us; also, that on both sides there may occur grievous mistakes. But my question all along lies, not with "quicquid delirant reges," but with what, under the circumstance of such a collision, is the duty of those who are both children of the Pope and subjects of the Civil Power. As to the duty of the Civil Power, I have already intimated in my first section that it should treat the Holy See as an independent sovereign, and if this rule had been observed, the difficulty to Catholics in a country not Catholic would be most materially lightened. Great Britain recognizes and is recognized by the United States; the two powers have ministers at each other's court; here is one standing prevention of serious quarrels. Misunderstandings between the two co-ordinate powers may arise; but there follow explanations, removals of the causes of offence, acts of restitution. In actual collisions, there are conferences, compromises, arbitrations. Now the point to observe here is that in such cases neither party gives up its abstract rights, but neither party practically insists on them. And each party thinks itself in the right in the particular case, protests against any other view, but still concedes. Neither party says, "I will not make it up with you, till you draw an intelligible line between your domain and mine." I suppose in the Geneva arbitration, though we gave way, we still thought that, in our conduct in the American civil war, we had acted within our rights. I say all this in answer to Mr. Gladstone's challenge to us to draw the line between the Pope's domain and the State's domain in civil or political questions. Many a private American, I suppose, lived in London and Liverpool, all through the correspondence between our Foreign Office and the government of the United States, and Mr. Gladstone never addressed any expostulation to them, or told them they had lost their moral freedom because they took part with their own government. The French, when their late war began, did sweep their German sojourners out of France (the number, as I recollect, was very great), but they were not considered to have done themselves much credit by such an act. When we went to war with Russia, the English in St. Petersburg made an address, I think to the Emperor, asking for his protection, and he gave it—I don't suppose they pledged themselves to the Russian view of the war, nor would he have called them slaves instead of patriots if they had refused to do so. Suppose England were to send her ironclads to support Italy against the Pope and his allies, English Catholics would be very indignant, they would take part with the Pope before the war began, they would use all constitutional means to hinder it; but who believes that, when they were once in the war, their action would be anything else than prayers and exertions for a termination of it? What reason is there for saying that they would commit themselves to any step of a treasonable nature, any more than loyal Germans, had they been allowed to remain in France? Yet, because those Germans would not relinquish their allegiance to their country, Mr. Gladstone, were he consistent, would at once send them adrift.

Of course it will be said that in these cases, there is no double allegiance, and again that the German government did not call upon Germans in France, as the Pope might call upon English Catholics, nay command them, to take a side; but my argument at least shows this, that till there comes to us a special, direct command from the Pope to oppose our country, we need not be said to have "placed our loyalty and civil duty at the mercy of another" (p. 45). It is strange that a great statesman, versed in the new and true philosophy of compromise, instead of taking a practical view of the actual situation, should proceed against us, like a professor in the schools, with the "parade" of his "relentless (and may I add 'rusty'?) logic" (p. 23).

I say, *till* the Pope told us to exert ourselves for his cause in a quarrel with this country, as in the time of the Armada, we need not attend to an abstract and hypothetical difficulty—then and not till then. I add, as before, that if the Holy See were frankly recognized by England, as other sovereignties are, direct quarrels between the two powers would in this age of the world be rare indeed; and still rarer, their becoming so energetic and urgent as to descend into the hearts of the community, and to disturb the consciences and the family unity of private Catholics.

But now, lastly, let us suppose one of these extraordinary cases of direct and open hostility between the two powers actually to occur— here first, we must bring before us the state of the case. Of course we must recollect, on the one hand, that Catholics are not only bound by allegiance to the British Crown but have special privileges as citizens, can meet together, speak and pass resolutions, can vote for members of Parliament, and sit in Parliament, and can hold office, all which are denied to foreigners sojourning among us; while on the other hand, there is the authority of the Pope, which, though not "absolute" even in religious matters, as Mr. Gladstone would have it to be, has a call, a supreme call on our obedience. Certainly in the event of such a collision of jurisdictions, there are cases in which we should obey the Pope and disobey the State. Suppose, for instance, an act was passed in Parliament, bidding Catholics to attend Protestant service every week, and the Pope distinctly told us not to do so, for it was to violate our duty to our faith—I should obey the Pope and not the Law. It will be said by Mr. Gladstone that such a case is impossible. I know it is; but why ask me for what I should do in extreme and utterly improbable cases such as this, if my answer cannot help bearing the character of an axiom? It is not my fault that I must deal in truisms. The circumferences of State jurisdiction and of Papal are for the most part quite apart from each other; there are just some few degrees out of the 360 in which they intersect, and Mr. Gladstone, instead of letting these cases of intersection alone, till they occur actually, asks me what I should do if I found myself placed in the space intersected. If I must answer then, I should say distinctly that did the State tell me in a question of worship to do what the Pope told me not to do, I should obey the Pope, and should think it no sin, if I used all the power and the influence I possessed as a citizen to prevent such a bill passing the Legislature, and to effect its repeal if it did.

But now, on the other hand, could the case ever occur, in which I should act with the Civil Power, and not with the Pope? Now, here again, when I begin to imagine instances, Catholics will cry out (as Mr. Gladstone, in the case I supposed, cried out in the interest of the other side) that instances never can occur. I know they cannot; I know the Pope never can do what I am going to suppose; but then, since it cannot possibly happen in fact, there is no harm in just saying what I should (hypothetically) do, if it did happen. I say then in certain (impossible) cases I should side, not with the Pope, but with the Civil Power. For instance, let us suppose members of Parliament, or of the Privy Council, took an oath that they would not acknowledge the right of succession of a Prince of Wales, if he became a Catholic: in that case I should not consider the Pope could release me from that oath, had I bound myself by it. Of course, I might exert myself to the utmost to get the act repealed which bound me; again, if I could not, I might retire from Parliament or office, and so rid myself of the engagement I had made; but I should be clear that, though the Pope bade all Catholics to stand firm in one phalanx for the Catholic Succession, still, while I remained in office, or in my place in Parliament, I could not do as he bade me.

Again, were I actually a soldier or sailor in her Majesty's service, and sent to take part in a war which I could not in my conscience see to be unjust, and should the Pope suddenly bid all Catholic soldiers and sailors to retire from the service, here again, taking the advice of others, as best I could, I should not obey him.

What is the use of forming impossible cases? One can find plenty of them in books of casuistry, with the answers attached in respect to them. In an actual case, a Catholic would, of course, not act simply on his own judgment; at the same time, there are supposable cases in which he would be obliged to go by it solely—viz., when his conscience could not be reconciled to any of the courses of action proposed to him by others.

In support of what I have been saying, I refer to one or two weighty authorities:

Cardinal Turrecremata says, "Although it clearly follows from the circumstance that the Pope can err at times, and command things which must not be done, that we are not to be simply obedient to him in all things, that does not show that he must not be obeyed by all when his commands are good. To know in what cases he is to be obeyed and in what not . . . it is said in the Acts of the Apostles, 'One ought to obey God rather than man': therefore, were the Pope to command anything against Holy Scripture, or the articles of faith, or the truth of the Sacraments, or the commands of the natural or divine law, *he ought not to be obeyed*, but in such commands is to be passed over (despiciendus)."—*Summ. de Eccl.*, pp. 47, 48.

Bellarmine, speaking of resisting the Pope, says, "In order to resist and defend oneself no authority is required. . . . Therefore, as it is lawful to resist the Pope, if he assaulted a man's person, so it is lawful to resist him, if he assaulted souls, or *troubled the state* (turbanti rempublicam), and much more if he strove to destroy the Church. It is lawful, I say, to resist him, by not doing what he commands, and hindering the execution of his will."—*De Rom. Pont.*, ii. 29.

Archbishop Kenrick says, "His power was given for edification, not for destruction. If he uses it from the love of domination (quod absit) *scarcely will he meet with obedient populations.*"—*Theolog. Moral.*, t. i. p. 158.

When, then, Mr. Gladstone asks Catholics how they can obey the Queen and yet obey the Pope, since it may happen that the commands of the two authorities may clash, I answer, that it is my *rule*, both to obey the one and to obey the other, but that there is no rule in this world without exceptions, and if either the Pope or the Queen demanded of me an "Absolute Obedience," he or she would be transgressing the laws of human society. I give an absolute obedience to neither. Further, if ever this double allegiance pulled me in contrary ways, which in this age of the world I think it never will, then I should decide according to the particular case, which is beyond all rule, and must be decided on its own merits. I should look to see what theologians could do for me, what the bishops and clergy around me, what my confessor; what friends whom I revered: and if, after all, I could not take their view of the matter, then I must rule myself by my own judgment and my own conscience. But all this is hypothetical and unreal.

Here, of course, it will be objected to me, that I am, after all, having recourse to the Protestant doctrine of Private Judgment; not so; it is the Protestant doctrine that Private Judgment is our *ordinary* guide in religious matters, but I use it, in the case in question, in very extraordinary and rare, nay, impossible emergencies. Do not the highest Tories thus defend the substitution of William for James II? It is a great mistake to suppose our state in the Catholic Church is so entirely subjected to rule and system, that we are never thrown upon what is called by divines "the Providence of God." The teaching and assistance of the Church does not supply all conceivable needs, but those which are ordinary; thus, for instance, the sacraments are necessary for dying in the grace of God and hope of heaven; yet, when they cannot be got, acts of faith, hope, and contrition, with the desire for those aids which the dying man has not, will convey in substance what those aids ordinarily convey. And so a Catechumen, not yet baptized, may be saved by his purpose and preparation to receive the rite. And so, again, though "Out of the Church there is no salvation," this does not hold in the case of good men who are in invincible ignorance. And so it is also in the case of our ordinations; Chillingworth and Macaulay say that it is morally impossible that we should have kept up for eighteen hundred years an Apostolical succession of ministers without some breaks in the chain; and we in answer say that, however true this may be humanly speaking, there has been a special Providence over the Church to secure it. Once more, how else could private Catholics save their souls when there was a Pope and Anti-popes, each severally claiming their allegiance?

## Conscience

It seems, then, that there are extreme cases in which Conscience may come into collision with the word of a Pope, and is to be followed in spite of that word. Now I wish to place this proposition on a broader basis, acknowledged by all Catholics, and, in order to do this satisfactorily, as I began with the prophecies of Scripture and the primitive Church, when I spoke of the Pope's prerogatives, so now I must begin with the Creator and His creature, when I would draw out the prerogatives and the supreme authority of Conscience.

I say, then, that the Supreme Being is of a certain character, which, expressed in human language, we call ethical. He has the attributes of justice, truth, wisdom, sanctity, benevolence and mercy, as eternal characteristics in His nature, the very Law of His being, identical with Himself; and next, when He became Creator, He implanted this Law, which is Himself, in the intelligence of all His rational creatures. The Divine Law, then, is the rule of ethical truth, the standard of right and wrong, a sovereign, irreversible, absolute authority in the presence of men and Angels. "The eternal law," says St. Augustine, "is the Divine Reason or Will of God, commanding the observance, forbidding the disturbance, of the natural order of things." "The natural law," says St. Thomas, "is an impression of the Divine Light in us, a participation of the eternal law in the rational creature" (Gousset, *Theol. Moral.*, t. i. pp. 24, etc.). This law, as apprehended in the minds of individual men, is called "conscience"; and though it may suffer refraction in passing into the intellectual medium of each, it is not therefore so affected as to lose its character of being the Divine Law, but still has, as such, the prerogative of commanding obedience. "The Divine Law," says Cardinal Gousset, "is the supreme rule of actions; our thoughts, desires, words, acts, all that man is, is subject to the domain of the law of God; and this law is the rule of our conduct by means of our conscience. Hence it is never lawful to go against our conscience; as the fourth Lateran council says, 'Quidquid fit contra conscientiam, ædificat ad gehennam.' "*

This view of conscience, I know, is very different from that ordinarily taken of it, both by the science and literature, and by the public opinion, of this day. It is founded on the doctrine that conscience is the voice of God, whereas it is fashionable on all hands now to consider it in one way or another a creation of man. Of course, there are great and broad exceptions to this statement. It is not true of many or most religious bodies of men; especially not of their teachers and ministers. When Anglicans, Wesleyans, the various Presbyterian sects in Scotland, and other denominations among us, speak of conscience, they mean what we mean, the voice of God in the nature and heart of man, as distinct from the voice of Revelation. They speak of a principle planted within us, before we have had any training, although training and experience are necessary for its strength, growth, and due formation. They consider it a constituent element of the mind, as our perception of other ideas may be, as our powers of reasoning, as our sense of order and the beautiful, and our other intellectual endowments. They consider it, as Catholics consider it, to be the internal witness of both the existence and the law of God. They think it holds of God, and not of man, as an Angel walking on the earth would be no citizen or dependent of the Civil Power. They would not allow, any more than we do, that it could be resolved into any combination of principles in our nature, more elementary than itself; nay, though it may be called,

---

* "Whatever is done in opposition to conscience is conducive to damnation."

and is, a law of the mind, they would not grant that it was nothing more; I mean, that it was not a dictate, nor conveyed the notion of responsibility, of duty, of a threat and a promise, with a vividness which discriminated it from all other constituents of our nature.

This, at least, is how I read the doctrine of Protestants as well as of Catholics. The rule and measure of duty is not utility, nor expedience, nor the happiness of the greatest number, nor State convenience, nor fitness, order, and the *pulchrum*. Conscience is not a long-sighted selfishness, nor a desire to be consistent with oneself; but it is a messenger from Him, who, both in nature and in grace, speaks to us behind a veil, and teaches and rules us by His representatives. Conscience is the aboriginal Vicar of Christ, a prophet in its informations, a monarch in its peremptoriness, a priest in its blessings and anathemas, and, even though the eternal priesthood throughout the Church could cease to be, in it the sacerdotal principle would remain and would have a sway.

Words such as these are idle empty verbiage to the great world of philosophy now. All through my day there has been a resolute warfare, I had almost said conspiracy, against the rights of conscience, as I have described it. Literature and science have been embodied in great institutions in order to put it down. Noble buildings have been reared as fortresses against that spiritual, invisible influence which is too subtle for science and too profound for literature. Chairs in Universities have been made the seats of an antagonist tradition. Public writers, day after day, have indoctrinated the minds of innumerable readers with theories subversive of its claims. As in Roman times, and in the Middle Ages, its supremacy was assailed by the arm of physical force, so now the intellect is put in operation to sap the foundations of a power which the sword could not destroy. We are told that conscience is but a twist in primitive and untutored man; that its dictate is an imagination; that the very notion of guiltiness, which that dictate enforces, is simply irrational, for how can there possibly be freedom of will, how can there be consequent responsibility, in that infinite eternal network of cause and effect, in which we helplessly lie? and what retribution have we to fear, when we have had no real choice to do good or evil?

So much for philosophers; now let us see what is the notion of conscience in this day in the popular mind. There, no more than in the intellectual world, does "conscience" retain the old, true, Catholic meaning of the word. There too the idea, the presence of a Moral Governor is far away from the use of it, frequent and emphatic as that use of it is. When men advocate the rights of conscience, they in no sense mean the rights of the Creator, nor the duty to Him, in thought and deed, of the creature; but the right of thinking, speaking, writing, and acting, according to their judgment or their humour, without any thought of God at all. They do not even pretend to go by any moral rule, but they demand what they think is an Englishman's prerogative, for each to be his own master in all things, and to profess what he pleases, asking no one's leave, and accounting priest or preacher, speaker or writer unutterably impertinent, who dares to say a word against his going to perdition, if he like it, in his own way. Conscience has rights because it has duties; but in this age, with a large portion of the public, it is the very right and freedom of conscience to dispense with conscience, to ignore a Lawgiver and Judge, to be independent of unseen obligations. It becomes a licence to take up any or no religion, to take up this or that and let it go again, to go to church, to go to chapel, to boast of being above all religions and to be an impartial critic of each of them. Conscience is a stern monitor, but in this century it has been superseded by a counterfeit, which the eighteen centuries prior to it never heard of, and could not have mistaken for it, if they had. It is the right of self-will.

And now I shall turn aside for a moment to show how it is that the Popes of our century have been misunderstood by the English people, as if they really were speaking against conscience in the true sense of the word, when in fact they were speaking against it in the various false senses, philosophical or popular, which in this day are put upon the word. The present Pope, in his Encyclical of 1864, *Quantâ curâ*, speaks (as will come before us in the next section) against "liberty of conscience," and he refers to his predecessor, Gregory XVI, who, in his *Mirari vos*, calls it a "deliramentum." It is a rule in formal ecclesiastical proceedings, as I shall have occasion to notice lower down, when books or authors are condemned to use the very words of the book or author, and to condemn the words in that particular sense which they have in their context and their drift, not in the literal, not in the religious sense, such as the Pope might recognize, were they in another book or author. To take a familiar parallel, among many which occur daily. Protestants speak of the "Blessed Reformation"; Catholics too talk of "the Reformation," though they do not call it blessed. Yet every "reformation" ought, from the very meaning of the word, to be good, not bad; so that Catholics seem to be implying a eulogy on an event which, at the same time, they consider a surpassing evil. Here then they are taking the word and using it in the popular sense of it, not in the Catholic. They would say, if they expressed their full meaning, "the *so-called* reformation." In like manner, if the Pope condemned "the Reformation," it would be utterly sophistical to say in consequence that he had declared himself against all reforms; yet this is how Mr. Gladstone treats him, when he speaks of (so-called) liberty of conscience. To make this distinction clear, viz., between the Catholic sense of the word "conscience" and that sense in which the Pope condemns it, we find in the *Recueil des Allocutions*, etc., the words accompanied with quotation marks, both in Pope Gregory's and Pope Pius's Encyclicals, thus: Gregory's "Ex hoc putidissimo 'indifferentismi' fonte" (mind, "indifferentismi" is in quotation marks, because the Pope will not make himself answerable for so unclassical a word) "absurda illa fluit ac erronea sententia, seu potius deliramentum, asserendam esse ac vindicandam cuilibet 'libertatem conscientiæ.' "* And that of Pius: "Haud timent erroneam illam fovere opinionem a Gregorio XVI deliramentum appellatam, nimirum 'libertatem conscientiæ' esse proprium cujuscunque hominis jus."** Both Popes certainly scoff at the so-called "liberty of conscience," but there is no scoffing of any Pope, in formal documents addressed to the faithful at large, at that most serious doctrine, the right and the duty of following that Divine Authority, the voice of conscience, on which in truth the Church herself is built.

So indeed it is; did the Pope speak against Conscience in the true sense of the word, he would commit a suicidal act. He would be cutting the ground from under his feet. His very mission is to proclaim the moral law, and to protect and strengthen that "Light which enlighteneth every man that cometh into the world." On the law of conscience and its sacredness are founded both his authority in theory and his power in fact. Whether this or that particular Pope in this bad world always kept this great truth in view in all he did, it is for history to tell. I am considering here the Papacy in its office and its duties, and in reference to those who acknowledge its claims. They are not bound by the Pope's personal character or private acts, but by his formal teaching. Thus viewing his position, we shall find that it is by the universal sense of right and wrong, the consciousness of transgression, the pangs of guilt, and the dread of retribution, as first principles

---

* "From that polluted spring of 'indifferentism' flows that absurd and erroneous opinion—or rather delusion—to the effect that everyone's 'liberty of conscience' is to be asserted and vindicated."
** "They do not hesitate to foster that false opinion, called a delusion by Gregory XVI, that 'liberty of conscience' is a right belonging to every human being."

deeply lodged in the hearts of men, it is thus and only thus, that he has gained his footing in the world and achieved his success. It is his claim to come from the Divine Lawgiver, in order to elicit, protect, and enforce those truths which the Lawgiver has sown in our very nature, it is this and this only that is the explanation of his length of life more than antediluvian. The championship of the Moral Law and of conscience is his *raison d'être*. The fact of his mission is the answer to the complaints of those who feel the insufficiency of the natural light; and the insufficiency of that light is the justification of his mission.

All sciences, except the science of Religion, have their certainty in themselves; as far as they are sciences, they consist of necessary conclusions from undeniable premisses, or of phenomena manipulated into general truths by an irresistible induction. But the sense of right and wrong, which is the first element in religion, is so delicate, so fitful, so easily puzzled, obscured, perverted, so subtle in its argumentative methods, so impressible by education, so biassed by pride and passion, so unsteady in its course that, in the struggle for existence amid the various exercises and triumphs of the human intellect, this sense is at once the highest of all teachers, yet the least luminous; and the Church, the Pope, the Hierarchy are, in the Divine purpose, the supply of an urgent demand. Natural Religion, certain as are its grounds and its doctrines as addressed to thoughtful, serious minds, needs, in order that it may speak to mankind with effect and subdue the world, to be sustained and completed by Revelation.

In saying all this, of course I must not be supposed to be limiting the Revelation of which the Church is the keeper to a mere republication of the Natural Law; but still it is true, that, though Revelation is so distinct from the teaching of nature and beyond it, yet it is not independent of it, nor without relations towards it, but is its complement, reassertion, issue, embodiment, and interpretation. The Pope, who comes of Revelation, has no jurisdiction over nature. If, under the plea of his revealed prerogatives, he neglected his mission of preaching truth, justice, mercy, and peace, much more if he trampled on the consciences of his subjects—if he had done so all along, as Protestants say, then he could not have lasted all these many centuries till now, so as to supply a mark for their reprobation. Dean Milman has told us above, how faithful he was to his duty in the medieval time, and how successful. Afterwards, for a while the Papal chair was filled by men who gave themselves up to luxury, security, and a pagan kind of Christianity; and we all know what a moral earthquake was the consequence, and how the Church lost, thereby, and has lost to this day, one half of Europe. The Popes could not have recovered from so terrible a catastrophe, as they have done, had they not returned to their first and better ways, and the grave lesson of the past is in itself the guarantee of the future.

Such is the relation of the ecclesiastical power to the human conscience; however, a contrary view may be taken of it. It may be said that no one doubts that the Pope's power rests on those weaknesses of human nature, that religious sense, which in ancient days Lucretius noted as the cause of the worst ills of our race; that he uses it dexterously, forming under shelter of it a false code of morals for his own aggrandisement and tyranny; and that thus conscience becomes his creature and his slave, doing, as if on a divine sanction, his will; so that in the abstract indeed and in idea it is free, but never free in fact, never able to take a flight of its own, independent of him, any more than birds whose wings are clipped; moreover, that, if it were able to exert a will of its own, then there would ensue a collision more unmanageable than that between the Church and the State, as being in one and the same subject-matter, viz., religion; for what would become of the Pope's "absolute authority," as Mr. Gladstone calls it, if the private conscience had an absolute authority also?

I wish to answer this important objection distinctly.

1. First, I am using the word "conscience" in the high sense in which I have already explained it, not as a fancy or an opinion, but as a dutiful obedience to what claims to be a divine voice, speaking within us; and that this is the view properly to be taken of it, I shall not attempt to prove here, but shall assume it as a first principle.

2. Secondly, I observe that conscience is not a judgment upon any speculative truth, any abstract doctrine, but bears immediately on conduct, on something to be done or not done. "Conscience," says St. Thomas, "is the practical judgment or dictate of reason, by which we judge what *hic et nunc* is to be done as being good, or to be avoided as evil." Hence conscience cannot come into direct collision with the Church's or the Pope's infallibility; which is engaged on general propositions, and in the condemnation of particular and given errors.

3. Next, I observe that, conscience being a practical dictate, a collision is possible between it and the Pope's authority only when the Pope legislates, or gives particular orders, and the like. But a Pope is not infallible in his laws, nor in his commands, nor in his acts of state, nor in his administration, nor in his public policy. Let it be observed that the Vatican Council has left him just as it found him here. Mr.

Gladstone's language on this point is to me quite unintelligible. Why, instead of using vague terms, does he not point out precisely the very words by which the Council has made the Pope in his acts infallible? Instead of so doing, he assumes a conclusion which is altogether false. He says (p. 34), "First comes the Pope's infallibility": then in the next page he insinuates that, under his infallibility, come acts of excommunication, as if the Pope could not make mistakes in this field of action. He says (p. 35), "It may be sought to plead that the Pope does not propose to invade the country, to seize Woolwich, or burn Portsmouth. He will only, at the worst, excommunicate opponents. . . . Is this a good answer? After all, even in the Middle Ages, it was not by the direct action of fleets and armies of their own that the Popes contended with kings who were refractory; it was mainly by interdicts," etc. What have excommunication and interdict to do with Infallibility? Was St. Peter infallible on that occasion at Antioch when St. Paul withstood him? was St. Victor infallible when he separated from his communion the Asiatic Churches? or Liberius when in like manner he excommunicated Athanasius? And, to come to later times, was Gregory XIII, when he had a medal struck in honour of the Bartholomew massacre? or Paul IV in his conduct towards Elizabeth? or Sextus V when he blessed the Armada? or Urban VIII when he persecuted Galileo? No Catholic ever pretends that these Popes were infallible in these acts. Since then infallibility alone could block the exercise of conscience, and the Pope is not infallible in that subject-matter in which conscience is of supreme authority, no dead-lock, such as is implied in the objection which I am answering, can take place between conscience and the Pope.

4. But, of course, I have to say again, lest I should be misunderstood, that when I speak of Conscience, I mean conscience truly so called. When it has the right of opposing the supreme, though not infallible Authority of the Pope, it must be something more than that miserable counterfeit which, as I have said above, now goes by the name. If in a particular case it is to be taken as a sacred and sovereign monitor, its dictate, in order to prevail against the voice of the Pope, must follow upon serious thought, prayer, and all available means of arriving at a right judgment on the matter in question. And further, obedience to the Pope is what is called "in possession"; that is, the *onus probandi* of establishing a case against him lies, as in all cases of exception, on the side of conscience. Unless a man is able to say to himself, as in the Presence of God, that he must not, and dare not, act upon the Papal injunction, he is bound to obey it, and would commit a great sin in

disobeying it. *Primâ facie* it is his bounden duty, even from a sentiment of loyalty, to believe the Pope right and to act accordingly. He must vanquish that mean, ungenerous, selfish, vulgar spirit of his nature, which, at the very first rumour of a command, places itself in opposition to the Superior who gives it, asks itself whether he is not exceeding his right, and rejoices, in a moral and practical matter to commence with scepticism. He must have no wilful determination to exercise a right of thinking, saying, doing just what he pleases, the question of truth and falsehood, right and wrong, the duty if possible of obedience, the love of speaking as his Head speaks, and of standing in all cases on his Head's side, being simply discarded. If this necessary rule were observed, collisions between the Pope's authority and the authority of conscience would be very rare. On the other hand, in the fact that, after all, in extraordinary cases, the conscience of each individual is free, we have a safeguard and security, were security necessary (which is a most gratuitous supposition), that no Pope ever will be able, as the objection supposes, to create a false conscience for his own ends.

Now, I shall end this part of the subject, for I have not done with it altogether, by appealing to various of our theologians in evidence that, in what I have been saying, I have not misrepresented Catholic doctrine on these important points.

That is, on the duty of obeying our conscience at all hazards.

I have already quoted the words which Cardinal Gousset has adduced from the Fourth Lateran; that "He who acts against his conscience loses his soul." This *dictum* is brought out with singular fulness and force in the moral treatises of theologians. The celebrated school, known as the Salmanticenses, or Carmelites of Salamanca, lays down the broad proposition that conscience is ever to be obeyed whether it tells truly or erroneously, and that, whether the error is the fault of the person thus erring or not.[1] They say that this opinion is certain, and refer, as agreeing with them, to St. Thomas, St. Bonaventura, Caietan, Vasquez, Durandus, Navarrus, Corduba, Layman, Escobar, and fourteen others. Two of them even say this opinion is *de fide*. Of

---

[1] "Aliqui opinantur quod conscientia erronea non obligat; secundam sententiam, et certam, asserentem esse peccatum discordare à conscientiâ erroneâ, invincibili aut vincibili, tenet D. Thomas; quem sequuntur omnes Scholastici." ["Some hold the opinion that an erroneous conscience does not oblige. St. Thomas holds a different opinion, and it is a certain one, namely that it is sinful to act in a way that is inconsistent with an erroneous conscience, vincible or invincible. St. Thomas is followed in this by all Scholastic writers."] *Theol. Moral.*, t. v. p. 12, ed. 1728.

course, if a man is culpable in being in error, which he might have escaped had he been more in earnest, for that error he is answerable to God, but still he must act according to that error, while he is in it, because he in full sincerity thinks the error to be truth.

Thus, if the Pope told the English bishops to order their priests to stir themselves energetically in favour of teetotalism, and a particular priest was fully persuaded that abstinence from wine, etc., was practically a Gnostic error, and therefore felt he could not so exert himself without sin; or suppose there was a Papal order to hold lotteries in each mission for some religious object, and a priest could say in God's sight that he believed lotteries to be morally wrong, that priest in either of these cases would commit a sin *hic et nunc* if he obeyed the Pope, whether he was right or wrong in his opinion, and, if wrong, although he had not taken proper pains to get at the truth of the matter.

Busenbaum, of the Society of Jesus, whose work I have already had occasion to notice, writes thus: "A heretic, as long as he judges his sect to be more or equally deserving of belief, has no obligation to believe [in the Church]." And he continues, "When men who have been brought up in heresy, are persuaded from boyhood that we impugn and attack the word of God, that we are idolators, pestilent deceivers, and therefore are to be shunned as pests, they cannot, while this persuasion lasts, with a safe conscience, hear us."—t. l, p. 54.

Antonio Corduba, a Spanish Franciscan, states the doctrine with still more point, because he makes mention of Superiors. "In no manner is it lawful to act against conscience, even though a Law, or a Superior commands it."—*De Conscient.*, p. 138.

And the French Dominican, Natalis Alexander: "If, in the judgment of conscience, through a mistaken conscience, a man is persuaded that what his Superior commands is displeasing to God, he is bound not to obey."—*Theol.* t. 2, p. 32.

The word "Superior" certainly includes the Pope; Cardinal Jacobatius brings out this point clearly in his authoritative work on Councils, which is contained in Labbe's Collection, introducing the Pope by name: "If it were doubtful," he says, "whether a precept [of the Pope] be a sin or not, we must determine thus: that, if he to whom the precept is addressed has a conscientious sense that it is a sin and injustice, first it is duty to put off that sense; but, if he cannot, nor conform himself to the judgment of the Pope, in that case it is his duty to follow his own private conscience, and patiently to bear it, if the Pope punishes him."—lib. iv. p. 241.

Would it not be well for Mr. Gladstone to bring passages from our recognized authors as confirmatory of his view of our teaching, as those which I have quoted are destructive of it? and they must be passages declaring, not only that the Pope is ever to be obeyed, but that there are no exceptions to the rule, for exceptions there must be in all concrete matters.

I add one remark. Certainly, if I am obliged to bring religion into after-dinner toasts (which indeed does not seem quite the thing), I shall drink—to the Pope, if you please,—still, to Conscience first, and to the Pope afterwards.

# V

# APPENDICES

## APPENDIX ONE:
## GLOSSARY OF THEOLOGICAL TERMS
## AND HISTORICAL REFERENCES

The following is a selection of names and terms, figuring somewhat prominently in Newman's writings on development, that may be less than familiar to readers having no special background in theology. The identifications are not only very brief, but deliberately slanted to reflect Newman's characteristic interests and perspectives.

**AFRICA:** The Christian communities of that part of the Roman Empire extending, in modern geography, approximately from Morocco to Tunisia, which early adopted the Latin Bible and liturgy. Among leading theologians were Tertullian, Cyprian, and Augustine.

**ALEXANDER:** 4th-century bishop of Alexandria, who excommunicated Arius.

**ALEXANDRIA:** Major Egyptian center of both Christian and Jewish religious culture. Alexandrian theology, strongly influenced by Platonism, was highly valued by Newman. Leading theologians included Clement, Athanasius, Origen, and Cyril.

**AMBROSE:** 4th-century bishop of Milan, strong defender of orthodoxy, and courageous resister of state interference in church matters.

**AMBROSIASTER:** Name applied to a 4th-century commentator on St. Paul erroneously thought to be Ambrose.

**ANTIOCH:** Major Egyptian center often in theological rivalry with

Alexandria. Newman distrusted its typical methods and regarded it as the source of several heresies.

**APOLLINARIANS:** Adherents to the 4th-century heresy of Apollinaris, which denied full humanity to Christ.

**APOLOGISTS:** Christian writers, mainly of the 2nd century, who defended Christianity against pagan and Jewish detractors. One of them, Tertullian, was a major theologian.

**AREOPAGITE:** Dionysius, a 6th-century mystical theologian strongly influenced by neo-Platonism, erroneously believed to have been converted by St. Paul on the Areopagus in Athens.

**ARIANISM:** Heresy fostered by Arius, which denied full divinity to Christ. Newman, who wrote extensively on Arianism, tended to regard it as typifying heretical movements.

**ATHANASIAN CREED:** A principal Christian profession of faith, probably from the 5th century and mistakenly attributed to St. Athanasius.

**ATHANASIUS:** 4th-century bishop of Alexandria and leading adversary of Arianism. Newman, who admired him greatly, found in his life many significant parallels with his own situation.

**AUGUSTINE:** 5th-century bishop of Hippo and most influential theologian of the Latin church. His teachings on grace have been at the center of many major controversies, including those of the Protestant Reformation.

**BACON, FRANCIS:** 16th–17th-century British philosopher whose empirical and skeptical methodology Newman considered inappropriate for dealing with questions of religious faith.

**BARROW, ISAAC:** 17th-century Anglican scholar who wrote a major critique of papal supremacy.

**BASIL:** 4th-century bishop of Caesarea and defender of orthodoxy, especially against Arianism.

**BELLARMINE, ROBERT:** 16th-century Jesuit theologian, especially influential for his teaching about the Church and his criticisms of the Protestant Reformation.

**BULL, GEORGE:** 17th-century Anglican bishop and theologian whose writings are in a number of respects strongly supportive of Roman Catholic teachings.

**BURTON, EDWARD:** 19th-century Anglican theologian whose views on ante-Nicene doctrines as compared with those of Nicaea were similar to Newman's.

**BUTLER, JOSEPH:** 18th-century Anglican bishop and philosopher whose teachings on analogy and probability greatly influenced Newman.

**CHALCEDON, COUNCIL OF:** 4th general council, in 451, which reaffirmed earlier formulations of orthodoxy and rejected the errors of Eutyches on the duality of Christ's natures and of Nestorius on the unity of his person.

**CHILLINGWORTH, WILLIAM:** 17th-century Anglican theologian critical of both exclusive reliance on the Bible and Church claims to infallibility.

**CHRYSOSTOM, JOHN:** 4th-century bishop of Constantinople, renowned for eloquence and courageous pastoral reforms, greatly admired by Newman, who wrote a historical study of him.

**CLEMENT:** 2nd-century theologian of Alexandria who strove to supplement Christian revelation with Greek philosophic reasoning.

**COMMUNION IN ONE KIND:** Reception of Holy Communion under the species of bread only, common from the Middle Ages to the Reformation, occasional in earlier centuries, opposed by Protestant Reformers.

**CONSTANCE, COUNCIL OF:** 15th-century general council, concerned to end division of the Church by claims of anti-popes. It approved communion in one kind.

**CONSUBSTANTIALITY:** Oneness of substance or being, applied especially to the persons of the Trinity.

**CYPRIAN:** 3rd-century African theologian whose views on the roles of bishops and pope influenced Newman.

**DAMASUS:** 4th-century pope very active in suppressing Arianism and other heresies.

**DAVISON, JOHN:** Oxford scholar, with Newman at Oriel, whose intellectuality had a moderating effect on his more extreme early religious attitudes.

**DIOCLETIAN:** 4th-century Roman Emperor responsible for major persecution of Christians.

DIONYSIUS: see AREOPAGITE

DOGMATISM: Belief in the indispensability and reliability of intellectual formulations of orthodoxy established by church authority.

DONATISM: African schism which denied the validity of sacramental ministry exercised by persons who had yielded to persecution.

EPHESUS, COUNCIL OF: 3rd general council, in 431, called to settle the Nestorian controversy, which proclaimed Mary to be "God's mother."

EUSEBIUS: 4th-century bishop of Caesarea, called the "Father of Church History," who had strong pro-Arian sympathies.

GIBBON, EDWARD: 18th-century author of "Decline and Fall of the Roman Empire," whose scholarship Newman admired while lamenting his secularism and contempt of supernatural claims.

GNOSTICISM: Many-sided movement inside and outside Christianity that sought salvation in esoteric divine knowledge and emphasised a fundamental antagonism between spirit and matter.

GUIZOT, FRANÇOIS: 19th-century French historian and conservative political leader whose interpretation of early Christianity contributed to Newman's views on development.

HERESY: Denial of a defined doctrine of the faith.

HOMOUSION: See CONSUBSTANTIALITY

HOOKER, RICHARD: 16th-century Anglican theologian who defended the form of government of the Church of England as a legitimate development.

IGNATIUS: 1st-century bishop of Antioch whose letters, written on his way to martyrdom, urge the role of bishops in ensuring unity in the faith.

IMMACULATE CONCEPTION: Doctrine that Jesus's mother Mary was conceived without original sin.

INCARNATION: Doctrine that the second person of the Trinity took on "flesh," that is, bodily humanity.

INDULGENCE: Remission, total or partial, of temporal punishment, in Purgatory, for sins committed during life.

INFALLIBILITY: Immunity from error in defining doctrines of Christian belief, attributed to the Church and to the pope.

**IRENAEUS:** 2nd-century bishop of Lyons, who opposed Gnosticism and defended Church tradition. He is regarded as the first great Catholic theologian.

**JEROME:** 3rd–4th-century Latin translator and commentator on the Bible.

**JESUITS:** 16th-century religious order founded by Ignatius Loyola, which Newman regarded as exemplifying great organizational strength and resolute obedience.

**JUSTIFICATION:** Doctrine of the restoration by God's grace of sinful human beings to righteousness, differently interpreted by Protestants and Catholics.

**JUSTIN:** 2nd-century Apologist whose view that elements of Christian faith were anticipated by pagan thought was shared by Newman.

**LEO I:** 5th-century pope who inculcated the doctrinal supremacy and enhanced the political prestige of the bishopric of Rome.

**LOCKE, JOHN:** 17th-century British philosopher whose rationalistic approach to religion Newman deplored.

**LUTHERANISM:** The developed teachings of Martin Luther, regarded by Newman as exemplifying the corruption of doctrine over the course of history.

**MANICHEANISM:** Teachings attributed to a 3rd-century Persian, Manes, based on belief in a primordial conflict between satanic darkness and divine light, calling for severe asceticism. It maintained a following until the high Middle Ages, and for a time included Augustine among its adherents.

**MARTYRDOM:** Sacrifice of one's life in loyalty to one's Christian faith, believed to remit all punishment due for sin.

**MERITORIOUS WORKS:** Good actions, assisted by grace and supernaturally motivated, rewarded by God in accordance with divine promises. The doctrine, retained by Catholics, was opposed by Protestant reformers.

**MILMAN, HENRY:** 19th-century Anglican historian, who regarded as alien to Christianity pagan elements which Newman considered to be wholesome assimilations.

MONOPHYSITES:  Heretics who believed Christ had only one, a divine, nature.

MONTANISM:  2nd-century movement attributed to Montanus, which anticipated an imminent end of the world, heralded by prophets and prepared for by severe asceticism. Tertullian joined the movement.

NESTORIANISM:  Heretical doctrine of Nestorius that Christ comprised two persons, one human and one divine.

NICAEA, COUNCIL:  1st general council, in 325, called to settle the controversy over Arianism. The beginning of the history of dogmatic definitions of Christian belief.

ORIGEN:  2nd–3rd-century Alexandrian theologian, greatly esteemed by orthodox writers, including Newman, although some of his teachings were condemned as heterodox.

ORIGINAL SIN:  State of sin in which, since the Fall, human beings enter the world. Western interpretations of the doctrine, dominated by Augustine's theology, have been intensely controversial.

PALEY, WILLIAM:  18th-century Anglican scholar who attempted to defend Christian belief on the basis of rational evidence.

PETAVIUS:  17th-century Jesuit whose studies of the Fathers contain early anticipations of some of Newman's teachings on development.

PURGATORY:  State or place of temporal punishment after death for sins committed during life. The doctrine was rejected by Protestant Reformers.

RELICS:  Bodily remains or objects closely associated with saints, veneration of which by Catholics was considered superstitious by Protestant critics.

SABELLIANS:  Adherents to the theology of Sabellius, which, in the 4th century, obscured the distinctness of the Son from the Father in the Trinity.

SATISFACTION:  Penitential suffering interpreted as not only expressing contrition, but fulfilling a debt of reparation owed to divine justice.

SEMI-ARIANISM:  4th-century theology which sought a compromise formulation in the interest of reintegrating Arianism into Christian orthodoxy.

SOCINIANISM:   16th-century movement, led by two Italian scholars named Sozzini, which stressed divine unity to the prejudice of Christ's divinity.

TERTULLIAN:   2nd–3rd-century African theologian, apologist, and controversialist, whose rigorist tendencies led him to Montanism.

THIRTY-NINE ARTICLES:   16th-century set of Anglican doctrinal norms, which Newman interpreted in ways favorable to Catholicism.

TRANSSUBSTANTIATION:   Doctrine, opposed by Protestant Reformers, that the substance of bread and wine in the Eucharist is replaced by the substance of Christ's body and blood.

TRENT, COUNCIL OF:   16th-century general council called to deal with issues, doctrinal and practical, raised by the Protestant Reformation.

TRINITY:   Doctrine that the divine unity comprises three distinct persons in one divine nature.

VINCENT OF LERINS:   5th-century monastic theologian who proposed criteria for determining authentic Christian doctrine, based on scriptural revelation interpreted by constant universal tradition in the Church.

# APPENDIX TWO:
## FOR FURTHER READING

For a balanced, comprehensive biography, making use of all available primary source material, and situating the history of his ideas within the context of his personal life, read Ian Ker, *John Henry Newman: A Biography* (Oxford: Clarendon Press, 1988).

The most influential modern critique of Newman's theory of development, comparing it with approaches by earlier writers to the same problems, is Owen Chadwick, *From Bossuet to Newman*, 2nd edition (Cambridge: Cambridge University Press, 1987).

A thorough analysis of Newman's work on development, including comparisons of different works and successive editions, is Nicholas Lash, *Newman on Development: The Search for an Explanation in History* (Shepherdstown, West Virginia: Patmos Press, 1975).

Of Newman's own writings, in addition to those included in the present collection, there are at least two which have significant and direct bearing on this subject. One, written in Latin, has not yet been translated, *De Catholici Dogmatis Evolutione*, reprinted as "The Newman-Perrone Paper on Development," edited by T. Lynch, *Gregorianum* XVI (1935) 402–47. Another, seriously neglected in the past, which discloses a whole new dimension of Newman's thought, exists only in the form of a long preface, written in 1877, to a work published forty years earlier: "Preface to the Third Edition" of *The Via Media of the Anglican Church* (London: Longmans, 1901), Vol. I, xv–xciv.

# ABOUT THE EDITOR.

JAMES GAFFNEY is Professor and Chairman of the Department of Religious Studies at Loyola University in New Orleans. In addition to many other articles and books, he has published studies of Newman's thought in *The Heythrop Journal, The Journal of Religious Ethics, Horizons, The Linacre Quarterly, The Catholic World,* and *Catholic Education Today.*